Tranquility on the Razor's Edge

ALSO BY ERIC WEISSMAN

Dignity in Exile:
Stories of Struggle and Hope from a Modern American Shanty Town
(with Nigel Dickson; 2012)

Tranquility on the Razor's Edge

Changing Narratives of Inevitability

Eric Weissman

Rock's Mills Press
Oakville, Ontario
2017

Published by
ROCK'S MILLS PRESS
www.rocksmillspress.com

Cover image: Nigel Dickson.

Library and Archives Cataloguing in Publication (CIP) data is available from
the publisher. Contact us at customer.service@rocksmillspress.com.

For "E."
and all edge riders everywhere

Acknowledgements

I wish to thank a number of people and organizations. First, I want to thank the people I have met over the years, too many to write down, and who have contributed their stories and experience to this work, especially Brian and Eddy who passed during the making of my films. To Ibrahim and the folks at R2DToo; everyone at Dignity Village and in Oregon: Dave Samson, Ptery, Brad, Mitch, Lisa, Scott, Israel; Mark, Andrew, Wendy and Heather; all the great minds that have contributed to my research. To Concordia University's INDI Program, Ketra and Darlene; my committee: Greg, Eric and Satoshi, and Elizabeth and Meir in Soc/Anthro, and, my good friend Domenic Beneventi at Sherbrooke; in Texas: Jerome and Dan, the IMH—thank all of you for working things through with me, during my dissertation and into the book.

My entire family has been extremely supportive to me: Peter, Andrea, Cassidy, Renay, Mark and Zev—thank you. Quite honestly, without their love, expressed in many ways, I might find the edge again. Very special thanks to Barry Callaghan for his mentorship and critical discussions about the meaning of my work. And to my Mom, Claire (Weissman) Wilks, who has just passed: one cannot explain just how special she was. She rode an artist's edge all her own.

I need to also thank my recovery fellowship and the friends I have made in those rooms, especially Mark J. and John B. and Krista M.

Many other people have contributed their ideas, time and skill sets to this project. Thanks to: Sgt. Steve Wick (Houston), Dr. David Buck and Dr. Fann (Houston), the UTMB Institute for the Medical Humanities, Robert Goldhirsch, Magnificat House, Ellie and the women of Ada's; in Toronto, Lorne Tepperman, Dennis Magill, and Stephen Gaetz; thank you, Steven, for the excellent foreword.

Very special thanks' to Nigel Dickson for the use of his stunning images, and to Michael Callaghan, publisher of Exile Editions, for allowing the use of excerpts from the book we made together; Keiki-Alexander for the use of some of his images; and to David and Jen at Rock's Mills Press, for working this unusual hybrid text into a readable form.

Lastly and importantly, to the Indigenous Peoples on whose territories my life and all the stories contained herein have taken place, thank you.

ERIC WEISSMAN

Video and Web Links

Readers will find videos of many of the people and topics covered in the book at the following sites.

- Personal website: www.ericpaulweissman.com.
- Introduction: The author speaks on CBC about the 2015 Housing Report: https://www.youtube.com/watch?v=e8oND--dVNg&t=25s.
- Chapter One: *Subtext: Real Stories*, version 5, 2016: https://vimeo.com/126702110.
- Chapter Two: Brian Dodge and the power of self-reflection on changing narratives of the self: https://www.youtube.com/watch?v=Sg8f7VoAtek.
- Chapter Two: Montreal student protests, 2012: https://www.youtube.com/watch?v=aVHfPHKbPMo&t=143s.
- Chapter Two: Eddy: https://www.youtube.com/watch?v=s4zJKiNuGBo.
- Chapter Six: Introduction to Dignity Village: https://www.youtube.com/watch?v=rHaFa8w430g.
- Chapter Six: More on Dignity Village, 2011: https://www.youtube.com/watch?v=lN8pe-dCnQQ
- Chapter Six: Jay, expelled from the Village, 2011: https://www.youtube.com/watch?v=zdtWpTxY4Zg&t=22s.
- Chapter Eight: Dignity Village activism: https://www.youtube.com/watch?v=gWwBPs4XmRs.
- Chapter Eight: Introduction to Ibrahim Mubarak: https://www.youtube.com/watch?v=f-VXe9KzNbk&feature=youtube.
- Chapter Nine: Michael Jackson in Galveston; Art, Community and God; Juneteenth in Galveston: https://www.youtube.com/watch?v=OVCsSCscpe4.
- Chapter Nine: Subtext demo footage with images of Houston camps, 2014: https://www.youtube.com/watch?v=VJYtGEpEIP8&feature=youtu.beConc lusions
- Chapter Nine: National Housing Day with Cathy Crowe and Don Weitz: https://www.youtube.com/watch?v=Sg8f7VoAtek.
- Chapter Nine: Two fellows evicted from the street, literally: https://www.youtube.com/watch?v=OVCsSCscpe4.

Contents

Foreword

Forewords to books are often littered with descriptions such as "provocative," "thought provoking," "cutting against the grain." In reading Eric Weissman's book, one is readily drawn to such claims, but not in the service of yet again tossing around clichés. There is a lot in this book to consider at a time when we continue to struggle with how to address the problem of mass homelessness.

Weissman's book raises important questions regarding how we respond to homelessness, whether or not our approaches actually work, and what role people who experience homelessness should play in developing their own housing solutions. In doing so he demonstrates the value of an anthropological ethnographic investigation into the lives of people who experience homelessness. Weissman is an excellent writer and ethnographer. I would tell you to stop reading this foreword right now and go to the first pages of his introduction to see what I mean, but I suspect you would not return to these comments (which would be okay). His engaging style will draw you in not only to his way of thinking but to an evocative rendering of the daily lives of the people he was working with. One comes away with a deeper understanding of homelessness and the varied ways in which it is experienced. That he shares not only richly descriptive details of the lives of individuals he encountered but his own story of the lived experience of homelessness contributes to a fuller awareness and understanding of the ongoing challenges of addictions, mental health issues and trauma. While readers may be troubled by the decisions and actions of the people he engages, Weissman instead seeks understanding. I appreciate his comment that "something people tend to forget when criticizing an ill homeless person is that they are *ill*, not foolish." This is all significant because without these understandings, we cannot possibly consider what to do about homelessness, and what role people who experience this extreme form of poverty should play in determining the solutions that will work for them.

In thinking about how to effectively respond to modern mass homelessness, Weismann is unafraid of challenging some of the dominant paradigms and narratives that frame our current understandings. Through his travels across North America, he finds that in spite of efforts to shift from a crisis response, we still seem to be experiencing mass homelessness in community after community. He questions whether Housing First really provides long-term solutions to the lives of people with complex mental health and addictions issues. From there, he asks whether we can ever really live up to the promise of ending homelessness.

Whether you agree or not with Weissman's assertions and critique, it is important to assert that we need this kind of research. I don't agree with everything here, but I do go along with the notion that we need to consider provocative questions. We need to challenge and reflect on what we are doing and how we might do things differently. Most of all, we cannot be afraid of, in Weissman's terms, having "unpopular conversations" in order to move forward in our thinking about what to do about the seemingly intractable problem of homelessness.

The focus of Weissman's book is on "intentional homelessness communities" (IHCs) and the lives of people within them. IHCs are physical spaces for living organized by people experiencing homelessness that range from temporary or makeshift communities, including tent cities or shanty towns (at one extreme), to more organized and structured communities, including tiny homes communities, constructed by and for people with lived experience. What unites these approaches is the organizational intent of residents to provide housing and community for individuals who are generally excluded from both, through how we manage mental health and well-being, poverty, addictions and homelessness in North America.

In asking the question of how to consider the role of IHCs in our response to homelessness, Weissman doesn't attempt to valorize such communities or to present them in an unproblematic way. He addresses, from an operational perspective, both the strengths and weaknesses of intentional communities, and their impact on the lives of people living within them. He also looks at both the opportunities and challenges that come with engaging with the state to support the development of such communities. His ethnographic method compels us to consider whether in the end intentional communities are good or bad for people with complex problems. Short of considering IHCs as the solution to homelessness, he asks, more modestly, whether they reasonably fit within a more comprehensive response to homelessness,

The key contribution to this conversation, I believe, is about rights and dignity. It brings us back to Henri Lefebvre's question of who has the right to the city. When as a society we provide minimal supports for people who experience homelessness, we need to consider the consequences not only for those individuals, but for our towns and cities. Those minimal "crisis supports"—emergency shelters, soup kitchens, day programs—while well-meaning charitable efforts, are often demeaning, infantilizing (as housed adults, do we need a curfew? Do we need to demonstrate that we haven't been drinking before we get access to shelter?), unsafe and often without dignity. Moreover, we organize this crisis response spatially, providing places in the city that divide us in terms of who is homeless and who is not. We further reinforce this spatial division through policing the spaces in between—the sidewalks, parks, alleyways, bridges and abandoned buildings that people with no home must traverse and occupy when they have no other place to go to sit, visit, rest or use substances. Lacking private homes, people experiencing homelessness are necessarily thrust into public spaces, and ones that we invest considerable resources in policing, controlling and containing the "problem" of homelessness. This criminalization of homelessness is a manifestation both of our attitudes towards and how we address the needs of people living in extreme poverty, and a resultant desire to contain and control the spaces they move through and occupy.

There is very little ambiguity here regarding which spaces are for people experiencing homelessness and which are not. This is also how we produce and reproduce the concept of homelessness on a daily basis. It should not be surprising that many of the people Weissman engaged through this research reject the label of "homeless" (something that would not surprise most people working in the field), for it is a category and a stigmatizing label that we create through how we organize the lives of people living in poverty who lack access to their own shelter.

The creation of intentional communities is one way that people push back and claim their right to the city. Rather than wait to be selected for a housing program, or spend time in inhospitable emergency shelters, people with lived experience of homelessness in cities across Canada and the United States have worked collaboratively to make their own communities. In some cases these communities have developed on public land, with support from municipal governments and other community members. There are many examples where these communities seem to be achieving their goals, and providing people with better lives.

It is not all sunshine and ponies, however, in the land of IHCs.

Foreword

Weissman remarks on the unsustainability of many of these communities, and that for many individuals their personal struggles are too great to be solved or addressed through such new ways of providing people with homes. He even questions whether it may be necessary in some cases to do unpopular things regarding the rights of those with severe mental health and addictions challenges so long as the supports are first-rate and humane. He nevertheless concludes that there is value in IHCs, that "[i]t may be that we need to build spaces for people to live out their addictions and in which to die unfortunate deaths." In other words, in the end, and consistent with the name of one such IHC called "Dignity Village," it is about creating spaces for human dignity, for connection and belonging, and for people to be as they are, regardless of what we may think is best for them.

If you want your ideas about what homelessness is and what we should do about it challenged, read on. This is a book that is provocative, thought provoking and cuts against the grain.

STEPHEN GAETZ
Professor, Faculty of Education, York University, Toronto
Director, Canadian Observatory on Homelessness

Tranquility on the Razor's Edge

Introduction

I am going to tell you a story I found in a single field note I wrote after a hard day on the streets of Portland. This field note story, I've now come to see, lies at the heart of this book, this uneasy academic narrative about the struggle to be seen and to be heard by those homeless people I have encountered on the streets and in tent camps and intentional communities across Canada and the U.S. This academic narrative, my doctoral dissertation, somewhat revised, involves a social critique that weaves in and out of joy, despair, addiction, recovery, steps forward and leaps backwards. It involves decisions made for and by the homeless, and includes issues of rights and freedoms, and discourses on deserving and undeserving character. In other words, it is a complex narrative. Where better to begin, therefore, than with a simple field note written a year after this academic enterprise was finished, after certain awards had been won—a field-note story about a moment of a kind rarely encountered by ethnographers or everyday citizens; a moment that ties the issues surrounding, and the policies governing, homelessness into a single story of loss, a story, I might say, that has its own inevitability, an inevitability that is unsettling, at least to me, because it is an inevitability absent of epiphany. Or as Aristotle might have said, it was indeed a moment of pity or fear, but it was also a moment absent of any purging, absent of catharsis.

MARCH 13, 2014

I have been in Portland for three days (this trip). And I am really struggling to convey what it is I am feeling. Because, frankly, I should be feeling more than I am feeling. I sometimes feel that I am the narcissistic sociopath that Guylaine had accused me of being back in Montreal. I mean, a young woman died today; in a sleeping bag in a tent camp in Portland, and Kirsten, the camp "nurse" who did street work, and I, we each did several minutes of CPR on this girl and whereas Kirsten was filled with fear and grief during the process, I was rather detached, mystified by the wonder at whether or not CPR (which I'd taken a course in) would work.

Detached. Detached, and not at all grounded in that moment. And even afterward, as the poor girl lay there with Portland EMS and Fire trying to resuscitate her, I casually chatted with the cops. At some point, I even laughed at something the cop said, maybe about a fishing trip, or about the world in general, something I cannot recall, but I remember laughing, while a few metres away, I could smell the odor of whatever it was they were injecting into the girl, and I could hear the defibrillator pinging ... all this

1

while outside the Gates of R2DToo, residents waited anxiously to see, to hear what was transpiring in their shelter.

They looked on, pacing and marching along the sidewalk, gazing in real despair as one of their clan slipped into that place dead junkies and hobos go to; that place that, even though in my own using days I had tried to get there, I still had no idea where it was. Where did she go as my hands pumped against her and her body yielded with cracks and gurgles to my urgent pounding? Why was she staring at me? I see her eyes, the whites turning yellow to match the browning of her lips and her nipples.

Laughing. Again. And noisy. I hear the hum of the crowd. I hear cell phones going off. A helicopter scoots overhead, hovers, and then scoots off. What the fuck is with this laughter? The cops and EMS are laughing at something said, while they hover over the girl; what was her name again anyway? Emily, maybe? Or Emma? In all the confusion, for it was confusion, I lost her name. "Jesus Christ, did I do that right? Did I do it the way I was supposed to?" I have no idea what the cop is saying to me. I SEE his lips moving, and I hear his voice, but I am kneeling over E., and pumping away. And then more laughter. I lose names easily now, and I wonder if it is because of all the drugs I did back in the day. Well, at least I didn't die in a sleeping bag in a tent in an overdose, while strangers defibbed me and worked my sternum and pounded me so hard that puke came out my nostrils. And the cops are STILL laughing while the EMT stick tubes in her and pound on her, 5, 10, 15, TWENTY minutes—I can smell the aroma of the IV again, and still they pump, pump, pump—to no avail, and the cops are still smiling and chatting.

Beyond the picnic bench and all the stuff piled on it, I see the movement of the teams out of focus in a strange narrow depth of field, like the fine bokeh of an expensive prime lens, and with each shove of her weighty body I somehow see her fingers, her hand, shudder with each pound—I hear the gurgle and follow that sound up her chest, through her throat until her sepia vomit enters the intubation bag, and the cops are chatting, Kirsten is crying and I sit there watching the cop's lips move as I wonder if I have lost the capacity to feel.

Of course within minutes the speculation had hit the rumor mill; E. had OD'd on "benzos." Or on "meth," or anti-depressants, or…. Her husband, her fictive husband that is, Bob, or James, once again a name that might as well be the universe for how it eludes my memory and comprehension, is a junkie himself, and worried. He is wasted as he always is as far as I can tell. Drunk per se. He was a drunk. Was his nature, I had noted earlier that week. And his wife is lying there while strangers try to rescue her, though she was already dead, I thought … and he with this anti-freeze, anti-feel elixir of cheap booze and drugs in his veins to numb out how he MUST feel, really feel.

I mean, what more sincere a cry for passion is there than the death of a loved one?

Somehow even he is managing to feel through his poison. HE is crying, this wreck can cry, but not me.

And Kirsten who had given her mouth-to-mouth and swallowed some puke for her effort, even, perhaps, ESPECIALLY, she is crying. And I who had been compressing her chest with two flaccid, lifeless breasts hanging like wet sacks and who—OH FUCK DID I DO IT RIGHT? DID I COMPRESS RIGHT? AM I SHOUTING AND OBSERVNG AND DOING IT RIGHT—DID SHE DIE 'CUZ I FUCKED UP?

Sashimi and sushi. I am eating sashimi and sushi at this hip joint a few blocks from my hotel and the regular Thursday night crowd is watching me—this weird guy—writing notes down as he feeds himself. I wonder what I look like: every minute or two brushing my hand against my forehead as I used to do when I was writing my dissertation, rubbing kneading the tight skin on my temples and then back to work—yellow tail, a dip of wasabi ... another thought, more notes ... wrapped so tight, I want to crawl out of my skin.

No, of course I did it right. I did what they said. I compressed and compressed until the EMT's got there.

"Second one in an hour," he said. The cop. "We just came back from Bud Clark Commons. We go there a lot, though they don't always die." I looked at him and I said, "I think what has me weirded out is the laughing. And the chatter. They are laughing and chatting and she just died."

He looked back at me. Smiled. A different kind of smile than simply laughing, and he closed his notebook. Had he been taking notes the whole time I was talking? I wonder what they look like. His notes. Did I say something? Incriminate myself? Ah fuck, did I do it right?

"She was dead before you got to her. They usually are. There is nothing you could have done. Don't be hard on yourself. You get used to it."

Then the front gates opened to let the coroner in, and I walked out the sidewalk to commiserate with the people who lived in the camp.

Holy fuck, I am hungry. But I can't cry.

I'd felt pity, I'd felt fear for E. in her dying, but no emotional release, no purging and certainly no tears as evidence of any purging. In fact, I'd felt all the urgency caused by pity and fear but in quite a detached way, something I might describe as an almost cold remove while in the midst of urgency. What, I wondered was the nature of this detachment and what did that detachment tell me about the story itself?

This was getting complicated because this had not been the indifference that is inherent in most states of detachment, the detachment of the aloof bystander. Quite the reverse. This was the detachment of the engaged observer.

3

Me! The detachment of the storyteller engaged in his own story.

Perhaps this was what Primo Levi, the survivor and writer who'd come out of the concentration camps, meant when he said that, as a writer, he'd entered into a Grey Zone. After all, he tried to tell a story that—by its very nature—would have meaning, but it was a story about a place that by its very nature could have no meaning. He'd entered into a zone where he'd dealt with his own recollection of evidence that had its own terrible inevitability, an inevitability absent of any epiphany. Could this be what Wordsworth had meant when he'd said that the writer engages in a moment "of emotion recollected in tranquility"? If so, I would add that in our time we might describe this as a state of tranquility on the razor's edge

My task as a writer has been to engage and explore a contradictory and muddled world of abject poverty and the politics of care, the unrest between good people at loggerheads with other good people, addictions and abstentions, and on and on, through one confusing narrative after another, all the while hoping for not just resolution, but maybe even a redemptive moment, a moment that would give the narrative of struggle a positive degree of actual consequence on the street. But when E. died, all the conventions that had previously bound me to an academic tone and mode of storytelling disappeared into what I can only now call a *narrative of inevitability,* a mode of reportage, as I now understand it, that has an ending but no epiphany, an ending but no meaningful resolution in that ending.

That is why—though urgently engaged—pound-pound-pounding on heaven's door, I did not cry, I have not cried, and likely will not ever cry for those who perish on the streets. This is not because I am weary or jaded or have developed a thick skin. Hardly. After almost 20 years of being in recovery myself, having been periodically homeless in the '80s and '90's, of working in these unfortunate places, of making films about streets, squats and tent camps in Toronto in the early 2000s, of doing fieldwork in legal homeless campgrounds in Oregon and in Housing First Projects in Montreal and Houston, of having worked as witness to that pervasive dark, invasive poverty that has burrowed into underpasses, empty buildings and other dank places, I see that what I feel is not a need to weep, not a need to purge, but a fierce unfettered empathy, an empathy that is binding beyond any release that tears could provide.

This book, therefore, has been written so that the ideas I developed in my dissertation will resonate with those readers who have a need to draw solutions imbued with hope out of research and scholarship, readers who have a need for positive resolution, even if it is only implied.

What I have to tell these readers is that they should expect no resolution in the stories I have to tell but only a call to do, in the most determined way, what needs to be done from defeating moment to defeating moment, for inherent in the stories I have to report is a certain grating despair born out of an awareness of how implacable homelessness is in our time, in our metropolitan places. This has led me into what I call narratives of inevitability.

So there it is. I hadn't intended to go to the camp that day. I was going to go for one last walk in Portland and do some shopping. For no reason, I made a right turn instead of a left into an almost deserted R2DToo rest area. There was just me, and a resident serving as the lone security officer, and Kirsten in her tent, and E. dying in her sleeping blanket. The security guy and I heard Kirsten's cries—"911, 911 call the EMTs!"—and I ran to the sound of her voice and saw E. puking into Kirsten's mouth and she looked at me hoping I would say exactly what I said, "I can do this, I know CPR." She and I both hoped that we could do this—this being the saving of a poor person dying "on the streets." Had this not occurred, I might very well have flown back to Houston and thought in the best of academic senses about other things we had done that week, such as the experiment we had been conducting with cell phones and video conferencing as we tried to link a number camps for an upcoming political action, and talking to members of Dignity Village about using photographs online to improve their public image in a project we are still designing, called Digital Bridges, a project we feel holds real promise: images of problems and solutions originating in alternative housing spaces, intended to change our stories; offered up for all kinds of people to see and comment on posted on our web based visual elicitation tool, perhaps sufficiently to change the homeless narrative; images that by their very nature imply meaningful consequence.

Consequence of course is the conundrum that confronts us, that confronted me that day. Seated in that sushi bar, I was aware of myself on one hand as a red-eyed frenetic loner busy scribbling in a notebook while wolfing down ahi and yellow tail, while on the other hand I was in a strange state of tranquility: I was in possession of (or perhaps possessed by) a sudden clarity about what my work had meant to academia, and what it could now mean to those who were attempting a growing, sensitive awareness of homelessness.

After all the theory and all the methods, all the critical and clever talk was done and the controversial conclusions had been drawn, after all those hurdles had been overcome, this question remained: "So what does it really mean? Outside of the academic world, what does it mean that people are fighting for the right to build tent camps and that many, despite our best conceptual and constructive intentions, must continue to die on the streets and in other dark places? What does it mean that no matter how and what we try to do as a society in order to limit homelessness, it will continue to pervade our cities?" For some reason, it was those minutes spent pounding that woman's bare chest, the sound of her sternum snapping, the gurgling and somatic spasms of a dead addict's body, the voiceless laughs of the EMTs and the needless chatting, that led me to a mental space wherein, without remorse or any sense of failed redemption, I told myself, "You cannot end all kinds of homelessness, ever, and people are going to die." Or as the Irish sometimes put it: "No matter

what you've done or are going to do, they're piling up on the other side."
This is not a defeatist position. It is bold, empirically substantiated and openminded: as I suggested earlier, in the face of endings that have no dénouement, it is a call to action, a call predicated on our acceptance that we cannot end all forms of homelessness, but at our best, we can do that which is left to do for those people we will always find dodging prosecution, if not persecution, in our cities' negative spaces: we must accept that homelessness will, with crushing inevitability, always be with us, and what we must do is make sure we make homelessness livable.

How do I go about making the world embrace that contrary news? What can a narrative that has such an outcome really mean, particularly in the context of the progressive optimism that is in fact necessary to produce livable conditions and to keep them in place? In the case of this book, part of the way we can do this is to understand the historical and larger structural conditions that provide contexts for understanding poverty and homelessness and the types of spaces set aside for those experiences. We can look at laws, policies and programming artifacts, and at statements, activism and protest as evidence of competing narratives which, differently produced to compel social actors towards diverse ends, ask a simple direct question—in the tension between all narratives, particularly those that seem to be in conflict, is there the possibility for the different views of social change and social justice to find rendition?

The second part is to ask people who are homeless, people who work or otherwise have roles in these contexts, how they understand their experience and what they might do to change these experiences if they had new information to act upon. This part of the task is very complex; methodologically, it is a form of pragmatic investigation that I call pragmatic ethnography and it requires a serious dedication to field sites and to what Alain Badiou (2001) has referred to as a fidelity to emerging situations because the truth is always the "truth of a particular situation." It means writing amidst the muddle of contradictory experiences with as much non-ideological clarity as possible and doing so fearlessly, as if there were no other way, until the emergent experience signals its own end.

I understand that the ethnography I engage in is not only a sort of community activism but at times a form of social work. I understand that there are those, like the EMTs and the police outreach squads I've met, who encounter the situation I've described every day, day in and day out, but for me, I was obviously troubled that the emergency crews could laugh and talk about mundane crap while going through those motions that yielded to and acknowledged an inevitability; intubating and compressing with the knowledge it was all pointless and simply a requisite routine. Their experience allowed them to look at the arrival of the pale rider on the pale horse and survive through humor and chatter. Inured. This was their work, and admittedly, they would have gone mad without levity and distraction.

But, this book is intended to help people see connections between their defenses and their values and the defenses of those homeless people about whom they would not otherwise think about too much. We want to understand that tent camps and other intentional communities are not just about shelter, but about people needing attachments to others, or community. Once such connections are made, it is hard to hide behind exclusionary narratives.

On that day, seated at the picnic table, mindlessly rambling on with the cop, I was able to observe how—while the EMTs worked on E.—the camp had been cordoned off from the actual residents of the rest area. Within the fencing, we who were immediately involved with the mechanics of her demise did what we had to; I gave details to the cops of how we tried to help her, the EMS shot stuff into her veins and defibbed her. But no one else was allowed inside the gate. Outside the gate were dozens of people, and their focus was on what had transpired inside. None of these people were laughing or telling jokes or deflecting. They were residents and members of that tented community, of the rest camp's neighborhood, and many were local supporters who had heard the shout go out over cell phones that there was a problem at R2DToo. Death on the streets was not new to them, but they suffered for her loss, openly lamented over what her loss represented to people fighting for the right to camp. Of these folks, not all were homeless or activist, but were people who could not tear themselves away from the unfolding drama because they were connected to the issue and the person, street poverty and the E.'s they all knew.

Ibrahim Mubarak, the leader of the rest area, arrived, grief stricken that E. had died. It was the first time in the camp's three years of struggling against public opinion that anyone had died there. In fact, it is a drug-free camp, and had been gaining leverage with the city because of its success, so he was not only wondering in pragmatic terms how it had happened, he was terrified that the press would tell the story in a way that would favour critics of the emergency camp movement. But then, turning the whole experience on its ear for me, because it had its own migrant buoyant tone, there was, if not love, then certainly gratitude. Mubarak hugged me and thanked me for being a stand-up guy, and I actually said nothing, odd for me. What had needed to be done had been done. I had no way to know what else to say.

About 10 minutes after the coroner and police wheeled E.'s body out of the camp, Ibrahim took all the passersby and the members of the rest area to a nearby non-profit organization called Sisters of The Road. "Sisters," as it is fondly—very fondly—known in Portland, is a sort of intentional community center organized around food and conversation, advocacy and participation. People meet, eat and work there. Ibrahim and his non-profit, Right To Survive, which parented Right 2 Dream Too (or R2DToo and sometimes, R2D2), immediately gathered at Sisters to hold a healing circle. While they were there and the camp was empty except for the lawyer and I who had remained to keep an eye on things, two street guys, members of that broader street community, came running across the busy intersection and with great urgency, they asked us to step outside so they could smudge the camp before E.'s spirit departed the grounds.[1] "Were you here?" one asked. "I did CPR on her," I replied. I suppose I looked forlorn. The other fellow said, "I should smudge you. May I smudge you?" I had never been smudged but in short order they lit a wick of Sweet Grass and with their hands laid the smoke on my body.

The following day I made my return to Galveston and the University of Texas Medical Branch where I was doing a visiting scholarship at the Institute for the Medical Humanities. I sat on the plane staring at the two pages of notes I have just transcribed. I haven't written another word since about that experience, even though I have tried. I didn't look at my notes except to shuffle them around from folder to folder until yesterday when I wrote them down here. I have done exhaustive searches of literature to find out what others who have had my experience might have said about how such a wrenching, hands-on experience might have impacted their entire epistemology. There is surprisingly little in the literature about ethnographers who have failed at hands-on interventions, though there is some literature that looks at driving people to hospitals for emergency care or advocating for them in doctors' offices as types of interventions that can have unintended consequences. Still, there is very little written directly on the kind of emotional trauma that befalls one trained to study life and lives, after failing to save one.

When I landed, I had more texts and phone messages from the folks who ran R2DToo and even one from Dignity Village, which seemed to be a revelatory statement about how the two activist sites were detached from one another. I had hoped that in the time since I deposited my dissertation, an enterprise very much focused on how to improve Dignity Village's connections to other activist groups, they would be very much present in Portland's housing collectivity. That they showed little interest in this crisis at R2DToo was very disappointing, but upon post-dissertation reflection, not so surprising. I had entered my program imagining the "homeless camps" I was studying in a certain positive light, but I'd finally had to conclude that they were in fact failing to live up to their declared missions, a failure we will critique in this book. Understanding the role of critique in changing the narratives we impose on social problems is central to this book, just as it has been key to both Dignity Village and R2DToo in their fight for legitimacy during the era of Housing First and rapid rehousing.

This is very important: the pervasiveness of literal and chronic homelessness requires drastic and wildly creative experimentation, and that is what this latest research has been designed to survey—what kinds of alternatives seem to help, and is the present-day conventionally housed citizen prepared to have "homeless camps" in his or her backyard? This is not a new way of approaching old problems; in the 1930s Franklin Delano Roosevelt, who implemented the first ambitious national social security measures in the U.S. in his New Deal, had said, and I am paraphrasing, that the U.S. required "bold and persistent experimentation." Given that his comment was directed at problems that still persist today, I am asking the reader to do several things.

First, we will have to talk about some of the key concepts that helped me organize my research. We will have to understand how our key case studies, Dignity Village and Right to Dream Too in Portland and Tent City in Toronto, came to be and why they have had divergent outcomes as communities. We will do this largely by reading about my own journey out of addiction and homelessness and the way that this experience shaped the questions I asked. So we will look at a lot of literature on poverty and homelessness. We will have to look at what freedom and "rights" mean as underlying values in the housing activist movement, and how such rights have been interpreted over time in the U.S. as aspects of economic rather than moral being.

Since I finished my dissertation my work has changed somewhat and I will represent that shift in this book. Elsewhere I have suggested that I currently do work on social policy at the intersection of political sociology and social inequality, where these meet the welfare regime as it applies to vulnerable people, especially the homeless. As such there is a merging of broad historical and comparative welfare analysis, similar to the work of Esping-Andersen (1993) and Richard Titmuss (1974) within the University of Chicago tradition of ethnographic data collection.

So we will have to look at how to go about doing ethnographic research in unusual living spaces, and how pragmatic and critical forms of ethnography help us to attach our research to the communities we work in. We must address the question of what is meant by social critique and power, since the former and the latter are in essence two sides of the same coin that is tossed over time to produce dominant discourses. My work comes to be anchored in a Foucauldian (1991) model of power and critique that binds to the pragmatic sociology of Boltanski (2011) as part of the larger comparative and historical analysis and interrogation of institutions and the origins of justifications. This step is particularly important because in order to understand the various narratives that people apply to the same situations, for which each person sees their own sense of "inevitability," we need to understand where their critical dispositions come from. Applying a broad sense of Mills' sociological imagination to look at individuals' biographies and social contexts helps us to understand why some actors impose truth onto situations to determine their inevitability, and others are willing to enter contests to prove different truths.

So, we will look at some theories of power and space. Because we are looking at homelessness and tent camps, which we will here begin to call intentional homeless communities (IHC), while asking people to consider unusual narratives about how to care, we are also asking people to question their own social critiques, views on right and wrong, deserving and non-deserving, and so on. And we have to do all this before we can talk about where the narrative is now and where it looks to be going.

The current dominant narrative on solving homelessness in North America is a conversation about rapid rehousing popularized but not limited to the model of Housing First. We have a situation where harm reduction philosophies are strengthening the sense that IHC can play a role in our strategies, and in which the Tiny Home Movement is popularizing small homes and intentional communities. In this frame, where having a home—an apartment, a house and other conventional spaces—is considered desirable, it seems to many to be more urgent to create the sense that without such places, E.'s experience would indicate failure of an alternative housing model. But some of us don't think that this is true. We look at sites that present intentional community in a very critical way and we try to discern what works and what doesn't, and, then after that dust has settled, you and I, we, can decide whether an acceptance of inevitability constitutes failure or not.

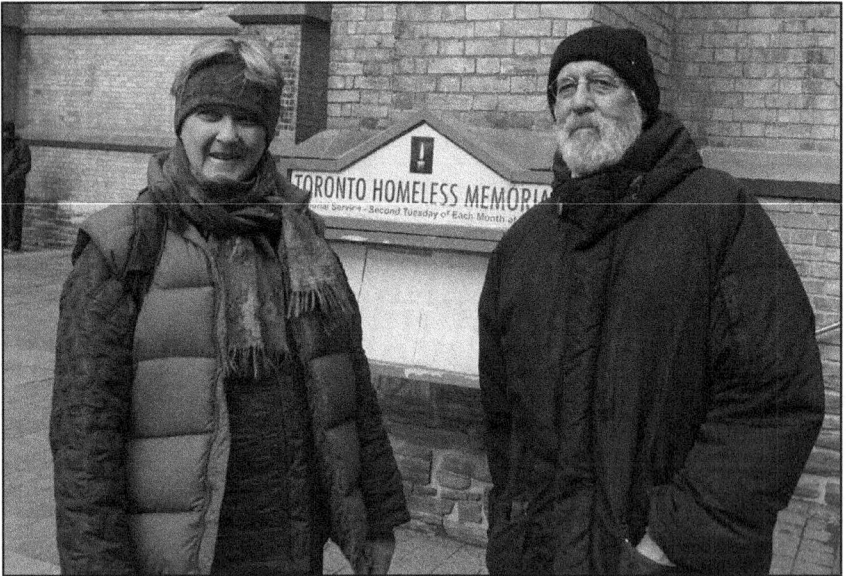

Cathy Crowe and Beric German at the Toronto Homeless Memorial, 2016. Almost 20 years after leading the Toronto Disaster Relief Committee and the fight for Tent City, they are still championing the fight for the rights of people experiencing homelessness. Since the mid-1980s, over 800 people have died as a result of literal homelessness. Photo: Eric Weissman.

Chapter One
CONDITIONS OF POSSIBILITY

1.1 Sociologically Imagining the Case

In *The Sociological Imagination* (1959) C. Wright Mills argued that social scientists must remain in touch with the values and senses that frame their perspective and the perspective of those they study. Without understanding

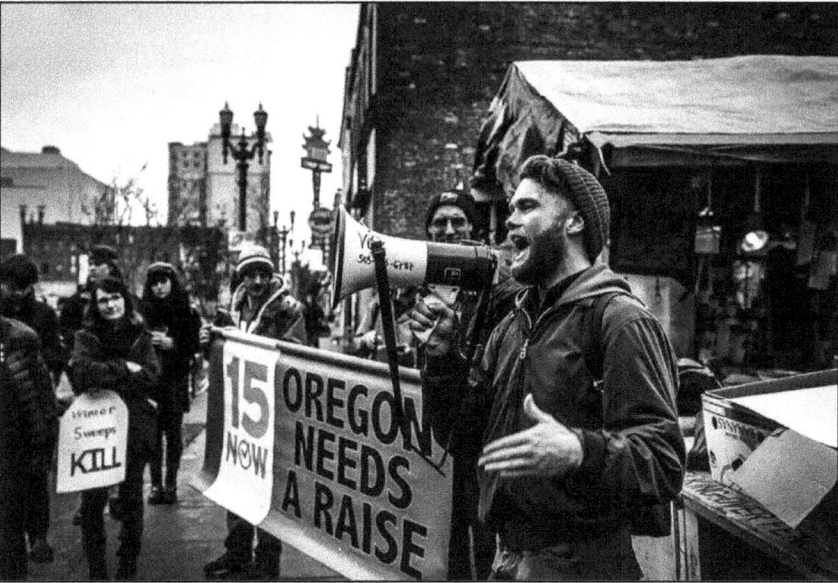

March to City Hall. Photo: Keiki-Alexander, 646Studios.

the values on which such orientations are premised, the individual in society and the scholar alike are both vulnerable to domination by existing power structures. Mills emphasized the importance for ethnographers of integrating biographical, social, historical, economic and political values of the individuals they studied into the "social milieus" in which discussions about society at large are set (1959:64–68). Put simply, in Mills' view, sociologists should study people and their communities within the contextual frames that give their human condition meaning.

This chapter introduces some of the concepts that elucidate an understanding of the intentional community known as Dignity Village in Portland, Oregon and by extension, the general discussions made in this book. Mills' model encourages us to understand the biographies, histories and social-political context of the "others" we are examining. But in addition, there is sufficient room in my own sociological imagination to suggest that scholarly authorship today requires ethnographic writers to reveal the origins of their own ideas and biases as well.

First, then, are the circumstances under which my research took place, as well as the contours to the social problem that had attracted my interest. The size of a social problem and its distribution across cities helps explain the degree of urgency and the directions social policies will take. In addition, it is valuable to be aware of how different values collide in the debates over given policies. In this case, terms like *community* and *shantytown* are often invested with moral-normative commitments that are odds with one another. Furthermore, because homelessness is about people who do not possess spaces to live, attitudes towards how space ought to be used are central to larger debates about rights and moral behaviour. Most citizens accept encoded rules and bylaws as a sensible means of evaluating how urban spaces may be used. But when a group of marginalized citizens whose roles in society are ill-defined and whose lifestyles are counter-hegemonic claim a city block on which to camp, it is no surprise that conventional citizens are confronted by a new set of issues and claims. So we need to examine how the liminal nature—what is often thought of as a state of limbo—attributed to homelessness impacts these claims. Furthermore, to understand the issues facing communities such as Dignity Village, it is key to understand the concepts of freedom and democracy in the context of isolation and poverty. We will apply these concepts in the later chapters to the cases presented in order to destabilize certain powerful narratives about homelessness and housing. Throughout this work, one of the key questions for me remains, "Is fighting for the right to live in a shack on a remote swept-off tarmac, located next to a garbage facility an example of democratic freedom?"

1.2 The General Context of This Research

In 2011, when I carried out my participant observation fieldwork in Dignity Village in Portland, it was estimated that close to 146 million Americans had difficulty paying for at least one of the following: rent, food, clothing, medicine and transportation.[2] In the U.S.—a country that in 2012 was ranked seventh in per capita wealth by *Forbes* Magazine—47 million people out of these 146 million were considered by the US Government to be living *below* the poverty line (NAEH 2011; HUD 20012). Of these, some 3 million persons suffered from some form of homelessness. According to the most lenient definitions such as those employed by the Department of Education, this homelessness could have been temporary, episodic or chronic. The majority of homelessness was found in urban environments among people who came from ethnic minorities and/or were male.[3] *Chronic* homelessness—that is homelessness experienced multiple times or over extended periods—still confounds housing authorities as a pervasive and historically troubling urban problem.

Three years later, in 2015, U.S. figures estimated the number of people in poverty at 15.8%, or approximately 50 million people (NAEH 2015). In 2016, it was reported that 33 states had shown declines in the number of homeless people, while 16 had shown increases. Despite increases in the number of rapid rehousing units and supportive housing units, the rent burden of most poor Americans had increased by as much as 2.1% over the previous year (NAEH 2016).

Certain categories of homelessness are growing more rapidly than others: people doubling up in other households, so-called couch-surfing or staying with friends; but perhaps the most troubling of all are skilled and educated young adults who are ready to work and start their own lives, but who remain in their parents' homes. All these categories have shown alarming increases. Since the Great Recession of 2007–09, the number of poor households experiencing extreme rent burdens (>50% of income) has increased by 27.7%, despite the subsequent economic recovery (NAEH 2016:3). And these figures are hard to nail down because homelessness itself is a complicated concept, one which takes a range of forms: *literal* (having nowhere to sleep at all), *chronic* (using shelters or having nowhere to sleep multiple times in a 12-month period), *episodic* (a number of literal or chronic experiences over a long period of time) and *in-jeopardy of homelessness*. Recognizing all these forms as types of homelessness underscores its pervasive nature and seeming inevitability.

Currently the United States federal government supports a *Housing First* and other *Rapid Re-housing* approaches to deal with the homeless problem. Nation-wide programs such as Obama's *Opening Doors* provide competition-based funding for cities, which comply with this model. The former relocates people directly in apartments or other housing, sometimes with supports, before addressing issues of addiction or mental health. The mantra here is housing first, issues later. The latter intervenes with families who are in jeopardy of losing housing because of lack of rent or loss of jobs by offering temporary rent relief and family assistance. Such preventive and restorative programs currently constitute the backbone of widely adopted Ten-Year Plans to End Homelessness, a widely implemented national strategy initiated by the Bush Administration in 2003 and embraced by Obama's Opening Doors program. This strategy is by now well established in the long-term strategies most major cities pitch to federal funders for housing monies. In the U.S., neither the federal government nor the cities have been effective in ending even sporadic homelessness.

Very often, the chronically homeless have had no choice but to pitch a tent, or to otherwise illegally inhabit empty urban spaces. An historic tension between so called street-engaged homeless people and city governance leaves the homeless subject to arrest for urinating in laneways or sleeping on sidewalks. A citation for relieving oneself in a public space can lead to a charge of sexual indecency; that offence can render access to housing programs impossible. Many on the streets have only the scant shelter offerings of charitable organizations and poorly run shelters that offer a finite number of beds and services. At times, out of sheer necessity, street-engaged homeless people group together and occupy bridge underpasses, abandoned buildings or parks in order to "squat"—establishing places to sleep and congregate.[4] In most cities, police and municipal workers sweep such camps within 72 hours of posted warnings of trespass (De Pastino 2003; Mitchell 2003; National Law Center on Homelessness and Poverty 2007, 2012; Mosher 2010). American cities by and large have not been kind to squatters and homeless tent camps except under unusually dark times. The Great Depression is an example of such dark times, but even then such camps were seen as temporary, secondary alternatives to "proper" or conventional housing (DePastino 2003).

At the national level, recent foreclosure actions in the U.S. have spiked the numbers of persons entering homelessness for the first time.[5] The impact of the Great Recession and foreclosures of 2007 and 2008 is still expressing itself in the form of personal and business bankruptcies, foreclosures, and rising debt. Despite the tens of thousands of empty homes and rental units in American cities—which, it should be noted here, are easily capable of offering adequate housing—a growing number of municipal governments have been forced to tolerate tent camps and large-scale homeless squats in their homeless management strategies.[6]

These tent camps, however, remain outside of ten-year planning language. Since 2014, the cities of Seattle, Washington, Eugene and Ashland, Oregon, San Francisco and Sacramento, California, and Austin, Texas (among others) have formed alliances with housing activists, tiny home entrepreneurs, religious charities such as Mobile Loaves and Fishes, and homeless people. These alliances are designed to explore the possibility of building transitional housing camps, affordable tiny homes for the poor, or for extending the rights of those camps and shelters already in the midst of critical displacements. In other words multiple groups are in the midst of establishing themselves through protest, direct action and court battles within local strategic emergency housing policies. Many of these camps have succeeded in obtaining the legal, and that means the judicially sanctioned, right to space on which to build emergency housing, even if on a temporary basis. In August 2015, the City of Dallas, Texas entered into a formal arrangement with a local Non-Profit called CitySquare to build the "Cottages at Hickory Crossing," an intentional community for the homeless. We will later discuss how such places differ from our case studies, particularly in view of the millions of dollars in funding they have received. But since they are being recognized as legitimate Housing First programs, it could be that an important shift in policy language could take place, pending outcomes here and elsewhere.

A note on terminology: the inhabitants of "camps," "tent camps," or "homeless camps" by and large reject these names. These inhabitants remain adamant that they want to avoid the stigma of such names. Ibrahim Mubarak, founder of the emergency rest area Right 2 Dream Too in Portland (and many of his group along with him) refer to themselves as "houseless." They want to argue that home can be in any kind of structure, even a tent, and that "houses is what they need." Beyond the debate between houseless and homeless, common labels seem inappropriate: there are few tents in such places, and the idea of a camp suggests impermanence. Dignity Village member Dave Samson has argued that such a term "sort of limits the horizon, right? I mean, you call this place a camp, and then what can you really expect from people here? Not much." Clearly, the idea of home is both a spatial—or physical—matter, and a mental-imaginary one.

This excerpt from *Dignity in Exile* (*2012*) might help explain this:

> Later that day, I showed the residents an early version of my film, *Subtext*.[7] It was a way for them to get to know me and to understand how I saw things, and to decide whether they wanted me to come stay there. The response was surprising. Most notably, villagers felt that they had seen mirror images of themselves in the squatters in Toronto's defunct Tent City. They were equally angry at the way Tent City was demolished, and several remarked that Tent City probably would have had a chance at it if only they had had more structure and were able to negotiate a lease with the city.
>
> After the viewing, Brad remarked that he was even more grateful to have his shack. He, like most people in the village, dreamt about having a home or a subsidized apartment, but the odds against actually finding mainstream housing were high in Oregon, as they were in most of the U.S. And as Brad suggested, "I can see all kinds of possible drawbacks to having housing that I never imagined before, and it makes me think."
>
> At dusk, after the village had quieted down, Brad and I concluded our first interview, though, looking back at it literally in digital form, it does not feel like an interview. If there was such a thing as conversational anthropology, this surely was it. I was fairly certain that these folks at the village were homeless, but that the painted shacks, the gardens, the flags flying and the smell of meals being cooked on various barbeques were all symptomatic of a housed community. Brad didn't agree.
>
> "I'm still homeless."
>
> "But why? You have a house?"
>
> "Technically, I'm homeless."

"According to whom?"
"The city, the state, the federal government."
"But what about in your state of mind?"
"Homelessness is a state of mind. Home is where your heart is, so you are never without a home."

Language and terminology are understood by successful organizers of these communities to be powerful tools. For this reason we have come to embrace camps as socially organized, politically driven forms of intentional community. Communities specifically built around an organizational goal are called intentional communities; in this case, the organizing categories are *emergency* and *transitional* housing. Homeless tent camps, shantytowns and tent cities are all intentional communities. For strictly analytical purposes, in this book I refer to them as *Intentional Homelessness Communities (IHCs)*.

The success or failure of proposed and existing IHCs is hard to predict, given that they occupy a difficult discursive space in an emerging struggle between institutional housing models and grassroots solutions. By that I mean that the general public and policy makers can grasp the difference between the sudden appearance of unplanned and desperate tent camps, and publically funded Housing First programs. People can take a position towards either on several moral and political grounds—are they safe, are they too expensive, and should public money go into these? But the IHC inheres the grassroots orientations of random tent camps, with the organized rule-driven structures of HF, and therefore people tend to ask: "Are they shelters or are they something profoundly different? If they are not merely desperate claims on space, are they some new way of doing housing that threatens our expectations for officially sanctioned housing space?" "NIMBY" is an acronym for "Not in my backyard" and it speaks to the dilemma conventional publics face when IHC start to become sanctioned living spaces. I will expand on this below, but for now it is worth noting that these varied perceptions are very much at the heart of the debates I encountered.

Political shifts on city councils, bad press from camps, and failed action by housing activists undermine the negotiations. For example, in June 2013 the city of Seattle decided to abandon some of its historically "tolerated" homeless camps such as the infamous "Nickelsville" and began to argue in favour of shelters and affordable housing projects. By contrast Eugene, Oregon christened its first city-sanctioned camp "Opportunity Village" in August of 2013, and is currently (2015) working on plans for another. Different regions have different value systems, emerging from their own local contexts and history. These differences influence the case a given group of housing activists must make.

1.3 The Portland Urban Imaginary and Dignity Village

Responses to homeless solutions have been warmer in Oregon, where there is a tradition of grassroots communitarian responses to poverty. Oregon's longstanding resource economy and vast wild territories fostered a legendary hobo and migrant worker economy spanning much of the 19th and early 20th centuries. Mobile labor was needed, traditionally involving relocating to different camps in search of seasonal work. In addition, unemployment rates fluctuated. These factors have fed into what we can think of as a common value system, or to borrow a term from critical thinking, a *symbolic imaginary*[8] (here I use the term as it has been defined by Jacques Lacan [(1971) 2002], Castoriadis [1987] and Wright [1997]). I use this term to think about a shared system of (urban) identities and attitudes towards the use of space that, in this case, understands rough sleeping and impoverished shelter communities as part of Oregon lore.[9]

Portland in particular has a strong grassroots environmental and communitarian tradition, and has enjoyed a creative artistic urban imaginary that includes community-based alternative cooperatives like *City Repair* and the *Village Building Convergence*. These initiatives have questioned the monopoly of urban space by the wealthy for over twenty years.[10] Activist groups have periodically occupied abandoned lots and built communal gardens, taken control of neighborhood streets, transforming them into parkettes and communal tea stations. These activists are champions of the emerging "tiny house movement."[11] Portland was a city of 598,000 people in 2011. Census data from 2013 records the population at 609,456. As the largest urban center in the state, it has borne the brunt of demands for social services in a period of economic recession and rising poverty rates. Such poverty has not been seen there since the early 1960s, when Johnson declared his national War on Poverty. In the years since 2008, some 120,000 people have crossed into poverty, bringing the total to 596,000. This number is only slightly smaller than the total population of Portland; it is nearly double the population of Oregon's next two largest cities, Eugene and Salem. The U.S. national poverty rate stands at an average of 14.3%,[12] close to 47 million people. Oregon's poverty rate sits above the national average, close to 15.8%. Almost 7.2 percent of Oregonians live in "deep" poverty (an example of this would be a family of three that earns less than $8,687.00 a year). Poverty is worse in Oregon, as it is in most places, for people who are not white. White, non-Hispanic poverty sits at about 13.1%. For people who are not classified as white, the rate jumps precipitously: 23.1% for Native Americans, 28.8 % for Latinos, and 39.0 % for blacks. By 2010, the number of children in poverty had increased to 1 in 5, or 16.9% to 21.6% (Oregon Center for Public Policy, Fact Sheet 2011). Given the widespread distribution of poverty, homelessness can be difficult to define or to measure in static or uniform terms, both in Oregon generally, and Portland, especially.[13]

17

Between 2010 and 2012, the number of people identified by the Portland Housing Bureau's various street counts as being "literally homeless" increased by 7% (from 2,542 to 2,727). A different kind of count was made by the U.S. Department of Housing and Urban Development (HUD). The HUD counts people who are "unsheltered"—living in hostels or vouchered in motels. But such groups are difficult to enumerate, is likely well below the actual number of people living on the streets. The real number may be twice as high.

Cities that receive funding from Housing and Urban Development are required to send out researchers at various points in time to calculate the numbers of homeless. This is known as the "Point in Time Count." In the 2013 Point in Time Count, the city of Portland recorded increases in all four categories of homelessness (COP 2013). The broadest definition includes people who literally have no shelter, people who are in shelters, people in transitional housing and people doubling up at other people's places. The difference between this and other definitions is its reflection of a broader and more facile grasp of the complications associated with homelessness at any given time, complications that are greater than most large funding agencies had imagined. The traditionally popular definition of homelessness meant *being literally without shelter*, having nowhere sleep except shelters, if that. But the definition of what homelessness means now, for reasons we will examine in greater detail in other chapters, has shifted to include inconveniences like couch surfing or temporary housing because these experiences are on the rise across urban populations.

In October 2014, the Canadian Press covered my dissertation award. Many people I had known found out that I had identified as homeless. I was faced with a number of very heated and critical debates about my identification. I was told "you better be careful, someone in your position, when you call yourself, homeless; you were never homeless, not homeless like we think of homeless." My response to such cautions was simple. I had identified with this broader definition because I had slept outside, couch-surfed, been evicted during my years as an addict. We have come to understand that these experiences befall millions of people in North America who are not addicts but who end up without a home. I had to remind my critics that enlightening them about just how complicated homelessness had become (and perhaps had always been) was exactly the kind of lesson I hoped my work would provide.

In my research in the U.S., it has become clear to me that agencies charged with delivering social services and providing essential basic institutional care, like schooling, tended to support broader definitions, while agencies that funded such programs tended to restrict the definitions to specific classes related to literal or frequent homelessness. The tendency then is for funders to try to manage numbers, and for providers to try and manage the human condition.

By the broadest definition employed by other government agencies (including the U.S. Department of Education), the number increased from 14,451 to 15,563. This figure includes people couch-surfing or doubling up on housing as a result of economic hardship. This group tends to be ignored by average people when they speak of homelessness, but it is more difficult to accept for those concerned with the general wellbeing of people, because it is about 2.62% and more than twice the national average of people literally without housing. Along with all the cities in the U.S. and Canada that had promised to end homelessness according to 10-year plans, Portland has failed to do so. The total of the broadest category of the homeless population in the Portland area is now as high as 15,917 (ibid). Portland remains a city with one of the historically highest per capita poverty rates in the U.S.

Because of a history of high numbers of homeless residents, camping and squatting in the Portland area have not been uncommon. In 2000 homeless activists challenged the city in the Supreme Court of the state of Oregon. Part of the reason the decision was in their favour was the pre-existence of an urban value system that understood campgrounds and rough living as part of the regional identity. In June 2013, Dignity Village celebrated 12 years as an avatar of the emotional and protracted debate about the place of emergency intentional homeless camps in modern American cities.

The debate over Dignity Village surges every time the city announces proposals to extend the village's contract, or when the village is due for fire department and other city-led inspections. Contract negotiations are lengthy and pit different internal factions and visions of the village against one another. As recently as August 12, 2013, a local activist[14] in the Portland area drew attention to the village's ongoing drug problems on the grounds that such exposure would help residents "get on track."

A recent column in the *Oregonian*—a popular newspaper that is often critical of the Village—claimed that Portland's homelessness problem is not the result of economic problems, but rather because the city has become a symbolic magnet for transient homeless people from across the state and the nation (Pindyck, E., September 1, 2012)[15]: "It's not because of the temperate weather, or local demands for housing, but the problem it seems, has more to do with our collective attitudes than anything else." Permissive idealism is depicted as the real problem, an orientation toward homelessness that enables the homeless population to continue growing. Here, the homeless belong in shelters, housing programs, and jails. The problem is one of attitudes, not numbers.

Activist websites like the *Portland Occupier*[16] and grassroots magazines like *Street Roots*[17] frame the issue differently; here, permissiveness is seen as a recognition of human rights and basic needs for the poor. Both individual communities as well as the state as a whole have a responsibility to help them.

Furthermore, so-called guardians of this permissiveness argue that the home-less have the right to help themselves by occupying city space and building camps. This is because the American Constitution grants them the right to shelter, and because the help they *deserve* is not forthcoming. This echoes the popular position espoused in current state "Homeless Bill[s] of Rights"; these bills seek to table and establish legislative sanctions in favor of the poor, including repealing anti-loitering laws, outlawing discriminatory zoning and rental practices that exclude the homeless and their organizations and other practices that violate the rights of the poor.[18] These bills of rights currently exist as law only in Rhode Island and Connecticut, but are being explored in several states, including Oregon and California. Even though such bills have seen limited success, lawmakers are being asked to recognize that there is room within conventional urban imaginaries for the homeless.

Some people are troubled by the notion of imaginaries, but I find it an elucidating concept. Variations of this concept are also elucidating, such as "urban imaginaries." My use follows two critical scholars who have studied attitudes towards urban life. Castoriadis (1987) and Wright (1997) each invoke a Marxian lens in crafting imaginaries in which the material value of space and of social behaviour in spaces (or perhaps one might say "lived experiences") vary widely between urban and other locations. Imaginaries produce narra-tives that members of communities consume about space, morals, right and wrong and so on. Expectations per se inhere narratives of inevitability, and imaginaries try to tell us what to expect from our social worlds. Wright in particular demonstrates that current attitudes towards the use of urban space are the results of mediations over time between competing views on accepta-ble reality and spatial values under late neoliberal capitalism (1992, 1997, 2000). This is not to say that spatializations of poverty such as homeless camps are widely accepted as legitimate (that is, legally and politically acceptable) forms by members of conventional imaginaries, even in Oregon. More accu-rately, such attitudes are understandable in the symbolic, narrative, and imagi-nary concepts Oregonians use to organize their feelings and ideas about poverty, constitutional rights, and community uses of space. A key reason for this apparent "permissiveness" lies in the historical roots that people recog-nize, even if they disagree with it on moral or other grounds.

This goes for homeless Oregonians as well. Since the emergence of Dignity Village, urban developers—along with others for whom city space is a matter of capital investment—continue to raise questions about the validity of this use of space. Tension remains between the use of public space for profit versus for people; space as part of the network of basic human rights. This tension comprises a central critical dynamic to debates about intentional communities for the homeless. This is not simply a classic Marxian conflict between the rich and the poor, where space is a commodity (Castells 1983; Harvey 2008). Most critics of the village would be delighted if it lived up to its mandate as a transitional community with a moral duty and legal mission to help wayward souls back into the neoliberal fold. Villagers would be deserving of the space, that is, if they earned it, by doing something positive for society, even if just to conquer addictions or find work and pay taxes. Though this tension is hardly surprising we need to recognize it for what it is; an attempt by powerful and dominant groups to impose on lesser and weaker ones a moral normative position on where and how to live. In Portland, like every city in North America, there are wealthy people and poor people. And like every city, good people with some wealth debate what to do about the homelessness problem. What is of particular interest in this case—and others involving IHCs—powerful groups are being forced to ask what to do with a solution proposed *by* the homeless *for themselves*, what are often called intentional communities. At some point, the question arises: what makes one deserving of assistance, and how far should that assistance go?

Under neoliberalism, *deserving subjectivities* are by and large seen primarily in terms of economic roles.[19] Conservative imaginaries want the village to live up to its transitional promise, and return homeless people to self-governed lifestyles. The promise, however faint it might be, of transition from prior failed roles to conventional and socially useful ones, is a basic goal of most long-term shelters, transitional housing, rehabs, and other "workfare" projects. This promise of transition rests at the heart of the social contract that makes such uses of space sensible to conventional imaginaries. Hence Fairbanks Jr. (2004) has used Foucault's (1991) *governmentality critique* for understanding tolerance for spatializations of service for the poor. Governmentality, understood here as the range of techniques employed by government to produce self-regulating subjects, is a critical anchoring point for my research for many reasons, but at this juncture, I point out only that Foucault argued that suitable self-conduct, that is the government of one's self, was a basic requirement of neoliberal citizenship, as a certain expression of freedom (1991). Criticisms of Dignity Village and other camps, center on the assumption that in these places people do not self-govern well. They do drugs. They do not move out of the village. Neo-liberal urban imaginaries do not like people who visibly fail at self-governance, especially when they are allowed to do so on land for free while others pay rent. Land has value and part of good self-governance is learning how to pay for space.

In North America, the cleansing of urban cores has been happening for decades, with conventional urban planners and housing providers confounded by the pervasiveness of abject homelessness on city streets. The battle has raged in particular in those cities where Business Improvement Districts (BIDS) have been implanted as a means of organizing capital against the street homeless (WRAP 2008). Polarization over the spatial rights of the homeless increasingly is defined by the objections of capital though BIDS, and the claims of activists, communitarian movements, and non-profits in the name of their homeless members. While the presence of wealthy, powerful BIDS suggests a classic Marxian conflict between capital and the exploited classes, the fact that some of these intentional camps have been recognized by the state as legitimate—if not temporary—responses suggests that one must abandon strict conflict-based perspectives in order to understand how homeless activism gives power to the very poor in order to politically defeat capital. In Portland, BIDS, Economic Improvement Districts (EID), and since 2010 "Ecodistricts," all tend to spearhead the debate over how to develop the city core and to improve its standing as a vibrant and sustainable community.[20] City-council debates over how to make the city richer and better to live in continue, all the while homeless people queue for shelter beds and food, or sneak into the night to sleep in laneways and abandoned lots. Housing activists contest the use of this private city space too.

Skyscraper and R2DToo.
Photo: Keiki-Alexander, 646Studios.

1.4 Spatial Concerns and Liminal Spaces

The concept of space is of key importance to my research. Space is what is under dispute. Homeless claimants want an address, and a certain amount of space on which to build small shelters. While chapter six discusses this in more detail, here we may begin with the premise that space itself has no essential value. Its value originates with what humans impose on it, usually monetary. In 2000, Dignity activists were able to exploit a loophole in state law that granted cities the constitutional right to build two emergency campgrounds. This enabled them to build their community. The city's response was to force compromises on that decision involving how much land, how many buildings, how close or how far they should be, their distance from the center of town, maximum occupation laws and so on.

These are all measures of what Soja (1996) has called "firstspace." Firstspace is the physical vector of space; that which can be counted, measured, and commoditized. It is in this sense the space of domination and control; space that can be made accessible to those who govern well in the manner described above, or withheld from those who fail to do so. It is the space that is parceled into square metres and lots and on which a fee is imposed for its use.

Beyond firstspace is what Soja calls "secondspace": this is the mental vector of space, the experiences that we imagine to go on in certain spaces. It is a concept worth understanding for my own research, given that a certain tension exists between how conventionally housed people see the normal home ideal and the failure of such camps to support this myth.

Soja argues that the classic antagonism between space and time in social theory originates with the traditional cleaving of space into these two vectors. In his model of "thirdspace"—his term for the unanticipated qualities of space—Soja unites Lefebvre's (1974) representational space (that part of social space where ideas and critique abound) with Foucault's (1984) heterotopias (temporary sites of counter conduct or resistance) with the notion of abstract space (or physical). This allows space to be metaphorically torn open, available to a near-infinite array of interpretation, be it emotional, historical, light, dark, safe, tangible, imaginative, and so on. This allows us to more easily recognize the diverse critiques that space represents rather than a simple binary construction. IHCs constitute those zones of living in which people are caught up in what may be thought of as "the uncertainty of life"; with this term I am thinking of narratives of inevitability that seek to impose control and order by measuring empirical experiences against the imagined concept of home. In fact, one of the reasons why these places are so difficult for many citizens to accept is the ambiguity they present. They pose a conundrum to people who see human life as being guided by narratives of what might be described as inevitable order. For such a space to become legitimate, organizers of successful IHCs must brand their model in a way that suits dominant critical powers. The reality is that even the powerful are leery of ambiguity and especially of uncertainty.

Another concept that helps us think about space is liminality. *Liminal* is a descriptive concept that originated in late 19th century psychology to represent the emergent capacities of certain undesirable personality conditions. The idea is rooted to the base plank of a door, or *limen*, which is a sort of threshold one must cross on the way to somewhere else. Undergoing transitional experiences or liminal events seems vital not just to individuals, but also to entire social groups; this at any rate is the argument of French folklorist Arnold Van Gennep in *Les Rites Des Passages* (1908). Van Gennep, in his discussion of rites of passage, describes transitional stages in individual lives when they are removed from antecedent social contexts and roles on the way to achieving new ones.

In recent years, some attention has been paid to the liminal nature of homelessness, and to homeless people as *liminal personae*—Victor Turner's (1969) name for members occupying spaces of liminality like festivals or ritual processes (Turner 1969, 1985; Baumhol 1996; Hopper and Baumhol 2004; Leginski 2007; Weissman 2012). The term liminality has common usage in the social sciences, and even reaches into many areas of social and cultural analysis (Myerhoff 1982; St. John 2001; Harper and Baumhol 2004; Topinka 2010). Liminal mental and physical spaces are dark and suspicious, ambiguous, and very often the source of fear and anxiety. People stuck in liminal phases (or undergoing it) were and are seen as unclear, impure, and not-yet-characterized as being successful; the reason is that their transition to expected roles and status is incomplete. Turner suggested that inverting and experimenting with roles and statuses was vital to social structural stability. He envisioned a ludic (what we might call frivolous or playful) and experimental space for this called "communitas" (1967). Communitas suggests a kind of temporary space, such as those found in festivals or performances; in this way, it does not bear the mantle of responsibility for transiting people from ludic to "real" statuses. This expectation for successful transition is part of the redemption narratives I alluded to above. It is almost a stereotype or cliché to think of adults who "act like children" or never grow up; in every culture there is an expectation that members will transit through statuses necessary for the social world. We pity those who fail, and we rejoice when the same people overcome obstacles to redeem their failed nature. This was my own story, which I discuss in more detail in chapter three.

However, while the village I participated in was replete with childish behaviour, there was nothing funny about it, so I exclude this concept from my discussions of IHC because homelessness is rarely ludic. Homelessness is, in fact, increasingly permanent. In the West, liminality amongst the homeless is under-theorized [21] but we do know that the length of homelessness is associated with the severity of addictions, mental illness, physical disabilities, and high mortality rates (NCH 2011; NAEH 2012; HUD 2012).

Intentional homeless communities of the kinds we are discussing are relatively new to North America. Yet the mission statement of many of these insists that building community is essential to helping homeless people reclaim themselves. A central question in this book is to what extent the struggle for intentional homeless communities or residency in such places helps people transcend liminality.

Such communities are liminal spaces—ostensibly designed and legally encoded to facilitate transitions from marginal to conventional—but they are often characterized by unanticipated outcomes, even failures. For this reason, in order to theorize their role in the world of homeless strategies, we cannot try to reduce these experiences into simplistic frames of understanding. Such simplification is precisely what Latour argues leads to social critique "running out of steam" (2005). Social critique too often seeks the reduction of complex situations into simpler applications of a few essential criteria to a given problem. Such reductionism is impossible in liminal spaces—this, at any rate, is the basis of my argument.

Rather, ambiguity and diversity are most fruitfully envisioned as the basis for meaningful social critique. This allows us to look at how life reveals itself through what Soja called a "thirding" (and many today would call a "queering") of such spaces, a realm in which we come to understand that there will always be a number of outcomes for different inhabitants. Individual IHCs, regardless of how they are envisioned or how they present themselves in the media, have many faces. It might seem obvious that we now live in a world of increasingly complicated domestic households, many of which defy simple definitions. But the open-mindedness of any given outsider is rarely so perfectly ubiquitous. When alternative uses of public space are brought into the debate, the tensions between established powerful groups and claimants increase—at times violently.[22]

Recognition of the liminality of homelessness is due in part to the enormity of the problem. Since the 1980s a new kind of poverty has emerged: mothers and children, young people, able-bodied white-collar workers cast aside by the economy. Every decade since the 1980s, the percentage of first-time homeless people, white-collar deportees to limbo, and others have contributed to the economically and socially destabilizing effects of millions of people moving into and out of homelessness. Less concern was paid to the antecedent avatars of homelessness—the drunk men and women who lined laneways and begged on street corners. These were understood as tragic "worst cases," collateral damage to be managed by local charity in a system that creates poverty, addiction, and psychiatric patients just as it produces wealth (Marcuse 1983; Rossi 1989; Davis 1999; Bourgois and Schonberg 2008). The system has also been quite successful at depicting flawed individuals as the root cause of homelessness. Many researchers have observed that it has taken 100 years to change that understanding (Riis, 1905; Wilson 1911; Andersen, 1923; 1975, Liebow 1967; Bahr, 1968; Wagner 1995; Wright 1999; DePastino 2003).

Drugs, alcohol and mental illness do not cause homelessness. Homelessness is caused by rising levels of poverty, a retraction of long-term care for addicts and patients, and a lack of affordable housing (NCH 2010; NAEH 2011; HUD, "Opening Doors" 2012). In the current U.S. context, in which 52 million people live below the poverty line and are therefore close to homelessness, the 3 million or so who move in and out of homelessness constitute a base number. This number will rise if economies and governments do not shift their focus (NCH 2011; NAEH 2011).[23] With shelters and government housing filling up with women and children, and with cities increasingly clamping down on homeless sleepers in parks, the usual places available to the homeless are decreasing. What is available is also less safe. These individuals have by necessity needed to form camps. While this is something that unsheltered persons have always done, more than ever before they are willing to fight for that right. Part of this fight emerges from desperation: they have nowhere else to go. But equally, part of the fight is related to the presence of sanctioned intentional homeless communities that offer hope of winning the right to self-govern in intentional community.

To return to the concept of liminality: it may be understood as a threat to the person stuck in it, as well as to the social structures that depend on people moving successfully through socially necessary roles. For the individual the threat is actual and corporeal; people need places to live and roles to live by. A large number of people stuck in homeless limbo is a cause of concern to authorities. Such a situation is characterized by unpredictability and the range of possible critical moments—crime, rebellion, occupations and so on. Poverty in and of itself is relatively little concern to neoliberalism. Neoliberalism produces, polices, and protects poverty and the poor. An entire industry is built around criminalizing, warehousing, and servicing the poor. But concentrated spatializations of poverty are a relatively new phenomenon as far as neoliberalism is concerned. In fact, these camps are just beginning to be understood by the homeless, the state, and researchers like myself for their diverse potential to produce social critique, as well as for the roles they happen to be playing in the fight for shelter and home, even if cities do not recognize them officially. The role they play is to help people change their perceptions about poverty, housing and social justice. As much as the IHCs we talk about are about housing per se, they are also about changing the way we look at solving social problems.

Beyond the unpredictable ideas and actions such spaces might produce, the liminality of the village is also a spatial concern. Van Gennep and others have spoken of the importance of "passage" in the social, spiritual, and physical sense. In many cultures, passages are clearly marked, whether by sign posts, flags, anthems and border crossings. Such markings act as ritually symbolic designations of passages from place to place. In the design of some ancient walled cities, citizens lived within the protection of the gates; others whose character appeared to be of a more questionable nature were expelled to the regions beyond its safety. In this case, the city of Portland pushed Dignity Village as far away as possible from the city center—from the core of social services and other homeless networks that the villagers actually need. This was because the businesses in downtown Portland were unwilling to accept the presence of Dignity Village anywhere else. It was also a kind of demonstration by the city that it had control over the village.

Today the inhabitants of Dignity Village are so distanced—in both the geographical as well as the social sense—from the world in which they could find employment or housing that their social marginalization is reinforced. In this way, the village has liminality built right into its metaphorical foundations. It becomes virtually everything, *an island of misfit toys* as Mitch Grubic and Dave Samson—both ex-village council members—have said repeatedly. So the liminality of the village is perpetual, with very few people ever successfully moving from there into homes or to jobs. Put simply, these post-liminal roles no longer exist, and certainly not for misfits. And failure to advance out of this state of permanent liminality is part of the negative frame drawn around the Village by many authorities; widespread acceptance of such a negative frame makes the Village appear all the less viable or desirable by the wider public. The further the camp lies from conventional, established roles, the easier it is to protect the moral-normative vision of "home" that fuels neoliberalism. Successful IHCs have the potential to threaten such visions.

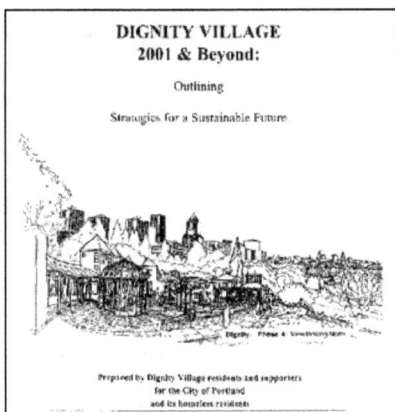

DIGNITY VILLAGE
2001 & Beyond:

Outlining

Strategies for a Sustainable Future

Prepared by Dignity Village residents and supporters for the City of Portland and its homeless residents

Cover page of the Village Plan, 2001. From the mission statement: "The Village will integrate itself within the city so as to be a contribution to the life of Portland, presenting a public face that will invigorate the life of adjoining streetscapes and public areas. Consistent with the structure of Dignity thus far, the Villagers will actively participate in the design and will literally build the phases of the Village through their own sweat-equity. The Public spaces will be designated, path and roadway infrastructure laid out, and the tent pods will be sited in anticipation of more permanent shared-housing structures to be built in Phase 1."

1.5 Community, First

There is disagreement about whether nor not Dignity Village and places like it should be considered communities or not. Moreover, if they are accepted as communities, how can people living in "nice" suburbs or small recognizable neighborhoods reconcile that they fall in the same category? While the notion of community is vague, there is value in claiming it. At very least, community is an idea that bridges unusual uses of space like tent camps with conventional ones. Moreover, community is also suggestive of the structural and infrastructural ties each has with the other. These ties are stated goals of IHC, but rarely do urban neighborhoods declare themselves to want to be good members of the local homeless community. In other words, IHCs understand themselves to be looking for a place within the broader community; however, broader communities are uncertain whether or not IHCs should exist at all. Opponents (like many of the writers of op-eds appearing in the *Oregonian* newspaper) prefer other terms: tent camp, shanty town, or (grudgingly) homeless community or community of shacks. Even so, residents and proponents of the IHC model can argue, as I will in the following pages, that such spaces are in fact specifically communities first, with specific orientation and ethical ideals by which people in them are to live. A number of community ethnographies have influenced this study of homelessness. Important studies include Snow and Anderson, Wagner, Ward, and Bourgois, all of whom have influenced my own work significantly. These studies have demonstrated that despite the drugs, the mental health issues, the poverty and other stigmatizing generalizations made about poor communities, life there continues; life that is inclusive of love, pain, suffering, marriage, friendship and death. But what these generalizations tend to demonstrate for me is that the stigmatizing features of marginalized neighborhoods and the ways of life they represent can easily be applied to conventional living spaces as well. In fact, all they really do is confirm the fact that the homeless are people too, and their social networks and spaces they occupy are communities just like yours in the ways that matter.

Framing my research as it happened as part of the community dynamic—that is emplacing this pragmatic ethnography as part of the communities it discusses—helps to reveal how this research was constructed in real situations. For Casey (1996)[24] *place*, after all, denotes a setting, a context and a sense of lived experience and is the basic component of ethnographic understanding.[25] Looking at my work, I tend to use the words *space* or *spaces* in relation to the size, location, and structural parameters of a given location. My understanding of place is as a way of uniting human action and lived performances in temporal and spatial terms. Casey says, "Places are not added to sensations any more than they are imposed on spaces. Both sensations and spaces are themselves emplaced from the very first moment, and at every subsequent moment as well" (1996:19).

As the "basic component of ethnographic understanding," a community like Dignity Village, and intentional communities in general, are perhaps the best if not the last manifestation of the ideal community model in the sense that they are intentionally demarcated by measures of space, such as fence lines and gateways, thresholds and passageways encoded and enshrined in planning documents, building codes, site maps, rules of conduct and the actual spatialization of structures on sites. Each of the above is a type of physical measurement for defining the zone of action for the community as a *firstspace*: the place, Dignity Village is at 9401 NE Sunderland, in Portland. It is populated by members who come to know and recognize each other as members of the same community. In fact, as we will see people enter the village as "guests", then become "residents" and finally "members." Each of these titles is collectively and ritually expressed. Within the governance of that community, then , each person is compelled to follow rules of conduct that unite people across a range of possible behaviors whose important ethnographic measure is understood as everyday experience, as time spent in *secondspace.* This, we recall, is Soja's name for the part of spaces that we experience but can't measure mathematically.

If nothing else, villagers agree that community implies a sense of belonging to a group and of that group to be grounded in a given location. Set off to the margins of the city, and to the margins of capital, inclusive identities—*member, community, friend,* and *villager*—become meaningful at a level most of us in conventionally understood housing take for granted. Rocky, a resident of Dignity Village, and one of the few homeless women veterans I met, once said: "We're a family out here. We look out for each other. And nobody judges no one, cause we all been there. Even if we had a 'beef' back there (on the streets). I mean no one understands homelessness until they get here. God forbid. That's what makes this community different than normal (laughs) ones. We might be a bunch of fuck ups, but we all know we belong here, together. Hell, who else is 'gonna' let us live like this together. You tell me where?" (Phone chat, December 2012)

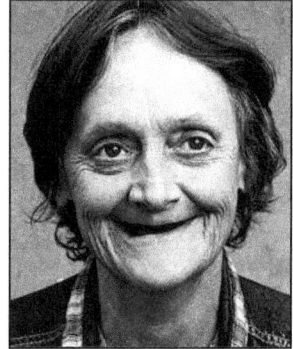

Rocky, 2011.
Photo: Nigel Dickson.

This statement, as simple as it is, suggests that there is some value in understanding the fence, the gate, the sign and the property that contains Dignity Village as delineating a unique kind of community space. A villager's social relations may not be wholly bounded by that geography, but even so, for those who live in that space, the integration of conventional and homeless social and symbolic imaginaries yields social relations of particular import to the community that mirror the conventional. While it may mirror the conventional, however, these spaces "would largely be rejected by it, if they happened anywhere else" (Stacey 1975 in Brunt 2004:89; Mosher 2010; Weissman 2012).

Dignity Village is called *Dignity Village* on purpose. Ex-founder Ibrahim Mubarak explains that "we called it a village because it is a community first, and most important." In 2012, I had an instructive conversation with Dave Samson, then security head of the village:

"Where do you want to be in a year, David?"
"You mean, aside from save the whole planet in general and myself?"
"How long will you be in the village?"

"I am thinking a year. And then a bunch of us are trying to build a new intentional community. I don't want to live in Rome anymore. Our civilization is Rome
and it's gonna fall. But to carry the message, first you have to build it, not just
building it, living it. My carbon footprint is small. I don't want to contribute to the
garbage and consumerism culture. I want to contribute to healthy, positive, sane,
sober living. Sane behavior. People treating each other with dignity and respect.
Human beings and animals are not trash, they are not disposable items."

"Okay, okay. So beyond the rhetoric, which I don't disagree with, what can the
village do for people in the short term?"

"Relieve survival anxieties."

"And in the long term? Maybe some of them get jobs, some might get housing,
and some will go back to the streets?"

"Yeah. I hate to say it," Dave concedes, "but some of them can't be saved. But
as long as we offer safe communities for people, a great number more can be saved
than the current system model offers."

"David, let's end this right now. What is dignity?"

"Well.... having or getting the sense returned to you that you are a human
being, you are worthy of time and place and community."

"Okay. Leave it on that, Dave" (*Dignity in Exile* 2012:132).

Dave Samson.
Photo: Nigel Dickson.

One of the important insights gained from community ethnographies has been to recognize
that local communities can no longer be understood outside of, or free from, power relations
and struggles with other communities or levels
of government (Brunt 2004:84). Dignity Village
created its own space within an extant regime
through critical action and protest, and invited
the city to rule over it.[26] Put otherwise, by framing its claim to existence as a democratic and
constitutional right, and by agreeing to specific
terms of cooperation in its contract with the city,
Dignity Village asserted itself into a pre-existing political, economic and social
context. As such, Dignity Village became a transitional housing camp, in a
lease with the city. In this sense, it is a community, but the power dynamic
that encapsulates it is best understood as a tactical agreement between the
state and the protesters. In this dynamic, the spatialization was conditioned by
the encoding of the activist community's function as an alternative path to re-
producing self-governing individuals—the same purpose that rehabs and
transitional shelters serve. The Village won the right to be an alternative part
of a strategy for containing homeless people on the grounds that it would be
self-governing according to the law as expressed in a formal agreement (and
later, in a contract with the city). For its part, the city placed a range of
prerequisite codes of construction on the Village. This was one of many

aspects of city control over the space and people who reside there. At the same time, in 2002 the Village was located on the outskirts of Portland as a sort of statement that, in terms of the city symbolic imaginary, this spatialization had no proper place, except as far away as possible.[27]

One might assume that size of the community expresses a certain structural complexity, of which the village might be a simpler type. This idea, we know from Van Gennep and Turner, suggests that "simpler" societies present less complicated critiques of identity by more effectively moderating and regulating rites of passage, which are ways of establishing identity.[28]

Community studies have been valuable in overturning any notion that community life is homogenous. Durkheim (1893) argued that life in smaller communities is simpler, and understood in similar terms by each member. Solidarity in these small communities is achieved by the necessary and mechanical dependence of people on one another. By contrast, life in large industrial cities is far more complicated, such that solidarity is achieved by far more complex means. These means are more likely to regulate social relations rather than unifying ideas; in larger groups, then, identity is much less of a real marker. However, community studies perspectives help us to see that the need to see simplification within the complicated organic context can lead to unsatisfied expectations. In small communities like the village, where people with similar histories and experiencing similar common problems: poverty and homelessness, and who willingly participate in a local government, it might seem logical to assume that at some level the effect of power has been to produce a similar mechanical subjectivity amongst them, and also then, potentially similarly motivated political actors. In other words, in a small community, if the bonds are mechanical and the community identity closely wrapped up in each member's immediate social relations, it would seem likely they might act together to meet political and other threats. And in cases, this is true. But not at Dignity Village.

When I visited Dignity Village in 2011 at a time of political crisis, I observed very little political unity. This was true even in a small community of only 60 people. We will see in chapter six that villagers not only debated how to interpret the bylaws of their community, but they also organized around pseudo-militant factions that used expulsion and threats to quell opposing points of view (viewpoints about, for example, how to deal with the city or how to improve the village's political and economic horizons). So while we can agree that Dignity Village is a community, it is one that remains very much divided. Because the village is a community linked to others physically and discursively as part of the bigger narrative on homelessness, the internal issues are very problematic. Later in the book, we are going to see how the problems faced by Dignity Village were recognized, critiqued and overcome by new discursive forms of IHC, in order to avoid that narrative inevitability.

1.6 Critically, Critique

Inasmuch as the village's claim to land was presented to city governance as a cooperative democratically self-governed space in which homeless people could work at recovering their lives before transitioning back into mainstream communities, Dignity shares some similarly to drug rehabs, treatment programs, and other self-help programs for the poor. In this way Dignity appeals to, but is not limited to, critiques of governmentality (Foucault 1991; Tsemberis 1992; Mitchell 2003).[29] How does one reconcile the divergent critical actions of residents at Dignity Village, given that they are subjects of the same shifting political and social structures within and outside of the village? Put otherwise, if they are subject to the same art of government, how does a truly activist moment come to be? If governmentality is everywhere under neoliberal governance (as Foucault might argue), how are these diverse and often disintegrating village identities to be reconciled?

For my earlier work, the key was to locate the potential for critique that resided in Dignity Villagers, and to understand why that potential was not being converted into empowering action for the village as a community. As other types of IHC gained steam during the course of my research, it has become instructive to look to members of R2DToo along with other players in order to uncover ways that they have overcome the crisis of community that Dignity has endured. I do this throughout the book by asking key actors to express their critical imaginings about homelessness, housing policies, and strategies for actions in their own terms. I then consider how these arguments night make sense in these other frames of analysis. What does the actual critique say about critique? In helping Dignity Village to identify the source of its political impotence and social limbo, we have come across a number of observations that are essential to making IHCs viable in the power struggle that is defined by the era of Ten Year Plans to End Homelessness. So we are really looking at the narratives or scripts villagers tell themselves and how these impact the community as a political entity.

In Dignity Village, a number of such scripts exist because to some the village is a permanent residence; to others a temporary space en route to housing or back into homelessness; to activist members, it is a secret place in which to plan protests and experiment with social economy; for others (including myself when I was there), the place was ambiguous and uncertain. Critics of the village cling to this latter position, and therefore the village comes to be both feared and rejected. These observations suggest to me that experience is often understood in terms of mental and physical dimensions, distinct from one another. If firstspace consists of the physical and built urban environment and secondspace embodies the expectations we hold of those structures, then the continuum of debate I have mentioned is largely to be understood in terms of disagreements over narratives describing how the latter should be carried out

in the former. Understood as a "Firstspace-Secondspace bicameral confine-
ment" (Soja 1996:3; Anderson 2002:301), such a perspective restricts critique to
one or the other category of experience, or argues for the normalcy of certain
experiences in certain spaces, and misses the myriad ways time and space are

John Boy Hawkes and Brad Powell, June 2010. Photo: Eric Weissman

imbricated and experienced by actors. The notion of community transcends
this bicameralism, but is ambiguous. For this reason one might want to know
what members of a community understand it to be.

For example, on my first day in the village in June of 2010, Brad Powell,
then CEO, took me on a tour. He described his own past:

> I've only been here for a little over three years. I was homeless, camping out
> on the [Columbia] river a little ways, on one of the sloughs, and one day, the
> city came in with one of their crews from the jail and took our whole camp
> ... took everything, straightened the blades of grass out ... I had nothing ex-
> cept for the backpack on my back ... I had gone to a day-labor place to work
> and when I went home there was nothing there, and I had a friend who had
> lived out here and he told me about it. And I shared the same social stigma
> [towards it] about a 'dirty bum camp'. And when I got here I was amazed.

For Brad, the amazement refers to a psychic shift resulting from actual
experience of the village. Very few people in Portland had even heard about
the village. In the days before I entered I had toured around and talked to shop
owners and tourists. If they had heard of Dignity Village, it had been a long
time ago in a news story. Few people had any idea that it was still there. Brad

was very insistent that daily routines and social structure were important (and not to be confused with structure or structures, the terms they also use to refer to their shacks).

"It saved me. Saved him too," Brad said.

"What exactly?" I asked.

"Structure. Order, I mean rules, not being afraid of rules. I mean we make the rules here so it's better for us here than out there."

1.7 Structure, Agency and Freedom

Living in the village requires homeless people to at least consider the debates that produced the village, its history, and its failed traditions; they may also involve themselves in the current debates about what directions the village can evolve as an experiment with a ticking clock. At the time of the writing of this book, 1½ years remain on a contract that many feel will be the last. Other villagers care little for this deadline and suggest that what really is problematic is that after 14 years the village has progressed little toward its stated goals. Villagers debate how to resolve their poor public image and the administrative incapacity of the village. These debates draw attention to popular values homeless actors employ in the self-reflective process that help them to come to understand themselves as deserving or underserving "selves." We will discuss this in chapter two as a matter of *dialogics*, a process by which actors involved in communicative acts work through their fundamental beliefs and logics to arrive at new understandings. Such self-perceptions impact the choices they make towards critical action. Taking agency to mean the ability of the individual to make her own choices, structure is often counter-positioned to this, as that institutional part of society, which imposes the values and means by which individuals are directed to exercise this agency if at all (Bourdieu 1972; Foucault 1975; Giddens 1976; Bakhtin 1993, 1982; De Certeau 1986; Latour 2005; Isin 2008; Nielsen 2008).

The debate over agency and structure is an important one. This is because in advanced liberal society, citizenship requires involving regular citizens with others in the formal practices of decision making such as elections and campaigning or marching in protests; we call this democracy (Rose 1999:84). Isin (2008) distinguishes between an *activist citizen* whose act is an inversion or break with habitus, and an *active citizen*, who engages in these other practices of freedom that we confuse with acts. An act of citizenship then is unusual and questions these practices in search of social justice. I will test these distinctions as we go along, because of the way these two identities tend to divide villagers in their critical orientation to housing justice.

Critique of housing is also part of governance. That is, those who govern must be critical of their own attempts to provide solutions to housing. Indeed, a major expenditure for social policies like housing is the amount of self-analysis and evaluation that governing officials must employ. If governance could see IHC as politically viable and cost effective, IHCs might be more widely adopted. These are the kinds of qualities we discuss in the final chapter of this book. The claim made about city space by homeless actors is a form of resistance to the power of city councils and welfare programs. But critique is not something only done by angry actors. City councils, the general public and law makers, in this case, make critiques of the same housing problem and are in a position to resist the claim. Governors can stall procedures, use their legislative powers to rescind or amend bylaws governing housing and so on. Resistance, like power, is a concept we will have to question and we do this in chapter four.

Activism is not just about changing conservative aspects of society and reforming them into left-of-center visions of social justice. Even though we commonly think of activism in terms of radically minded people wishing to challenge dominant systems, the truth is that activism is any attempt to mobilize popular action towards perceptions of socially just causes. Conservative and Liberal, left, and right, all use activism. I want this to be clear to the reader. When we read about the Dignity Village activists, we will also have to look at the conservative activists who fought and continue to fight against these IHC models. Understanding both poles on this imaginary continuum of debate as activisms, allows us to look for the way power becomes central to understanding the future of IHC. If the IHC is seen as resistance to powerful narratives with built-in inevitabilities, then activism, on both sides and in other places along this continuum, is the way regular citizens are asked to pipe in on the constitutionality and place of IHC in our cities.

This book then looks at the critical action between villagers as actors in a tentative democracy, and also between the village and broader systems of democratic governance that are powerful too—how do they perceive the claim? What made the claim for better housing, or for a piece of land on which to build a camp, deserving of consideration not only for homeless people, but those in a potentially powerful position to have rejected it, such as city councils or business groups? Perhaps most importantly, what do villagers understand as the means to keep this critically powerful place in the discourse on housing?

Beyond the village, critics look at IHCs as unjust occupations of public land by undeserving squatters, and as a failed transitional housing experience. Supporters prefer to see them as bold and laudable housing actions by deserving citizens. In the former, the villager is imagined as a lawless drug infested den of iniquity; in the latter, a self-governed tribute to democracy in the making. Hence, it is not easy to define the village in terms of what *kind* of place, or community, it is. It is more apt to understand the diversity it represents because actors from within and without the village comprehend it in very different ways. Understanding the possibly infinite meanings that attach to the village helps understand the range of actions people might take in favour or against such places. My concern has been to understand how the debates and competition between villagers over ways of seeing the village impair the collective power.

The question is vital to me because at the time when I was there, I saw little collective critical action. Those few activists I did meet at the village were afraid of powerful factions who threatened to kick them out. This left me wondering: what exactly does democracy mean? As it turns out, the inherent difficulty of democracy—that is, the innate conflict out of which democratic governing is possible—is that it is never a completed project, and is constantly emerging, transforming, changing; in essence, it is a kind of liminality disguised as politics.

1.8 Liminal Democracy: A Conversation with Ibrahim Mubarek, Co-founder of Dignity Village, Founder of R2DToo (July 13, 2011)

Well into my stay at Dignity Village in July 2011 my perspective on intentional

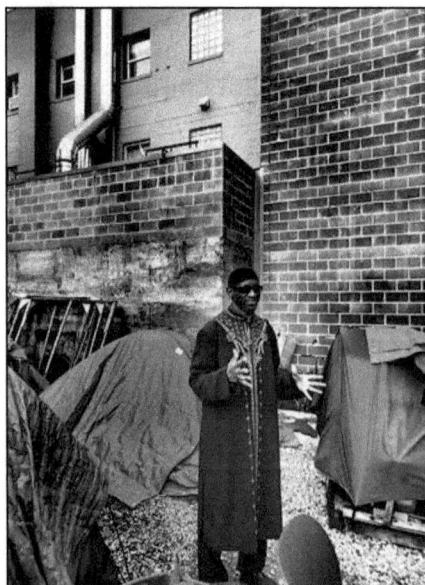

Ibrahim Mubarak at R2DToo, 2013.
Photo: Eric Weissman.

housing camps had changed drastically as a result of the horror stories I had heard from visitors to other tent camps, like Seattle's Tent City 3 and 4. My greatest source of anxiety was the absolute reversal of the community spirit I had witnessed a year earlier. Experiencing day after day the negativity and lack of motivation within Dignity Village, I began to question the validity of such communities. I had been told that I should talk to some of the founders who were in the Portland area. I tried over a period of several weeks to speak with one in particular, but he was always out on "activist business," engaged in an action or a meeting or a protest—in other words, busy with various housing actions, one of which included the planning stages of a well-thought-out occupation of a piece of prime downtown Portland. It would come to fruition some months later as "Right 2 Dream Too" (R2DToo), a tent camp that is by legal definition an "emergency rest area," supporting up to 50 street persons with emergency sleep, showers, and food on a non-resident basis. This emergency camp has since come into existence.

Finally on July 16, 2011, we met. I walked through downtown Portland with Ibrahim Mubarak. "Ib" had been a co-founder of Dignity Village from 2000 to 2004. He had left the village once it was up and running shortly after that and moved in and out of homelessness, kicked his own crack addiction, but continued to remain engaged in homeless activism in the city.

When I met him, he lived in a house with a few other members of his activist network. A couple was camped in his backyard and another couple slept in their minivan on his driveway. It was a modest house, the gardens lush and full like most in the damp Portland climate. Ibrahim, like most of the activist community in Portland, had stopped visiting Dignity Village. Ibrahim had said something that echoed clearly the sentiment of what most housing activists as well as the street homeless themselves had said to me in my jaunts downtown: "When they gave up fighting for the rights of homeless people, we had to start fighting for us, not them living up there—they got themselves housing. We're down here dying on the streets. They just don't know how much they need us too. We need each other."

The rest of the city, the state, the country, and activists around the world had particular views on Dignity Village, views that generally reified the alternative and sustainable qualities of the place. My presence there had soon revealed a darker if not downright stagnant side to life. When I told Ibrahim this, he did not appear surprised. He looked at me and smiled. He is a tall man, Black, Muslim, devout; still proudly American. Gold-capped tooth. When he smiles, his charisma is overwhelming. His smile seemed to say, "Duh. What did you expect?" That is not something he would ever be likely to utter aloud, however. He is a man of dignity, and dignity meant respect both for one's self and for others in Ibrahim's worldview. The following is a transcription of video I shot and my own comments.

He started: "It's like the American country, when the forefathers fought against, England, the British, they had a concept, and they wanted that freedom. They had that fight in them. And now people that's born in this county take it for granted, you know they say: 'this country's good, bam, this country's here, this is a good country,' whereas, you know in other countries people are still struggling. And I don't think the hard-core homeless [in the U.S.] don't struggle as much as people in third block countries. So they're here with you might say a so-called silver spoon in they mouths. And that's what happens to [homeless] people when they go out there to Dignity Village—they say: 'Wow, I don't have to do nothing, I can just stay here and exist.' And there's more to life than just existing. It's a difference between life and survival, man."

One of the reasons I had wanted to meet him was to understand how it might be that the political factions who were controlling the village's democratic government might be overcome, and a more representative voice created.

"The leadership now is only seven people, and it is supposed to be 22." I take the statement as a question. "Yeah, well ... no. No, everybody there's a leader, you just have spokespersons, that's the way it's supposed to be."

I nod because I know how it is supposed to be because I, like most other outsiders, have read the web site and had seen the village promotional videos. "But no these cliques really control who gets into power ... and that's really a problem," I have to insist.

Ptery, 2011. Photo: Nigel Dickson.

He agrees. "Yeah, that's a problem, right. And like I said they get that from grade school. We're taught cliques and power. It's like the Blacks hang out with each other. The Whites hang out with each other. The women hang out with each other. The sports guys hang out with each other.... And it takes a community, an effort of all people—people don't understand the Quran much here in this country, so I usually go to the Bible and I tell them about Babel, and how they was one people and then how God caused a confusion to come on them. And they had different language, different lifestyles. So they was stuck with the people that could understand. And that's how cliques form—and the only thing that was missing was an interpreter. So ... Dignity Village need an interpreter to interpret rules, to interpret life. To interpret how to survive with self-sufficiency. You know I went to the U.S. social forum in Detroit last year, I saw how that city is destroyed by greed and laziness, but now they's starting to rise up with communal living. You got people living together—you got people growing gardens together, feeding off the land, and that was the Dignity Village model—a community ... that's why we called it 'village.'"

He pauses briefly, smiles, and looks at me again with those eyes and that grin, and in a questioning tone, he says/asks, "It takes a village? So that's what they were doing and they need to stick together and figure out a way to survive, 'cause everybody got a right to survive." He smiles, looking for acknowledgement from Ptery, one of the Dignity Village activists who came with me to introduce me to the active side of Portland. The smile capriciously framed around the phrase "right to survive," the name of his housing activist group.

Ibrahim was very much the professional activist. He had that charismatic capacity to impress ideas on people. He was not imposing.

"So they need to start growing their own vegetables, they need to start cooperating again, they need to stop fighting from inside. Cause that's what's gonna destroy them. The city, you know the city's just sitting back and saying, 'okay, just watch it, watch them mess up' and that's exactly what they're doing because they're free ... and they don't know how to make their decisions because they used to people telling them, 'wake up at 6 o'clock, go out in the rain, come back at 7, but we gonna be feeding at 6 ... at night, we gonna be feeding at 12 at noon, and you can use the showers at this time or the next day,' and then, 'we got this amount of fresh clothes ...' they always being told—dictated to—they don't know how to make their decisions. Like I said (earlier) they took their will power away from them and instead of making them independent, they made them DEE-pendent, so that's why they sit out there with their palms up—gimme gimme gimme and waitin' waitin' waitin'. [At the village they say:] 'If I sit here long enough somebody gonna bring something to the village, I don't ever need to leave the village... I can stay here.'"

"And they don't leave," I interject.

"I know," he says, "they stay calm, they stay in jail ..."

"Even their drugs come to them," I add.

He pauses slightly. Looks again with that smile. "And that's a sin and a shame." (This is accompanied by a nervous chuckle.)

I implore him. "You need to come and be a voice, just one voice. Maybe just one day even —?"

He laughs. I am not sure if he is being humble, or if he finds some irony in this. He was the original voice of Dignity Village: Ibrahim, Jack Tafari, some others. He is one of the loudest voices in Portland now. Ptery who introduced me to Ibrahim is learning from Ibrahim. His smile I surmise reveals the confidence that his voice is louder than I know. But then why aren't all the folks at Dignity listening? What happened to that voice that created the moment that became Dignity Village? I suggest it to him again, "You really need to get out there. They need to hear it."

"God's will," he says, "God's will." Laughing, laughing, nervously.

There is a hesitance in Ibrahim's voice. He looks over at Ptery.

Ptery, who has been living at the village for a year, was attracted to Dignity Village for exactly the model of sustainable democratic community that was pitched to him when he arrived. Since then, the other villagers cloistered in their idleness and hands-out comfort, a sort of terminal liminality I had been calling it when at the village, had been hard on Ptery, discouraging his activism. This was, it seemed to him and me, a complete abandonment of the ethos that was behind Dignity Village's triumph as the first city-sanctioned *emergency transitional campground* in modern US history.

Ptery and I glance at each other. Hesitant to speak, I finally offer to Ibrahim, by way of a polite challenge, "I don't know what your hesitance is, I know there is emotional stuff there, I know you have emotional and painful attachments there to the place, still ... that lingers for you, and I know to go back there and to speak to them is a heavy duty thing for you ..."

Ibrahim looks serious, and pensive. "It may be heavy duty, I may be strict and firm on them to let them know what I would like for them to get a congregation together and walk with me.... Ptery and Brad Gibson are good representatives and they should let those people be ambassadors for Dignity Village and come (out here) and learn and let what Ptery and Brad learn be brought to them so they can learn to be leadership. And they can get involved in things what happening in the city—go to city hall and see what city hall is doing. You know it's like they sitting out there with the laws, the unjust laws being imposed on (homeless) people down here, and they not going to be affected by it. Well they wrong, they're wrong."

"Well, there's problems out there too," I add.

Brad Gibson, 2011. Photo: Nigel Dickson.

"Right! Right! So the first what they gotta do is put a blockade up around Dignity Village and kick everyone out who's not following the bylaws...."

At this point Ptery and I are a little shocked. I mean, no one follows all of the bylaws.

"Tell them to leave!" he adds shaking his head resolutely.

"But who's gonna tell them?" I ask.

"You have people on the council doing shit [drugs or dealing drugs]," Ptery adds.

"People on the council are all doing shit," I confirm.

Ibrahim looks a bit more serious. "Now that's where you come back to your constitutional rights. Everybody in there got constitutional rights.... If the government ain't doing for you what the people voted them to do, they get impeached. They don't get voted back in. They should be replaced. So that's the same thing in Dignity Village.... What they need to do is follow the old concept of the village—you have to be in good standing. You have to come out and do activism. That was one of the things they had—they have to do—come out do activist work for the homeless community—the leadership, the council, the chairman, the vice-chair, the treasurer, the secretary, they the ones who need to be out here doing that work. How can they know how to run and teach the people at the village, if they ain't getting no kind of education. Their job ain't to sit around there and do nothing."

Ibrahim was for all intents and purposes the iconic villager activist. He was patient, and motivated during our interviews. I had to add, "You really need to come talk to these people and let them know what it was like and what it was meant to be."

"God's will."

"I am pressuring you, but in a friendly way," I offer.

He laughs deeply. Ptery's eyes roll.

"I just know that if ... that place needs a shaking up, and if someone like you doesn't come and shake it up, I just know it's gonna fail." He nods. Commits to coming out before or after Ramadan.

I ask him what he would say to people in my world, outside of Portland about places like Dignity Village. Should other cities let there be Dignity Villages? He and I both knew about or had visited some of the dozen tent camps and intentional communities, some permanent and vying for legal rights, in the Oregon-Washington corridor. But Dignity Village was a legally self-governed corporation; it had rights. Should there be more?

"Do you think what you guys started there more than ten years ago, could be adopted in others cities, or should be?"

He didn't even have to pause to think about his response. "I think it should be adopted in other cities where the government should give people a chance to redeem themselves. It used to be, you commit a crime, you pay just dues for it by doing community service, going to jail or whatever and you can get back to the floor of society. We become an unforgiving nation where we don't forgive easily. We hold people down from being progressive. And this [the village] is a way for people to get their self-esteem, their motivations, their scruples and their principles back together into being somebody. Now this is what happens when you know your constitutional rights. You can achieve this because nobody above their constitutional rights and you can do that but you have to do that and think of everybody, not just yourself, and one individual. And this should be done, and it can be done, and it will be done, or this country and every country like it is going to fail."

Some hours later, I went back to my shack in the village. There was so much bickering and fighting over stupid things, mundane nonsense: who received more donations than the next guy, why Whitefoot got the last piece of fried chicken, was Mitch going to use more than his share of electricity sanding wood for the mirrors he was making: all mundane nonsense. There was no discussion whatsoever between villagers about the new city-imposed contract, or about community issues like how to raise funds for the servicing of the outhouses. No one ever, ever, engaged in spontaneous communication with others about the 3,000 or so homeless men and women on the streets or about what the village should be doing to help out these others. In the village, citizens were consumed by their personal needs and this just didn't seem right. "They are like spoiled children," I had jotted in my field notes. They were critical of each other but of critique, I found no evidence, at least not then.

Was Ibrahim imagining a whole other place? I wondered.

Ibrahim's conversation with me reveals many important contradictions about what democratic self-governance means. In the same breath he talks of an alternative and self-governed community in which people have rights and freedom. He then goes on to speak to the need to curtail, restrain and structure those actors in accordance with fundamental village principles. At the same time as he speaks of the need for more communities where homeless people can govern themselves; he insists that these places need to confirm extant constitutional and legal codes. Freedom and constraint issue forth in the same rhetorical commitment to alternative community. He calls for the village and the leadership to be critical and conformist, at the same time, from within the same mental and physical living space—to at once work on new narratives to fight the inevitability of entropy, but to also cling to extant narratives of duty, freedom, and liberty that tend to reinforce broader experiences of inevitability. How can this be? There is a sense of the idealistic and normative value of such space, and what it could represent "if only," or perhaps as might have once been, or might be, *one day in the future*. There is too a certain naïve practical hopefulness to achieving these ends that emerges in his discourse. While he professes liberation through democracy, he reiterates examples of how this liberation requires a degree of domination.

Derrida (2005) famously instructs us that democracy is yet to come, constantly being invented. I would argue that if this is the case, democracy is perpetually liminal. Furthermore, participants in democracies are—by virtue of this very participation in it—in some sense liminal political personae. It is perhaps a Catch-22, a vicious cycle, or some other cliché of ironic despair. But the village is a socially produced space that is failing to be what Lefebvre understands to be more than a "mere container for human action" (1991:27). If we critically examine what people who live there say, then we must admit that it has come to resemble what De Tocqueville (1840) argued was all that is good all that is bad about American democracy:

> Although men cannot become absolutely equal unless they are entirely free, and consequently equality, pushed to its furthest extent, may be confounded with freedom, yet there is good reason for distinguishing the one from the other. The taste, which men have, for liberty and that which they feel for

equality are, in fact, two different things; and I am not afraid to add that among democratic nations they are two unequal things.

And a few lines later: "The advantages that freedom brings are shown only by the lapse of time, and it is always easy to mistake the cause in which they originate. The advantages of equality are immediate, and they may always be traced from their source" ([1840] 2004 Book Two (1): 1).

De Tocqueville means that one's relative equality (under the law) is understood to be a commensurate measure of having freedom; being *politically equal* to participate (understood as freedom) satisfies the immediate need of gratification that homelessness imposes on the people I study. They do not see a "greater" freedom, because it had been taken from them by life's events. The freedom they have is available, while a greater freedom seems unobtainable. And in any event, life in the village is better than a life on the streets. A certain desirable quality or experience in the moment, a room in which to sleep, food to eat, drugs to sniff, to shoot, the rush, a few hours of bliss, are generally more secure and surely more satisfying, or so they think, than more freedom down the road, which might cost them the relative equality they now have (a shack, donated clothes and food stamps).[30]

Even in critiques of social justice such as debates over poverty, housing, and gender equality, it is not given that a successful claim—one that achieves certain goals which are always unique—renders power and inequality unimportant for organizing social life. The best one can hope for is that the fundamentally just issue at the heart of the critique is recognized by the action. But there is still power—that social force that alienates some and manipulates others. Human history itself, in addition to the example above, demonstrates quite clearly that this can never be equally distributed among all persons and at all times. From the very beginning, the pragmatic critique that led to the building of Dignity Village was oriented towards these unfortunate ends. Quite simply, an issue of fundamental justice no longer binds the group together; nor does it help to foster a sense of collectivity that compels them to search for such an issue. If any individual village can acquire sufficient internal support to be powerful, he or she can make any critique work in the village. This is true even if it the critique itself potentially damaging to the community. Following Derrida (1994, 2005) this orientation is understood as emblematic of an "auto-immune" or inherent flaw in democracy: a flaw in which emancipating possibility of its inherent logic is always questioned.[31] The flaw is equally highlighted by Ibrahim's testimony. In the sense that democracy means that the freedom of some must displace the freedom of others, there is an inherent tension between actors seeking different ends, regardless of means, or the same ends but through different means.

Michels (1949 [1915]) presented the notion of the *Iron Law of Oligarchy*, which claims that in all democratic societies leadership eventually produces systems by which to dominate and oppress its members, largely through the expansion of bureaucracy into the daily lives of members (Hyland 1965). In large societies, this has been well argued to be very true (Michels 1915; Lipset 1959; Jung et al. 2010). In smaller groups, mostly studied as small political parties, such as unions, there is some sense that democracy works better (Lipset 1956; Enjolras and Holmen-Waldhal 2008). That is, members have more direct influence on decisions and methods by which laws are carried out. Lipset (1956) identified the means by which trade unions are able to avoid the oligarchic usury that Michels had expounded. Lipset also argued that economic development was directly related to democratic capacity (1959). In the absence of economic diversity and wealth, this capacity decays into factions and disarray. Participant observation in the community of Dignity Village by Mosher (2010), as well as that carried out by me for this book (2010–2013), showed how democratic self-rule led to a series of impeachments and entrenched factions that over time crippled the village in direct action and protest, and battered the village's image to its critics. This tends to support Lipset's hypothesis. Rather than engaging citizens in a process where they can express themselves freely by voting for or against ideas and principles, as autonomous citizens, the social reality now requires villagers to align with and vote for the representatives of powerful factions in the village in order to secure protection and support in village affairs. This action is governed by practical concerns disguised in a rhetorical idealism, which they call *democracy*. To me this is oligarchic factionalism. Oddly enough, Mitch Grubic, Dave Samson, Lisa Larson, and Brad Gibson, each a past or present member of the village council, understand this as normal democratic "politicking."

This is part of the auto-immune deficiency of democracy that Derrida had described. We can think of this auto-immunity as evidence of what in his deconstructionism Derrida (1996) would call *aporia*, which is the logical and irresolvable contradiction inherent to a way of thinking, a theory or a critical position; but in this case we are talking about a feature of the system (democracy) that forces it to contradict the very ethos on which it professes to matter. Following his earlier thoughts about "la démocratie à venir," in *Spectres of Marx* (1993) and *The Politics of Friendship* (1994), in *Rogues: Two Essays on Reason* (2005) Derrida in my most simple terms suggests that democracy as we understand it is always an attack on itself from within. He explains this as an auto-immunity in two important anti-logical dimensions.

First, democracy suggests emancipation from sovereign rule by extending the power to affect change to all citizens. Democracy needs to express liberty and equality in those terms. Yet democracy also needs to lock all participants in a closed sovereign system of political and civic associations—the nation or the village for example. Each democratic nation, or organization of any kind, presupposes the existence of equally free citizens who are at the same time united under a sovereign set of codes and rules, sometimes called a constitution or charter of rights. This sovereign set of principles is often called upon as the arbiter of rules governing acts that push this interpretation of freedom beyond popular understandings. Freedom of speech, of expression, and so on are not unlimited. This suggests that democracy cannot exist without sovereignty. Even the terms of freedom and liberty that one might find in the village documents and bylaws provide a sovereign set of standards and so in our deliberations about how to fix the community or how to find places for IHC, there is always this sovereign Other which exists as an implicit backdrop to our pragmatic actions.

Second, very simply put, the villager recognizes her freedom as paramount, and that all others are equally free. It is only in this way that democracy makes any sense. The auto-immunity is that the citizens' incalculable freedom is impossible where others have power over others. *That* is democracy, as we know it. While the obvious tension between these aspects suggests the impossibility of idealistic democracy, Derrida argues that democracy is yet to come. It is not guaranteed that this will be a peaceful or emancipating transition. There will be more and less democratic emergences in this perpetual event of becoming, but it suggests that in a very basic way, all citizens who claim to be democratically governed are in part liminal personae within the system itself, and internally, as persons coming to know what democracy and freedom means to them. The village provides a unique place: it rides the emergent issues raised by its own liminal and self-regulated "democracy of poverty" (as Dave Samson has called it), which produces a variety of local understandings. It also rides currents of debate about housing and shelter within the larger democracy, of which it is merely a part. Each of these competing levels of democratic identity contributes to the villager's sense of right and wrong, and therefore to what degree they might be willing to fight for the village or remain suspended in liminality.

At a very fundamental level essential to the formation of political sub-jectivities, participants in my research create stories and narratives to make sense of personal, social, and political actions they take; or, more importantly, they create narratives to make sense of those actions that they do not take. If one does not have a clear erudition of what it is like to live in abject poverty with severe survival anxieties, these narratives could easily be interpreted as escapist rationalizations, perhaps even excuse-making. But in understanding how these anxieties get in the way of people's mental or spiritual capacity to commit to critical action, it is easier to understand why the village as a whole fails to live up to its activist manifesto. These narratives amount to an essentially pragmatic critical attitude about how villagers understand their freedoms and liberties and the nature of homelessness. They also touch on

American neoliberal democratic thought and the unique interpretation of democracy in the village.

1.9 Summary

As it stands, it seems that neoliberal governance has found an alternative place for the worst-case homeless. It is no longer on the streets, or in the shelters, and certainly not in decent affordable housing. It is in these camps. While cities claim to be spending more on housing, the numbers of first-time homeless continue to rise. And so does the number of camps. Dignity Villagers made an unofficial count of homeless tent camps on the West Coast—those that are recognized and have names, are fighting for rights, and might obtain them. In 2012 there were 55 official sites, from San Luis Obispo, California in the south to Seattle in the north. And these do not include the hundreds of temporary camps, the unorganized ones, and the ones that are popping up as I write this. Between 2014 and 2015, Dallas, Eugene, Seattle, and Austin, all important and large cities, entered into officially recognized and legally sanctioned arrangements with NPOs to build IHC as part of their housing plans. In order to look at these places differently—that is to say, in order to see them in a more deserving light—one must understand what provisions have emerged to help them overcome the madness and despair I saw at Dignity Village. When I left the village after my fieldwork, filled with a sense of doom about the prospects of such spaces to serve basic needs well, I was in the quiet and internal process of changing the narrative of inevitability I had in mind. Was the malaise and the factionalism necessarily harbingers of an inevitable failure of the village? Would such places; could such places actually achieve their goals? Every once in a while a note or a message would come way from one of the villagers that reinforced my apprehension about Dignity's ability to overcome—to change its inevitability. Note the following Facebook message (original spelling unaltered) from Dave Samson, who had been a resident at Dignity twice.

> *December 13, 2011:* ... just gettin up and havin some coffee. getting things done in a habitual manner is the key to all things for me so i shall start with coffee i do it every morning so why not take the time to send a few text while i am at it !! sounds right!. mmmmmmmmmmm coffee! any way things here on the island seem rocky and the beach smells bad lol. i love the way the ice crystals covering all the broken things shine! i think that morning is the best time for me to focus and write before my head fills up with the days crap. i will be sending you some nice island in winter pics. its a different place in winter the vibe is very low. The frozen moral hangs off every house like a sickness striped of summers brite colors. the walking dead suddenly seem like what they are in clear sharp contrast. the portalets reek of last nights self medication like a john in a bar. the islanders stumbling around in

recovery from there own filth and decay. complaining of things they carry with them. but unwilling to drop the load as if it where some valued commodity. clinging to there broken luck as if it will bring them warmth. lending hard looks at any one that dare look happy. as if the happy where some disease the needs to be eradicated. and running from the truth like birds from cats. my inner voice screeming drop the load and be free! but they can not hear. to focused on the baggage to hear any thing but the song of misery the emanates from there own actions. i think making the switch to writing seems hard but the further i go in that direction the more it seems the best path. art just dos not convey the richness of thought that seems to fill my head. imagery seems to be taking a back seat to all other thoughts. not that i don't get lots of really beautiful pics in the head but they just don't seem to answer any of the really strong impulses. but the idea of starting from scratch and remaking my self leaves me feeling a little intimidated OK a lot intimidated!!! lol. but i have just got to know what i have been hiding in my shadow (a line from the tool song 46+2 about transformation) things have been going well on the stay sober front. i am going to quit smoking as well. i had a dream that the time for that is at an end. and i am going to start to listen to my self more seriously. learning how to trust my self. is some thing that i have all ways had a little trouble with! you are the closest thing to a strong and guiding brother that i have ever had so forgive me if my lack of faith in my self seems harsh or that it seems i don't believe you. this will take some time but hey i have got lots of that lol. peace for now. your bro all ways ... dave ..."

I made the following note after reading this.

It's a dream, some *Cuckoo's Nest* of a horror show. I left the village earlier than I wanted because watching the people there medicate and do nothing, caught in limbo day after day—bitching and complaining, debating each other at every turn was suffocating and unhealthy for me. I could see the big picture, they could see the big picture, but they were wrapped tight. Tight into each other's shit, thinking small. No escape. Poor Dave, I want him to get out of there. I want him to find his way. It should be possible.

As concerned citizens we cannot help but to worry about the implications of enduring social problems like poverty and homelessness. Discussing social problems is not only about the suffering person. We are involved in their experience, but the world is designed so we don't have to look at that interconnection. We often fail at that recognition; we let governments or activists worry about it. Instead we hide behind narratives that blame those who suffer their own suffering, or to religious beliefs that justify suffering as part of this plane of living, or we understand that success for some must occur at the cost of others' well-being. We feel a moment of sadness perhaps for those who die on the streets and we are reminded to do everything we can to

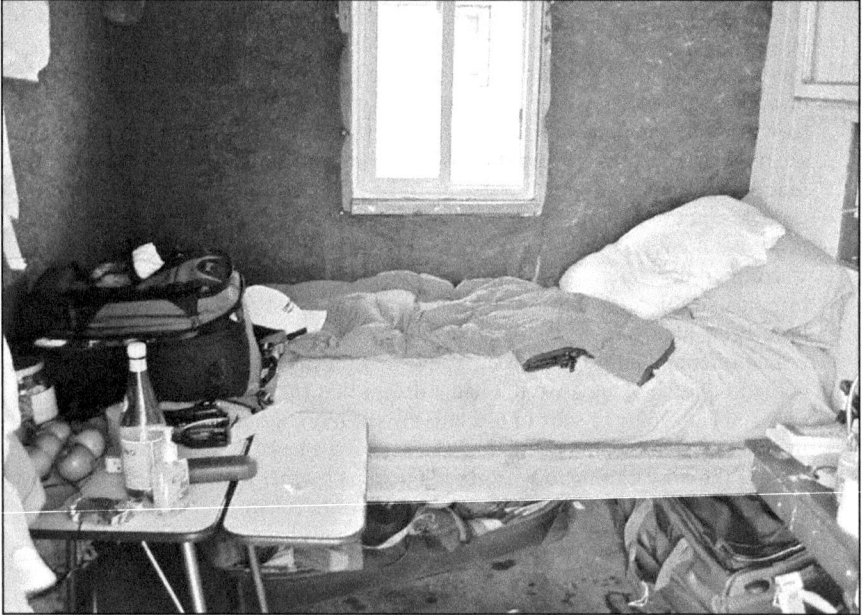

Interior of my "dorm," June 2011. All new guests spend early days in a 6' X 8' shack like this until they get a structure of their own. Photo: Eric Weissman

avoid that for ourselves and our families. Neoliberalism, which has been the ideological and structural undercurrent in the West bridging two centuries, has implanted the narrative of the failed identity and self-governance into the stories we tell ourselves when confronted with disturbing situations arising out of poverty. E.'s death, after all, is understandable on the streets, and according to the neoliberal narrative of inevitability, streets and shelters are where such failed persons should end up. Those who are not failed tell these stories.

They are also stories that many who have failed fit into their own self-narratives, and they are therefore stories—only stories, mind you—which have origins we can unearth and rewrite. This is a very difficult job. It requires looking at ourselves as those who do the investigating, at the contexts we grew up in and the narratives that shape our points of view, at the historical conditions that shaped the kind of poverty we have looked at, at the meanings that the participants in our research bring into situations and impact their choices about how to act, and then at how, given new ways of thinking, they might act differently. Then and only then can we truly understand what inevitability really means.

Any discussion we are going to have about homelessness, solutions to it, or the role of IHC in plans to end homelessness will necessarily be complicated because all the voices in these discussions are valid and often sit in opposition to one another. The BIG question we are addressing, then, is not about homelessness per se, but how to look at pervasive and enduring social problems in a way that compels us to eschew the safety of gray zones and get into the tough discussions about what we can do differently. I look at homelessness and housing and it is through the lens of my experience in these areas that I am going to suggest a way to change the narratives that we hide behind.

For me, doing this starts with a form of ethnography that is critical of the pragmatic nature of human actors. It must be open to the reader, open in the sense that the reader can understand how in this work, truths are constructed and narratives learned. We will ask people concerned about their poverty and concerned about social problems how they see their world and how they are going to change that—what I call *pragmatic ethnography*.

R2DToo, 2013. Photo: Eric Weissman.

Chapter Two
PRAGMATIC ETHNOGRAPHY OF CRITIQUE UNDRESSED

R2DToo, on the right, sits on valuable downtown real estate. Photo: Eric Weissman.

2.1 Ethnographic Roots

Over time, we North Americans have come increasingly to think of social problems and their solutions in terms of monetary costs and effects. Homelessness has been pervasive; a number of solutions have been proposed, and some actually tried. For example, temporarily rehousing homeless people into immediate shelter, such as a market-valued apartment, is part of the paradigm we call *rapid rehousing*. Researchers who study how this type of housing helps once-homeless people can tell you that in many cases, and with the proper social and medical supports, their quality of life improves, as does mental and physical health. Has this led to the expansion of the rapid rehousing sector to the degree that we have solved homelessness? No. Such programs are perceived in different ways in the public eye, and so supporters of such models need to find ways to transcend opposing public opinions. Housing First (HF) is the most prominent rapid rehousing program model in the US and Canada. It is being widely adopted because it has been shown to be cheaper than street living. This cost efficiency is its most compelling argument in the court of public opinion. And so as HF grows, other models (like the IHC) that are characterized as types of rapid rehousing must, as actual and worthy housing program models, learn to change the public narrative surrounding them if they are to grow as well.

One of the most compelling arguments about HF is that it satisfies the key to self-governance, which under neoliberalism is maintained in the myth of the normal home. This myth suggests that it is normal or, at least, desirable to live in a self-contained unit of dwelling in a market-valued space such as an apartment or house. The kind of public housing for the worst-off most acceptable to public opinion is usually in conventional open-market apartments or in specially built housing, but it always points the narrative in the direction of the normal home myth: the idea that people are self-contained, self-sufficient, and good neighbors. It is easier to say that people are going back to normalized living conditions and that it is cheaper to house people than to leave them on the streets, so public resistance is reduced. HF costs about $24,000 (Canadian) per year per person. And people stay housed; eventually most seek medical and addictions assistance and generally fare better. By contrast, the average homeless person living on the street costs society about $100,000 per year. So, overall, HF is a good thing. This is not to suggest that there is no resistance to HF, because much does remain. Even so, the program is adoptable by governments for two reasons. First, HF generates quantitative data that researchers can use to measure cost-effectiveness. Second, the types of transitional experiences people have under HF programs appeal to the public desire to see recipients of assistance take steps in the right direction to becoming "normal" residents again. Hence, one can say that HF models conform to the moral normative and cost-efficient values of neoliberal citizens.

I noted above that in the U.S. IHC is more popular but does not receive the same level of funding as does HF. In Canada there are currently no official IHC communities. IHC programs like Dignity Village cost less than $1,000 a year per person, but even so they have many critics. There are many reasons for this. One is that Dignity Village does not fulfill the city's data requirements. Cities want these housing spaces to generate data on intake, expulsions, costs, demographics, length of stay and so on. These reporting requirements are noted in Chapter 5. But since villagers are so incapable of running things and often unable to carry out their village jobs well, there has been little usable data from which to generate persuasive quantitative studies that might be used to persuade the public of the validity of IHC.

Ethnographic analysis of Dignity Village has been also wanting. In newspaper stories and scholarly articles, the village is often portrayed as either a dark and suffering place or an enlightened and wonderful example of how people with deficits can overcome their challenges. These image systems attach to the many IHCs discussed in this book. Some people praise them for the good they do as emergency housing and others find them dubious options at best. The lack of economic and social participation is also questionable to neoliberal moral normative lenses. After all, communes and lifestyles where self-improvement is not demanded are counter-intuitive to the neoliberal subjectivity. These two problems clearly need to be addressed to improve public perception.

This is the basis of what I have called the *pragmatic ethnography of liminal critique (PEOC)* in my dissertation and which as you read this chapter we will begin to think about as simply a form of critical pragmatic ethnography. Living with the villagers helps generate qualitative data about that lifestyle and about inhabitants' attitudes. The village is a liminal space where roles and transitions rarely fulfill their expectations. So we are gathering information about unfulfilled transitional life experiences, which in itself is troubling for the people caught up in that mess and for many who want to understand the place IHC might have in their communities.

My focus was on the best use of this information. I asked how we could use the information generated to find out what rules of conduct and political participation and which managerial processes worked or failed to contribute to the village's ongoing struggle for legitimacy within the city structure. Perhaps more importantly to me, as someone who had to struggle with regaining relevance in the world, I pointed our collective criticism to understand how certain petty and anti-social attitudes were getting in the way of the village by suspending most people in mid-transition—they exercised their rights against each other, rather than against public opinion and those who questioned the village's right to be. In very simple terms I used ethnography to tell the stories of the village and the villager and then to ask people what stories needed changing. A critical look at these narratives of inevitability that were rooted in the people's stories allowed for a certain rewriting of more successful stories. While this process was less than successful at Dignity Village, it has helped other IHCs, as we will discuss below.

First, a quick note on terminology: *Ethnography*, which originates from the Greek words *ethnos* and *graphos* quite literally means *writing people*, or later, "writing culture." Ethnography refers to a systematic analysis of people and customs, usually presented in a written text (*Merriam Webster Dictionary* 2011). Ethnography had long been the key methodology of social and cultural anthropologists, a tradition began in the mid- to late 1800s. By the early 1900s it already resembled our current definition of social and cultural anthropology. Ethnography is not undertaken only by anthropologists. And observing and writing about human culture alone does not necessarily constitute ethnography. Broadly speaking, however, and owing to its roots in anthropological field work, ethnography is a systematic and serious attempt to observe and record social and cultural practices rooted in our *participation in them*: by that I mean that we live, work, eat, learn the language and the jargons, in order to experience that rich and deep familiarity with the people we are studying. It is also informed by the concepts and critical debates inherent to social sciences.

In this book I employ a form of critical and pragmatic ethnography that links the critical attitudes of individuals, such as opinions about each other's conduct, material priorities, religious or spiritual beliefs, interpretations of how the government should work in the village and so on, to the individual's desire to engage in broader social justice issues. As we will see in Chapter 5 and as I mentioned before, the village and these IHCs are politically discursive sites and they are housing. They will never be merely another subdivision, even though that is what they might desire. They are claims on public space that force everyone to reevaluate their own beliefs about home. But to remain valid in a world where other forms of housing are better funded and more respectable to the public, the spirit of housing activism built into Dignity Village and other projects like it is vital in order to understand how to help these places become effective housing. Just as a shark must always keep water flowing through its gills, Dignity Village in particular needs to keep that activist spirit flowing or else it will simply fade away. That spirit affords the only way for the village and the villager to have sufficient power to fight for their collective rights as a community.

I am particularly interested in the larger social structural conditions that constrain or enhance the choices made by these individuals, something of a departure from the traditional anthropological focus on basic cultural practices such as rituals (Howes 2014). Much of this activism and the ties to broader social structures are presented as actual conversations in Chapter 5 and 6, but this chapter examines the method of getting to those conversations, illuminating this departure from traditional ethnography.

A quick overview of ethnography is helpful here. One of the defining characteristics of social and cultural anthropology at least since Malinowski's famous study of the Tobriand Islanders in *Argonauts of the Western Pacific* (1922) is attention to fieldwork, specifically our own participation in the cultures we study. For this branch of anthropology, fieldwork was seen to be superior to any observations made about culture from archives, notes, or other peoples' research (sometimes called "armchair anthropology" [Howes 2014]). Ethnographic observation speaks to how different cultures inscribe the social world with possibility and constraint. So we look at immaterial things like religious beliefs or food taboos, and material things like tools, technology and buildings, all examples of aspects of the social world that tend to make social life possible, but vary greatly between different cultures. Written descriptions about one's experience of these aspects of culture have traditionally been seen as the most important contributions an ethnographer can make. My own work incorporates video and stills with written accounts, and represents the kind of hybridized and future-looking forms of writing culture that are becoming popular.

Several early studies began carving out space for visual ethnographies. Two key examples are the snippets of film produced by Cort-Haddon's Torres Straits expeditions in 1898 and Edward Curtis' (1907) famous photo archive of *The North American Indian*. The critical analysis of such pieces, which determines their ethnographic soundness, rests on the degree to which the visual narrative conforms to the requirements of a "rigorous and systematic study of culture," as a paraphrase of early anthropological provisos.

Eric Weissman

Jay Ruby (1975), a well-read ethnographic film critic, commented that ethnographic films, including such classic examples as Curtis' *In the Land of the War Canoes* (1914[32]), Gardener's *Dead Birds* (1963), and MacDougall's *Forest of Bliss* (1986) are forms of anthropological texts. He argues that they present a visual narrative informed by anthropological concepts and theories, such as understanding the technological basis on which different cultures evolve, or key institutions seen universal to cultures, such as rituals and kinship. In looking at common focal interests, Ruby argued that such visual texts, along with all other ethnographic texts, should invoke directly or indirectly the lexicon of anthropology. They should also bring new information to the way culture per se is understood (Ruby 1975).

What makes a text ethnographic? It might seem obvious, but it is worth reiterating that ethnographic methods cross a range of academic boundaries and are characterized by legitimate social inquiry deriving information from people and their experience. Early social anthropology emerged out of British colonialism, such that anthropologists were often interested in cultural differences as a way to catalogue lesser peoples and justify empirical hierarchies. Not only do we now recognize the powerful nature of ethnography and use it more fairly, we also look at matters closer to home. The ethnographic lens is now increasingly focused on our own cultures (Lohmann 2007; Strathern 1987; Hastrup 1992; Oakley 1992; Bourgois 1995; Fabian 2001; Pink 2001; Rapport 2006; Gallinat and Collins 2010).

In respect to poverty and homelessness in particular, urban sociologists and symbolic interactionists have long been committed to fieldwork. An early player in this area was the Chicago School of Sociology, which fostered urgent and practically minded ethnographic research into urban social problems such as poverty. The Chicago School bridged classic anthropological attention to cultures and sub-cultural practices with sociology's discussions of larger political and economic structures as a means to steer practical social change. It gave rise to the social psychological approach to understanding social worlds, in which social knowledge, the meanings people attach to self, others and symbols, contribute to a sense of human ecology, and are understood to be far more important than simply structures or rules or classes. Symbolic interaction grew from this approach and includes the seminal work of G.H. Mead (1934).[33]

In addition to my interest in homelessness, an even more urgent focus for me is to make sense of how people become engaged in thinking critically about their world, finding the motivation to address stubborn problems, and then mapping out how effective their efforts can be in the social structures that produce the conditions of poverty in the first place. I am using ethnography to understand a certain capacity to tell important narratives. Perhaps I am writing about the culture of the place to eventually understand how it is that some cultures produce ineffective social critiques. I have called this *writing critique*, as a play on "writing culture."

We can write Ruby's proviso as follows: *Ethnography is the production of representations about culture and society as they come to be experienced by any researcher's dedicated and reasonable efforts in various lived fields of experience.*

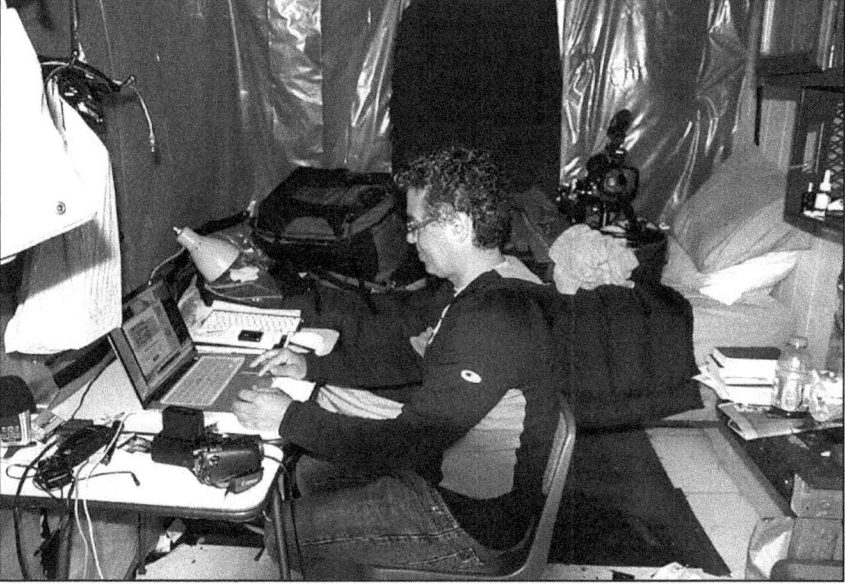

The author at his structure in Dignity Village, typing up field notes, 2011.
Photo: Nigel Dickson.

Regardless of the larger debate, ethnography is an inherently qualitative mode of inquiry, and one very different than a quantitative method. Quantitative methods include widely distributed surveys, questionnaires, and census data. More recently, they include the tracking of user data on computers and Internet sites, by which scientists gather large data sets; these may be useful for making very broad generalizations and depicting long historical trends. Such methods may yield considerable information that speaks to the size and frequency of a dependent variable, such as poverty. A look at the distribution of poverty over a large North American population reveals the fact that independent variables such as race, age, degree of disability, education and family size (among many others) impact the occurrence and severity of poverty. This large data set suggests how to concentrate our collective efforts to help reduce or ameliorate the impact of poverty.

Sociologists often use statistics to look at crime and deviance and other

rates of experiences that are problematic at the social level. Quantitative studies help gauge the size and distribution of a social fact like poverty, and to
measure how it changes over time. But such measures reveal little about the
quality of that experience. We have to turn to qualitative analyses to do that.

Ethnography has its place within these larger studies or on its own as a diverse set of tools that help us understand what those larger experiences look
and feel like at the level of everyday experience. Ethnography can help us
understand the scale and size of experiences in a smaller group. It also helps us
compare what, for example, crime looks like in one culture, or what might be
considered as deviant or desirable in another. Of course, the foci of the social
sciences are much broader than crime and deviance, but these are two peren-
nial concerns that tend to be measured often in terms of both their quantitative distribution in societies, and qualitatively, in order to understand how different cultures handle each problem in culturally diverse ways. My own methods involve a pragmatic form of ethnography employing fieldwork-based
observations as a way to ground the way struggling people see their potential
to change social circumstances within broader systems of economic and
political power. My approach is qualitative, but frequently large data, such as
distributional numbers about poverty and so on, are used to situate the context in which the ethnography is performed. One of the goals of this book is to
bridge quantitative measures with qualitative descriptions of poverty and
homelessness in our cities.

It is important to note that to many people, especially indigenous persons
and homeless groups, research is a dirty word. Since the early days of anthropologists like Cort-Haddon[34] and sociologists like Anderson,[35] research has
been a tool for colonial control and the municipal planning goals of large cities. Research was a way of expanding the academic appreciation of culture, but
so too was it the scientific basis of racist and expansionist development programs based on the presentation of relatively underdeveloped nature of *lesser*
and needy people.

For urban sociology, fieldwork—including surveys and numbers taking, as
well as journals and written analyses—became essential for helping cities and
governments identify social problems and to gauge the measure or responses
they required (Park 1915; Anderson 1923; Hughes 1952; Bahr 1973; Gans 1991).
By way of addressing definitional issues, Denzin and Lincoln use the term
qualitative research to include observation, interviewing, participation and ethnography, and to describe it as a "field of inquiry in its own right," one that
"crosscuts disciplines, fields and subject matters" (1994:2). For these authors, it
is possible to discern patterns in how we have gone about doing qualitative
work. In other words, we can see historically how field notes and long term
immersion in foreign cultures has shifted to current online interviewing and
video conferenced participant observation. The authors suggest an historical

periodization based on what qualitative methods were dominant at different times.[36]

The most impactful of these periods for ethnographers was the well-known *Crisis of Representation stage, which* occurred in the 1980s and is generally subsumed between the covers of Clifford and Marcus' *Writing Culture* (1986). This fourth period is marked by the deliberation of "truth." There are those current students and scholars who suggest abandoning discussions of this period because it has passed and, worse yet, never really was; after all, even Foucault, who is often blamed for this period, never saw himself as a post-modern thinker. But since we are concerned with looking at how certain ideas pass themselves off as truth in Dignity Village and in other communities where popular uses of space are debated, 1 want to explain how this period makes applied research difficult. My work is very much an answer to the question left by the Crisis period: in a world where truth is unstable and objective reality constantly socially constructed, how can social research be effective? What truths are we questioning? Into what gap in a capricious objective reality are we applying our knowledge?

The key to the Crisis period, and to the problem with asserting truthful accounts, is a twisting of our faith in written texts. Early in this period, social theory emerges as a tool for understanding the widely held view of an essentially socially constructed nature of social life and culture (Berger and Luhmann 1966; Giddens 1973; Foucault 1977; Bourdieu 1977; Clifford and Marcus 1986). We reach a certain paradox: everything we understand as truth is truth only because of how we construct that understanding, and those constructions are learned, not absolute. So, what is truth? Under the scrutiny of a post-modern gaze, all theory and representation becomes suspect and debates about objectivity, "scientificness" and fiction come to dominate the social sciences, including anthropology and sociology (Fabian 1983; Sanjek 1990; Denzin 1994). Gender, age, ethnicity, and class are once again reunited with critiques of knowledge construction and the production of ever evasive productions of truth (Denzin and Lincoln 1994: 17–18). The suggestion that writing and doing fieldwork provide a gap in the representation of experienced realities very much lies at the heart of the problematizations facing ethnography today. Writing—simply laying out in words what we observe—is demonstrated to be a sort of fictional writing; this in spite of ethnographers' claims to truth. Since the mid-1980s, a variety of experimental written forms of ethnography have emerged. Sometimes defined as *messy texts*, these forms are always incomplete, self-reflexive, and resistant to totalizing theories (Denzin 1997:245; also Strathern 1991; Foley 2002; Law 2004; Lather 2004; Chiapello 2005; Turner 2008; Drache 2008; Isin 2008).

Since then, ethnography has enjoyed a sort of renaissance. This is because the products we produced—texts and films—no longer had to be "true." What had come to matter was that the deliberations and methods we used to arrive at conclusions became as important as the observations we made. Ethnographic accounts, no matter how derived, are recognized for the fictional qualities they possess as well as for the recognition that the true authority is not the "subject" nor the author, but the reader. This suggests that in the end all truth is of a second- or a third-hand nature.

The narrative aspect of ethnographic texts had, to this point, been largely interpreted as a direct and honest comingling of the observer with the observed. That is why anthropologists have called their fieldwork *participant observation*. For the reader of the texts (or in the case of film, the viewer), the better ethnographies gave the impression that one was really present in a different time or place. Hence, anthropologists or Chicago School ethnographers and the like had always spoken or written with a certain trustable authority that instilled faith in the veracity of an ethnographic present—a moment offered up to the consumer as a rare touch of different realities.

As discomfiting as it might have been to traditional ethnographers, the "turn" has also suggested that in a sense we have always had a virtual or exterior presence to what we wrote or observed, regardless of how much effort was made to produces a narrative written in the tone of the observed (Fabian 1983; Sanjek 1991; Denzin 1997; Law 2004). We could say that ethnographic truth was always in some ways mythical, a delusion that we could package a model of different realities and gift them to the world as truth; delusional in the sense that the truth was in fact a sort of fiction (Clifford and Marcus 1986).

According to the *Sage Handbook of Ethnography* (2009), "Whatever the range of data collection techniques, we believe that ethnographic research remains firmly rooted in the first-hand exploration of research settings. It is this sense of social exploration and protracted investigation that gives ethnography its abiding and continuing character" (Atkinson et al. 2004:5). Given the destabilizing of its authoritative rank since the "turn" of the 1980s, how then can an investigative method that has been found wanting in its quest of "writing culture" be conjoined with the complex notions of critique?

Social criticism is a mode of thinking that looks for ways to identify problems in the social world, particularly where injustice, exclusion, abuse and marginalization arise. Social critique explores such issues from the perspective of a particular epistemology or a world-view that sets up the meaning of social justice and argues for the use of certain criteria in affixing blame for social problems. Marxists critique all social problems by highlighting the antagonisms between capital and labour. Classic liberals such as Adam Smith (1776) see too much government as the cause of social problems. A critique, then, evaluates certain problems via a given premise.

2.2 Critical Time and Emancipation

The goal of social critique is to identify the means to overcome extant power systems that render social life unjust. This means that one way of imagining the world wants to obtain sufficient power to displace another from its privi-

March on City Hall. One thing R2DToo is very good at doing is engaging critical narratives, including participations in actions like this march on City Hall.
Photo: Keiki-Alexander, 646Studios.

leged place in the order of things. Marxists want to eliminate capitalist patriarchy and replace it with a socialist framework. But has such change ever rendered life better than it was before? The question is often debated in sociology. The Soviet Union and China are used as examples of that critique gone wrong, so wrong that each of these entities has returned to essentially capitalist political economies. So, it takes time to fully understand what happens in instances where critique displaces power, an example being when, for example, a Marxist-led peasant rebellion takes over government, only to replace old systems of power and domination with new forms. Larsen (2011) argues that time is necessary, given that the course of successful critical ideas can only be evaluated after they have transformed existing power relations. In a sense, then, all critical action, whether it be done by a person in pursuit of her rights or a group seeking to change a certain policy, inheres a liminal phase. In the presence of criteria of justification, we can gauge how well the social issue has been resolved by bringing the test of criteria into our observations. These tests and criteria are not fully developed or expressed in liminal spaces, so we have a hard time understanding them in terms of success or failure.

Let me put forward a concrete example. If we take the space to be a transitional housing setting, it would seem that the logical criterion of judgment would be the successful transition of people into permanent housing. In Dignity Village, very few people transition from that space into secure housing, the clear measure of success that would allow Dignity to meet the terms of its contract with the city. While a transition might be made, at least from the streets to a shack in the village, there is no way to say it is a successful or complete transition in the sense we discussed in Chapter 1, unless there is a code of some kind that defines what that transition should be. And there are such for Dignity Village, so we will look at the codes and definitions of transition in Chapter 5, and then ask if the village is completely failing to be that defined place, or is bearing witness to a certain natural progression in the evolution of its community. Many residents stay on for five or more years; some have no intention of leaving. For these individuals, it is a functional and suitable permanent home. So the ethnographic experience tells us this is not a transitional housing camp, but one with varying meanings no matter how it is legally defined. But because people there have so different ideas on what their residency means, it also means they identify the terms of their just residency differently as well, and that means they may or may not be inclined to help fight for competing visions of the village.

Because of the different ways people understand their residency, and the vested interest they might have in living there, they find cause to either support the transitional or residential visions of the village. They also form internal political alliances on the basis of those competing criteria. People in the village rarely agree with one another over solutions to the village's administrative or public image problems. Even though they tend to share affinity for the "American Dream," they dispute legitimate means to arrive there. They argue over what real emancipation and freedom means.

In 2001, eight activist homeless campers filed under Oregon law for status as 501(c)(3) non-profit; with this, Dignity Village Oregon became the first city-sanctioned emergency transitional homeless camp in the U.S. It has always been controversial, itself the product of a critical separation between the activists who founded it. The original divide was between two elements of the "Out of the Doorways Campaign," as it had come to be known. The first group, known as the Housing Liberation Front (HLF) would not compromise with the city: they wanted their own land on which to govern themselves without any interference from the city. Moreover, they rejected capital and wished to reclaim a right to the city. A larger group from the same bank of activists, "Camp Dignity," exhausted by the struggle, having moved from occupation to occupation seven times in a year, established themselves under Portland's Fremont Bridge, and accepted a city-regulated compromise for temporary use of city-owned land on the outskirts of town. Where the more radical faction envisioned a way to opt out of the system by fighting for the right to its own land, as a rejection of neoliberalism's core values, Dignity Village began as a democratically self-governed transitional housing community, tenants of the city, as a means to giving the homeless the same rights and access to prosperity as other citizens. These were two very different views on what emancipation from street poverty meant.

Scott Beck suggests:

> Emancipation eludes definition, and its very meaning will differ significantly from individual to individual and from culture to culture. Out of this ambiguity we might posit two alternate visions of emancipation: emancipation as inclusion, where the oppressed individual or group acquires equal rights of participation in the existing social or political structure, and emancipation as revolution, or the wholesale eradication of the existing social structure, with the assumption that that very social structure itself is both the cause of oppression and beyond reform. (Accessed online from the website, June 5, 2013).[37]

In the latter, critique wants to lead to an entirely new way of organizing personal relationships or social life. Here, perceptions of the conditions of exploitation or domination that created an issue of justice are eradicated. In the HLF case, a normative vision of a just way is imposed on extant relations and the critique is towards a new totality; ownership of their own land, no contracts and sustainable community and cooperative self-government for people denied both. In the former, critique seeks a better piece of the pie for the claimant without changing the ingredients; the normative evaluation of the system doesn't change but people's access to power within it is enhanced through shelter, a safe community and a say in village affairs and a chance to get back in the game of being a citizen. The critique is about the right to participate in an extant system, not to change the system, so contracted inequality is okay so long as inequality makes everyone's life relatively better than if it did not exist (Rawls 1971).

After six years of Dignity Village's proving itself compliant, in 2007 the city handed down its first official contract to the village, firmly setting out the condition by which their tenancy was sanctionable. The village was pitched to the city as a utopian, green, sustainable and democratically self-governed nonprofit community, and as a critique of Portland's treatment of the homeless. The articles of incorporation, the mission statement and other documents we will read clearly spell out these utopian goals and also the compromises included in the agreements with the city that rendered them impossible, a compromise that has created this case of perpetual liminality, in the added sense that the villager now lives in a world that is betwixt and between the ideals set out in the mission statement and bylaws, and the realities of living in poverty. Villagers each share a similar inability to know where they are headed. Moreover, if they have goals, they do not always know how to achieve them in practical terms. It could be argued that this is not so different than the rest of the world; a competition between criteria and visions of justice very much defines the world today. It would be almost derisory to call up names like ISIS or Al-Qaeda. But legally sanctioned IHCs have explicitly stated criteria of justification that rationalize them within broader governance like the city, such as bylaws and articles of incorporation. They have mission statements.

Bruno Latour is skeptical of the usefulness of social critique, stating "our critical equipment deserves as much critical scrutiny as the Pentagon budget" (2004:231). Put differently, Latour doubts the veracity and competence of those in positions to make important observations. He rebukes Baudrillard, who mysticizes the attack on the Twin Towers as some effect of capitalism. He argues that the world has been (over)taken by conspiracy and weird forms of truth that somehow pass as critique when they are nothing more than *matters of concern*: opinions impossible to prove but consumed as critiques of government, science, capitalism, the CIA and so on. Latour is arguing that critique has come to mean little more than skepticism and suspiciousness to the point of a common faith in delusional conspiracy theories. Later he adds:

> My argument is that a certain form of critical spirit has sent us down the wrong path, encouraging us to fight the wrong enemies and, worst of all, to be considered as friends by the wrong sort of allies because of a little mistake in the definition of its main target. The question was never to get away from facts but closer to them, not fighting empiricism but, on the contrary, renewing empiricism (2004:231).

In his view, critique needs to attach itself more fully to an understanding of objects as facts; matters of fact, that is, rather than matters of concern. Matters of concern tend to paint objects with a certain truth, as if they were *facts* (243). All objects are created, as are all matters of fact, out of concern, or as objects of matters of concern, but that does not mean that the computer created to compute is merely that thing without social and political implications. For Latour, things have agency when they are implicated in social, economic, and political social arrangements. A critique of any of these areas must attach to ideas and things. This should lead to a broader under-standing of the implication non-living and living agents have in affecting other aspects of reality. In sum, Latour is simply arguing that critique needs to rejoin with realist positions that ascertain how certain matters of fact come to be understood that way.

His call to see multiplicity instead of simplicity, inherently not a deconstructionist but in fact a sort of expansionist critique, suggests not the reduction of ideas and facts to a basic underlying *aporia* or truthful principle, but, rather, to find "*more*, not *less*, with *multiplication*, not *subtraction*" (248). In his view, social critique passed away many years ago, because of its tendency to reduce what is observed critically to a simpler state of affairs, a truth, a function, a theory, a moral imperative or normative diagnostic precept. He puts it to us that in order to look at things critically we must look for the way the world around us mediates, integrates, assembles and deploys (248).

I agree that a certain critical attitude needs to be extended to the relation-ship between our social lives and non-human elements of the lived life. I agree also that we have to a degree sought to reduce social problems through cri-tique to key elements and to empower this simplicity through the application of narrow visions of legitimate criteria. We can critique social movements on the basis of the ideologies they profess to resist, but it would serve us well to see how the integration of people in the movement expands social complexi-ties by linking directly and transitively an almost virtual assemblage of things, resources and *actants, actants being the uniting of agents in a socially relevant performance.*[38]

I don't see Latour's indictment as the end of critique. Rather it is a call to arms. It poses a challenge to researchers to produce empirically and critically important work. My goal is to pay close attention the empirical reality of the places I am studying. They do not look like the images they present of them-selves in their design, in their contracts, and in their mission statements. The conflict that splits the village apart and renders it ineffective is in part due to a competition between critical attitudes that get in the way of community action. But how is this best communicated?

Self-transformative political subjects are often seen as vital to critical action (Foucault 1991, 1984; Archer 2003; Shragge 2003; Boltanski and Thé-venot 2006; Mosher 2010). The emphasis is on an actor who can transcend the micro critiques of daily life and engage in deliberations with issues of emanci-patory justice of a greater scale and in the process *become* a political being. Very simply put we have styles of critique that see a dominated actor in need of emancipatory knowledge—the truth—in order to be powerful or those that see power as truth, and so actors are inherently critical, and their collective action is part of the regulatory needs of structure. Dignity Village does not fall easily into the purview of either category. It is easier to explain the emergence of Dignity Village through an approach that unites aspects of several approaches.

One of the dangers of pragmatic and critical ethnographies is the very uncontrollable and often-unpredictable kinds of information that are revealed in groups, when the simple dogmatic truths that help them organize their poverty are uprooted. The safe, simple, and convenient patterns of dependence and order that homeless citizens of the village tend to ride—"the safety of structure" as one commentator put it—explode into messy, confusing, and seemingly unmanageable patterns when brought under a critical and reflexive mode of examination. What was considered a simple relationship with the head of the IT department in the village, for example, soon comes to look like a different problem. It becomes an issue of how access to the computer passwords presents complex possibilities for alignments and conflicts. The current grip on the village by the city is not the result of some legal code in a democratic constitution, but because no one will fight for another way to see this code. The villager does not want to know that because on his or her own they cannot imagine how life would be better by making this change. It is easier to cede a potentially critical position to the more powerful when a given individual does not know how to create a response. Similarly, residents of R2DToo are asked to join in critical actions as part of their membership.

The problem for changing narratives, then, is not that the alternatives do not exist, but that the criteria on which they are made must become knowable and then made usable by a number of parties as a part of the process by which they are incorporated into popular discourse. For those who favour rapid rehousing over these intentional camp models, the narrative is even more delicate, for the value behind rapid rehousing is to get people off the streets very quickly. This is what these camps do well—well, that is, unless the camps are painted as an extension of the streets, as a means to empower a conventional narrative. So critique is not always about making room for new things; it is often about excluding others.

Latour argues that it really is not the place of the researcher to critique anything, because society, or visions of society are largely fictional, "a *cosa mentale*, a hypostasis, a fiction" (163). How do you critique fiction after all? Since the origins of critique lie in a false sense of a reality, then the critique is a fiction too. Critique then contributes to the construction of the social as much as it tries to excavate it, and to this I agree, but this does not make critique pointless. Latour argues,

> Thus, all things considered, critiques of sociology of the social are misdirected if they forget to consider their extraordinary efficacy in generating one form of attachments: the social ones, or at least that part of the social that has been stabilized. There cannot be anything

wrong in forming, formatting, or informing the social world (226).

Latour's argument, hard to simplify, is that critique cannot stand outside of the observations it makes or the justness that it tries to see. His criticism attaches to critical approaches that pretend to be outside of the world they are critiquing, outside of the reality they are presenting, but for pragmatic ethnography (PEOC) as I practice it, this is not a problem. He says,

> To add in a messy way to a messy account of a messy world does not seem like a very grandiose activity. But we are not after grandeur: the goal is to produce a science of the social uniquely suited to the specificity of the social in the same way that all other sciences had to invent devious and artificial ways to be true to the specific phenomena on which they wished to get a handle on ... (136).

Latour argued for the deployment of the actor "as part of networks of mediations" (136). In the context of the liminal communities we have been discussing, everything is mediation of a kind, and the point of view that guides us through them is the actor.

One way to understand how narrative inevitability works at the level of social justice is to identify how a given set of criteria is put to critical tests by a given set of actors. Biesta and Stams (2001) offer the terms *critical dogmatism*, *transcendental critique* and *deconstruction* as three main taproots from which "to be critical" can be understood (2001:1). It should be noted, however, that where dogma resists inclusion of other ideas, criticism could be inclusive of ideas that come from positions often thought of as divergent. Furthermore some dogmas might be correct. "Love your neighbor" is perhaps an acceptable dogma. Dogmatism is a valid approach to explaining the world, as long as it reveals its underlying assumptions to debate.

Critical dogmatism requires the application of criteria to evaluate a "specific state of affairs" (Biesta 1998:475–477; Biesta and Stams 2001:60). This kind of critique is dogmatic because the evaluation is geared toward using the criteria to produce new knowledge but the criterion, a sort of "truth," resides outside of the field being evaluated (Biesta and Stams 2001:60). In this case, the occupation of a park by homeless campers is argued by opponents and supporters on the basis of its constitutionality, a value defined in laws that exist outside of the action: people have a constitutional right to shelter, as one of the freedoms of being American, and this is transcendent and fundamental to all citizens. However, what freedom actually means to differently held dogmatic versions of the truth becomes the source of a struggle for power.

Transcendental critique also conceives of the critical operation as the application of a criterion but whose meaning is open to dispute and argumentation. Originating in Kant's notion of transcendental philosophy, moral actors are rational, and as such they choose to act morally because the repercussions are favourable, or rational, to them as beings.[39] In this sense, the individual's freedom and autonomy are to be found in the liberty to act morally. Liberty and morality come to be understood as ideas manufactured for the domination of unwary individuals understood as resources under capitalism.

For the Frankfurt School of Critical Theory, under Adorno (1947, 1951, 1966), Horkheimer (1930-38, 1947), and Marcuse (1933, 1940, 1964), that proposition undergirded rich and convincing discussions of how narratives in powerful media "convinced" people unknowingly of the naturalness of inequality. Transcendental critique suggests a style of critical thinking that looks to find performative contradictions. In other words, it is a kind of internal critique that takes as its starting point the presence of actors or ideas in the context of a group or a community. Here, actions often betray rational or accepted values about performance that pivots on a central criterion. The performance of ideas and values, therefore, can be put to a test: we are duped or betrayed by ideologues and capital, but we can debate alternatives. Hence a proposition or alternative is presented in terms of whether it is rational in that context: I wouldn't try to explain to a union of autoworkers that plant closures were the result of divine providence. But I could try. Very often what seems most lacking in either of these two approaches is understanding how individuals, experiencing the same habitus, or functioning with similar psychological and comprehension capacities, might act differently than one another, or perhaps better put, might address social justice and its remedies in alternative ways.

Ideally, in Habermas's critical theory, the key to collective critical action is an actor's functionality within communities of communication, so maybe if I were able to spin that yarn well, they might buy into it (Habermas 1987; Biesta and Stams 2001:65). That would be easier, of course, if I were a superior orator and the audience was more apt to believe what they hear. Once again, ideally members of groups where criteria are being tested share similar communicative capacities. The ability to present arguments and to comprehend the debate is essential to understanding how alternative means can achieve legitimate and just ends. For example, how can we convince people who live in a two-bedroom home with good plumbing and doors that lock that the shacks in Dignity Village are also legitimate forms of home? The question is so large: it asks us to decide what is home, what is safety, what is comfort, what are basic needs, what are rights, and on and on. There is no simple way to reduce the answer to a given criterion or a set of criteria, because no matter what the force of habitus or the weight or a moral argument might be, there is conflict and there is social change.

Another critical school that presumes the existence of stable objective realities that we can question and change is *critical realism*. Critical realism stems from the premise that through our primary senses we are linked to objective physical truths about the world, yet our secondary perceptual senses often misinterpret this "pure" information. So it is necessary to be critical of realism (Sayer 2000; Bhaskar 1975). From a critical point of view, this means we must be wary of what we sense to be real, because, given the same set of physical stimuli, a variety of misinterpretations might arise among individuals, so we are faced with the likelihood of narrative complexity rather than inevitability. This could make social life quite difficult. The opposition of the two ways of knowing is between a *mind-dependent* experience of the world that tries to comprehend a *mind-independent* reality. In a very broad sense, this approach suggests that the representative value of objects, and by extension, events often linked with objects, are constitutive of basic perception, and therefore, as I see it, perceptions about reality that undergird narrative inevitabilities are key to our understanding of critical processes.[40]

An important critical realist is Margaret Archer. Archer (1995, 2001, 2003) had argued that sociology suffered from the problem of conflation in the sense that the tendency of sociology to present social phenomena as oppositional— structure and agency as exclusive categories of analysis, for example—has created a situation where we tend to see causation as a unilateral or one-sided affair. In the sense that structure is seen as causal, one speaks of *downward conflation*. In the case of agency affecting structure, one speaks of *upward conflation*. *Structuration*, as proposed by Giddens (1984) suggests *central conflation* whereby each, structure and agency are mutually implicated in the agency of actors (Archer 1995). The key to reproduction of social injustices and "ways of seeing" then is to implant narrative structures and meanings in the minds of potential actors.

In a very basic sense this is the way functionalist and conflict theorists critique neoliberal social structures. Whether there is a lot of room for change to happen or not is less important than the fact that all ways of seeing see *some* room for change to happen. Once again, the possibility of changing the way things are done—for example, the way we look at housing spaces or deserving and undeserving character—emerges out of the tension between antecedent narratives and emergent discourses that respond to new ways of doing old things. The point of my work has been that this potential for change, the fight for new forms of housing, for example, is a liminal phase where new narratives must compete with the old in order to move society in progressive directions. So why do some people cling to old information and resist new knowledge? Bourdieu said we learn to perform the same epistemology we were trained in. Critical theorists say it is because we are duped by capitalist-run idea machines. But Archer and others are suggesting that structures are real but in part produced by actors. This would suggest that actors who are subjected to institutional influence beginning at birth must have influence in bringing forth new ideas and thereby have impact on institutions. But how could this be so?

Archer's *analytical dualism* (1995:165-94) starts with the assumption that structures exist, and are real, but not directly observable. However, she argues that it is possible to trace the elaboration of the articulation between agents and structures—to unpick them—through a process of analyzing what she calls *morphogenetic sequences* (ibid). Looking at independently oriented actor-structure sequences, which contribute to overall social systems, allows the researcher opportunity to discern how such sequences were internally produced—what their internal dynamics were. In this way Archer finds means to link agents and structures in social outcomes because we can see how common narratives more or less contribute to stable patterns of social life, and how counter-narratives are met with resistance. [41] We will discuss resistance in more detail when we get to Foucault in Chapter 4.

Within this perspective, the critical goal of social science is to reveal the objective reality that exists beyond our primary sensory apparatuses, because without this guidance we don't perceive it. This is not to illuminate the excluded, as is the call in deconstructionist modes of critique where there is no basic form to reality. On the contrary, this position states that structures are real, and not necessarily exclusionary, regardless of the impossibility of seeing/witnessing them directly. So, if we want to change things we see that disturb us, if we have social justice as a goal, how do we do this? Archer (1996, 2003) has sought to explain how actors enter into processes of critique and critical action by defining a new locus of freedom: the individual's inner self that is already composed by its experience of other mechanisms and linkages.

The key to understanding reality, the key to engaging in a critique or to understanding broader social communities of critique, therefore, cannot be found outside of the intimate thoughts of the individual. The main thesis of Archer's *Structure, Agency and the Internal Conversation* (2003) is that social agents compute and imagine the results of thorough reflexive deliberations about their ultimate concerns in an existential and deeply personal context to which they commit themselves as the result of an "internal conversation." The causal powers of mechanisms, the links between structure and agency are mediated in a thought process that determines how actors align themselves with the social or political projects that create the *appearance*—literally appearance in a phenomenological sense—of this agency. In other words, it is not the case that actors are engaged in all actions that might take place in a social system, but that they choose to be engaged or not on the basis of deliberations that take place in their imagination. I am arguing that we can give these analytical force by looking at them as stories people tell themselves and others about how to navigate daily life.[42]

In line with Bourdieu's (1977) *generative structuralism,* the internal conversation takes place in the actor as she mediates her places in a field though her perception of habitus. Society therefore is either reproduced to the degree that actors act commensurately with habitus, or it might change to the degree that situations arise where the internal conversation creates the need for alternate ways of doing things. Actors are determined, not by structure, not by agency as such, but by the way an internal conversation produces agency in various alignments with established practices or towards to new ends. This has implications for practical undertakings for social scientists, especially in regard to critical action and critique.

Mechanisms do not produce the same outcomes for all actors. Even in direct acts of resistance, the experience of critical actors will vary within the particular action, such as squatting in Portland, or between other cases classified as resistance, such as a protest march down a city street. While each such action is likely to be resisted by dominant institutions, the shape of this counter-measure is impossible to determine and will vary in each case. So when Dignity Villagers and other IHC builders want to set up in urban imaginaries where there is little room for concentrated poverty, the decision they have already made and the particular kind of fight they are about to face will give that act of resistance a unique character that one can try to predict, but the reality of which can only be understood as it takes place and goes off in unknowable directions.

So resistance in the name of freedom, which is often the moral call to squats and fights for space, as an example of action towards issues of justice, is not about a universal freedom, because there are others who fight the squats wishing to be free of the homeless and other ne'er-do-wells. (This is sometimes called the NIMBY or Not In My Back Yard position.) If this is true, resistance, as one way of arguing for competing narratives, offers no predictive value. In a sense this ultimate potential for action suggests that there are always mechanisms, but that the engagement of actors within them is merely latent, so there is no way to determine how agency will affect structure nor vice versa except in concrete terms, as these events become, or afterwards as a form of recounting. It has been suggested that this is a general weakness of the critical realism model; despite claiming to be a model of social transformation, it "does not offer much in the way of an interpretation of how social change happens" because there is no concrete model of events and actions, actors and mechanisms that provides any kind of anticipatory capacity.[43]

The implication of this brand of critical realism for understanding critical narratives and vague experiences like freedom and autonomy is that ultimately choice resides in the individual and she has the power to reconcile the influence of various mechanisms internally. Hence, predictability is not so likely from a critical realism perspective; understanding an event or a consequence, unraveling the links between mechanisms and consequences back though time in order to see their current status, is very much the end result. The other weakness for me is that there is little attention to understanding historical contexts, which contain the DNA of how certain narratives come to be persuasive over time.

Each of the previous modes of critique suggest that sociological critique can identify how *domination* happens as the result of objective and asymmetrical distributions of power. In other words, the key to understanding freedom and social justice is the eradication of domination by more powerful just criteria. They suggest that narratives based on transcendent truth about a just state of affairs, such as an idealization of freedom, can be mobilized to overcome inequalities and domination, as a way of giving the dominated power to overcome objectively understood structures of domination. The people can be rallied together to overcome. They also understand the role of the researcher or social scientist to be in a better position to understand these hidden systems or internal mechanisms than the person with only common-sense awareness and whose critical capacity is really limited to their own firsthand experience of situations. This places a moral burden on social critique and social researchers to determine means by which to identify the just cause and to pursue it. Put another way, the mission of critique is to demonstrate how narratives about the truth of objective realities are dominant and to argue for means out of this oppression—to take an active role in changing the conversation.

The usefulness of these three approaches is subject to debate. For my purposes, I see the importance of structural tendencies to control actors as a matter of concern for freedom or for critical action. Critical theory is weak largely because it cannot prove a false consciousness; in my fieldwork, even the worst-off have often stated a very broad awareness of the social and economic conditions of their humanity, and recognizing the inherent inequality the system produced remained solidly in favour of it over any other option. Its value to my work is to consider the implicit and unpublicized ways that power works to control others—to dominate, if you wish, though media, powerful institutions in the service of capital, envisioned in my work as central to neoliberalism and the governance that oversee Dignity Village and other alternative spaces.

Bourdieu, if taken in the generous parameters I have extended, leaves room for actors to act, but he has very much underplayed the unique and common-sensical types of critical moments that impinge on the choice to act, in the sense of activists' breaks with habitus. Critical realism wants to give it all to us, a sort of holistic critical perspective, but it is difficult in several ways. First, it assumes that there is a basic structure to the world, and 1 in agreement with Latour have said earlier that 1 do not see this. Furthermore, there is no way to understand how the critical attitudes expressed in conversational types link up to lead to acts of resistance, or to form socially transformative narratives, nor to anticipate how research might impact this. 1 find the idea of an inner conversation very interesting, but 1 cannot see its applicability to anything but ideal situations. The idea of conversational "types" is difficult to support in reality. People change their arguments frequently and often say and act in contradictory ways. My mission as stated earlier is to understand how such conversations change, and if actors are stuck in "types" then this is unlikely to happen.

Furthermore, as 1 stated earlier, all three of these positions suggest that there is truth out there that must be known to the actor for her to act. And they leave no room for anticipating or understanding action generated in spaces or modes of living that are poorly formed in terms of structural or other cultural values. For ambiguous and liminal cultural spaces like the lHCs, they are of little use in that sense.

Each of the previous modes uses criteria external to the case to create narratives about inevitability and, therefore, about what is just in a given situation. But this suggests that external narratives, often understood as "ought to be" or "should be" statements, have more power than actors in a real living situation to claim another way. The appeal of critical dogmatism to my work in IHC is that 1 often hear from very poor housing activists that freedom and democracy are essential qualities that people want, and that their inalterable rights to autonomy and to participate freely make IHC reasonable. But no one can tell me what freedom and dignity really are. As you will read, in these camps these key concepts remain aloof as defined criteria and so we will have to address the problem such noble ideas present to practical activist work in Chapter 6. Still, we want to watch for how external criteria are used in the context of my fieldwork.

Transcendental critique is interesting for the promise it gives to communities of communication where contests can take place over just criteria. But in this formulation, ideas are trying to exclude others, and that means that justice must be based on exclusion of less powerful ideas. Since power at this level is based on consensus and that is an essentially social product, if one controls social relations, one controls the consensus. And so we have the perfect conditions for exclusionary democracy, which is in fact why IHCs struggle.

While we will pay attention to these ways of looking at the underlying criteria that guide the upcoming transcriptions, the goal of PEOC is to reimagine situations given new information. This is an approach to critique that seeks to include ideas that have been excluded, and understands inclusion of people and ideas in a diverse social world to be key to social justice. This view links my work to another approach understood as *deconstruction*.

Jacques Derrida is often considered the father of modern deconstruction. Derrida's *metaphysical exigency* is the tendency of Western philosophy to look at "presence" in terms of its natural, whole, and self-sufficient qualities, instead of interior qualities of decay, complication and accident (Derrida 1988:93).[44] Derrida argues that we can never isolate ourselves or our inquiries from this tendency because it is the tradition out of which we have emerged as cognizant and articulate beings. Hence, all ideas, representations and critiques, all narratives we use to make sense of life, inhere some dogmatic qualities. His project is to show that "being," along with ideas about any "thing," cannot be understood without discerning how they come to make sense in relation to other beings, states or ideas or things, sometimes referred to as *elements*. This is a pseudo-metaphysical issue. There are no self-sufficient meanings. So the goal is to discern how things achieve meaning by their articulation with other things in *that* structure their togetherness produces (1978, 1991).[45] Perhaps we can think of this as the mediations of ideas in networks of ideas. It is through a process of deconstruction, of dismantling, that this articulation is made knowable. One way of looking at difference is the way Dignity Village is viewed by conventional Oregonians, as a bad, dark, and less than desirable situation, which it is, to my thinking. It has this meaning because its origins are the street, its problems are street problems and so it is inflected with "streetness." However, when successful professionals build "Tiny Home" communities, this becomes an interesting experiment in reducing carbon footprints, and drug use or mental health issues in the community do not come to define it. How we look at things in terms of what they appear to exhibit and what inevitability this proffers is a constructed narrative.

Deconstruction has a unique way of contributing to critique. Instead of asserting the validity of rationalized criteria to matters of justice in a fixed and objective social system, deconstruction tries to open up such systems to an awareness of how imagining the system in that way excludes other valid criteria; deconstruction affirms knowledge not simply of what is known to be excluded from the system, but affirms what is wholly other, what is unforeseeable from the present as it *appears* to be (67-68). The key to this is exposing the conditions that make an idea or state of affairs possible. For this, however, there is no word; rather, there is just a specific way that elements impact the future possibility of others. Derrida called this *différrance*. Derrida insisted deconstruction was neither method nor form of analysis and as such, this "non-method" does not seek to contain ideas or to re-present the conditions of possibility for extant notions; it seeks to suggest, perhaps more correctly than to say *to understand*, the inevitability of invention, of the "otherness" contained in systems and programs and anticipations (Derrida 1991:27). Biesta and Stams (2001:68) suggest it is this concern to find or to understand what is wholly other from a system that makes deconstruction not merely critical, but something that seeks justice as its outcome by revealing how what we take to be the natural state of things can be opened up to new ways of doing and being. Inequality and domination are not natural vectors of association simply because we experience them. Something has made them so. In their sense of it, the justness of the deconstructive method is opening up to inclusion, what has been excluded, and this then is the matter of social justice.

The judgment deconstruction offers comes from a different place than dogmatic or transcendental critique. There are no absolute truths, so no way to impose a dogma of any kind. There is no inevitability that *must* be, only those that happen as "results" of deliberate choices. There is no way to argue the case for an idea in fair and reasonable communities of consensus. The reason for this is that Derrida himself would argue that there is no way to guarantee language is capable of expressing the un-expressible—which is quite literally the point of différrance. Unlike the former, it is not pitched onto an idea from behind the rationale construction of an external ideal or truth; unlike the latter, it doesn't result from within communities of communication as the result of actors' judgments about performance of a criterion because the "universally" just criterion cannot really be known, since the identification of the criterion is generated by the same system that generates its need. Capitalism creates poverty and homelessness and then capitalists produce visions of a solution. The solution must be preferable to that narrative or it would not happen, except under peculiar conditions. And the sites we have been talking about are exactly examples of that possibility. In these cases, for example, activists reduced the idea of home to a basic constitutional right to shelter first, and the courts agreed. The form of this housing became mostly the concern of the activists.

The contribution of deconstruction is that it points to the fact that critical criteria are not self-sustained or self-actualized units of meaning; rather, they require events or information outside of themselves to become relevant. When the city demands in Chapter 5 that Dignity Village live up to its contract but it cannot do so, there is a reason to understand why the current form of things is ineffective. Suddenly the very spirit of the old contract is called into question for the ways it excludes other ways of seeing the village in pragmatic terms. On a broader scale, the elements of activist critique of homelessness are meaningless without the housing policies to critique. IHC could not be framed as rapid rehousing until that paradigm and other examples of it like HF emerged and created a new way of looking at IHC.

For IHC dwellers, their self-meaning becomes structured by their very connection to one another in the structures of resistance produced by homelessness. Otherwise they become mere wards of the state. But how do people become aware of the structures in which they are oppressed and forced to suffer? What role can ethnography play in the directions and choices made by communities of struggle? I will not pretend that I have not played a role in the outcomes described below. But neither will I pretend that an objective reality made itself known to me, towards which I could apply a transcendental notion of right and wrong. These places are so unique and in such early periods of their emergence as discursive sites that they defy easy description or categorization. This book, part anecdote and part method, is precisely a response to trying to make sense of a very messy truth.

Being critical in the sense we are using it, then, means taking a position. In light of the post-modern, post-structural turn, how can an ethnography that says something, that takes a position towards understanding critical action, be valid, if reality is unknowable, or at the very least, is constantly shifting? Is a post-structural/post-critical ethnography possible? Ultimately, I argue that following Denzin's (1997) heuristically conceived "eight moments of qualitative inquiry," the *fractured future* of ethnography rests in a pragmatic ethnographic approach to critical action, in politically motivated activist ethnographies, rather than its traditional and impossible role as an arbiter of truth told from a position of exteriority. Denzin and Lincoln suggest that "[t]he eighth moment is now" and that only the most tentative legacies and causal links can be made. They leave the latest period wide open for the interconnecting of methods, theories, and multiple criteria for adjudicating validity. Researchers "have never before had so many paradigms, strategies of inquiry and methods of analysis to draw upon and utilize" (20). Looking forward they offer that we are in a moment of "discovery and rediscovery out of which new ways of looking, interpreting, arguing and writing are debated and discussed" (ibid). Pragmatic ethnography of critique emerged out of the problem-oriented work I do with villagers, in which ethnographic knowledge has been used to steer various political actions. This type of ethnography is thus pragmatic, critical, and also risky.

2.3 Ties to Critical and Reflexive Ethnography

Critical ethnography has a long and rich history in anthropology and the social sciences (Conquergood 1991; Smith, G. 1991; Thomas 1993; Carspecken 1996; Davis 1999; Denzin 2001; Lather 2002; Smith D. 1999; Kinsman 2006). Foley (2002) provides one of the more complete examinations of the roots of critical ethnography:

> Such empirical investigations are often founded on the following general ontological and epistemological assumptions: (1) All cultural

groups produce an inter-subjective reality which is both "inherited" and continually constructed and reconstructed as it is lived or practiced. This shared cultural reality is external in the sense that Bourdieu defines "habitas" (Bourdieu and Wacquant 1992). It is a distinct, lived historical tradition "objectified" through structuring practices (laws, public policies, cultural conventions). The habitus of a lived historical tradition is marked by a collective memory of particular ecological, geo-political, embodied, spaces/places; (2) A well-trained, reflexive investigator can know that historical, socially constructed reality in a partial, provisional sense through an intensive, experiential encounter with people who live by these cultural constructions of reality; and (3) A reflexive investigator, who has experienced this unfamiliar cultural space and has dialogued with its practitioners, can portray this cultural space and its people in a provisionally accurate manner (2002:43).

It is impossible to pinpoint in history the exact origins of critical ethnography. Yet it is increasingly becoming the mode of critical qualitative analysis across disciplines, where there is a need to understand the lived experiences of actors who are often in critical performance-oriented positions. We find this kind of work attached to the critique of institutional settings such as education and medicine (Vandenberg and Hall 2011), and of political movements (Smith 1990). This endeavour reveals how such roles and identities are wrapped up in systems of order, domination, and power struggle. As such the critical ethnographic enterprise has the important capacity to inform socially transformative experiences, but only under certain conditions.

Foley argues for a certain detachment of the ethnographer from the critical enterprise. In my work, which I have often argued is a type of critical ethnography, I do not present myself as detached from the enterprise. I have already suggested that my past experience of homelessness enables this. I also want to suggest that we are not always looking at a system of domination: rather, we are looking at a system where people are dominated or controlled but from within, and that given the tools they can find empowerment. That is the point of my enterprise. For this to work, open lines of communication must be maintained. This works better in situations wherein the researcher has something in common with those people with whom he works. I live in or near the cities where I do my work. I was an addict and episodically homeless, I speak the same language and reside under the same legal system, and so on. For this reason, I disagree with Foley. It is correct that we may be better authorities on the science behind our work, but at the same time we must acknowledge that all our portrayals are "provisionally accurate" and that often, commonality with the culture provides insights we could not have from a distance (Collins 2008; Gallinat 2008; Coffey 1999).

Critical ethnography at last is about understanding action directed towards social justice. As an extension of the Marxist project to reveal orders of inequity, critical ethnography in practice departs from the external role of observer and aligns or integrates with the action of individuals in critical action as a tool of empowerment. Far from pretending to be external or objective, the critical ethnographer adjoins the "transformative endeavor" and "emancipatory consciousness" (Kincheloe and McLaren 2000:291). In developing the notion of a *subjugated knowledge*, that is, of how frames of reference come to be shaped in the field by institutions and other regimes of knowledge, these authors *present* the case that language and communicative action are aspects of power and of dominated subjectivities.[46]

Once again, this is how critical ethnographers have understood themselves. I want to suggest that "critical," in the sense of doing work in one's own culture, can attach itself to one of the two levels of emancipation I have mentioned already. We do not have to disclose contradictions and domination to eradicate the system that predicates them, but we can indicate how to participate more fully in them. This is very different than the classic Marxist expectation for a sudden and massive revolution against capitalism. Yet it does suggest that the work is designed to transform social relations in favour of those individuals for whom the current system has created socially unjust experiences.

Because my work focuses on an impoverished and marginalized community, I expected to hear a kind of indictment of capital. In fact, however, most villagers do not reject the inequality that capital produces. PEOC really messes things up. There is no way to see things in a "certain way" if one is pragmatic and critical. In the sense that a PEOC embraces a means to understand how truths are produced, argued, and moved into the worlds of social actors, it presents an "exquisitely tormented" understanding in how it completely undermines the bedrock of delusions that undergird grand narratives and allegedly foundational truths that researchers and participants alike might hold (Derrida 1996:55 in Lather 2004:481).

"Moving across levels of the particular and the abstract, trying to voice a transcendent purchase on the object of study, we set ourselves up for necessary failure in order to learn how to find our way into post-foundational possibilities" (Lather 2004:482). The wonderful predisposition of the deconstructionist aspect of this position is its very lack of predisposition in the academic sense (ibid). As ethnographers we can no longer try to fit the assumption of daily experience into neat, conceptual categories and systems of classification. As a direct nod to the legacy of the turn, Lather adds, "given the demise of master narratives of identification, perspective and linear truth, such ethnography draws close to its objects in the moment of loss where much is refused, including abandoning the project to such a moment" (2004:482, also Haver 1996 in Lather 2004:482).

In terms of the authority of the researcher, a deconstructionist critique leads to the destabilizing of traditional power relations in critical research. Successfully undertaken, this kind of ethnography "problematizes the researcher as "the one who knows" (Lather 2004:482), since in a critical ethnography the point is to understand how truths are constructed by researcher and actors, and by the actions in which they are engaged. Furthermore, and in my work especially, I am free, if not frequently asked, to offer my educated opinion as it were, and this is very often rejected.

Lather (2004) and Denzin and Lincoln (2005) among others remind us that since ethnography has represented a form of surveillance and discipline (Foucault 1998; Said 1989; Clifford and Marcus 1986; Fabian 1983), critical ethnography situates research in a position to fail; indeed, it counts on reaching points where understanding is pressed to the limits of capacity to inform. I went to Dignity Village in 2010 and found Utopia. Over the following year I worked on developing a model of the village based on its ability to *resolve the life traumas of homeless people* by forging them into happy and useful citizens. This was the common perception held by outsiders based on the web links and other propaganda produced by the village.

When I returned in 2011, the community was completely dysfunctional and close to imploding. What had happened to Utopia? Once again, I had reached a point where my understanding was insufficient to make sense of or to remedy the problems of community that villagers faced. Often when I was there, a villager asked about my solutions to political or social problems, and more often than not this led to heated arguments and debates. On a few occasions, some of the villagers chose to no longer work with me because I had taken a hard line on idleness and low morale.

Was I was acting outside my ethically participative capacity? Maybe. But this debating and argumentation was exactly what villagers did in their own time, and so it was expected of me, if I was to be an actual participant, to take sides, to argue, to appear aligned with others and to be understandable by these attachments. Those who remained outside of such "factions" were not trusted because their motives and feelings were largely unknowable—they were "outside of things." Perhaps I was forcing villagers to unravel the miserable state of affairs for me, but in order to do so they had to confront the fiction in their own narratives about the village. And in turn I had to confront my own contradictions and assumptions about the village and the complexity of the people who lived there. In the following excerpt from an earlier monograph I wrote about the Village, we can see how arriving at knowledge is not based on objective truth but on the interplay of people creating narratives about shared experiences:

Eric Weissman

MICHELLE (from *Dignity in Exile* [Weissman 2012:95]):
One day, before I went to New Seasons Market to buy my daily salad, I filmed a few of the villagers who were trying to figure out what to have for dinner based on the meagre canned goods they had stashed. It was a few days until the food stamps were issued, and the usual Sunday leftovers from the bar down the road hadn't arrived. Normally, the restaurant brought its entire Sunday brunch buffet leftovers; bacon, sausage, pancakes, bread, eggs, fruits and rich desserts. Villagers pounced on the food. I refrained from eating it because, in all honesty, watching them claw into the stuff with their hands made it unappetizing. But it hadn't come that Sunday, so as we ended filming I offered to pick up some food for Michelle and a couple of friends. I didn't know her too well but I knew her well enough to appreciate how hard it must be for a single woman to be living in a 6-by-8-foot shack without a support network. Left to fend for herself on the streets, she would, if the stats were correct, have to hook up with a man or a group of street people, to ensure her safety and that things like food and shelter were found. In the village, she was one of only a handful of single women. I knew she was angry most of the time. I knew she could rocket into incredible rants. I also knew she had a good heart. This place was her last hope. I knew, even if she didn't say so....

I walked away. She chased after me and said, "I'm embarrassed.... I'm not working.... I'm living off Washington State food stamps." It was embarrassing to her because she had real skills, but nowhere to use them. She was a journeyman carpenter, and was a card-carrying union member. But Michelle, like many other single moms with threads of mental health issues and personal trauma, could no longer transform her skills into long-term stable employment, even though she had a pretty impressive resume of carpentry, framing and other construction gigs from Seattle to Portland.... "And, half the time you can't find a place to even squat because the cops are all working for the banks and the banks are all working for the capitalists."

Michelle at her dorm, 2011.
Photo: Nigel Dickson.

78

Her tone became loud when she talked about the liturgy of her life, as she always engaged in the classic Marxian ideas about the alienation of the laborer and then shifted to her disgust of the police and the mental health system, wherein less than a year ago she had been diagnosed as manic depressive and committed to a mental health facility for a few weeks. Her switches were many and they turned on and off in unpredictable linkages. Her circuits overloaded, her body, her face, her gestures transformed instantly, blurting things so quickly and so nonsensically that she welled up and her cheeks flushed. "I'm sorry, I'm sorry," she said. "I know I am not supposed to get angry. I know you don't like that on camera." "No," I told her, "that's not it. I just, well, I don't know how to help you...."

A long pause. We just smiled at each other. A transformation in her. From anger to apparent tranquility.

"But anyway," she went on, "I feel great here, man. Portland rocks! And the sisters, the 'sparky sisters.' The electrician sisters, are really reaching out to me and helping me to feel included, people are really helping me to feel a sense of inclusion, even though I am embarrassed that I am home-less...."

... After couch surfing, using shelters and sleeping behind a church, she'd become involved with one of the several temporary camps strewn across Seattle. What is today known as Nickelsville—a city-recognized, but not legalized, tent encampment that is now in its fourth year—became her home. She had unfortunate memories of that place. At first she'd felt it had great potential. The community was really fighting for land claims by the homeless. But, organized under the auspices of an activist NGO—Share/Wheel31—Michelle insists the community's fiscal arrangements and outreach were soon being overseen by a management team, rather than by the actual members. "They try to make us think we have some say, but it's way worse than here at the village. If they think they have factions and all that crap here, they should see up there. And one guy was getting two bucks a head for everyone who stayed there. Two bucks a head a night."

"So over a thousand a week?" I asked. "To watch the village?"

"To be a manager," she said sarcastically, fingers gesturing quotation marks. "The tent master. Anyway, I helped build the place. I worked on the structures and I had good friends there. I never did dope or caused any trou-ble. And I left one time to try my business, my vintage clothing thing. And it worked for a while. But it was hard, Eric. Really hard. So there I was again. I was living at the Harborview, but it was no good. So I followed some people I knew, from the U-district parking lot. We took the bus down to Nickels-ville. And I had busted my butt for that place. I'd never got barred from that place, never been disciplined, and they turned me away at midnight with-

79

out even a blanket onto the streets of Seattle, and that was my repayment from Nickelsville. That's how they repaid my hard work and dedication—by turning me away when I did need help because I didn't have ID."
"But they knew who you were?"
She nodded, "But they didn't care."
When she'd heard about Dignity Village and had come to it, it was like the angels were singing and heaven had opened to her, finally.
"But we can speak up here and have a voice. And I love this place. Just the place itself, and the real, uh, community, man. And, you know, now I really want to be about activism. I need a purpose in my life and I just want to spread a message of unity and I just been through all that like spirituality and I just think that we all gotta get it—you know, sometimes I'm the worst you know for going 'oh that person's got money, oh, oh, oh'... and I don't want to be that way. I just want us all to unify and take our lives back, and I want people to move back into their houses. And that's what got me down here in the first place. Just seeing all the foreclosures and the tragedy in the place I lived for 44 years."
"Seattle?"
"Yeah, yeah. Sorry ... sorry."
"Don't be sorry, don't be. This is hard stuff to talk about."
She smiled. "It really is."
"But maybe it's good to talk about it?"
"I totally think so."
"There are people who need to hear your story."
"Thank you." She wiped her eyes.

As only one example of the deep structure to even mundane critical attitudes, Michelle's story illuminates the difficulty of writing culture without the reflexive commitments to which I speak. *This was a relationship.* There is no way to talk about her without revealing how she and I articulated our ideas together. She suffered. She suffered from psychiatric and personal issues, and I can't imagine producing an external summary of what I learned from her (just as this last sentence feels awkward, even unnecessary).

Understanding that all cultures construct privacy and secrets in their own fashion, it is still absolutely necessary to be "present" in the storytelling as a way of showing trust and loyalty to the participant (Moor 1990; Pink 2007; Svenningsson Elm 2008; Aull Davies [1998] 2008). This is very different from pragmatic inquiry that asks questions, looking for answers that conform to an overall agenda. In *The New Spirit of Capitalism*, Boltanski and Chiapello (2005) employed ethnographic methods including interviews. The questions and goals of the interviews, however, were to address the issue of "justifications";

by contrast, in my work, the participant guides the direction of inquiry, opening and closing subjects, providing contiguous and separate sets of ideas to the ones I might have been interested in when I sat down with them. In Michelle's case, she leaps from deeply personal agitations to points of view— critiques of entire economic systems, communities and governance. She came to know me as a person she *could talk to* and she told me when I should or shouldn't record our conversations because she had an idea of what she "wanted to put out there."

In opening up investigation to its own contradictions and biases, the ethos of deconstructive ethnography should aim for what Lather has called the three "Aporias of Practice" (2004:482). The first aporia concerns ethics and is resolvable by recognizing research as a form of knowledge construction that is constantly negotiated and negotiable, where a reflexive style of representation can illuminate the "field of play" (ibid).[47] The second aporia concerns authenticity, representation and voice. In this, Lather suggests, "my attempt is not so much 'against' authenticity and voice as it is a double economy of the text to move toward de-stabilizing practices of 'telling the other' (McGee 1992) in ways that displace the privileged fixed position from which the researcher interrogates and writes the researched (Robinson 1994)" (484). The final aporia is the "Interpretation and its Complicities." Lather suggests the problem is that as noble as it might sound to be reflexive and to avoid "othering" informants, they will never be "me" because they are unique individuals. We can try to speak as truly to their words and ideas as we can, but we are never a direct channel to their experience. How does one respect the collective experience of doing fieldwork with another "person" or "persons" and yet pay respect to the qualities of their experience that are theirs and therefore are different? In other words, allow your narrative to exist without comprising the *other* in the "other"? Ultimately she quotes Visweswaran (1994:80): "Reflexive ethnography authorizes itself by confronting its own processes of interpretation as some sort of cure towards better knowing, while deconstruction approaches 'knowing through not knowing'" (in Lather 2004: 486). This, in the manner I understand it, is essentially a type of pragmatic issue.

A reflexive platform is the only way to look at how my actions helped to generate the understanding that I ultimately represent. We look back at the field experience in notes or on video in order to arrive at an understanding of what we have missed. As Lather argues, "we don't know what we are seeing, how much we are missing, what we are not understanding, or even how to locate those lacks.... My interest is, rather, Derrida's ethos of lack when lack becomes an enabling condition" (Lather 2004:486). Hence at the root of the deconstructionist critique is the point we reach at which we don't know where the fantasies we understand as truth collapse. From these positions of lacking, new knowledge emerges that makes critical moments happen.

This knowledge may be about how powerful narratives and rules have victimized us, or shed light on the ways we might obtain power to fight for our rights, where such things were not imagined before. Such knowledge may come as a revelation of the capricious forces of governance that are wreaking havoc on the morale of the village but had hitherto been seen as benevolent: the mobile health services, the city assessment teams, the freedom to live on a composting tarmac. These are all delusions in governmentality (of poverty) to manage a troublesome population. How do actors come to know this from within the experience of it? Where does the critical impulse to challenge this compliance come from, if it all?

Insomuch as the village claim made in 2000 drew attention away from city practices towards housing and made the homeless position a priority, it can be argued that a shift in extant power relations took place. From Larsen (2011), one might suggest that this is yet another example of how such power transformations shift the "spotlight away from authorities and those who exercise power, in order to focus almost exclusively on the subject of power, i.e. the student (or in this case the homeless claimant)" (38). What these critiques share is an indictment of hierarchical power and the use of knowledge from outside of the movement itself—from educators, social sciences, media and other activists, in order to present and claim alternate visions (38).

Dignity Village is a case that supports the idea put forth by Larsen, that "when critical ideas are effective in displacing power relations, the ideas themselves are easily turned inside out in the same process" (38). PEOC is useful in establishing how linkages between various critical positions help us to actually gauge critical capacities and action, and, in the case of this book, asks that we look at how neoliberal critiques of the state and governmentality "claim to govern as little as possible, but still develop ever more elaborate techniques to extract the most of human capital" (39).

Several critics have observed that there is danger in this critical approach: revealing the hidden structures to unwary participants is a destabilizing moment for the participant (Vandenberg and Hall 2011:25-30; Kincheloe and McLaren 2005; Denzin 1997). The authoritative stance of the researcher as the harbinger of important information is at once taken seriously and often taken as inevitable; the net effect is to confirm the inevitability of domination and to suspend the critical moment in a sense of hopelessness. Hence a number of researchers (Lincoln 1995; Hall and Callery 2001, in Vandenberg and Hall 2011) argue for the extension of the relations of field knowledge creation to the participants, as both a means to access the critical resources of actors and to democratize the production of truth about critical action.

One of the ways this is done is through abandonment of the traditional privy status by the researcher and the use of a highly reflexive manner in the field. So in this project 1 have shared what few notes 1 took with people;

showed people photos I was going to use to get responses; shared the videos we shot of the village and discussed how to edit them properly; and very importantly, when I wrote *Dignity In Exile*, I checked each section with the people about whom the stories were written and in some cases adjusted them to fit the facts as better seen by them. Then I sent the book back to the village, and this book, these portrayals came to be the primers for much of what you will read in Chapters 6 and 7 in this book. It is a much more labour-intensive process to share all this work with participants.

However, I argue that we are also compelled to be as openly reflexive as possible because this is not just research, but research with the goal of impacting how people will see themselves and then make new choices to act. I consider working towards critical knowledge as a type of act in the sense that Isin (2008) and Nielsen (2008) have suggested. This is so because the basis on which pragmatic storytelling and oral traditions unite is a certain dialogic experience in which the use of language and communication to arrive at new knowledge is in itself a break with common practice. That is because it is new and unfolding, and also because it inheres answerability to an "other" outside of the participants—the critique, itself. And this might seem to be a tough chew, but it is vital to understand how it is that the pragmatic critical ethnography attaches to the ongoing emancipatory project. This kind of ethnography, to me, is not about telling other people's stories but about social relationships, which evolve around changing a situation.

2.4 Reflexivity and Dialogics

Dialogics is the recognition by two participants in a speech act that each position is mutually constitutive despite the myriad possibilities for rejoinders around them (Bakhtin 1982:271-2). The idea here is that in our conversations with one another, we are implicitly referring to or speaking to prior conversations with others or prior experiences that we, knowingly or not, associate with the present exchange of ideas. Furthermore, not only is the observable communicative act related to prior experience, it inheres participants' expected or desired outcomes. So we cannot take the qualitative experience simply on its own terms but must recognize its ties to "others," not only people but also causes, or morals, or other sovereign principles. Very often, the other, sometimes written with a capital "O," is the communicative act in itself.

Since it is possible that an actor could be establishing meaning with a number of others who are not present but may reside in memory, and that the dialogic moment is a unique one, if it is to have analytic force in critical ethnography, the grounds on which that unique act took place need to be known by those in a position to interpret the investigative act, to act on the basis of its suggestive courses of action. This tells us what other information was excluded, or why some information was included, and contributes the answerability of the investigation to the just cause (the Other), which I explain presently.

Dialogics is very different than *dialectics*. In human communication, dialectics is a mode of communication that seeks closure and resolution to the conflict or competitions between ideas. It follows the Hegelian tradition of synthesizing a solution from a thesis and antithesis. Words express ideas, which then lead to conflict or new cumulative knowledge, which then needs to be thought of or expressed in a new way, with new words or ideas. In this way, it is a way to reduce complexities to simpler terms and is often used, especially in the Marxist literature, to identify and disrupt class- and power-laden discourses as a solution to social injustice. The dialectic is a way to set actors and narratives against each other. The result is either resolution or conflict.

Dialogics is very different in that it speaks to a kind of listening that is open-minded to the implicit and subtle intentions of the actually spoken word. Dialogics looks at where the choice of language and tone come from; and rather than trying to impose a conclusion to communicative acts can be less competitive and open to diversity. Instead of reducing the interview or the conversation to a simple synthesis of ideas, it recognizes such simplification once again as merely a way of twisting a vision of truth from a mop-head of experiences. One of the keys to Bakhtin's dialogics is the moment where one actor must reflect on the ideas just shared with another and in so doing becomes able to generate or modify her own new ideas, which are ultimately recalled as past experience. Working in critical ethnographic situations presents particularly complicated dialogic conditions, because participants are asked to revisit their words and statements—their positions relative to a "cause" or an issue—and then to discuss where that thinking comes from. The goal is to seek out ways that powerful but invisible structures of knowledge and oppression lead us to believe certain things, when, in fact, there are other ways to think them.

A reflexive mode of representation is required to account for the dialogic nature of such acts. An underlying premise in my research is that no matter what I am told, there are other voices speaking; friends, enemies, supporters, ancestors and therapists and more, who are not present in the corporeal sense, but exist at other levels of experience, in memory, imagination, just out of view, or on the temporal horizon. So part of the pragmatic aspect of my work is trying to understand where certain critical attitudes originate in villagers as a way to account for the diversity. In Michelle's case, her entire current emotional and political point of view is strongly correlated with her evaluations of prior experiences, which we can see for ourselves in her reference to other camps, her children and the Oregon area.

Understanding how people, including me in my own deliberations, come to think and act as a matter of personal contexts helps to explain diverse responses to situations that appear to be the same, to those of us outside of them. Bakhtin speaks of centripetal and centrifugal forces that respectively unite and pull apart the meaning of language and ideas (ibid). When I speak of the investigative work I do as an act of sorts, I am, in a sense, trying to understand these forces in the critical deliberations that occur between the villagers and me, but also trying to know how those forces existed in their knowledge-forming prior experience. Reflexive openings to this kind of information don't appear immediately, not all of the time, and so often it has been the case where revisiting an experience with villagers has revealed new knowledge that they came up with upon a period of self-reflection.

Reflexivity is a dominant if not essential element of current ethnographic anthropology and of social research in general (Bourgois 1992, 1995; Church 1995; Pink 1997; Bourdieu 2004). There is in general the sense that in any social research where the investigative "eye" is turned outward, it must also be turned inward. I would argue that reflexivity has always been a vital part of ethnography and of the general study of humanity. The social psychology of George Herbert Mead in *Mind, Self and Society* (1934) asserts the social nature of "being human" and the essentialness of reflexivity for the formation of the self. "It is by means of reflexiveness—the turning back of the experience of the individual upon himself—that the whole social process is thus brought into the experiences of individuals...." (in Straus 1956:211).

Similarly, in *Towards a Philosophy of the Act* (1993), Bakhtin constructs the I-other architectonic as the once occurrent state of being, where individuals aesthetically contemplate others, and upon returning into oneself, can proceed to understand, to empathize and to act. While Mead does not situate reflexivity directly in the process that occurs between the "student and the studied," Bakhtin implicates the dialogic process of interpenetration (persons gaining knowledge of one another) and self-reflection in the investigative act (1993:4). And so when we get to the very critical ethnographic sections in Chapters 5 and 6, this dialogic process will be seen to clearly impact the nature of the truths we are trying to uncover.

Bakhtin has shown clearly that there is a difficulty in interpreting what actors do when they act based solely on pre-existing concepts as if the actors come with a set of contingent-specific potentialities installed within them, and that the investigator cannot be free of his, or their, own value-laden "point of view." The "act is already folded into an event and thus into an order" (1993:28). The traditional "rules" of social fieldwork participation, as I stated earlier, purport objectivity in making observations about an event or deed and so on. In a perfect *I–other* event, the "actors" would act as if they were merely present in the event, and that what was *occurrent* issued primacy over what was valued or expected. In either case, as Engin Isin points out, if one does not make some kind of a judgment based on pre-existing notions, "one may have nothing to say at all about the act". Isin calls this the "paradox of acts" (2008:28). And it is this paradox we try to resolve by making the paradox itself, the subject of disclosure when we do pragmatic ethnography.

Critical fieldwork is an act in the sense that we have discussed earlier; one that twists, inverts and breaks with habitus in the sense that Bakhtin suggests, precisely because it attaches itself as part of a uniquely emerging experience. In *Towards a Philosophy of the Act*, Bakhtin unfortunately spends relatively little time specifically on that point. However, what he does demonstrate is that in studying or investigating an act per se, one articulates not the world produced by the act, "but the world in that act becomes answerably aware of itself and is actually performed" (1993:31). Bakhtin is certain that all acts, speech or political, inhere a once-occurrent eventness—that means they occur only in the moment of their emergence—and, therefore, an ethnographic present, that portrayal we produce in our accounts of fieldwork, presupposes the necessity of the observer and the subject in a "shared" moment of becoming. Hence the observer and the observed comingle and the traditional authority of a privileged researcher is usurped by an answerability to an emerging representation. And so writing ourselves out of the story is quite impossible.

The only truly ethical ethnographic moment is the one where this duality of roles (and there can be a multiplicity of roles with multiple actors) is both recognized and accounted for, and performed, by the observer-become-subject. In this book, pragmatic ethnography suggests re-presenting how knowledge is made available in a co-production between the villager and me, and is therefore a reflexive moment. My tone in the discussion with Ibrahim from chapter one is a clear demonstration of how I try to include my thoughts, feelings and interpretation of things in that exchange of ideas. Unlike a survey or a structured interview with a set agenda, this more organic emergent form of doing ethnography can lead us into areas of learning we might never have anticipated.

In previous fieldwork with shanty dwellers, it has been shown that the material that poses the greatest difficulty to assemble includes the moments in which intimate information, secrets, feelings and disappointments come into the presence of the ethnography. This happens as a result of this destabilization of roles through a fidelity of both or all performers to the once occurrent event of the ethnographic present.

As an example, consider Eddy Johnston. I met Eddy in his shack at Tent City in 2001. Eddy had committed a murder earlier in his life. He had served time at the Kingston penitentiary in 1971. During the time he was incarcerated, he knifed a pedophile who had been raping young inmates, and to whom the guards had turned a blind eye. He stabbed him 42 times as a message to other "diddlers" and the guards, that the rest of the prison population wouldn't stand for the presence of rapists in their midst. Eddy was given an extra 17 years for that "intervention." This helped to kick off the infamous Kingston riots.[48] He is known as one of the original "Kingston thirteen." He was also a resident at Tent City when I did my fieldwork there in 2001. We became friends over the next six years until his death (related to crack use and other poor choices, despite his having earned a place in Toronto's rent supplement program). When we first met, I had some difficulty reconciling his past with the friendly, outgoing and loyal man I encountered in 2001. But then he would smoke some rock (crack), and this other Eddy appeared. There was so much "pain inside" him that he smoked to "kill the pain." It made him not hurt, not feel, "not care about nuthin.'"[49]

When Tent City was paved over, Eddy and Terry (mentioned above), both good friends, asked me to keep in touch. They had my phone number. When,

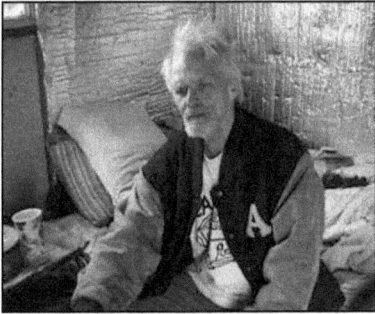

Eddy in his shack.
Photo: Nigel Dickson.

in 2002, Eddy and Terry along with the other 113 residents were evicted from Tent City and forced back to the streets, we kept in touch infrequently; it would have been easy to draw their part of the story to a natural close. That would not be the case, however, because as housing programs for the victims of Tent City were announced, Eddy and Terry got back in touch with me. They felt they (along with others from Tent City) had won rights by aligning with housing advocates in a fight for rent supplements. A new chapter in their story was beginning. They told me that this was part of their story too, and that I should follow it. This anecdote not only links their voice to the authorship of all my subsequent work about Tent City; it also links my willingness to help them produce a certain range of knowledge about their experience. This, they hoped, "would help other homeless people." Most importantly for how this experience informs my present work, my work with Eddy has shown me that ethnographic moments are completely open-ended if continuity exists; that is, if researchers and informants manage or need to continue "where they left off." Once occurrent events, yes, but what are the temporal bounds on the event?

In Eddy's case, it was interviewing him in his apartment, three years after our first meeting, that demonstrated to me how in such cases, the aporia—the moment where the informant's truth, what is true to him, is revealed—often takes years of "showing up" and being present.[50] I encourage you to look at this clip. If we had not continued to be present and to do this work over time, then the meaning of his prior stories would have a diminished value, and his truth would be lesser known.

As narrator, I say, "Even early in his housing Eddy seemed calmer, reflective, as if being housed were a balm to his mental health, and after losing a second child to the CAS, Eddy seemed well on his way to confronting his pain."

Eddy says, "I cost myself the kids because I didn't stop (doing crack)." He sits back on a large lounge chair. Holding a mug of coffee. Eyes welling up. He looks away, then back. He's sad. I have come to know that when he is sad, he turns to humor. "Not bad for fifty years, eh? Lose only two out of twelve?" he quips, but it doesn't work. His eyes well up.

Brian Dodge, 2012. Brian and I became good friends, but it took years of telling each other stories about ourselves. We often attended social housing functions together. Here he is at a screening of *Subtext*. A shining star he was. Photo: Eric Weissman.

Brian Dodge, another ex-resident of Tent City, is there. We have become a trio of sorts. They live in the same housing project near the airport. He was in Kingston penitentiary with Eddy. "Pops," as I call him, is very uncomfortable with Eddy's tears. Perhaps to Pops, tears are a sign of weakness. Eddy has always been the tough guy and the leader of their little group. Housing has changed certain things about him.

Eddy rises, walks towards the window. He can't speak. He is travelling somewhere, in his head. I keep the camera on him. He is hardly aware or does not care. He quietly says to me: "It's okay, buddy. Someday I'll sit and talk with ya. I'm the uncaring, unfeeling whatever I am ... just addict, don't care, don't feel about nuthin', nobody, nowhere...." He walks a bit, looks out the window. He's sniffling. "Anyways," he adds, as he walks over to me, "ya spun me buddy," and he laughs as he pushes my camera away.

Here we see that moment where new knowledge occurred because of the reflexive and critical engagement of researcher and participants over time.[51] But it is a span of time that you the viewer/reader are invited to experience. Eddy and I become answerable together to a greater Other—a truth perhaps, a critical awareness, and that awareness is partly yours. In the words of Bakhtin, one might add, "An event can only be described participatively" (31). In terms of observation, "it is not a world of objects that theorizing acts creates but relations amongst those objects and subjects as they unfold to each other and the investigator" (Isin 2008:30). Two facets of Bakhtin's model stand out here in the context of how I see my work. One is that for an investigator, his study is always in the process of becoming and is never finished. "An object that is absolutely indifferent, totally finished cannot be something one becomes actually conscious of, something one experiences actually" (1993:32). Hence, defining ethnography in terms of some temporal index, a beginning, middle or end, is quite impossible and referring to the object of an investigation in terms which reflect its *current* status in the *event of being* may be more appropriate. If one argues that from the point at which I began my fieldwork to the point at which I left the village is a time frame, then the argument can be made that there is a clear beginning and an end, but that speaks simply to *in situ* fieldwork; the critical moment, the answerability is ongoing and will go on, because you and others can now deliberate these ideas.

Regardless of the source, suffice it to say that "reflexivity is thus the constant awareness, assessment, and reassessment by the researcher of the researcher's own contribution/influence/shaping of intersubjective research and the consequent research findings" (Salzman 2002:806). [52] Insomuch as reflexivity reveals the researcher's life experience, beliefs, and goals at the onset and though a variety of techniques during the ongoing ethnographic process, the experience we report is about these, and it is about the group with whom the ethnography is made. The reflexive stance generates a knowledge-creation dynamic in which various actors come in and out of the process as contributors to the organic emancipatory project. Furthermore, reflexivity hinges on reciprocity; it allows for actors to critique the research, to assess the researcher's motives as a means of argumentation, and to suggest alternatives.

2.5 Visual Ethnography, Time, the Other and the Practical

Much of my current work is the result of videographed research I had undertaken many years before returning to school and doing my dissertation. That research was what we call a *filmic reportage* following no script and, as I suggested, in a Latourian sense of actor networks, following the ideas and imaginings of people I met into their social worlds. So it had been difficult to decide when to end shooting or to consider the project finished or complete. My feeling had been that my responsibility was to the people I was working with and I deferred to their perspectives when deciding on how to craft different versions of my work for viewing. I did this—sought participants' advice on what to show—because using a recording device like video opened up a whole new set of ethical and mechanical issues to ethnography. But in the end the benefits it offers surpass any of the ethical or methodological issues that might arise. The

Eric Weissman

main problem is this: given that truth is difficult to prove or to demonstrate in traditional textual forms, the use of images to tell stories is a more powerful way to convince people of truths. "Seeing is believing," as the saying goes. The use of images to support research requires particular openness about the choices made about what was represented, and how.

Johannes Fabian (1983) argued that anthropology's traditional handling of time as part of history or evolution was weakened by its subordination to the visual. We painted pictures of faraway places and presented this image-laden narrative as a snapshot of a culture in its own time, a time almost always behind our Western one. For Fabian the problem of anthropology was looking at cultures as if frozen in time relative to our own sense of progress, which was to deny them their own history and was the "the denial of coevalness." We envisioned the textual snapshot we took of other cultures as frozen in that moment. We did not problematize that current frame as the nexus of history, present and future possibilities—as an emergent state of affairs whose future is unknowable. Visualism had for a long time stood in the way of understanding coevalness because of its insistence of seeing difference in progressive measures of time. Now it must be understood that Fabian's critique was addressed to traditional anthropology and its focus on "simpler" or different cultures. Hence, a problem for him was that ethnography tended to look at others in terms of how far away they a were in temporal, spatial and therefore cultural senses; above this, ethnography tended to treat them as if its accounts of these cultures were fixed in a different time than its own. Sanjek (1991) argues:

> Fabian is concerned with the artificiality and the freezing of time that descriptions in the present tense may impart. Ethnography written in the present tense implies a view of human behaviour as conventional, predictable and rule-determined—a "culturology." Such writing conveys none of the independence of rule and action experienced in the ethnographer's own world, nor does it present behaviour as contingent, situational or deliberate.... The ethnographic present, for Fabian, functions to take the society so described out of the time stream of history in which ethnographers and their own societies exist (612).

As a means to resurrecting the notion of an ethnographic present, Sanjek (1991:609) posits four interconnecting angles of the ethnographic present. These are as follows: (1) the present state of ethnography; (2) the mode of presenting ethnography; (3) the ethnographer's presence during ethnography; and (4) ethnography as a material product like a gift. Video satisfies Fabian's problem of coevalness by offering a rich record of events and knowledge creation, as they were experienced. Video also affords participants a way to revisit what I call "originating moments," in order to amend the knowledge that was created to suit new categories of experience. In this way basic problems with ethnographic presence and the problem of coevalness are answered. I agree with Sanjek that we must not be lost in romantic notions of the deconstructed other, of the fear of ignoring the dialogicism of "real" interaction (618-19).

In terms of observation, video affords all involved a chance to revisit moments and to construct new meanings out of old. Beyond this, recording fieldwork on video captures field events in terms of a coded digital time sequence, which unites participants in a duration where their co-mingling is revealed as a series of interconnecting frames and data codes that are evidence of their coevalness in a time, a sense of time, neither theirs or mine, but ours— digitally compressed as tangible evidence of what happened and in what sequence, if that matters. There can be no more coeval a presence than this. If this video record stands as a sort of objective account of the raw experience— raw data, as it were—then it can be revisited and edited to be used in a number of ways. It can, for example, be used to review events and solve problems, or to inform others of issues that need to be addressed. It can also be packaged and presented as a summary of events or cultures (an ethnographic account) or used to promote goals or as an educational documentary device. Importantly for this book, video provides the basis for my transcriptions and informs my critique of the IHC movement. It is also available to you, the reader, as a companion to this text.

In the last ten years, I have learned that some methods afford collaborators reasons to revisit these unique field events better than others. Very few of the informants I worked with were willing to read or review my notes, but all of them felt engaged by more explicit visual representations. Video shot in an openly reflexive manner is one such method. However, I suggest that ethnography must "engage with issues of representation that question the right of the researcher to represent other people...." (Pink 2007:22). Can a video ethnography satisfy the rules of this engagement? In this sense, one of the biggest questions we face is that of legitimation. An ethical ethnography to me is precisely the one that meets many of the requirements of what Denzin has called "a critical post structural ethnography," a response to the "legitimation crisis" (1997:7). Further, it is one in which a stable other and a stable subject do not exist. It is recognized that both parties inform the construction of knowledge and have the power to make decisions regarding "truth." In my work, video serves as a method of recording field moments, as a tool for analyzing situations, and as a method for representation. In terms of mining this data, I have chosen neither to code nor to quantify what is essentially a series of conversations that are spontaneous and fluid. Certain themes become apparent and I make witness to them. You may find others.

Using markers such as "credibility," "comprehensiveness," "ethnographic-ness," "triangulation," "satisfaction with life scales" (SWLS), and so on would be to argue for a measureable world out there that is truthfully and accurately captured by the researcher's methods (Eisenhart and How 1992; Atkinson 1992). In my current research where we are using images to prime online conversations, these kinds of measures are important to us. I discuss that in the concluding chapter. But in the research I did in IHCs for this book, I wanted to argue against positions that state a (visual) text becomes valid if it satisfies some or many of the rules: here, the author can claim a text's validity based on these statistical measures and the results can then be taken "seriously." The danger with this is that the idea of validity means that only observations or situations that satisfy that test are seen as important enough to address. And there are problems with the way such tests are designed to necessarily exclude some variable as and to include others. These choices represent the objective world as understood by the researchers and do not make it true in any fixed reality, except the context in which it is being rationalized.

Video and film can reproduce the same misdirection. The power of film and video, and the major reason we must use a self-revealing methodology when doing visual work, is because the stories we tell are seen and heard, and they appeal to our ocular-biased Western sense of being real—that they can be seen suggests there must be some truth to them (Ruby 1975; Loizos 1993; MacDougall 1998; Tomas 2003). This places visual representations like video in line for even greater scrutiny and critique than written forms because there is sense of chicanery here that can trick those who watch our films into thinking that such things speak to some truth.

Speaking of photographs, Barthes wrote that a "sort of umbilical cord links the body of the photographed thing to my gaze: light, though impalpable, is here a carnal medium, a skin I share with anyone who has been photographed" (1984:81). I would bring this observation to bear on film, and onto the video data I am watching as I write this, in high definition on my 27-inch monitor in crystal-clear perfection, which in many ways surpasses the unconscious haptic and psychic power of images; combined with the support of HD-quality footage, brilliant stereo sound, lighting, effects and motion effects, this power to trick the viewer into buying into a film's credibility is greater now than ever before. In my daily ongoing post-fieldwork, which is a routine for me, I look at previously shot footage. I am digitally extending my ethnographic presence virtually forever: revisiting footage, starting new conversations, reiterating and refining what I had previously taken to be true. I see and hear things I did not before, because here at my desk all I have to do is look and listen and note, whereas in the field I was debating and acting and creating the reality I now play back and forth on a timeline. I see these experiences that happened in camps and on the streets in an entirely different way than when I was involved in them. It is quite different than the images I see when I recall that day in the camp. And this suggests to me that some things ought never be recorded, because some life events can never be treated in an objective sense.

Fabian (1983, 1985) had argued for an objective anthropology, and though I have some difficulty in accepting that objectivity, like reality, exists in any stable manner, I share with him the belief that we need to examine "what is performative in ethnographic communication, including aspects that are play-like." We do this not to uncover the objective value of our work but to see where outcomes are shaped by the researcher in unforeseen ways. One of the great problems I confront in my attempts to be ethical/faithful to the unfolding story is an awareness that other embodied senses are working with and against my own sight and my own intuition. Fabian (1983: preface, 106, 123, 179) argued well that visualism had traditionally placed the eye at the top of the hierarchy of senses, eliminating the place of all others and thereby creating a distance between what one saw and oneself. Vision requires distance from its objects; the eye maintains 'purity' as long as it is not in close contact with "foreign objects." In so doing he had suggested that observability, and hence the instructions for participant observation, had evolved into a method that replaced the senses and the body in knowledge production, supplanting it with signs, symbols and representation. Whether objectivity is possible or not is topic for another time. Clearly I do not believe it can be. I, like Fabian, must query whether we "can give to intersubjectivity a more concrete, palpable meaning than that of an abstract "condition" (31). Working with the villagers and others through video was a way, as you will see, of achieving this intersubjectivity.

Video has a special place in PEOC for the many ways it contributes to reflexivity and criticality, and for the way it offers a pragmatic link to emerging intersubjectivities. I have introduced the idea of *reflexive time* into my videography. In this case I bring the video we have shot over the years into people's lives at points where they think it is important to understand new life events. In the example below, Brian, a long time participant in my films, joined the church and found God. He felt he had experienced a revelation, a life-changing moment. I went to see him and brought the films we had made so he could reflect.[53] He died in June 2014, following a long battle with cancer, but his contribution to this critique is vital.

Brian helped me develop this model of reflexive time. In 2011, I visited Brian at his home, a geared-to-income apartment in Toronto. It had been ten years since we met at Tent City, and we had seen each other three or four times a year when I visited Toronto. We did interviews and discussed how housing had changed his life. On one occasion we sat down and looked at the cumulative work we had been constructing. Each year, we had made new cuts of old footage to reorganize how these events and new ones aligned in his own understanding of his story. Most recently he had beaten lung cancer and then found God. The world had become a different place to him by then. By that point, he found the experience of viewing the original *Subtext* footage was all-but-perplexing. In *Ethical-Traces*, there is a scene where I ask him why, back in the days of Tent City, it took him 17 interviews to tell me about the crime he committed that sent him to Kingston. He told us he had been to jail, that he had robbed banks, and reiterated many other stories of a dark nature, which held up to verification and which are included in the film. Then one day at lunch in a nearby diner, a year after I had met him, he finally told us about slitting a man's throat in a movie theatre in Ottawa. "That's the best part (of not telling people everything)," he says, "because I don't want people running away from me, because I've changed. I don't know if I changed for the good or the worse."

When we looked at the footage, I asked him why he had not told me and my colleague at the time, Jeff Mayhew, this important detail before, or why it had taken that long—a year of seeing and interacting with him daily—for him to tell us. Ten years later, in reviewing that footage, while seated on his balcony, healthier, off drugs, healed from his first battle with cancer, king of his castle and successfully implanted in a conventional identity since joining his community center and the church, he sat back and said, "Because we got to know each other a whole lot better, I got to know you better." The simple lesson, then, one that supports Bakhtin's reflections, is that there is no truth except that which emerges between actors in moments of creating such truths. And if these experiments (if I can call them that) with Eddy or Brian have demonstrated anything, it is that the truth changes over extension of such experience, through the fidelity of actors reaching critical moments together over time. Perhaps it is the visceral linkage between sound and seeing and the waves and photons inherent to each, that link Barthes[54] found so interesting, or hearing one's own voice as a trace of one's past, or perhaps the conceit of seeing oneself on the screen; very often in video informants are captivated and pensive about their role in producing truth and fiction. Finally, to paraphrase Brian, you never really remember the past as it actually was unless you see somebody who reminds you of something, or (he tapped the computer) "you see this, you see it on this ... the reality will come back to you."[55]

Very often it is in these moments that critical self-awareness is stimulated, perhaps re-ignited, but in any event there is no way to deny that seeing and hearing oneself as a critical character on video—in the sense that Brian was a key informant in a study on housing and that is how he sees himself—creates an opportunity to remain critically engaged with the truths those moments had represented. Videography contributes to critical ethnography in extremely practical ways: as a way to collect, review and re-visit ethnographic present(s). When people see themselves in the contexts that others perceive them in, it often changes the pragmatic deliberations they make in choosing actions towards themselves, others and critical positions.

STEVE AND CAROL, July 2011 (from *Dignity in Exile*)
One morning early in my stay at the village, I noticed Steve lurking around the five Portalets that the 56 of us shared. It seemed odd to me, he just stood there. Shifting, looking around, back to the Portalets, as if he was protecting something. A few minutes later, Carol appeared from the outhouse. She handed Steve the household roll of toilet paper, and they walked away towards their shack, a quaint structure, about double the size of mine. Steve met Carol about 12 years ago and was clean at the time. Nevertheless, when they met, it was love at first sight, despite her drug use. He started using again, and they have been together ever since, happily in love and to my knowledge and within my experience, more or less peaceful and devoted to one another. On the streets, in hostels and squats, "a man watches over his woman, man. Ya got to. Do you know how many freaks and assholes there are out there?" Steve laughs. Not a nervous, neurotic laugh, but because he is a laugher. My understanding of him is that he has a mechanism that helps him find some humor in everything, however dark it might seem to others. "Man, she's my lady. I know nothing's gonna happen to her here. But I look after her. It's what we do." In the time I was at the village, Steve and I spent some quality time together. "I ain't gonna lie about anything" he says in one interview. "I only speak about me, and no one else," he told me, "so I ain't got no problem saying nuthin'." Steve was tired of all the misrepresentations of people who live on the streets, of all the reporters "dissing" the village and homeless people. He once told me, "It's like they condemn us for using drugs, but they never talk about how we try to get off it. Because if they do, they gotta talk about how they can't help us. I want to get off drugs, Eric, I don't like using heroin, but it's a fucking bitch, man." He laughs again. "Anyway, we got a script [from a street health organization], and we're gonna get on the methadone ... next week I think ... as soon as we can get to the pharmacy. At least we got housing now, so at least here ... in the village we can try to get clean.... The village is a low-cost place to live and good chance to pull your head out of your ass and get your shit together, get a job and get your life back going on again."

I ask him, "So that's why I ask you what is your game plan—to get off the crap, to get off the heroin and get stabilized. So, that's like three, four months, right?"

"We'll see ... well, I'm gonna be doing a diversion program here in a few weeks."

"A what kind of program?"

"A diversion program for a DUI I got. I crashed a motor home. It's an alcohol treatment. They teach ya to recognize alcohol patterns and what to do to prevent it. And the outcomes and the responsibilities of being an adult drinker. Of adult drinking and not endangering people's lives."

"And when does that start?" I ask.

He rolls his eyes. "August first or something."

"And do you have to leave here ... or—?"

"No," he smiles. "It's an outpatient. AA meetings [rolling his eyes] and stuff like that."

He seems unconvinced. Rolling his head and eyes as if to mock the process. I am wondering if he knows the program can work. The desperate part of him that frequently complains about the stupid things he does when he is high, is overwhelmed by the cynical part of him that wants to believe in his helplessness. This is a key point in the structural violence of biopolitics. The debate over treatment and cure is not a battle of words but is waged in the living breathing person: Steve, in this case. On the one hand, his addiction, symptomatic of his traumas and bad choices made on the streets, keeps him tied to that lifestyle, and his desire to overcome it keeps him chained to a system that fails to actually help him. The idea that complete abstinence, like normalized housing, is a valid goal for everyone just might not be true. Overcoming Steve's addictions might just not be possible. The debate between treatment and harm reduction places people like Steve on a teeter-totter of policies and expensive programs that find their place in many addicts' lives only because of court decisions—as a means of a avoiding jail and rarely as the actual choice of the addict. He keeps going back and forth between a few days of jonesing to get off the drugs, a few minutes of hope that a diversion program might work, and then the realization sets in once again, that after a lifetime of such attempts, there probably is no point. He doesn't know what the answers are. We talk about whether the responsibility is his or not. But he comes to rest on the probability that addictions and alcoholism are produced in his world, the street, to fuel an industry that caters to treating these problems, hopelessly and endlessly. With a success rate of about 5% at best, even popular 12-step programs are not cures.

"Well, you know I have hadn't a drink in 16 years?" I ask.

"Yeah, yeah, and you must have a wicked case of cotton mouth," he laughs. "I've been to the meetings. I've done the steps—the thirteenth step...."

"The thirteenth step?" I ask.

"Yeah.... Well, the one step we're not supposed to do. That's the mythical one—where you pick up women at a meeting.

"Not supposed to do that," I suggest.

"Why not? Why not? Women are people too. They got rights to be at my meeting."

"Yeah, but you're not supposed to pick them up there."

"Why not?" His head is cocked and he looks at me like a prosecutor might, just before accusing the witness of lying or something.

"Because people aren't, women aren't...." I can't finish my sentence.

"— Stable? At meetings...." He twists my thoughts. "How do you know? They are people too, they got rights to meet other people. How do you know where another person's state of mind is? How do you know?"

"At a meeting? I guess because they are at a meeting?" I offer.

"Well, how do you know how long they have been in treatment, how long, maybe they are ready to take the next step, and progress with life. Isn't that what recovery's all about—is progressing and getting better ... moving forward ... You're moving backwards if you ain't moving forwards...."

"Yeah, but there are rules.... I mean you can get laid and have sex, but...." (I want to tell him that we just don't use meetings to meet girlfriends, especially in the early days, but he is

Steve, 2011. Photo: Nigel Dickson.

on a roll. His addictive personality has completely taken over.)

"Yeah, yeah. First you get a plant and then you get a fish and then you get a puppy ... and then you get an 'old lady'—Why?" he demands.

"Well, you know what the state of denial is then?" And I am hoping he doesn't say what inevitably every active addict who has gone to meetings and not stuck it out says: "Yeah, it's somewhere over in Egypt."

Steve's affable enough. He is smiling the whole time we have this exchange. He has thrown almost every cliché I have heard about recovery at me. Clearly he has been around it enough to know that it doesn't work for him. He does not want to offend, and instead of going to an angry place out of his frustration with the way things are, he chooses to joke and play around. But the truth is there.

"I am not here to convert anyone," I tell him.

"No, no, I'm good. I'm good. You're just asking me questions and I am just being straight honest with ya. It's just my opinion."

"Everyone's got one."

"Yeah, like assholes, and some of them stink," he laughs.

"Dude, I just want you to be happy, is all."

"And I am happy. I could be a lot more happy and comfortable and secure in my own skin, but it is what it is right now, and it can only go forward from here."

"And how does it go forward from here?" I want to know.

"Well, just by pulling my head out of my ass and doing what I need to be doing, you know, fighting back. You know, get that monkey off my back, kick him to the road and get rid of him."

"What has Dignity Village done for you, in a positive sense?"

"It's given me a sense of security in that I got a place to live and stuff and have an address ... and be able to take showers and be clean, and do the work in, in moving forward. Anyway, I have to get on the methadone ... it's part of the diversion program. I have to take a UA [urine analysis]. Mandatory UA. If I test positive I could do a year in county jail. And I don't want to do that."

"Well, the pot stays in your urine a long time. Do they test for that?" I ask.

"They're gonna have to get used to it," he smirks.

Steve and Carol did not want to become members of the village. They were housed in the unit next to mine. But they preferred to remain residents without the status of membership. I was never too clear on why they felt this way. Residents and members are still required to do the same hours and to pay the same dues. The rules have changed since then. While I was there, residents could decide to become members after 30 days' resident status. But the original language of the village automatically makes a resident a member after 44 days. In 2012, this was reinstated as part of the new leadership's campaign to return to the values that made the village what it once was, a thriving community based on social and political participation by all residents who must become members, or citizens if you will.

Still, back when I did this interview, Steve and Carol preferred to remain outside of the contentious politicking that membership required. Members from time to time are required to attend mandatory political meetings where votes are taken on village business, new members and so on. Both Steve and Carol were hesitant to get involved in the politicking and backstabbing that framed many of the members' alliances with one another.

But Steve has opinions about what needs to be done. "Somebody needs to do something, because it's out of control. There's cliques and they have all the control. And it's, well, they're all on council and crap, there's nothing anyone can do or a say about what they do." I suggest to him that it is because they have been here so long that they are pretty entrenched in the structure of the village. And also that people just feel that if they tried to get on council, it would cost them socially or materialistically. He agrees.

"Yeah, and so they pretty much run the camp any way they wanna," he insists.

I ask him, "What would you do if you were on council?

"I would take the grey area out of the bookwork."

"What's the grey area?"

"Well, the rules are black and white and then there's the grey area. Where it depends on how good a friend you are and how bad we are going to punish you, you know? It's black or it's white. It's right or it's wrong. I have a lot of friends here, you know, and Dave and Laura, a bunch of others.... Bubbles, I have trouble with Bubbles. He's just too negative. Negative all the time. I don't need that. It may not seem like it, but I have enough trouble staying in a good mood."

As only one example of the way personal stories collide with the collective, Steve's story summarizes the sense of frustration that I encountered when working in the Village. The subtext to Steve's story is a very long history of addiction and crimes committed in order to service that lifestyle. But at another level is a very clever, very reasonable and self-aware man who brings a set of meanings and values to the Village and its social dynamic. We can learn much about people and the social groups they are in, even if those are shanty-towns or IHCs, by understanding how people imagine their world and what they think might have to change for them to change within that world. This is a pragmatic concern.

2.6 Pragmatism Meets Critical Reflexive Ethnography

Pragmatism originated in the U.S. in 1870. Its most notable founders were Peirce, James and Dewey (*Stanford Encyclopedia of Philosophy* [SEPA], accessed Aug. 12, 2003). Pragmatism is not just a philosophical way of contemplating the relationship between ideas and action. Pragmatism, as an essentially anti-foundationalist approach to understanding the relationship between ideas and action, and in turn the practical potential for social change, appeals to the social sciences more broadly since the post-structural turn of the 1980s (Riles 2003:1; Hamner 2003:1; SEPA, August 9, 2013; Knight 2002). Its practical extension into sociology in Boltanski and Thévenot's pragmatic sociology of critique (e.g. 2006, 2010), and the reason I use it in my work, is its pragmatist maxim of seeking to understand hypotheses by their practical consequences (SEPA, "Pragmatism," accessed August 9:1).

Hamner (2003) discerns an early American pragmatism rooted in Peirce (1958) and James (1977) that imagines acts and social relations as outcomes of

Eric Weissman

knowledge of the "self" rooted in Puritan imaginaries (2002:39). In this inherently anti-nominalist form, reality is formed around concepts that are understood as real *in se*. James had tried to relate values and morality, posing the question: Why do things have value? And as I mentioned earlier in this chapter, as part of the deconstructive ethos of my work I ask people how they imagine things like freedom: What does it feel like to you? Or how do they imagine making self-government work?

Peirce was more concerned with how understanding ideas could lead to solving problems. Dewey's instrumental pragmatism blended the two former styles as a means to understanding how logical positions corresponded to actions directed at satisfying needs or values. For Dewey (Hickman and Alexander 1999), events, moments and experiences impacted the pragmatic orientation of individuals to ideas.

My sense of pragmatism follows Dewey and imbricates with what Hamner describes as European *praxis theory,* of which Marx and Gramsci had laid out theoretical underpinnings, and whose interest in the moral weight of social analysis Boltanski (2011) has recently avowed (Hamner 2003). In this nominalist form, the "self" is constructed out of ideas and knowledge that are produced for the individual and presented by powerful ideologies as if they were *in se*, and it is the moral imperative of ethnography in this case to expose the constructed nature of inequalities and domination that such power creates— though there are instances, perhaps, where ideology can present valuable ideas too; after all kindness and gratitude can be ideological (Hamner 2003: 38–41; and also [G.] Smith 1991; Boltanski and Thévenot 2006; Smith 2006; Boltanski 2010). Hamner's major study of American pragmatism (2002) sees it "as an extended and theologically informed reflection on how a self comes into being through action-molded beliefs and its belief informed actions (2003:28). And this rests in the center of my inquiries in Dignity Village.

Hamner argues that self and action are important considerations, to which American pragmatists, notably Peirce and James, had paid much attention. But they paid less attentionto social change, and so pragmatic views towards social justice were more likely to be understandable in the European approach.[56] European pragmatism was far more concerned with how ideas and actors' orientation around them are mobilized towards socially transformative movements. This is one of the central questions I began with: What abets or gets in the way of homeless people fighting for their rights and their communities?

Despite the departure in how "truth" or reality is experienced for American pragmatists or the praxis school, my pragmatic ethnographic method looks at important notions and concepts and the mundane personal and broader social consequences they produce in the same manner as Riles (2003) and asks: What would be the practical consequences to actors if another concept or another way of looking at things were understood as truth? (Riles 2003:1). Let us remember that PEOC is multi-textual, feminist, communitarian, wide-open and forward-looking, often visual in method and representation, and produces field and research situations that blur traditional distinctions between researcher and informant, such that the construction of the ethnographic relationship as a type of knowledge process in a "messy world" is a main current in the work (Denzin 1997; Riles 2003; Denzin and Lincoln 2004). Generalizing to pragmatic anthropology, Riles (2003) adds, "Here the subjects are theorizing alongside their anthropological interpreters, reading some of the same texts, orienting themselves towards similar political, ethical or theoretical problems" (2). The relationship, she adds, is more "one of sameness than difference." Understanding the pragmatic goals of this research, what makes it particularly ethnographic?[57]

For me, pragmatic inquiry focuses on the "consequences of practical actions" (Barbalet 2009: 200). It reveals the epistemic routing of ideas and values that shape and guide practical action. This process allows actors to act on the basis of beliefs or accepted knowledge, and this is the goal of the pragmatic ethnography of critique (PEOC), as presented in this book. An additional feature here is that very often the pragmatic considerations made by villagers interfere with the village's goals as a community. This *crisis of community* is important to my work: it was into that crisis I entered, and on which I have been asked to advise.

PEOC asks if the homeless people who fought for the right and in particular for the land upon which to build Dignity Village should be considered active citizens. This active citizenship exists given that their critique took the form and language of existing democratic scripts for protesting for change. And they can be seen as activist citizens, turning and twisting, finding new critiques and unusual means to carry this out. These two positions, set out in Isin and Nielsen's (2008) model of *Acts of Citizenship*, suggest that the activist citizen is the agent of acts that seek new moral possibilities, and that active citizens are caught up in predictable critical practices around which the concept of a democratic citizen might be understood (35–38). Following Isin (2008), I distinguish *acts* from *practices* in the sense that a practice is something the scholar observes and the subject *understands* only as *having happened* (see for example, Foucault 1975; Bourdieu 1972). An act contrarily implies a creative moment in the *experience of the actor* (the individual) which, while it might be shared by others, or experienced in the presence of others, is manifest of the volitions and movement of that individual through a unique space and time. Such acts often represent a break with common practice, and therefore are problematic for theories, which would try to solely explain acts as the *result* of forces external to them. In other words, these acts pose a challenge to customary or conventionalized modes of doing social things, such as being political, having sexual relationships, teaching and so on—there are many ways to do things, but for Isin and Nielsen (2008) an act breaks with the conventional way we do or resist. Hence the citizen who exercises critique by voting against his or her favourite political party is exercising freedom, but so too is the squatter who barricades him or herself within an abandoned building to protest gentrification. These are examples of two distinct ways of acting with a sense of justice, but which are perceived in dramatically different fashion: the former is a democratic right, while the latter is an occupation, an incursion of sorts, that brings constitutionally guaranteed rights to shelter into conflict with property rights. The choice made to express freedom in certain acts or practices is a matter of pragmatic understanding.

Barbalet (2009) says:

> The antecedents of action, especially external stimulation, while crucial to utilitarian accounts, are of secondary significance in pragmatism. Pragmatism, in understanding or forming a meaning of action, is concerned primarily with its consequence or outcomes. It follows that the distinction between thought and action is not accepted by pragmatism as implying that each is a different entity, as in Cartesian dualism, for instance, but refers only to distinct functions of engagement with the world. Finally, as each action necessarily changes the conditions for subsequent actions, pragmatism regards agency, for instance, and also interest, identity, and so on as things that are not given in persons prior to action but discovered, emergent, or constructed by them in the course of action (200).

Pragmatic ethnography attaches itself to this emergent experience as a way to know what is becoming known, and as a contribution to that knowledge. This participant mode of understanding helps me look at two vectors of action available to all actors. One is the act, which is a *result of practical activity* and reflects the person's potential to have or claim power. The other is a predisposition to action based on external truth. All citizens can transit in and out of active or activist roles. Moving beyond the apparent distinction between types of citizens, the work I did reveals actors who reside in both identities and move between them, as circumstances and the imponderabilia of daily life dictate. To summarize: when critique displaces power, the result is not always a permanent inversion or break with habitus. Rather, it may be a new, unjust habitus that results. To invoke Derrida again, a new democracy with its own set of internal confusions and tensions all too often emerges. The villager is constantly faced with an unstable set of affairs—a series of tensions between how that world is imagined and how it performs in reality—which means that pragmatic knowledge and action must always be contingent.

Similarly, actors do not need to remain fixed in one or another identity; they can move in and out of critical modes depending on how these tensions are understood. Towards some ideas they might fight for change, while for others they remain solidly resolute. An example that comes to mind involves the willingness on the part of a few of the villagers to support leaders who promise more computers and better distribution of the donations, but reject any attempt to hold 12-step meetings within the village community. The former action represents a progressive shift to address important and crippling issues in the village that appeals to their sense of immediacy and need, and the latter (in their perspective) is an attempt at mind control, regardless of their raving addictions and the practical need for help. To simplify, the link is that through participant observation, conversational storytelling and reviewing official documentation, my research has, in an openly unstructured format, inquired into villagers' views of themselves, and how they might like to see themselves. This is the pragmatic part. The critical part is that in the process we have often reached points of deliberation in which villagers came to question just how free and autonomous they really were—or, perhaps, just "how broken" things were in the village.

The starting point of my style of ethnography is the internal deliberations that people make during interactions with others. For this reason, critical and pragmatic ethnography, as I have framed it, asks that I include that deliberation as part of its analysis. Sometimes this looks like an autobiography. In the next section, I offer an autobiographical account of how my sociological imagination emerged over a number of years. These experiences led me to the questions I have been asking about IHC and homelessness. At one point I was mired in addictions, moving in and out of homelessness, and seemed to be heading toward an inevitable tragic fate. Yet a number of possibilities aligned themselves, allowing me to better control the direction of my own troubling narrative and rewrite my own inevitabilities. So here we go. How do we go about creating this possibility for others?

Chapter Three
EN ROUTE TO REDEMPTION

3.1 Autoethnography

> **Autoethnography:** A form of self-narrative that places the self within a social context. It included methods of research and writing that combine autobiography and ethnography. The term has a dual sense and can refer either to the ethnographic study of one's own group(s) or to autobiographical reflections that include ethnographic observations and analysis (Reed-Danahay 2006).

Recall our earlier discussion of Mills' *Sociological Imagination* (1959), in particular Mills' argument that researchers must contextualize the lives they study in the broader terms of their own experience. These terms include personal biography and history as well as the other social structural conditions that frame everyday life. In the last chapter 1 considered the dialogic nature of communication. It is not difficult to see how we always use, at perhaps a most basic level, a sociological imagination when making sense of what other people say and do. This is particularly true in those lived moments when we are interacting with others, caught up in webs of emotion and sensory stimulation. It is difficult to pause in such moments to ascertain the biographies of others, or their back stories. This kind of interaction is the work of ethnographers and for the rest of us, a certain gleaning of such information is the best one can do when caught up in social interaction. Still, the most successful communication we can have is that which tries to embrace the biographical and historical contexts of others, given that these conditions impact the reasoning that others employ when forming responses in conversation.

The form of ethnography 1 discussed is critical for its understanding of

The author as a young man, 1970.
Photo: Syd Weissman.

how participants are subject to and might acquire power. Consider that power does not simply emerge from identifying excluded ideas; rather, it must be earned, practiced, and defended within the research process. Power is also a pragmatic process, involving an inquiry into how participants envision their world. What ideas do they bring into the situation that confronts them? Also, how might they envision it differently, if given the tools?

The truth is not a static object. In the last chapter I discussed the tension between the traditional notion of an objective, measurable reality that tends to comfort social policy planners and critics of the welfare state and the fight that we can wage in order to produce alternative visions of truth as part of our ethnographic work. I argued that ethnography should be a very open affair, revealing the strokes taken to construct a certain vision of truths so that others—the reader, other researchers and the participants—can make informed decisions about the virtue of particular narratives of inevitability.

Part of the virtue of the work I do, then, is to reveal how the researcher comes to understand a certain situation. "Comes-to-understand" is not a moment or an event, but a process that takes time and is therefore hard to deliver in academic volumes or magazines or journals where word and page counts require significant edits. As an example, I was in a recent meeting with a participant from earlier work, Beric German, who had co-founded the Toronto Disaster Relief Committee (TDRC). He told me that he had been quite angry with some of the things I produced in my first *Subtext* film series. I responded by recounting the story below: about the many re-visitations I made with participants to rewrite the story as new experiences changed our views on prior recordings, about the way new categories of knowledge produced in the housing sector impacted how we saw ourselves and the IHC movement. Beric came to understand that my process had taken a long time, and that later products—a book, an article, two more films—all reflected how I came to understand IHC differently than when we had first worked together. It is difficult for those of us, and that really means all of us, who have adapted to comforting narratives of inevitability to allow ourselves the freedom to adapt our beliefs and values about people and places to new important information. Beric was relieved, of course but also encouraged because a certain respect to the process of coming-to-understand, and historical shifts in the IHC movement, was at least being given.

The last chapter discussed how researchers who engage in participant observation often discuss encounters with new cultures or social experiences in ways that are resonant with their own histories and biographies. This is especially true when ethnography is done within our own cultures, and where our own experiences give weight to the critical project (Strathern 1987; Hastrup 1992; Oakley 1992; Fabian 2001; Gallinat and Collins 2010; Rapport 2006). A certain autobiographical context is required to situate ethnographic work such that emotional, deliberative, and experiential knowledge of the field may be exposed before "entering" the fieldwork experience. This helps us understand how the representations we produce as ethnographers had been colored by these innate and precursor elements of ourselves (Collins and Gallinat 2010).[58] Framing investigation with personal experience invites the reader as well as the participants to ask the following question: "Is he really one of us; are they really like us in those ways?" We are intentionally trying to eschew the cultural distance to restore "coevalness"; these critics argue that the absence of coevalness creates a false sense of objective reality. In that sense, theoretical approaches have constraining power over us; they tell us what variables to look at and what criteria should govern the internal logic of our inquiries. But theories are essentially highly organized systems of ideas, and the way we theorize any perception of any reality is never simply the result of a body of postulates that exist outside of ourselves—or outside our way of imagining. In an autobiographically or autoethnographically informed inquiry, we are no longer forced to ask certain questions because they make sense theoretically. Instead, we can use our own experience as a metaphorical taproot from which to tell how a number of theoretical and interpretive issues became salient to us in our efforts to address an issue like homelessness. So for me the starting point was my own personal experience of homelessness. It was this experience that made me feel I had much in common with the issue and the people with whom I worked.

But does the fact that I declare myself to be part of a group's culture neces-sarily make that claim true? Collins and Gallinat (2010:9) point out that the identification of inclusion also means we should be able to understand the degree to which an ethnographer can claim membership in the groups studied on the basis of how knowledge of the self is equally obtained. This means that the claim must be based in self-referential experiences and ideas that link people in a collectivity. An author from a well-off family could never pretend to share the lived experience of poor housing activists. However, there may be aspects to his life—addictions or experience of abuse, for example—that might mean that his identity and sense of self in some way may allow him insight into the experience of others.

This section provides a reflective and reflexive history of my experience with addiction, recovery, homelessness, and early fieldwork on the streets of Toronto. To clarify my terms: "reflective storytelling" involves looking back upon experience through the lens of a pivotal or epiphanal experience; "reflex-ive storytelling" involves opening the story to its own contradictions and revelations, demonstrating how the narrative comes to be because of these meanders.

Insomuch as the ethnography here was done in cities and popular cultures that I call home, and with people for whom I had a deep and uniting camaraderie, as members of a tangible and imaginative community, there is no way to separate out myself from the "traditional" others in this work. So the work is reflective in that I retell my story, but it is reflexive because of the way this book comes to be informed by those experiences.

Recognizing and explicitly showing how we come to understand issues that are critical to individuals and their social relations is essential in pragmatic ethnography because pragmatism (as I discussed earlier) asks what meaning actors bring into situations and how these can be changed. If an actor challenged by street poverty brings a set of self-defeating and disempowering attitudes into a confrontation with police or with passersby, then they are likely to reinforce the unequal power relations that hold them back. If the same person can come to understand that the meaning they have brought with them into a situation was learned, and that there are other ways of seeing and doing, then these power relations (as well as other kinds of relations) can at the very least be challenged. There are two reasons why I include my own story when I work with people. First, it reveals a common a sense of struggle. Second, it provides a positive opening to the possibility that changing the narrative is possible.

Assuming that people living in the same cities or the same political economy or nations share certain values—like being Canadian or what acting democratically should look like—it might seem obvious that people who do not share the same symbolic imaginary would share fewer meanings. If we are communicating with people who share our meanings, even if that sharing is based on a disagreement, it is likely that the impact of the dialogic moment will have more immediate and substantial impact on us. The reflexive part of learning, that part that which is based on the use of new information to transform our own ideas, will impact the nature of our subsequent reasoning in more profound ways. At least that is an argument that can be made. Undertaking this kind of work can be mind-boggling; since no pretense to objectivity is tenable, we must take careful pains to render the autobiographical resonant with others.

Strathern (1987) recognizes the likelihood that a greater degree of reflexivity will occur in anthropology undertaken "at home"—what she has called *auto-anthropology*—but at the same time she argues that ethnographers claiming sameness is an ethical conundrum that borders on a kind of manipulation. In other words, pretending to be "like others" can be simply a way to get them to admit to or reveal what they otherwise would hide from strangers. I agree to an extent; when I went to Dignity Village and was asked to return to live there for a time for research purposes, I explained to them that I could not pretend to be one of them, and any work resulting from it would be published as the recounting of experience by a researcher living at Dignity Village. I would not be talking as a homeless person whose worldview started in the village because my worldview was anchored elsewhere and in other experiences.

Gallinat and Collins do not agree with Strathern. They find that the autobiographical ethnography to which Strathern refers is different than those wherein the ethnographer is a resource with others. Ethnographies from a solely personal perspective, where the self is the only resource, are essentially unethical. By contrast, when researchers, understood to be insiders, use their sameness as a conjoining element of the research, they can and do gain access to information that often is missed by other approaches (2010:7-11). Again, I agree to an extent. As a previous addict and occasional homeless person (what we now called "episodically homeless"), I shared some experiences with many of the villagers, and was able to establish bonds with others as a result of our sharing certain narratives of inevitability. For this reason I have always considered there to be three voices: mine; the voices of the people with whom I work; and the voice of our deliberations. In this last sense, the dialogic sense speaks to the Other, the emancipatory project that was my research. How each of these voices contributes to the narrative strength of this research is an important concern. Since there is no objective truth out there that I can force upon the world, here is how I came to understand what I now know to be true. One of the most compelling arguments about Housing First (HF) is that it satisfies the key to self-governance, which under neoliberalism is maintained in the myth of the normal home. This myth suggests that it is normal, or at least desirable, to live in a self-contained dwelling unit in a market-valued space such as an apartment or house. The kind of public housing for the worst-off that is most acceptable to public opinion is usually in conventional open-market apartments or in specially built housing, but it always points the narrative in the direction of the normal home myth: the idea that people are self-contained, self-sufficient, and good neighbors. It is easier to say that people are going back to normalized living conditions and that it is cheaper to house people than to leave them on the streets, so public resistance is reduced. HF costs about $24,000 (Canadian) per year per person. And, as the 2013 At Home/Chez Soi project found, people stay housed; eventually most seek medical and addictions assistance and generally fare better. By contrast, the average homeless person living on the street costs society about $100,000 per year. So, overall, HF is a good thing. This is not to suggest that there is no resistance to HF, because much does remain. Even so, the program is adoptable by governments for two reasons. First, HF generates quantitative data that researchers can use to measure cost-effectiveness. Second, the types of transitional experiences people have under HF programs appeal to the public desire to see recipients of assistance take steps in the right direction to becoming "normal" residents again. Hence, one can say that HF models conform to the moral normative and cost-efficient narratives of neoliberal citizens.

3.2 Roots and a Troubled Past

This research began as a sort of filmic reportage back in 2000.The major questions I am asking now must be situated in the continuum of efforts I have made for several years while creating films with homeless people, activists, and care groups. However, the experiences that governed my choice of a qualitative approach began much earlier in my life. Unfortunate as those experiences had been, those early struggles have become an important asset for my kind of work. Much of my attention has been guided less by theoretical dictums and more by an experienced eye. This perspective has not always been accepted in academic climes.

In 1998, in Toronto, I began writing about the homeless in a series of fictionalized short screenplays that included composite protagonists based on characters I had met on the street during my days as an addict and then later as a recovered person. At that time, my interest was deeply personal. I was writing not for scholarly reasons but because I felt an urgency to do this. There were troubling narratives in my own life I wanted—needed—to address.

At one point in my life I was an addict. I have now been in recovery for 20 years. I had been in recovery about two years at the point that I started writing, and four years when this research officially began. I have written elsewhere that I was one of the "lucky ones" because I knew why I had become homeless; I was an addict who preferred to get high rather than pay my bills. Put differently, it would be easier for us as a society to solve homelessness if the homeless consisted only of those who are in the grips of substance abuse, because then we could then blame an addicted individual's lack of self-control for their homelessness. There would be no need to look critically at industrial capitalism or neoliberal policies that have eroded access to affordable housing even for those who are not addicts. If addiction or mental health problems were the sole cause of homelessness, we could easily bid farewell to homelessness, by ambitiously addressing the root cause, addictions.

But addictions are not a good enough explanation to account for the vast numbers of people who are homeless. Nevertheless, addiction is its own special kind of madness and lends homelessness a peculiar flavor. To overcome addiction requires particular types of help and support. There are ways to control addiction. But there are particular conditions that make that recovery possible. You cannot get clean on the street. You have to have some form of housing to do it, and so we have a sort of Catch-22.

The first time I found myself with nowhere to sleep was not related to drugs. I was about 16, and had been scared out of our middle-class home in a good neighborhood in Toronto. My father and I had been fighting, as we often did; he had been damaged years earlier by a divorce, and in anger and heartbreak often became physically abusive. Years later it was suggested to me by a psychiatrist that my father sexualized his power over his children (particularly me). He attempted to reconcile the loss of his sexual claim over my mother (who had left him years earlier) by demonstrating his prowess and power over his oldest son, me. I came to see that this abuse was inexcusable, if perhaps explainable. In the stories I gathered from Dignity Village (and elsewhere), I came to see that this early experience of abusive parenting (often at younger ages, and most often even more traumatic) was the most common theme.

To return: I left the house that night at 16 because for the first time my father hit me in the face, albeit with an open hand. This was different, and very troubling. He did not send me to my room and force me to wait up there with the lights off until he had finished his coffee (his previous routine). At those times, I would sit there waiting for the footsteps to make their way up the carpeted stairs, slow and steady, determinedly, and I could always hear him unsheathe his belt just as he turned the brass door handle to my room. I wasn't allowed to turn on the lights. I sat there in the dark. He would push open the door and snap on the lights and in a fluid motion, as he ripped the belt off his waste, would say, "Why do you make me do this to you, eh? Why?" That had been the hard part. That was sheer terror. After that waiting and then anticipating and then the blaming, being spanked and whipped on a bare bottom was a relief. At least then my body would go into shock and my mind would produce drugs to ease the pain, and then I would shed tears. These were short bursts of tranquility on a dull razor's edge. But he had never hit me in the face before.

He honestly felt he was disciplining me, and I now think that the brutal force of his whips, successively stronger with each swing, reflected a horrible compulsion within him that was really a type of addiction. The reality about addictions is that at some point addicts cross a certain line from which he or she either finds a way to get right with the world, or perish. When he hit me in the face we had been sitting at the dinner table and it was as if he had wanted to say, out of his own displeasure, "I can do this to you." At 16, I knew there was a line that had been crossed. And though I had neither the need nor the desire to compare my experience to that of others, today when I encounter people on the streets who have been sexually, emotionally or physically abused, I suffer for them in a way only one who has been violated can suffer, with a visceral and somatic empathy beyond the merely imaginable.

In my case, that first time, I had left because it was clear he was going to hit me a second time. I felt determined this must not happen. I grabbed his arm and told him, "Never again." I slammed my plate. My grandmother and my younger brother—who maintains that he does not remember this night—looked horrified. But what were they to do? He struggled against my hold, and in that moment I think he realized that his days of beating me had come to an end. But I did not feel safe. I think my siblings too were traumatized by it, by the threat of violence. My father looked so angry and confounded that I had possessed the physical strength and the emotional resolve to stop him that I departed. In that moment, I did not know what the next level of his madness might have been.

I left and ran out the door and up to the nearby school yard and I lay down on the damp ground where the grass met the parking lot. I lay very low staring at the night sky, obscured from view of the street and the neighbors by a parking curb. I could hear his Delta Royale cruise by every so often. Caught up in the grief of the aftermath as he always had been, he was out looking for me. I knew it.

It is night in late spring, and you are crying and in shock, and you run out of the house into the night without a clue where you are going, without any recourse or safe haven in mind. You are not afraid. What was there to be afraid of? The vital blow had been made. You are so angry and indignant that you don't even realize until you make it to the dimly lit schoolyard that you have nowhere to go, but even this complete loss of center was more secure than living in a hostile situation. One's temporal horizons change in this mindset. We stop thinking about the future and what we would like to be, and caught up in the survival anxieties forced upon us we can imagine all kinds of alternative universes, even death. Lying there in that state of mind, even the idea of a family and having children and a house seems fantastic, in the mythical sense. These nights, these assaults did not happen every day. They happened enough that they have become part of the critique of my father. My friends and relatives who knew him often respond in utter disbelief when I recount these things. My younger brother admits he must have wiped from his mind these moments that I recall with crystal clarity. I am 54 and I still recall these moments. In fact I have found them in my new life to be motivational. I do not enjoy telling you or asking you to consider what these things feel like, look like. I imagine that if you are reading this book, you are already doing so in your own sociological imagination. My motivation is to infuse the academic with the personal as a way to deploy this kind of sensitivity when people have cause to judge the many thousands of young people who end up on the streets. The majority are not there because of good parenting.

I made it to a friend's house nearby and then stayed there for a few days until things at home seemed to calm down. I was not at ease. I smoked a few joints over that time period, as well as drinking a beer or two, but an association had been made in my mind that I could feel good by using.

One of the facts about this kind of instability is that there is no user-friendly way to anticipate when children might be in need of intervention. Child Protection Services and the police have the ubiquitous right to intervene in even suspected cases of abuse; however, with resources strained, and very few cases of victim self-reporting, many individuals slip through the cracks. Even if a young person does not leave home until the normal rite of passage, for university or a job, the psychological and emotional damage incurred in unstable housing can take many years to appear.

My family life was an example of unstable parenting that led to insecure housing. We learned to worry. My father made some bad investments and we had to move from house to house, each smaller and smaller. As my older sisters moved out, my younger brother and I fell more directly under my dad's lens. And we all learned to worry more than to feel secure. We worried about when the next bad decision would lead to the next move. We worried about my father and his anger. We worried and we lived in a culture that did not talk about these things openly as today. My drug use got much worse, so that by 19 I was high all the time, even though I was at university and doing fairly well, and working full-time as a shipper in T-shirt factory. In fact, I was leading quite an astonishing life, four full-time courses at the University of Toronto, full-time work, and still getting out to go fishing each week (one of the few skills my father bestowed on us).

I don't want to demonize my father. Most of the time he was really the hardest-working, most caring father you could imagine. He nurtured our interests: we had aquariums, gardens, rock collections, and art studios, and went fishing often. We visited our relatives and dressed well, ate well and had very good medical and other services. We were lucky in those ways. But troubled people have triggers, and the current literature now understands these often to be cyclical. We try to intervene if possible at the correct times to break these cycles, so that the harm does not occur. So in my case, for my father, bad luck at work or personal calamities meant this rage surfaced. Too often he took it out on us. This was in the 1970s before programs for divorced parents existed and before the literature we scholars use to create discourse included much discussion of this periodic abuse and the "cause to take flight response," as I like to call it. I only had cause to take flight a few times, and many of my friends grew up accustomed to this kind of periodic abuse and periodic vacations from our homes, but few have had cause to think on this as I have. In other words, this was not a narrative of inevitability in the symbolic imaginings of my good neighborhood. This kind of stuff only happened in ghettoes and tenements and so, for two decades, this narrative lay buried in fantasies about my dad, my neighborhood—buried, that is, until my own struggle meant this truth had to be confronted.

There is a madness that drives many addicts to the brink of overdosing; it is well that most people do not have to experience this madness. The human body is by and large ill-equipped to handle substance abuse. Addicts have a hyper-reactive nature. It is not simply a matter of becoming high; it becomes unthinkable to lose that feeling. We dread to "come down." It does not matter what the substance is. For me it was hash and pot, cocaine and large quantities of alcohol. In the literature, addiction is often lumped in with other problems, such as "mental health issues, medical issues and addictions"—as if addiction were not part of the other two categories. My understanding, and the one that many of the people I have worked with debate amongst each other, is that addiction, like cancer, is a disease. It is progressive, symptomatic and, left untreated, generally leads to the destruction of its host.

They call this the "medical model" of addictions. In my journey, people tend to debate whether this model is true; those who accept it as fact are more lenient towards housing the poor who are so afflicted because a disabling medical condition, after all, is not their fault. It is easier to forgive people with diseases than those who make bad choices or who display poor self-governance. In terms of addiction, however, there is no such thing as self-governance. This reality is in fact part of the popular definition of addiction, especially when talking with active addicts. As frustrating as it might be for the general public and social policy-planners to debate solutions to incessant drug use, the desperation is worse for many of us addicts who try to stop on our own but cannot. This *constitutional incapacity*, as it is termed in the *AA Big Book* (1937), is something people who are not so afflicted forget: addicts are people whose lives are governed by consumption of a substance, not young people occasionally doing foolish things with recreational drugs because it is a fun diversion. The ability to have a glass of wine or two, to smoke a joint on Saturday night, and to leave these things alone while at the business of living, is not something an addict possesses, even though most desperately want to. Addiction is physical in the sense that certain parts of the body (it affects all organs and the mind) are affected and can become dependent on the drug, and it is behavioural in the sense that people with addictions need the drugs to perform normal social activities. So some people have genes that, when stimulated by certain substances, produce a craving that cannot be satisfied. Other types of addiction—mine, for example—involve an habitualization of the relief that getting high provides. At a certain point, the addictive behaviour leads us to abandon self-conduct in favour of any act that will afford us the high and a certain uneasy and unsustainable comfort. And at this point, we make significant sacrifices, such as housing or anything that costs money, in order to service the addiction.

There are many people who are enabled by wealth and family support to survive with their addictions relatively undetected. We may not see the effect of their addictions because they don't lose material possession like homes or cars. For this reason, we assume that it cannot be present in conventional homes. This is not the case. Census data in Canada and the U.S. have shown that the use of recreational and prescription mind-altering drugs in cities is as high as 25% of the population. Moreover, Canada has the largest per capita use of anti-depressants, at almost 9% of the population (OECD 2013).[59]

These numbers are likely unreliable given that users often misreport out of fear of stigma or punishment. Even so, they remain an indication that addiction is most problematic when the disease is most visible—when the drug undermines the user's ability to live everyday life. There is no real data set about people who straddle the line between normal drug use and addiction, or those who take their prescriptions even when not required. There is no way to accurately measure usage. But there is ample evidence, anecdotal and quantitative, to suggest that prescribing drugs through accepted medical channels is normal in our culture. Anti-depressants and anti-anxiety meds, in order to be effective, produce an addictive response in the host. That is why getting onto (and off) the drug cycle is carefully managed in consultation with physicians. We essentially turn people into addicts for periods of time so they can cope with life, and then steer their withdrawal under medical care. This is not commonly defined as addiction, at least not in the popular understanding.

Use of prescribed medications makes assumptions about how that use is governed. To begin, there must be access to medical care and prescriptions. A culture with medical care is also a key feature of any ethos directed at controlling self-medication. In the populations I work with, there is generally no medical care, even though many people have mental health and other physical conditions that physicians routinely medicate through more conventional pharmaceutical protocols. Often people on the streets living in poverty medicate with drugs that are more common and accessible in their subcultures, such as meth, alcohol, heroin and marijuana. Both the privileged use of prescription medications and anti-depressants and the use of non-prescribed substances produce addiction. There are no accurate numbers[60] about numbers of addicts. The concept of self-control is of no use when speaking about addictions; it is as helpful as talking about "self-control" as a way to reduce the size of a tumor. Those who obtain medical advice and become "dependent" on prescribed drugs often cross the line too. One of the sad statistics is that the success rate for overcoming addiction in the long term is far lower than the cure rates for many types of cancer.

In my case, the progressive nature of the disease became self-evident as I

The author on his way to university classes in 1982. Five years later, he was a full-on addict and floundering.

left high school and entered university. There were no longer any physical conflicts with my dad, though we fought verbally all the time. We eventually made peace but continued to squabble. My brother, father and I lived together in a small apartment after a series of unhappy events in my father's life, including heart problems, losing our house again in the gold rush madness of 1979, and then a second failed marriage. Most of the time, the two of us could hardly bear to be in the same room.

By the second year of university I was getting high and drinking daily; I was not alone. It was the early 1980s and my drugs of choice were hash, coke and booze. In bars, clubs, and amongst dealers all over Toronto, these were abundant and popular. I had a small art business and was doing very well. I also had government support for my education so was able to move out. I lived on my own very near to school in downtown Toronto. In 1982, very few people thought of homelessness as the common problem it is now. My friends and I would stagger home from parties and pass by stoned bums sleeping in bus shelters, laughing at them, and swearing up and down to ourselves that that would never be us.

And things went well enough for me for a few years. Daily drug use and drinking did not seem to get in the way. Even though some relatives felt concerned because I was often high at family events and in public, no one worried that I had a "problem," given that I was thriving academically and professionally. Again, in the absence of any sign that my conventional practices were in jeopardy, no one said anything or thought of the drugs as especially problematic. I got good grades, ran my business, and got into graduate school, where I completed my M.A. in a year. The irony of this time period was that even as my disease was becoming acute, several parents of friends who were doing too much dope asked me to help, given what appeared to be my ability to manage drugs. In hindsight I wish I had revealed my dependency. Part of me knew I was living an impossible life. I began spending more time on activities that let me use, rather than on the work I had to do for school.

When that line is crossed, the inertia of the disease is like a juggernaut in the life of an addict. I led what is often called a "double life" in recovery literature; going to school, running my painting business, progressing through various rites of passage, getting one degree, moving onto another, having a personal life, looking after my own apartment, and all this "normal" stuff was less important to me than having a chunk of hash in my pocket or the free time I could spend getting high. I couldn't imagine going to class, or work or meeting friends and family without a mind alteration. So, soon, I reached that point where the disease became obvious. I knew I had a problem in the sense that I would go to any length to get high.

In the middle of the first year of my doctoral program, my grades were tanking, I was lost, and I was offered a chance to leave school and open an art

115

gallery. I took a leave to pursue my life as an artist. And that was the rationalization I gave to all my disappointed friends and family. I needed a break after six years of school and this was a chance to do art on a large scale. In fact, I had made a decision to turn my will and my life over to my addiction, and from that moment on, I entered into a situation of precarious living. Now, I can say that was the moment I had entered, by my own choosing, into precarious housing. If some knowledgeable person had been able to show me what was likely to happen if I stayed on that trajectory, I might not have ended up destitute, living off welfare and months from death.

And that's exactly where did I end up only a few years later. I lost my business, many of my friends, and dodged eviction notices. I also struggled to get high at any cost. Locked out of my apartment a number of times, I took refuge with friends. I had been dealing: moving good amounts of coke and whatever else I could. All of my friends at that time were of that world, and that world (the subject of another book) almost valorized couch surfing, taking over other people's units and manipulating others' home-spaces by supplying drugs to them. Today I wonder if I might have been spared the literal hell my life would become, had I had been caught, incarcerated and reformed....

On two occasions I found respite by sleeping on the balcony of a bar I used to frequent. Food was secondary to me. Housing—paying for housing— seemed unimportant when I needed to get high. And then there were always friends and family to prop up my rent or give me spending money or a place to sleep. In recovery literature, they call this *enabling*. A common complaint I hear from people is that they don't like giving homeless people with addictions public money to fund living space (such as HF) or to help them live (such as welfare) if it is just a way of enabling them to continue to get high. This is a faulty way of thinking on many levels. For example, not all homeless people are addicts, and second, addicts require housing to address their addictions. It is easier for people to complain about funding housing when they feel they have no personal attachment to the people they are asked to help. It is quite another experience for loved ones to watch a son, a brother, a friend struggle and to imagine them sleeping outside. The prospect of a family member on drugs killing himself or herself is especially horrifying.

The fact that I had enjoyed relationships with a few women and had shown great promise in artistic ventures only prolonged the inevitable for me. My drug use started off mild, then worsened. Each time I had any meagre success at work or at love, I felt I was doing well. But this feeling was misguided, leading to a prolongation of the inevitable: institutionalization, homelessness and death. I was to learn at a later date, while in rehab, that my disease enjoys equally success and failure. Success to keep me using, failure to keep me using. Failure especially was my excuse: the loss of each enterprise, each relationship provided me the state of mind to go even deeper in to drug use and to begin to care even less about myself.

I had lived with a woman in 1993–94 for over a year; it was her income that paid our rent, so when she (for good reason) left me, I had nowhere to live. I used up the three weeks left on our rent, and was evicted (again). My oldest sister took me in, and I lived with her family for a few months. My drug use scared them, however, and they could not trust me. I could not trust me. So when a downtown bar owner asked me to run his bar and offered me the small office upstairs to live in, I jumped at the opportunity.

I had developed a skill set uniquely suited to Queen Street West: I sold dope and people wanted to buy it from me. Where I went, people followed. Again, this world valorized dealing, partying hard, sex in washrooms, speakeasies and alternative music, alternative narratives.

So there I was living in a bar, sleeping on one of the pool tables and using the office as my personal space, and this was home. This was not a friendly

There are not many pictures of me at rock-bottom, but this is one.

neighborhood bar. This was a very popular place for real addicts because all of us who worked there or went there did so to push our limits. It was small, crowded, and dirty, with motorcycles hung up on the wall. Each morning we would sweep the floors and empty the pool-table pockets and the drug paraphernalia, the bullets and other artifacts of the nightlife, a syringe or a burnt spoon from time to time, were collected and immediately tossed in the trash. As crazy as I was, there were others who had good jobs and families who came there, drank, vomited on the bar, and continued drinking, and they never ended up homeless. But surely they were addicted like me. It was strange: there were times when I would look at someone and ask them, "Haven't you had enough?" I may have been buzzed out of my mind, but I could see the damage in other people. That may seem strange, but in the end, that ability to recognize madness might have saved me. I loved being in the bar. I had power there, and friends, and we were all quite mad. The place had a reputation. Movie stars, athletes, musicians would come there because my staff and I knew how to push the limits.

But all good things must come to an end. I built up the reputation of the bar sufficiently so that the owner could sell it to investors; I found myself homeless, jobless and lost. I was given $1500 as a settlement, which I used on drugs. I was forced to go on welfare. And I moved into a small studio space, my only furniture a futon I had found on the curb.

I got my nourishment from alcohol and my sustenance from drugs. I was 128 pounds, my teeth were stained and I was jaundiced. I owed drug dealers money, had used up every bit of goodwill I had ever had. An important point here is that I was desperate to stop, but I could not. Most of the poor souls who are on the streets or in shelters or begging for change are not there by choice. They might have chosen to leave home, but it is rarely for whimsical reasons. They have "cause to take flight," like I did. There are those who have endured this hardship for so long and have likely never had the guidance to talk about the reasons they ended up as denizens of the street or why they medicate. Later, during my doctoral research in Montreal, some of my street associates devised brilliant explanations of how they chose to live on the streets—that this lifestyle suited them, or that theirs had been a chosen path. Upon deconstruction, during our numerous conversations, we came to understand that this was just one way of understanding their truth. We almost always decided together that the narratives we had told ourselves about our demise and our choices were symptoms of our untreated, unmanaged mental illnesses. We were ashamed and powerless. We told crazy narratives about ourselves, just as the rest of the world continued to tell itself comforting narratives when it caught sight of us.

By 1995, after enduring a decade of daily drug use, I lay in bed one afternoon in that run-down studio—from which I was about to be evicted—waiting for some bad guys to whom I owed money to come and beat me to death. I heard the footsteps enter my studio. I really hoped it was the bad guys because I had neither the courage to end my life nor the strength to save it. As the steps neared my head, I did not turn to them but closed my eyes and waited, and heard a sob, and then another. It had been my sister's steps, and her sobs, and her voice that said, "You need help." I don't know why, that time of all the times I had heard it from her before, but I said: "Yes, I do."

That is why I am one of the lucky ones. That lens that let me see other people's madness was protecting a sense of self and dignity that ten years of rapacious drug and alcohol consumption could not strip away. I was not saved, yet. But I had reached a spiritual and physical bottom. I could go no lower, but someone cared, and risked their own emotional health and dignity to enter my tragedy and beg me to get help.

Shortly after that I met my sister's doctor, who remains my doctor to this day, given a fine ability to understand my disease. After a horrifying five-day detox at a facility in Barrie, Ontario, I entered treatment, the Jubilee Centre in Timmins. *Treatment* is a polite way of saying "Self-Government 101": for many, this is the first attempt to detox from drugs, to learn about the medical model of the disease and to understand simple tools for not relapsing. There are even programs that give people drugs to control their drug use or alcohol consumption, and others that give people anti-anxiety or mood modification drugs. Today there are companies that will attach a video camera and a breathalyzer to your front door and will not permit you entrance to your home if you blow over the limit. One of these devices is called Sentinel.® It is expensive, and is well known among some of the better-resourced families of addicts I know. It represents a last hope that their loved ones will live up to their promises of sobriety. None of these drugs or devices would have worked for me. I needed to be in a therapeutic, supportive housed environment where I could learn how to live with my disease.

In treatment, I learned a 12-step recovery program that taught me some simple practices about humility and decent behaviour towards others. I still go to the weekly fellowship meetings of one group in particular. The key to this program is that, based on its prior 60 years of practice, if we were to do all the simple things it asked, all would become well. All that we addicts had lost— financial, emotional, spiritual and other types of security—would return to us if we followed their prescriptions for good orderly direction. It is not a cult, or a religious group. It uses the power of conversation, belief in powers greater than our own will, and collective experience to help people not to use booze or drugs again. And these *promises* (as they are called) suggest that if we are dili- gent about our lives and about not taking the first drug, or the first drink, then we are likely to redeem ourselves and reclaim our conventional goals. This is the essence of good self-governance, which is the key to neoliberal citizenship. For most of the public, it is those of us who once had had a problem, got help, and then continued to help ourselves who come to be understood as deserving of second chances and public assistance to kick-start our lives. We go from being undeserving to deserving if we learn to self-govern.

Treatment is a kind of crash course, then, where all these ideas are drilled into us and then we either go to a long-term recovery and housing facility to learn how to actually live in this proper manner again, or we return to whence we came. I was homeless. I had nowhere of my own to go. But not everyone in treatment was homeless. We weren't there because of homelessness or unemployment. We were there because we shared an addiction. Most had wives or husbands, jobs and homes to which they could return. Not me. And my family had been instructed that letting me live with them might be unwise since I had been able to manipulate them in the past.

I returned to Toronto, on welfare, and lived in a room in a family friend's house. I stayed clean and sober for three months, and then relapsed. I had violated the conditions of my house stay. I was told to leave. It broke this person's heart. She is still a dear close family friend, but she was an experienced nurse and very strong. She was unwilling to enable my disease. The disease was so powerful that I went from sipping a non-alcoholic beer one night to using cocaine in less than 24 hours. I was powerless to resist. In my relapse, my need for drugs was so bad and my housing so insecure that I was "literally homeless" and came once again to know many of the places where people slept on the streets, sometimes trading drugs in exchange for a place on someone's couch or using drugs to enter the lives of housed people who liked to party so that they might let me hang around and sponge off them. There are people who do not want to recognize this period in my life as homelessness because I was able to find places to stay. But couch-surfing, trading drugs for a bed for a night, getting emergency welfare to pay rent, and then literally staying up all night so that during the day falling asleep in a Tim Hortons didn't look so bad—this is not housing. This is the kind of precarious, insecure housing with which our cities today struggle the most. And we will get to that topic soon.

Suffice it to say that by the end of a six-month relapse, I managed with the help of my doctor to enter the same treatment center for a second time. Following this I moved to the quaint town of Merrickville and became a long-term resident at the Buena Vista on the Rideau recovery house. This was a welfare-sponsored program lasting up to two years, where men could go to get over addictions—to booze, drugs, or gambling. It felt much more like a correctional institute or a halfway house than a recovery home; many of the men who went there were ex-cons, or recently convicted of drug or alcohol related vehicular offenses. These were not celebrities or rich kids. For all of us it was a last-resort kind of place. Our being there was the contingency on which returning to our worlds depended. The recovery process was handed to us— we were remanded to it—as a sort of punishment for crimes and infidelities, and recovery was to give evidence of commitment to self-govern once again.

A two-hundred-year-old mansion on the banks of the Rideau River, the rehab looked like a beautiful colonial building. There were no fences or guard posts, but it was a "facility," even though no one could tell just by looking at it. But the locals knew. Some of the townsfolk were friendly to us. But most of them steered shy of us, and if it hadn't been for the employment and revenues the center provided, they might have forced its closure. This was the first time I heard the acronym "NIMBY." It means "not in my backyard" and that is also a common sentiment amongst critics of welfare for addicts and the homeless—"Sure, help them, but not in my neighborhood." Aware of this, the center required us to volunteer in a number of local markets, festivals and other services.

The rehab program offered highly structured living, which included shared accommodations with no single rooms or private baths. It imposed on us daily and enforced routines as well as many "programs" about recovery that we had to pass in order to stay there. Almost half of the residents had come there as results of sentencing for DUI or assaults related to addiction, not because they were homeless and had nowhere else to go. Another quarter of the men were diagnosed with mental illnesses of various kinds and placed there to conquer co-addictions while waiting for funded long-term-care beds. For the rest of us, and the distribution varied as men came and went, the program and rules were preferable to fighting for a shelter bed, especially in January when I got there.

One of the staff members told me, "The place always filled up in winter, and cleared out come summer." A young First Nations man, who liked to be called Little Joe, arrived in late March from the Rideau Regional [Psychiatric] Centre,[61] having beaten his father to death in a drunken rage. The hospital itself, since closed, has a troubled past and is subject to ongoing litigation about mistreatment of the psychiatric patients who lived there. Little Joe told me that such abuses went on when he was there.

He would sit by the river in the evening, by himself. He was native and the rest of the guys hated him, because (like me) we were not from the Merrickville area. We were ethnic after all; I used Yiddish expletives like "Oi Vey," and he burned Sweetgrass. He was oddly serene. He had to do 18 months "sober time" at the Buena Vista before he could go back to regular society. I befriended him. If two men ever hit rock bottom from two very different starting points, it was the two of us: he, a murderer from the reservation, and me, an ex-drug-dealing cokehead from a good Jewish family. Both of us sat on the banks of the river, me fly-fishing for pike, he, praying to something I will never know. It was at Buena Vista that I began reflecting on the days leading up to that moment, the characters of the homeless—especially my own—and it was there where I learned that addictions do not need to cause homelessness. However, several of the men I met at Rideau or at recovery meetings had become addicted as a result of becoming homeless for other reasons. I began writing a chronicle of my time there and reading every bit of recovery literature I could find. It took me about three weeks to figure out that I was serious, and most others at Buena Vista were not. I hated it at first. I wanted to leave. I

121

developed an ulcer-like condition, as diagnosed by the local doctor. However, I also started gaining weight. I went in at about 135 pounds. Six months later, following treatment, I was 190 pounds. (I recall the tears in my mother's and my sister's eyes as they rejoiced at how plump I looked).

The problem with the *them-and-us* position, with either/or ways of thinking, is that they suggest that people on either side of a debate or a narrative are very similar. But even if we could draw up an imaginary continuum of debate about race or social problems with polar archetypes at each end, we could not say that all the pros and all the cons were expressed the same way. We find in fact that non-addicts, addicts housed, and unhoused people are unique across those vectors of identification, that they are far more complex as individuals and as groups, allowing for a number of convergent qualities that make such them-and-us positions untenable. Recently, at Christmas dinner, my relatives were talking to me about my research. They were very serious, but their cellphones went off several times during this conversation at the dinner table, and they could not resist answering and texting back to whomever was trying to reach them. This gave me cause to tell them about research I had done in the very early 1990s while a part of the Computer and Video Enhanced Communication and Technology Team (CAVECAT) at the University of Toronto. My graduate advisor and I were invited to examine what kinds of visual cues and behavioural ticks were part of face-to-face communication, and which could be integrated with Picture Monitoring Systems (PMS)—what we today call cellphones. One of the companies we had discussions with uses a fruit as its logo. The key to making these PMS systems work, they thought, was to make that use habitual. That is: they wanted to make us cellphone addicts. And we are. So how much "us" is there in "them"? There are studies that suggest cellphones and other social media are the new drugs for our youth to consume. Jim Roberts of Baylor Medical (2014), Roberts et al. (2014) in the *Journal of Behavioral Addictions*, and others speak to the growing sensitivity amongst researchers to the addictive nature of communication devices.

Admitting that we are all addicts of some kind does not make the them-and-us proposition easier to swallow. There is a strong sense that widely popular addictions—such as to cellphones—are acceptable, even though cell use impacts other people, and has caused many cities to impose high fines for using cellphones in cars. So, I want to suggest, when we point out the "other" as defective, it is often because we don't want to identify the "them" in ourselves.

Even if being unhoused is unconventional, and as much as housed people might not like unhoused folks, not everyone who is homeless or in recovery likes each other, either. That is to say that homeless people are a mixed lot; so are addicts, and even within these subcategories there is a sense of "us and them." These guys hated me, and I disliked them. But something miraculous if not completely mundane was to happen that would lead to a sort of detente between us.

After three months and completion of my relapse prevention program, I went for a visit to Toronto, where I developed an abscess in my upper jaw. I was granted permission to stay in Toronto with family for two weeks for dental surgery. And while I was there, two significant things happened. First, I realized just how messed up my family really was. I could see sick things people around me were doing. They say that part of the transition from active addiction to better health is a shift in how we see the world around us; learning, as it were, to understand the extent of spiritual and social illness around us. No longer medicated, we are forced out of a grayed-out zone and with some clarity we begin to see. I noticed that the normal behaviours I grew up with were problematic. Some people I knew well drank too much; others were terribly vain. As I wandered about the city, there was the general indifference people paid to each other. I actually wanted to go back to Buena Vista.

But I had to stay in Toronto until they removed four of my front teeth. And, perhaps surprisingly, that was the key to my spiritual awakening. Recall that many years earlier, my friends and I more than once laughed at the toothless bums in Allan Gardens or on Broadview. At Buena Vista I quietly ridiculed the other men because most of them were missing teeth. And there I was in the dentist's chair, transfixed by the mirror she had handed me, completely fascinated by the gaping space between my molars, laughing my head off. No one could understand what I found so funny. Ironic is more the word for it; and then strangely again, a sense of tranquility. If I had ever entertained any doubts about the nature of my addiction, they had vanished, and no matter how hard I had wanted to think of myself as a better addict than the bums, I, we, were and are the same animal.

I returned to Buena Vista late one Sunday night. At 6 a.m. I went into the washroom. There were four sinks. Every morning the guys without teeth would enter, take their dentures out of their mouths or remove them from a cup of Polident, and give them a good brush before putting them back in and heading off. Sometimes I had brushed my teeth a little longer as if to make a point: I had teeth. That morning, as usual, they didn't greet me or say hello even though I had just returned after two weeks' absence. No razzing, no polite hellos, just a safe distance between us. So when they started brushing their teeth, I reached into my mouth, pulled out my dentures and started brushing too. They looked amazed. The silence was amazing. Just running water. A couple of guys I had always sensed wanted to be nicer to me actually smiled. We looked at each other and one guy lent me his Polident. In stride, as if there had never been any narrative distance between us, we simply chatted; about what I can't recall, except that one fellow, Billy, asked me how Toronto was. "Leafs still suck?" is what he said, as I recall. But that was it for me. I realized that we were tied to one another no matter how hard we might have fought and debated it. One has cause to wonder how practical it would be to help all people find a source of unity like this, one that compels rethinking even simple narratives, because it seemed then and seems even more urgent to me now that it is these little doses of humanity that help change the broader and more profound discourses that are the subject of this book. And I started friendships with a few of the men there, men I had now come to understand were in their own ways eager to get sober, and I learned about their stories. Some of those stories I began writing down.

The men I got to know, almost 50 over a period of seven months, had become addicts for various reasons. Some were housed and some were homeless when I met them. So there was not a clear correlation between addiction and homelessness. Most of them had families and jobs waiting for them, and recovery was instrumental to returning to those lives; for many it was a condition of reconciliation with estranged wives and families, or keeping a job. Transition meant different things to different people, so transitional programs had to identify and meet disparate needs. For me, transitioning meant climbing up from the bottom, learning to manage my affairs, and addressing other personal hurdles, while for others it meant significantly less rebuilding. They had only to learn not to drink or drug, because their lives were otherwise intact.

Recall that the men in that home were not there because they were homeless. This was not transitional housing per se. We were there because of various addictions. It was a recovery house that gave men time to form an aftercare plan, which for those of us with nowhere to live generally included some kind of housing which might be transitional or permanent. I had arranged to move in with my mom and her partner, whom I refer to as my parents, until I was solvent enough to move out. At the time, and still today, "transitional" denoted a continuum of housing into which one entered after leaving Buena Vista. Usually for those of us without homes to go to, this continuum included treatment and recovery, managed conditional welfare-supported housing, and then regular market rental units.

Several men there (including me) were *literally* homeless, with no alternatives but the street. It seems almost redundant to suggest that all the homeless men I met there were addicts, and some were cross-diagnosed with various psychiatric problems; this was a recovery house, and it was *for* addicts. Statistically this seems obvious. However, having become friends or at least very acquainted with them over those months, and also with many of their family members who rejoined their lives as they recovered, I learned that they had not all been addicts or mentally ill when they lost their housing. Some had lost low-paying jobs, or been burned by the market collapses in the late 1980s

and mid-1990s; a few were mentally ill and their residential stays were termi-
nated by cutbacks. These men's psychiatric symptoms presented or became
worse when they lost their housing, and their addictions became worse or
appeared for the first time as a result of time spent on the streets, or when
access to prescribed medications was cut off. They had turned to street drugs
like methamphetamine, crack cocaine, cocaine, opiates (especially heroin), and
alcohol. All these were abundant, whereas the prescribed meds that might
have really helped them had been cut off or made contingent on humiliating
and oppressive medical diagnostic procedures.

It was not common at that time to think of the streets causing addiction or
mental illness. For the most part, the popular imaginary saw matters in the
reverse order. Of course, some of the guys there had lost everything as a result
of drinking and drugging or gambling. The early lesson for me was that drug
use of the kind associated with the streets—meth, sniffing glue, addictions to
Percocet and heroin—often occurs as a result of being on the streets, as coping
mechanisms or as the material basis for dependencies and alliances in street
relationships (Bahr 1973; Ward 1979; Bourgois 2002, 2009). One of the
interesting twists on my own perception is that I used to think an addict
would do anything to get high. That explained many of my own social
relationships and behaviours. But the reality is that people often enter
homelessness sober, and then become addicted. Maybe people do drugs on the
streets not just to relieve anxiety but because drugs, like other material
resources,   are   substances   that   facilitate   social   relationships   and
friendships. The current recognized truth is that a homeless person might do
anything to have friends and company, to get a bed or a protector, or to have
power, and this includes drugs (Ward 1975; Wagner 1991; DePastino 2003).

My recovery was very "white" and "male." The only women in my recovery
setting were therapists or drug counselors. There were no men of colour there,
except for two who identified as members of First Nations. The rest of us were
white. I heard both racism and misogyny. One guy was kicked out for calling
me a "fucking Jew" and threatening to "shiv" me (stab me with a sharpened
toothbrush, to be exact). Still, that recovery house was the first time I had to
recognize that homelessness and addiction are powerfully if unclearly interconnected, and that people of all races, religions, socio-economic background,
and education can end up there regardless of what distributive statistics suggest.

Residency at the recovery house was strictly governed. We were free to
leave anytime we wanted to. This was no prison. Many men who got fed up
with the rules did leave, usually returning to unhappy friends or family or to
later stages of addiction, perhaps to eventually end up on the streets. I did not
track any of the men who left the Buena Vista. We heard stories. Of the three
who left on their own accord while I was there, we learned that one had been

killed on the streets, another had returned to jail, and there was a rumour that the other had died, apparently homeless, on a park bench in Thunder Bay, Ontario.

For some of us, however, case workers were explicit about our not "fucking up" because we had nowhere to go, and getting into housing, finding jobs again or maybe going to school, and reuniting with family were contingent on good behaviour. As I said, this program was, in every sense of the word, neoliberalism's answer to the need for a good, healthy and self-governing citizen. This was Self-Government 201, treatment being the "101" course. It incorporated 12-step meetings, demanded regulated living where we were supposed to monitor each other, in addition to urine analysis, re-education and therapy. Of the 50 or so people I met there, only two of us had remained sober when I last checked in 2005. This is consistent with figures touted at 12-step regional meetings and in some recovery literature. For every 100 persons who seek treatment, between 2% and 8% get sober. Over time this number drops to less than 2% (AA Survey and Status Report 2007–2008).

In each case, we had become successful because certain conditions were in place. First, we had family who supported us during this process. We were loved. And though this is another hard subject for scientists, in some cases the power of love trumps the power of denial. It was, after all, a well-timed tear that saved me. We had education and skills. As I said, while there I wrote a chronicle of life in the house and did a very serious study of the Alcoholics Anonymous Big Book (1937) with my sponsor Pat Fortune, who has since passed away.

Perhaps more importantly than any of this, we had no place to go. This rocked our sensibility. We were living in Buena Vista, but outside we were homeless. The possession of a house is central to the imaginary that framed our identity as Canadians and as men. Faced with nowhere to live, if we continued our ways, we would be dumped into the streets when our tenure was over, or placed, like before, in some welfare hellhole. As humbling as this admission is, there is no way for me to prevent its disclosure here. That would be tantamount to a chemist ignoring the observations she made of acid burns she received as a child, or a biologist who pretends his swim with whales hasn't given his work a certain compassionate eye, or a fly fisherman writing about dry flies, having never studied hatches.[62] The homeless people I work with in my research are interchangeable in ways we will discuss throughout this work. In my case, it was the compassionate eye I developed towards the relationship between housing, home and self-worth that ultimately led to my work. I shared my past with all the participants in my research. This constituted the basis of trust for us. This horrible deficit, these defects of a troubled past, are priceless resources in the work I do. Most importantly, there is a shame to having no housing that is unimaginable for those who grow up housed and in a culture where the home is the center of the universe.

I stuck it out and completed my training. My family had rallied behind me. My painting skills had improved since I had time to practice free of drugs and booze. I was also writing again. I had come to enjoy the safe, structured life at the house, but I was ready to reclaim myself. My after-care plan was carefully constructed: return to Toronto and live at my parents' home, start work as a muralist again, save money, go to recovery fellowship meetings, move out and get into housing. And stay away from drugs, and keep my housing.

In June 1996, I returned to Toronto where, two days following my return, I re-started my business as a muralist and sculptor. I also began earnestly writing and reading about homelessness, addiction, and poverty. What just a few months earlier had seemed to be the biggest threat to my existence and stigmatized me among most of the people I had known prior to my experience with homelessness had now become my most valuable resource. Combined with my graduate training as a fieldworker in the mid-1980s, and my serious contemplation of rehabilitation and homelessness while in recovery, in the final analysis it was *shame* that provided me a certain eye to the homeless problem in Toronto.

3.3 Returning to Housing

From 1996 to 1998 I was earning enough as a painter and muralist to afford a cute studio apartment in Cabbagetown, historically known as part of Toronto's "poor white district." I owned a van, fished frequently, took vacations, attended fellowship meetings, dated rather poorly, and learned how to live a sober life. My family, weekly 12-step fellowship, and work relationships were key to this. In my "hood" there were still halfway houses, cheap rundown single room occupancy (SRO) hotels and shelters. It was being gentrified, as were all neighborhoods in the core. I was content with my living space, listening at night to the sounds of car windows breaking, footsteps running from the alarms, and I understood that the suffering went on. I met a lot of guys who shacked up together in rooming houses on Parliament Street, in the one section where such places remained, and we talked. A few said they recognized me from years previous, but they were mistaken; they were only trying to stimulate a sense of camaraderie so I might give them a dollar or two.

I did very well at business. By 2000, as the streets were literally filling with homeless people, I moved away from Cabbagetown to a two-bedroom apartment with my own garage in the area known as High Park, a "move upwards" one might say, but in the interim I had been writing, writing. I had written a number of short stories and a few screenplays. One of them, "The Horseman," was about an elderly man who had become homeless after losing his job as a racehorse jockey. His dying wish had been to ride again. In the script, he dies, and his street family duct-taped his cadaver to a horse at Woodbine racetrack for his last ride. It won a prize as best screenplay in a Ryerson University screenwriting course I was taking at night. It was black comedy, but comedy just the same.

Except that it was also very accurate. This character was a composite of various men I had met. I had learned, once again, that the homeless are not just junkies or alcoholics. Some people become homeless simply because they lose their job—often the only trade or skill they know—and are poor. When a person loses a job later in life and under unfair circumstances, the trauma is more than destabilizing; it is catastrophic. Today, middle-aged people lose their jobs frequently and this has become an increasing concern for governments and families struggling with the growing cohort of the homeless. These people are not addicts or mentally or physically challenged when they lose their jobs. Back in 1998, a man I used to talk with in Allan Park near Cabbagetown did not drink or do drugs. He had been on the streets for twenty years by then, a defrocked jockey who had been accused of throwing races. He had never got over the loss of his vocation. It had depressed him so much at a time (the late 1970s) when depression was rarely discussed, especially among men, that he floated from park to park, shelter to shelter, adrift in memories of past glories on the dirt oval. I met a social worker who had tried to get him housing and psychiatric help. He declined these offers, perhaps because accepting such services would be admitting guilt. In real life he didn't die (although I would guess that by now he surely has).

Beer Bottle. One of my first gigs after rehab was an agonizing six weeks building this 15-foot beer bottle for Molson. Each day I walked past 9 million cans of beer on the way to the cafeteria Photo: Eric Weissman, 1998.

A number of important works written in the 1990s to which I referred earlier, including Caton (1990), Wright (1993), and Gans (1991), speak to the immensity of the problem with homelessness and to the call for a paradigm shift in how we look at it. In fact, contemporary arts had moved beyond the Buster Keaton and Charlie Chaplin comedic portrayals of the poor vagabond: the wildly successful theatrical production of *Rent* (1994) helped the old popular imaginary shift by 2000, when I approached a contact in the movie industry about making this film.

We did not make the film, since his interests were now in theatre, but the script was good enough that they hired me to write character sketches of the people I was meeting in my jaunts about town for a proposed new musical on homelessness.[63] The Toronto representative of the American firm knew me as an academic, had witnessed my bottom, and was "thrilled" to read these stories as a symbol of my resurrection. Most of all, they were keenly aware that Toronto and other major cities in North America were beginning to present higher numbers of poor people and of different kinds than ever before. He wasn't interested in a head count: "Anyone can see how bad it has gotten," he said to me several times. As it turned out, he wanted stories like "The Horseman," about "people that don't deserve to be homeless." This was the first time I thought with any serious deliberation about what "deserving" and "undeserving" poverty actually were. His feeling was that within this vast sea of poor people invading downtown parks and churches, there must be more than merely drunks and criminals who deserve to be homeless. They wanted to put a face to what he implicitly understood to be neoliberalism's greatest indictment, abject poverty in the richest cities on the planet.

3.4 Toronto, Tent City, and Questions

In 2001, in Toronto, estimates of the number of the homeless ranged from 5,000 to over 20,000, depending on the source.[64] It was impossible to walk a block of the downtown core without being harassed by beggars or seeing tents and lean-tos in public parks. Street homelessness was not new to Toronto, but the homeless had never been so visible. I started out by meeting homeless people by chance on the streets, telling them about my theatrical work over a coffee, and then with an audio device and notepad taking down their stories. Those who participated, for the most part, felt that there was a sense of liberation in telling their stories. Very few of them believed me when I forced my story on them, so I let the interviews take on an organic feel. I abandoned the list of questions I had been asked to present. Instead we just chatted and as they got to know me, it became clear that I wasn't leading them on about my own difficult past.

By the winter of 2001, video handy-cams exploded onto the consumer market, and I progressed to a digital video device. While the character sketches I was compiling were not driven by any particular scholarly interest, the interviews I was acquiring and stories I was collecting provided insights into the lived experience of what was for most Torontonians a very distant unlikelihood, homelessness. Suddenly, articles, news stories, old books I hadn't read in years became important to me.

Opening frame of my film *Subtext.*

I had been employing a form of interpretive reportage, perhaps best understood as a sort of Actor Network or assemblage approach in which I was guided by individuals and their practical beliefs into the social assemblages that constituted their street life, and thus was able to see what their world looked like to them (Law 2004; Latour 2005).[65] Once again, this meant accepting the participant's point of view as "real" regardless of whether it made scientific or other kinds of sense. Some people I had met had been diagnosed with psychiatric disorders and seemed quite mad. But insomuch as what they were saying and showing me was their reality, and the social world they carved out of life was built on this madness, there was as much analytic validity in their point of view as would have been the case if they had sounded "normal." In fact, meeting their friends and doctors, sometimes their family, happened only because I went along with them in their daily excursions and experienced their social world, as they understood it. And it changed often. They followed certain rules, such as shelter curfews and soup kitchen hours of operation, and in that sense seemed very organized, but they had really lost the ability to care for themselves and most of the social services that had helped them were by then gone. Many of the people I met early on were driven not by power or ambition, but by the need for food, drugs, medication, clothes and other goods. Material objects had a lot of impact on the streets.

I was struck then, as I am now as I do work on the streets in Portland, Montreal and Toronto, by how the imbrication of human and non-human agents, people, places, things, materials—tough guys, passive loners, church parking lots, road underpasses, food, clothes, a bag of dope or bottle of Percocet—have as much to do with the choices made by street homeless as do the laws and other external contexts into which their lives are inserted by a sort of narrative fate. I recall driving for 11 hours one wintry night and morning to get a drug I wanted. Doing so led to a very near-death experience for me. In this case, one cannot pretend that the substance in question did not have agency. To the conventional world the way we act seems chaotic. And in comparison to the "good life" it probably is, but there is a certain repetition and institutionalization of types of behaviour that becomes structural.

Even if outsiders can only begin to imagine how chaos is structural, following homeless guys around and listening to their stories reveals discernable if not fleeting patterns around food, shelter, drugs, and friendships, eluding police and finding medical attention. All of these things were easier to do in Toronto than anywhere else in Canada, as nationwide devolution increased the numbers of homeless by cutting welfare and closing long-term care facilities. Even Buena Vista had been closed as a non-profit and reopened privately as a drug and addictions center.

By 2001, a visibly higher number of poor people had come from all over Canada (and other countries) to Toronto, especially the zone near St. Michael's Hospital, where there was and remains a concentration of detoxes, churches, soup kitchens, community centers, shelters and growing grassroots activism.[66] Toronto, being the largest and richest city in Canada, in due course found itself overwhelmed by welfare claimants and the poor from all over the country, looking for emergency welfare support, handouts, and shelter. To me, it seemed that Toronto was engaged in an outright war on the street poor, as police were forcibly rousting and jailing those who slept rough in various parks and other city spaces. Across the U.S. at the same time, cities were facing similarly high numbers of people on the streets.[67] In Toronto, there were so many squatters appearing in tents and sleeping bags on city parks that there came to be the beginnings of a collective struggle to make sense of these things. Newspapers and television newscasts began covering the "problem" and tended to emphasize the conflict between urban redevelopment and prosperity and the human cost of unaffordable housing.

The historical record shows that many North American cities were suffering a loss of inner-city industries and businesses concomitant with unprecedented rises of numbers of literally homeless persons, those who sleep rough outside or resort to shelter(Bahr and Caplow 1968; Caton 1990; Ward 1979; Leginski 2007; Hulchanski 2009).[68] The relationship of the two events was not causal (Burt and Aron 2000 in Leginski 2007). Rather, it reflected a connection between the government's unwillingness to spend money on the poor when such expenditures were portrayed by ideologues as negatively impacting the economy, regardless of performance. There was also the fact that such empty real estate was attractive to developers and city planners who had been encouraged by the state-supported ideology of urban renewal to buy cheap and redevelop broken inner-city cores.

The homeless problem increasingly became framed as an obstacle to revitalization of the downtown core of Toronto. And because it was mostly men left out of the shelters, the problem was with "drunk men." Traditionally they had occupied Toronto's version of the "Main Stem" and "Skid Row." At the turn of the twenty-first century, Toronto's skid rows—pockets of unused or poor-quality housing, isolated in small zones in the areas roughly bordered by Broadview Avenue and Church Street to the east and west, and Bloor Street and Lake Shore Boulevard to the north and south, were well into a phase of redevelopment.

I heard occasional rumors of a peculiar homeless utopia being built on the U.S. west coast in Portland, Oregon, some 2,500 miles away. It had mystical names like "Liberty Town" and "Dignity Land." It was apparently a rugged pioneer town imbued with dignity because it had been the zone of a major contestation between capitalist power and grassroots activists, something that the TDRC and OCAP had been trying to do with Toronto's street poor. We all wanted the fantasy to be true, and we began talking about it as if it were.

In fact, events in Toronto and Portland paralleled one another over the next several months, providing a sort of conjunctural frame of experience for those of us investigating street poverty at the time. Toronto and Portland as the largest cities in their respective geopolitical territories were absorbing the human fallout of a retracted social services system. Their respective urban imaginaries were to handle it very differently.

The presence of small gatherings of the homeless in tents along Toronto's Don River Valley was not new. They had been there for decades, but went largely undetected. In Portland, a fairly persistent occupation of the Columbia River Sloughs by lone indigent men and women in tents and lean-tos had by 2000 become something of an institution, having existed for over a century according to one man who had told me on my first trip there that he slept in and around the same site his father had used for years before settling in a small rural community outside of Portland. In every major city on the continent, the classic homeless nomad with his or her shopping cart had become a persistent historical form, and urban citizens seemed to be more comforted, perhaps reassured by their presence, a visual reminder that homelessness was isolated to the very worst of possibilities. These other worse-off cases squatting in the fringes rarely crossed our minds.

It occurred to me that congregations of homeless people by the hundred or more in several of Toronto's downtown parks bespoke the utter failure of one of the richest cities in the world to care for the poor. Moreover, secure housing—once the bedrock of the Canadian identity—was being derided for the way governments managed poverty. Newspapers, other media,[69] and concerned scientists from various universities engaged in a debate about housing policy and basic rights. I came to questions about how such abject poverty is reproduced over long periods of time in cultures that continue to create wealth and advance in other areas of medicine, science and most importantly, urban renewal. As a Torontonian, the fact that people should be camping in numbers and in full view of the public seemed to demand attention.

Homelessness is as old as history. Skid row, an infrequently used term nowadays, was the perceptual spatial embodiment of street-engaged homelessness for almost a century in North American cities (Bahr 1973:21; Ward 1979). It is, therefore, a relatively new concept and a North American invention, which resulted from a series of spatial mediations in the city over time that demonized the homeless man for his role as casual laborer and for his intemperate manner (Anderson 1923; Bahr 1973). As such, it occurred to me then—though only as an idea—that space is what we make of it, and that this usage shifts over time by the influence of laws we create to reign over it. Not all civilizations have treated the homeless the same way. For the ancient Greeks, the homeless were revered; Zeus was the God of "strangers" (Bahr 1973:20). And wasn't Jesus a friend to all beggars? The poor have always suffered material poverty, and some might argue that they have always been the embodiment of discourses about insanity, crime and all manner of deviance, a theme expressed in many early ethnographies such as Anderson's *The Hobo* (1923), Liebow's *Tally's Corner* (1967), and, most influentially, Lewis' *The Culture of Poverty* (1966).

Poverty does not equate with homelessness of the kind I am referring to here. In my early days on the streets, the housed urban imaginary in Toronto understood the street people we saw as a certain worst-off case; people like me who had little hope, were addicted or infirm. The perception was that, because most people managed to do well, such problems were idiosyncratic, and so the rising numbers of homeless were not the result of failing social systems. For most of us, poverty was an enigmatic aspect of our civilization managed by mysterious government or economic forces. In classic Marxian language, the poor in general were of some value within the urban imaginary as the *proletariat* or *workers*; the busboys, construction apprentices and factory slaves we saw about town, but these others, famously discussed in Marx's *The Eighteenth Brumaire of Louis Napoleon* (1852) as *lumpenproletariat*, a miscreant class fraction, were those that we chose to imagine as not willing or able to participate in the economy or the social world we understood.

Even today, poverty does not mean homelessness. Homelessness more recently happens to people who were never poor, when economies crash, investments turn sour, or major illness strips away one's assets. Still, in 2000, despite the work of Caton (1990), Marcuse (1983; 1990), Rossi (1989), and many others that spoke to diversifying "new poverty" in America, popular media and urban imaginaries remained fixed on a characterologically flawed poor person as the coefficient of homelessness and the basic actor in cultures of poverty. This position is still central to many debates about poverty and housing.

3.5 Legacy of the Culture of Poverty
Sociologist Oscar Lewis wrote *The Culture of Poverty* (1966), *A Study of Slum Culture* (1968), and *Five Families: Mexican Case Studies in the Culture of Poverty*

Eric Weissman

(1962). The determinism of this model is something I want to move away from in this book, even though it has had significant influence on how ethnographers examine poverty and homelessness and is experiencing a sort of renaissance today. Lewis' culture of poverty model works on the premise that through early childhood socialization, the tendencies of poverty are inscribed in the individual and henceforth in the culture, in much the same way Bourdieu (1972) later suggested the force of habitus exerts on the bodies and minds of actors.

Pierre Bourdieu is a highly influential figure in critical sociology. His approach explores how social structures limit a social actor's critical capacity by routinizing restraining cultural practices. In *Outline of a Theory of Practice* (1972), Bourdieu takes an important step towards integrating structural and subjective explanations of social realities by his use of *habitus*, which includes a system of dispositions developed by a given agent in response to structural forces (1972: introduction). The individual or subject as an actor with agency internalizes these structural forces in a personalized mental and somatic set of manners and behaviours within what Bourdieu called the *field*, be it art, politics, work and so on. In this way, the objective and subjective are synthesized and compatible.

In this model of "generative structuralism," Bourdieu explains that the subject has little (initial) say about his or her disposition towards choice, having been born into particular cultural and class-based value systems and narrative performances that code the body from birth, through ways of "standing, speaking and thereby of *feeling* and *thinking* (Bourdieu 1972:32; Bourdieu and Wacquant 1992; Vandenberghe 1999; Lizardo 2009). A *doxic* relationship emerges. Here, a *doxa* is a deep internalized set of beliefs and understandings in the agent, particular to field (setting-structure, like art, culture, food, work ...), which favour the "rules" of the field, and therefore satisfy the need of those vested powers and structures that underpin the field. The individual, by involvement in the field, submits to the implicit rule that acts against it are incongruent and unacceptable.

Predating contemporary feminist theoretical concerns with the body and embodied difference as both material and symbolic grounds for experience and subjectivity, Bourdieu (1972) argued that the body is the source of cultural reproduction; it is in the body that subjective qualities combine with the social and cultural world. Mediation of the "social/cultural" is a somatic process; the body mediates subjectivity and the "objective" world (32). We would have to live the stories we want to change to be able to make them possible. It seems counter-intuitive. But I tried to do this earlier in this chapter by relating my own cause-to-flight reaction. We will have cause to return to Bourdieu, but the analytical force of habitus is that it suggests that cultural practices are very hard to re-learn and overcome and so, if there is a culture of poverty, then solving homelessness must start with overcoming habitus.

Lewis' culture of poverty embodies the experience of the following:

(1) a cash economy, wage labor and production for profit;
(2) a persistently high rate of unemployment and underemployment for unskilled labor;
(3) low wages;
(4) the failure to provide social, political or economic organization, either on a voluntary basis or by government imposition, for the low-income population;
(5) the existence of a bilateral kinship system rather than a unilateral one; and, finally,
(6) the existence in the dominant class of a set of values that stresses the accumulation of wealth and property, thrift, and the possibility of upward mobility, and that explains low economic status as the result of personal inadequacy or inferiority (Lewis 1968:4-5).

Lewis' ethnographic realism suggests that there are dozens of traits that are generally associated (though not in any degree or order) with poor populations. These traits include the following: unemployment, absence of savings, lack of privacy, gregariousness, frequent use of physical violence in child training, predisposition to authoritarianism, inability to defer gratification, fatalism, mistrust of government, and strong feelings of powerlessness, marginality, and helplessness. Lewis was adamant that the culture of poverty was a sub-cultural aspect of capitalism (1968:20). During a period of economic prosperity among the wealthy in the United States, Lewis' realist approach was compelling. The image of a "poor" personality resonated well with claims that individuals and not structural conditions were to blame for poverty. Once again, cultures of poverty identify particular social roles and attitudes as the causal agents for poverty, and reduce the imperative for large structural changes. Bourgois (2001) has argued that the continued presence of Lewis' model in academic and scientific discourse corresponds with the historical manner by which others have been treated throughout US history:

> In the USA, irrespective of the theoretical orientation of researchers, most discussions on poverty polarize around value judgments concerning individual self-worth or around racial/ethnic stereotypes. U.S. attitudes towards poverty are rooted in the country's colonial Calvinist/Puritanical heritage and are exacerbated by the historical importance of racialized hierarchies that have legitimized genocide, slavery, colonization, and immigration control. This helps explain why the culture of poverty concept continues to generate so much emotional heat while shedding so little conceptual light. The uses and misuses of the concept offer a fascinating case study in the sociology of knowledge illustrating the political interfaces between

theory, empiricism, art, and ethnocentric moralizing in the social sciences (2001:906).

The moral call to recognize the embedded despair of homelessness in American society is quite old. Major works of note include Jacob Riss' photo-journalism[70] (De Pastino 2003:3), Jack London's *The War on Classes* (1905), Nels Anderson's *The Hobo* (1923), and, later, in Harrington's *The Other America* (1962), which takes a stand against poverty by arguing that the state and local communities had failed in a time of great technological innovation to induce any bettering of the poor. Whereas Anderson and others had recounted in novel and detailed ways the ethnography of being poor and of migrant labor, Lewis and Harrington each sought to redress the injustice of economic inequality by tasking regimes and states with services for the needy.

However, Lewis' position suggested a poor actor incapable of superseding his or her prescribed poverty. For Bourgois (2001:904), this characterization was an attempt to confirm the image of an undeserving and "pathologically" poor person, a negative *othering* that resonated well with the "blame the victim discourse" so prevalent in the West under capitalism in the 1960s and 1970s, and under neoliberal governmentality as it entered the twenty-first century. This narrative with its embedded inevitabilities is a powerful neoliberal critique of the poor that rewards the capable self-governed citizen.

By 2001, on the streets of Toronto, and across dining tables in the Greater Toronto Area, the debate over whether or not the poor were deserving of more assistance was a heated one. Mike Harris, the Progressive Conservative prem-ier of Ontario, had by then established his "Common Sense Revolution" that effectively closed over 20% of mental health long-term care beds and reduced welfare expenditures; Harris introduced "Ontario Works," a workfare program that required able-bodied welfare recipients to work for their assistance. This program, like U.S. workfare policies, reflected the belief that forcing people to work would redress the psychological deficits of poverty and replace idleness with an incentive to improve oneself though hard work. A basic premise we explore later is that the contradiction of having ability yet living in idleness are characteristics attributed to the undeserving poor under neoliberal value sys-tems. The ethnographic reality, however, if one accepts the works of Ward (1979), Wagner (1993), Bahr (1973) and others, is that the street-engaged home-less are amongst the most resourceful and busy people we can know. Simply surviving on the streets is difficult, but the founding and building of inten-tional homeless communities results from very serious and sustained efforts that most conventionally housed people cannot imagine, nor could they achieve given their utter dependence on others for most daily needs.

Perhaps this is what troubles me the most about Lewis' work (and any work that looks to individuals and their malfunctioning in general): this characterological diagnosis-based analysis allows neoliberal governance to blame the poor person for lack of effort, which in some cases might be true, but does not in itself explain systemic poverty.

It was not a lack of structural possibilities that produced my addiction or my homelessness: I *did* make poor choices. Once in that retrograde spiral of the streets and drugs, matters only got worse for me. At the same time, others I knew who were equally troubled did manage to escape that scene on their own and to become prosperous if not happy. There is no predestined or predetermined effect of proper socialization on the possibilities of emancipation from any debilitating condition. Should a poor person, as Lewis argues, be destined to be poor by a young age simply by learning it? Even Bourdieu (1971), who argued that culture is learned through *habitus* and difficult to unlearn, leaves room for people to find ways to change their ideas and to change the world. Should we solve poverty then by changing the thinking of poor people or by working on the economy and the school system to provide better opportunities? We are embracing again, whether wanted or not, the debate between structure and agency. In cases where homelessness is caused by addictions, from drinking to gambling, the route to homelessness needs to be identified and a treatment-based solution presented, if we want to avoid the point where that line is crossed. We will discuss the moral debate that presents in chapter 6.

Wasserman and Clair (2010) suggest that for modern capitalism in Western liberal democracies, the market ideal paves an equal path under fair rules of competition for *all* members of society. This has resulted in a situation where the same structures that conspire to produce wealth also conspire to produce poverty as part of the natural order of things (7). With Lewis' theory in hand, conservative forces in the United States during the 1960s began to ignore structural issues that might be related to poverty, and to focus on the visible dysfunction of the undeserving individual (Wright 1997:15). Opposition to Lyndon Johnson's War on Poverty, a proudly proclaimed but underfunded federal platform to create a "Great Society," was sufficient to ensure that the field of engagement, as it were, was limited in scope. This opposition was based on the power of the culture-of-poverty discourse. The onus of the government to provide was transferred onto the individual, who was expected to contend with his or her own problems through subsidized education and food programs that might abet personal management.

Lewis himself advised the U.S. Head Start Program that provided nutritional and social counseling and other services to children age 5 and younger.[71] Bourgois criticizes the effectiveness of a program that seeks to reinvent poor slum-dwelling children as bright-eyed, alert students by providing school meals and other supports, while failing to redress the violence, material depravity, and emotional pain of living in slum-like conditions (Bourgois

2001:1995). Once again we enter a moment where we need to avoid the either/or position. If Lewis' position is flawed, do we abandon it completely and deny the characterological components of homelessness? Does the fact that homeless people are resourceful and clever somehow make the fact of their existence more acceptable?

Bourgois points out that much of the negative response by academics to Lewis' portrayal has manifested itself in a political desire to demonstrate the able attributes of the poor, to otherwise shed this mantle of undeserving character cast upon them in the wake of their apparent "hopelessness." While Bourgois criticizes Lewis for his psychological reductionism, his weakly developed cultural model, and his inability to (genealogically) imbricate economic, gender and ideology and culture, he is more critical of the subsequent attempts by some academics to look past the intolerable violence and self-destructive behaviors that Lewis discusses as being universal and inevitable, and, which Bourgois knows from his in-depth field experience, are all too real (Bourgois 2001; Wagner 1993; Harvey and Reed 1996). These features of the life of the poor are empirically valid. They are the sort of symbolic and structural violence that Bourgois speaks to in his current work (2009),[72] by bringing many of Bourdieu's ideas to bear on ethnography of heroin injectors in San Francisco, and are discussed in some of the excerpts from my research you will read. Whether it takes the form of spousal or child abuse, violent assault or self-abusive addictive behaviours, or, more aptly for this book, of people governing themselves in slum-like living conditions without seeking transcendence from this rut, "none of the behaviours or personalities described by Lewis should shock anyone who is familiar with everyday life in the U.S. inner city or Latin American shantytowns" (Bourgois 2001:905).

I think what most of these positions point to is a question of empowerment. On one hand, Lewis measures the poor individual against a neoliberal sense of self-empowerment within an economic structure where one's power really is spending power, and the ability to be solvent. So when the very poor do remarkable things such as building a camp or finding their way into welfare-subsidized homes, conventional imaginaries can interpret these things as converging on popular ways to be a good citizen and obtaining proper power as a citizen.

It seems to be a truism that without a home, a person must be powerless. One of the biggest flaws of the culture-of-poverty debate is that it misinterprets the role of power. As such, it fails to grasp how alternative visions of power might be a useful tool for addressing how to unravel the problem of poverty. The assumption that poverty is the same thing as powerlessness has been a common problem for urban ethnographies in general. It remains so today. By looking at power in terms of its binary expression— less/more, powerful/powerless, dominated/liberated—the popular ethnographic discourses on poverty that emerged in the 1960s and '70s tended to isolate resistance in obvious or clearly observable phenomena such as protest, riot and rebellion. In other words, it defined resistant as the kind of work that *active citizens* might do. Hence resistance is hard to find, given that these responses are empirically rare.

Fairbanks Jr. (2004:49) argues that this "myopia" prevents us from understanding the ways "in which poor subjects are both *effects* and *measures* of political power, and therefore fully political entities." The basic conflict and critical sociological perspectives had tended to place the poor and the homeless under the weight of social-control discourses and the exigencies of the welfare state. Their political emergence was possible only in collective or mass revolutionary undertakings, or as the result of structural breakdowns where new forms of poverty had to be addressed by the state, such as during the Great Depression. Without eschewing the enormous inequalities that persisted and continue to persist between the haves and have-nots, an empowering pragmatic ethnographic approach seeks to understand where the enduring source of this power is imagined by the poor person herself, and for communities of poverty under neoliberalism and late capitalism.

For my generation, educated as we were at a time when the culture of poverty was still a very potent model, the idea that people who fell into the category of "poorest of the poor" were stuck there forever was very common. I include myself here, for I had never thought of myself as poor, nor had I been poor in the sense of being abandoned or exploited by capitalism. I had had full access to its opportunities; my poverty and my homelessness were self-induced. Prior to my own awakening—that rich and detailed life experience of poverty and madness—we had pitied them, if not felt completely helpless to understand how to really help them. I had felt completely hopeless. My own experience into and then out of homelessness and addiction completely shook the foundation of that very limited culture-of-poverty imaginary. And when I left rehab armed with the statistically valid likelihood of less than 20% success in remaining sober over an extended period of time, I sensed an immense frustration with how hard it would be to help others in my position. I was lucky in that sense. I had information that looking forward helped me to make better choices. Understanding which imaginary concepts and systems of knowledge governed popular belief became central to my work, but of more urgency was this question: "How might we change these perceptions: given certain new information, how can we change the world?" My friends and family thought I had been reborn and that my quest was too vast to pursue. But they were not the ones on the streets hearing old conversations about the origins of poverty clashing with newer visions of social change. There were, in places, small groups of homeless people who travelled together and looked out for each other. In fact, even the lone men I had met on the streets had key friends—

other loners—who looked out for them and with whom they had strong bonds. Often the small groups hooked up with others to watch over property and to mark the best squats.

The more I met people on the streets and carried out my research, the more it became clear to me that the streets and the homeless were far more organized than I had imagined, and that some individuals held a certain authority over others in their groups and other groups.[73] While the idea of street families, the fictive kin structures that emerge on the streets, was widely understood (Liebow 1967; Bailey 1972; Anderson 1975), the chronic homeless, the "lifers," had expressed on occasion that the streets were the only place they felt they could fit in or feel empowered.[74] This, we will see later, is vital to understanding Dignity Village and the IHC model, because for some this was the first spatialization of their poverty in which they found their voice and a sense of power.

Housing then satisfies certain material needs. Housing gives you a place to live. But housing is also a physical location in a social world. So there is reason to understand that part of people's goals from housing includes establishing social ties and feeling socially relevant. We understand these vectors of a person's social experience as empowering, and so being housed is part of how we in the West account for personal power. Lisa Larson, who has lived at the village for close to 10 years with her husband Scott, had often commented that living in the village was the first time she felt she could speak freely without being judged. Further, she reported that it was the first community that had offered opportunities to use her voice. While she and Scott imagine moving back into conventional lives, reuniting with friends, her children and family, they are not anxious to leave the safety and sense of community that the village offers.[75] They are content to live there, despite the often unhappy mood of the place, because they feel they have influence over the governance of the village and, therefore, over themselves. In June 2013, she led an impeachment of the CEO and took his place as leader of the village. In her own words, "Not every poor person wants to live with yuppies in neatly appointed neighborhoods." That is a sort of ethnocentric middle-class delusion. At the very least, the village model, and this extended to Tent City, had the promise of uniting people with many conflicting attitudes and personalities under a common locality-based cause and establishing socially dignified roles therein.

Back in 2000–01, however, with disturbing numbers of visible homeless on U.S. and Canadian city streets, it was easy for governments to identify this group as "the poor in general," which in fact left hidden the thousands of others who lived in dubious and insecure housing and poverty off the streets. The structural conditions producing poverty, and the real dimension of poverty and poor housing, remained hidden in the bodies of the visible poor on the streets or isolated in welfare programs.[76]

Insomuch as some people are empowered by the struggle of homelessness, I am in no way arguing that street life is more empowering or desirable when compared to conventionally housed lives. I am not a relativist to the point where I don't recognize unhappy people adapting to poor life conditions and describing them as beneficial. There is also a symbolic and a very actual conventional disempowerment on the streets that is vital to understanding the stigma that the city social imaginary attaches to *being* homeless in general. Concentrated spatializations of poverty like intentional camps confound this already dubious outlook on normal deviant behaviour. Bourgois' sentiment is exactly that we ought not to forget the deplorable human condition that structural violence creates in the lives of the homeless; we should not be distracted from discussions about how to redress systemic poverty merely because a few homeless groups have made successful claims.

Yet the imaginary continuum of debate I mentioned in the beginning of this book suggests that Lewis's legacy populates the imaginary that targets undeserving character in homeless populations, and thereby forces a certain kind of narrative inevitability on them. On the other end, we have views such as mine that try to find ways to empower poor people, or to find the sources of power available to poor people to help them avoid or get out of homelessness.

Chapter Four
POWER, JUSTIFICATIONS AND CRITIQUE

"America! America!
God shed His grace on thee,
And crown thy good with brotherhood
From sea to shining sea!"

Scott and Lisa's place, Dignity Village, 2016. Photo: Eric Weissman.

On July 4, 2011 when I sat with my friends from Dignity Village on the secluded banks of the Columbia River in a little cove, hidden from the public and the cops, looking at the fireworks, they sang "O Canada" for me, as a tribute to my nationality. They didn't know the tune, so it came out in the harmonies and rhythms of "Happy Birthday." It was eerie: Laura B., Dave M., Steve and Carol, Lisa and Scot, all wasted on beer and smoking joints; the bonfire lighting up their faces, as for miles, literally 60 miles up and down the Columbia, fireworks went off to celebrate American independence. I was straight, of course. But the energy and the lighting, the drugs, the explosions, the American flags ... it was like that scene in *Apocalypse Now*, where they reach the last bridge on the river. Every day as the army built it up, the Cong demolished it. They continued to do this while American soldiers died, to allow the generals to claim that they were "keeping the road open."

They sang "Happy Birthday, Happy Birthday, O Canada to you ..." because they had no idea what the words were, but they figured that I was like them—a patriot, above all else. It seemed almost indecent to me that they would be so enraptured in celebration of the same system that marginalized and trivialized them. As I filmed this display, I had to wonder how they could feel so strongly towards a country that was failing them at so many levels. Rather than blame the way that their democracy and the economy worked, they accepted the mistakes they had made, and there they remained. They could see the flaws in their system, but it was easier to blame themselves because they could not see other systems as a solution. I was Canadian after all, and to them, my country was *socialist* because we had universal health care. But patriotism, loyalty, and perseverance mattered most. A month into my fieldwork in 2011, they were at the point of awareness where going any further would have had to lead to an indictment of their perceptions of the American Dream, and that they were not prepared to do. They sang and insisted that I join them but I told them I had a sore throat. I felt that as a result of the conversations we had been having up that point, they had, as Lather had said earlier in this book, entered Derrida's moment of aporia, where to go any further into this discussion of whom and where they were, would lead to the impossibility rather than an inevitability of reinvention. They would not step any closer to that "exquisitely tormented" understanding, but preferred to remain high, and hidden, blinded by the fireworks—the bombs bursting in air. Happy Canada, Happy Canada to you.

4.1 Finding the Power to Act/Acting to Find Power

Based on the three philosophically rooted critical traditions we discussed in chapter two, five key critical sociological approaches can be placed into two groups. The first group includes critical theory of the Frankfurt School, Bourdieu's critical sociology and critical realism. We spoke of these in chapters two and three. In this way of thinking, structural and normative systems control how individuals act by creating narratives and values that can be contested and proven in an objectively knowable reality. Critical action then is empowered by a truthful normative proposition that is either widely held to be true, or that is presented in a contest over normative criteria. Criteria in these situations present certain propositions or moral narratives that people argue about and from which they find justification for their actions in pursuit of a just world based on these narratives of inevitability. Such critical positions stress a macro form of analysis

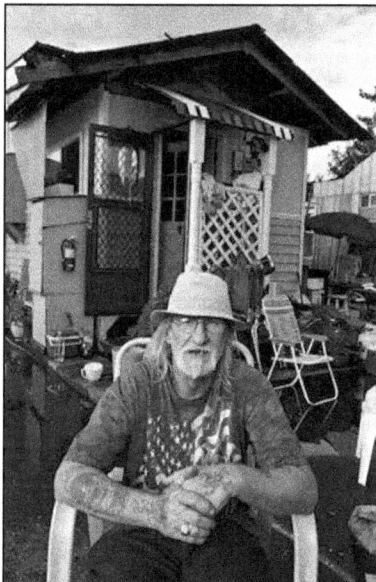

Dave Sullivan, long-time Villager, at his structure. Photo: Nigel Dickson.

where structural reality, observable or not as an objective phenomenon, im-

143

poses experiences of injustice on actors that cause them to question the distribution of power in society. In this case truth gives power, by providing
reasonable cause for action. We can look at Marxist critiques of capital as an
example of how such grand moral-normative critiques identify the truth about
domination and inequality and suggest means of redress. In each of these positions, the ideological root is a critique of very real and knowable capitalist
social structures. All inequalities are to be understood in terms of the way
capital-driven and inhumane systems of accumulation mislead people into
falsely accepting this reality, and that this acceptance is learned in the imbrication of physiological and cultural values that reproduce injustice as a stable
state of affairs over time. The inevitability of our station in life, of addicts
dying in camps is false, but we don't see it because we learn to perform our
roles and to expect such things.

There is a tie here with Lewis's work, as I discussed in chapter three. This is
not a case of people making choices, or having fair and equitable access to
power. Capitalist relations of production are designed to keep some people
down, so a few can stay up. The key to emancipation is to replace the system
with one that transforms the state of social inequality towards greater equality. To create a critical moment for social actors is simply to demonstrate the
falseness of their consciousness or to identify ways to make the criteria of this
truth effective. Truth is power. But it has also been shown that even when
charismatic and powerful leaders emerge to lead so-called revolutions of the
poor against the engines of oppression, just social systems are rarely, if ever,
the result. So these positions paint a pretty dim view of things for poor people
seeking to right social wrongs. Habermas's rejection of his colleagues in the
Frankfurt School was precisely that the imminent transcendence that they
spoke of—the overcoming of the false consciousness produced in them by
capital—failed to occur after World War II, and so simply identifying structural causes and social effects was ineffective for social justice critiques.

If power is seen as similar to wealth and to the ability to impose one's goals
on others (or to promote the collective well-being of one class above that of
other classes), the only just situation is one where the basic antagonism
between wealth and poverty is eradicated. Power is, in this sense, an ability or
a capacity that individuals and groups have, but in varying degrees. The
wealthy capitalists and the social and media institutions they command are
able to compel others to act in ways that are acceptable to them based on self-
serving criteria about what (for example) freedom or autonomy might
mean. So in this asymmetrically powerful social world, social justice can only
happen when equality in all senses of the word is made real. Perhaps that is
why this kind of justice is unheard of in the history of this world. While we
continue to work towards perfect democracy, towards more equal distribution

of resources, we continue to produce inequality and homelessness. We actually need to rethink what power is. Maybe competing visions from beyond the conventionally applied criteria are, whether we like it or not, part of this big question.

A second group of approaches to critique includes Foucault's (1967, 1975, 1991) genealogical critique and (here I emphasize his conceptualization of governmentality) and Boltanski, Chiapello and Thévenot's pragmatic sociology of critique (1996, 2010, 2011). For this group of thinkers, truth does not provide actors with power; power *is* truth. These are largely discourse-oriented approaches that look at how knowledge created about subjects or by them, is empowering and also, potentially overpowering. Understanding how discourses and information become powerful and can create truth often requires a micro level of analysis. Looking at interaction, at how people establish meaning to the world, helps us to understand the ways that individual actors experience power, and come to be political in critical self-transformative processes that occur in a socially constructed and therefore objectively impossible world.

In this model, powerful groups—groups that are not necessarily evil or willing to crush and alienate others—create stories about the world through education, socialization and a number of other dynamic processes and institutions. We produce and employ such narratives in pursuit of our social and personal interests. We want to understand how we see ourselves, argue our position to others, or pursue our goals, and thus "feel" original and free. If we look closely enough, however, we can discern how we have participated in social practices and contributed to narratives that reinforce popular perceptions of justice and self-worth. It is important to note that being taught or convinced to see things a certain way is not always evil. Powerful discourses don't have to alienate us, or be a form of chicanery. In the competition of popular discourses, certain narratives tend to become dominant. In cases where harm and inequality persist, where persecution and violence might occur, we want to understand how certain powerful narratives fuel the social relations that ferment antagonism and persecution. The institutionalization of mental illness and the criminalization of poverty result from the way groups of people with certain ideas come to populate and control knowledge systems, which produce the truths we can consume. They are powerful because they produce the truths we live by. Even if these truths are not designed to oppress or restrain us, they are powerful. And there is room for other ways of thinking to become powerful, too.

To understand critique, then, we must reverse the fundamental arrangement of truth over power, arguing that you cannot mobilize truth to produce power because power is truth. The moral imperative of the three prior approaches was to align actors in just causes that reverse domination. Power is rarely seen as a good thing, but as a force used by the more powerful to subdue less powerful actors.

These last two perspectives understand resistance to other ideas as empowerment and as a necessary type of social relation that makes the social world possible. Power is a function of relationships and compelling narratives we use to navigate the social world and manage our own self-conduct. For these approaches, domination is rare. (Domination is specifically the repressive use of power and force in a social system that requires people to endure unjust situations.) Rather, argumentation, narratives, and discourses emerge over time and become powerful as they find ways of settling into the way people think about themselves, about others and about social problems. These perspectives consider how a social problem comes to be understood as a problem, and then again at how competing narratives on just goals can be learned, incorporated and deployed in the tug of war between competing powerful groups, out of which some things come to be seen as true. Resistance to power is not powerlessness but a form of critique that over time can have unforeseen results.

First, we discuss Foucault's genealogical approach to governmentality as a deconstructive form of critique,[77] in the sense that he seeks to understand how problems come to be imagined as they are by powerful people, subjects, groups and government. Essentially Foucault argues that there is no truth outside of power, that powerful institutions and groups create what societies take as true by delivering powerful discourse and providing technologies of the self though education, medicine, science and so on, by which subjectivities learn what power wants us to think about ourselves and say about others. So social critique wants to ask how a certain way of knowing has come to be thought of by regimes of power. In asking how certain narratives of inevitability come to be understood and embraced, we can begin to discern what has been excluded from that arrangement.

4.2 Foucault's Genealogical Critique and Governmentality

> Genealogy is gray, meticulous, and patiently documentary. It operates on a field of entangled and confused parchments, on documents that have been scratched over and recopied many times (Foucault in Rabinow 1984:76).

Genealogy is a difficult concept to define, and then even harder to easily compare to other forms of historical analysis, including Foucault's prior attachment to "archaeology" (1967, 1969). Foucault's work on governmentality[78] employs a genealogical approach, which has provoked criticism. "Genealogy is characterized as a diagnostic of the present by 'problematizing' taken-for-granted assumptions and *anti-anachronistic* refusal to read the past in terms of the present" (Dean 2010:3). Governmentality, however, is not simply about the government that controls us administratively, but is critical analysis directed towards understanding modes of constructing the self (Delanty 2011:83). Genealogical criticism stands out against classical "critique," such as that associated with the Frankfurt school, as a form of criticism under the frame of "universal norms and truths pointing to a necessary end" (Dean 1991:3). Most importantly, as Dean (1991, 2010) and others (Gordon 1991; Hacking 1999) note, Foucault's genealogical approach carries a certain *burden* of critique, and it cannot remain descriptive or contented with simple observations or the reduction of events to universalizing principles that bear no moral or ethical consequence for society. Genealogy requires us to examine how problems and ideas come to be thought over time by powerful groups or "regimes of truth" so that we end up with a current problematization. Homelessness today is understood in a number of ways that are linked to the negotiation of this definition over hundreds of years. Modern western neoliberalism, which provides the current political and economic context for the kinds of housing critique we are discussing, is the result of specific economic and political processes that are linked to ideas and the people who debated those. Neoliberal ways of thinking did not just appear with a rapid change in political regimes. For Foucault and me, at least, neoliberalism is difficult to pin down or to define, yet, under its grasp, individuals are burdened with managing inevitability while governments do little to interfere.

For example, Foucault asserts that neoliberalism is "not Adam Smith; neoliberalism is not the Gulag on the insidious scale of capitalism" (1978:131). Neoliberalism(s) describe an indefinite range of rationalities and references to a style of liberal government and therefore to speak of an ideal type of neoliberalism is impossible. Rose and Miller (1992) suggest that all rationalities are moral, epistemological and idiomatic. To understand a rationale, therefore, means to discern how these qualities are uniquely manifest.[79] My understanding of the neoliberalism that has governed my generation and continues to reign in the West is that it imposes on the actor the responsibility of self-care and conduct and produces this responsibility as a type of autonomy that, successfully achieved, confirms (the fallacy of) freedom.

Where did neoliberalism come from? In short, in the U.S., shortly after the Great Depression of the 1930s, economic and social policy emerged that was influenced by intellectual movements at the University of Chicago in which the social became re-described as a *form* of the economic (Gordon 1991:42). "Economics thus becomes an 'approach' capable of addressing the totality of human behavior...." (43). Gordon reminds us further that under American neoliberalism, classical positions on the subject—that is, man viewed simply as free-thinking, free-choosing economic man—no longer remain outside the reach of government but are transmuted; "*homo economicus* is *manipulable man*" (43). The manipulation is achieved through direct measures that stimulate economies and by reconfiguration of the worker's subjectivity. Hence the worker is no longer merely a labourer; under neoliberalism, workers are envisioned as producers and consumers—entrepreneurs of themselves (44). In the parlance of economic and political debate, workers become defined not only by the value of their labour, but by the knowledge that they increase their value through hard work, education, training and developing economic capital. A new code of conduct becomes infused with the values of the economy above other moral considerations. Under neoliberalism, the maintenance of this enterprise, this human product as it were, is what comes to be known as "care of the self" and is central to Foucault's critique of governmentality (Foucault 1991; Gordon 1991; Dean 1991; Rose 1993).

The simple narrative produced in this scheme is that of the man and wife and children: the man who works, the wife who cooks and the children who learn to re-enact this history. A citizen works, produces, learns, listens to instructions, follows the law and engages in normal sexual and love relations. A citizen does not engage with those who act out of the order of things. The implication of this for the homeless is that their poverty is a symbol of their failed conduct, and life on the streets is a sort of brutal punishment for millions of people who either chronically or periodically fall in and out of neoliberalism's expectations for conduct and personal government, two facets of life that are increasingly understood in terms of fulfilling economically sensible action. If one fails to self-govern, or cannot self-govern because of temperament or malady, these unfortunate outcomes are seen as inevitable.

Governmentality, "the art of government" as Foucault called it, is a rationalized system for ordering the conduct of citizens through their own self-governing actions, and by systems of government that make that inevitable. Those IHCs that become "legal" or have contracts with cities must encode the conduct of their members commensurate with the laws of the legislative governments that hold power over their charter. "Rules" must be in place. Below are the first five things a would-be Dignity Villager must know. Each one of these rules is violated several times a day by different people, and the rules are frequently used by powerful factions in the village to control the behaviour of villagers or to cast out others. *One must memorize these rules and sign the document*—after that, they are often ignored.

The Five Rules of Dignity Village
(reprinted from the Dignity Village Document 2011)
The following five basic rules apply to residents:
1. **No violence to yourselves or others.**
2. **No theft.**
3. **No alcohol, illegal drugs or drug paraphernalia on-site or within**

a one-block radius.
4. No constant disruptive behavior.
5. Everyone must contribute to the operation and maintenance of the Village. A minimum of 10 hours are required per week.
I understand that Dignity Village is incorporated as a membership-based non-profit organization. By signing this agreement, I become eligible for membership, according to the terms of the bylaws, and recommendation of the Tents and Population Standing Committee. In addition, due to the participatory culture of Dignity Village, I understand that it is sometimes necessary to convene meetings of the members or Village Councillors with less advance notice than required by ORS Chapter 65. Therefore, in signing this agreement, I agree to forego and forfeit all rights to advance notice of emergency meetings of the membership or Village Council, as provided by section 4.10.1 of Dignity Village bylaws. I have read the Dignity Admittance Agreement and agree with its terms and I agree to live by these terms and the rules of the village.
Signature: _____ **Date:** _____

Beyond being reasonable or practical, these rules are intended to make a statement to would-be villagers that their lives will be governed, and that they must be in charge of themselves. This is in essence what governmentality is: a particular way that those in charge govern, by insisting that citizens govern themselves. This is freedom under neoliberalism. Free to self-govern or free to fail. In phrasing this statement as I have, it reads as an indictment of the concept of freedom. This is not the case. This is a more an indictment of how neoliberal institutions and regimes of power benefit from the illusion that the potential to succeed in the world on the basis of freedom is evenly distributed throughout society. It is not. Neoliberal governments have a tendency to sacrifice the well-being of people for the well-being of economic and military complexes. The idea is that if people conduct themselves better, the neoliberal state won't have to look after them so much. To make better sense of this, we have to better understand the concept of conduct.

Foucault imagined *conduct*, as *government*, in very much the way it was used prior to the twentieth century; not only in the commonly used sense as an institutional or other system of managing a population, but also as the way a citizen imagines and proceeds to manage their spiritual and physical well-being, on their own. The government of a citizen's self is a sense of order in one's moral, spiritual and daily life. Hence governmentality is from the outset a concept that incorporates conduct of the group with conduct of the self. In another sense, governmentality implies that the way a citizen manages personal well-being also determines the group's well-being, and so one of the central problems of (neoliberal) governance, regardless of the level, is well-being; conduct should be directed towards the well-being of the self as a means of also achieving the well-being of the group.[80]

In his chapter on governmentality in *The Foucault Effect: Studies in Governmentality* (1991), Foucault offers the following conclusion:

> I would like to say that on second thought the more exact title I would like to have given the course of lectures, which I have begun this year, is not the one I originally chose. 'Security, territory and population': what I would like to undertake is something, which I would term a history of 'governmentality'. By this word I mean three things:
>
> 1. The ensemble formed by the institutions, procedures, analyses and reflections, the calculations and tactics that allow the exercise of this very specific albeit complex form or power, which has as its target population, as its principal form of knowledge political economy, and as its essential technical means apparatuses of security.
>
> 2. The tendency, which over a long period and throughout the West, has steadily led towards the pre-eminence over all other forms (sovereignty, discipline, etc.) of this type of power which may termed government, resulting on the one hand, in the formation of a whole series of specific governmental apparatuses and, on the other, in the development of a whole complex of *savoirs*.
>
> 3. The process, or rather the result of the process, through which the state of justice of the Middle Ages, transformed into the administrative state during the fifteenth and sixteenth centuries, gradually becomes 'governmentalized' (Foucault 1991:103).

Under neoliberal governmentality, power is not just repressive or dominating. Government is creative and unites citizen subjects with knowledge produced by society. Government's very purpose is the creation of freely choosing subjects as a function of political economy (Dean 2010; Delanty 2011; Rose 1999). As Lemke (2000) suggests, for Foucault,

> *Domination* is a particular type of power relationship that is both stable and hierarchical, fixed and difficult to reverse. Foucault reserves the term "domination" to "what we ordinarily call power" (1988b, p. 19). Domination refers to those asymmetrical relationships of power in which the subordinated persons have little room for manoeuvre because their "margin of liberty is extremely limited" (1988b, p. 12). But states of domination are not the primary source for holding power or exploiting asymmetries, on the contrary they are the effects of technologies of government. Technologies of government account for the systematization, stabilization and regulation of power relationships that may lead to a state of domination (Lemke 2000:6).

On the basis of this definition, then, we can say that domination exists but that it is not the most effective way to govern. So who is dominated and who is left to self-govern? We find that states are very good at dealing with those who do not self-govern well. They have two ways of doing this. On the one hand, they can ignore or underservice problematic populations, something they have done to the poor and the people with mental health issues for three decades. On the other, they can criminalize and prosecute unpopular expressions of freedom, such as squatters and those with mental illness who voluntarily go off their medications. Squatters are arrested and fined. Mental health patients are often remanded under mental hygiene laws. I include them in this discussion with the homeless because we find that the chronically homeless very often have a mental health diagnoses. This speaks less to the choices they make then the choices neoliberal states on how to govern problematic populations.

The central questions in governmentality studies are "how" questions: how we govern ourselves and how we are governed by others (Dean 1999, 2010). This approach differs from theories of the state. These theories are rationalist discourses and "may be characterized by: a state-centric position that anticipates the global environment as anarchical, political action is carried out by atomized independent actors; the bases for analysis is a positivist and clearly defined subject-object position where theory invests actors with predefined potentials, and the world with probable outcomes from certain types of actions; and actor's political agency is external to their social lives" (Che 2007: 3).

Elsewhere I have argued about a governmentality of the poor and the homeless that succeeds at imposing a sense of undeserving character on those we presume to have failed at their economic role. To flesh out this problem let me suggest, very simply following Dean (1991) and Foucault (1978), that historically for sovereigns the problem of government was relatively simple. A monarch held supreme power over life or death, and sovereign power worked though legitimate or illegitimate means (by taking that life or through authority of the right to take that life). The monarchy, claimed to be empowered by God, determined what justice meant. Poverty and charity were managed by local parishes, religious orders, and, until the advent of capital, the homeless were understood as divine in the sense that Christ was a peasant, charity was a virtue and poverty inhered the symbolic quality of piety (Bahr 1973; Marx and Engels 1975; Wrightson and Levine 1995). Marx characterizes the poor under monarchy, prior to capital, as "those whose property consists of life, freedom, humanity and citizenship of the state, who own nothing except themselves" (Marx and Engels 1975:256). Sherover (1979) reminds us that, according to Marx, the poor had the mystical ability to see beyond the materialist and vain attachment to gold and (in this case, an anecdote about wood thieves) wood (56). Marx said, "The poor are not deceived by an "abject materialism, which enthrones the immoral, irrational and soulless abstractions of a particular material object" (1975:262 in Sherover 1979:58). In the West, the poor therefore continued to inhere this essential, incorruptible simplicity that deserved pity if not compassion, at least until their poverty became a device for capital, and a problem for governance (Marshall 1950; Marx and Engels 1975; Dean 1991; Proacci; 1991). Governmentality is of no use to sovereigns or dictators because under sovereignty and fascism, leaders have irrefutable power usually enforced by oppression. Try to do "your own thing," in those conditions. Freedom is an end-game. It is something one reaps in the spiritual afterlife, despite whatever injustices she faces in this life.

Foucault reminds us that governmentality begins with the separation of the state from the direct service of the sovereign.[81] The state was very much concerned with proper management of populations and encouraging economic health. Thus the state for Foucault begins, "not in the negative and pejorative sense we give it today, but in a full positive sense. The state is governed according to rational principles which are intrinsic to it and which cannot be derived solely from natural or divine laws or the principles of wisdom" (1978:212–13).[82]

The ethical implications of "conduct" appear from the reflexive qualities of the word *conduct*. Insomuch as conduct as a noun suggests a form of behaviour exercised within or compared to the behaviour of others, "to conduct oneself" means to gauge one's choices of behaviour in relation to others, as a conscious decision and is therefore ethical and moral (Dean 2010:17). Government is dependent, therefore, on the way people come to know about themselves and the world around them; on language and vocabularies, symbolic systems and signs, and on administrative and bureaucratic mechanisms, each of which contributes to specific knowledge about a governable subject. There are two sides to governmentality, then; the first is a subject who is governed, and the second is a subject who governs him or herself.

In *Technologies of the Self* Foucault (1988) argues that knowledge created about a subject, and therefore, that can be held over it, creates power over the subject. Within this classification or narrative understanding of one's own subjectivity then, is the key to freedom, a freedom gained through self-control (Foucault 1988:18–19).

> I conceived of a rather odd project: not the evolution of sexual behavior but the projection of a history of the link between the obligation to tell the truth and the prohibitions against sexuality. I asked: How had the subject been compelled to decipher himself in regard to what was forbidden? It is a question of the relation between asceticism and truth" (1982:16).[83]

Foucault was interested not only in how sexual rules come to be thought of over time, but also, in a more general sense, how it is that a person will act in

ways that are forbidden to them by some ways of thinking, or that bear some heavy cost.
Foucault writes:

> As a context, we must understand that there are four major types of these "technologies," each a matrix of practical reason: (1) technologies of production, which permit us to produce, transform, or manipulate things; (2) technologies of sign systems, which permit us to use signs, meanings, symbols, or signification; (3) technologies of power, which determine the conduct of individuals and submit them to certain ends or domination, an objectivizing of the subject; (4) technologies of the self, which permit individuals to effect by their own means or with the help of others a certain number of operations on their own bodies and souls, thoughts, conduct, and way of being, so as to transform 1 themselves in order to attain a certain state of happiness, purity, wisdom, perfection, or immortality (ibid).

There is no way to anticipate that the personal habits or conduct of populations will embody all that is ideally framed for them in rational policies or rules. It is out of this range of practical reason employed by subjects towards or away from normalized practice that the state finds reason to exercise its disciplinary power[84] to control or suppress. It is also within this range that individuals can define for themselves the habits or actions they accept or reject and is, therefore, the source of their own freedom, their own power. It is perhaps why people in the village behave so inconsistently—as a means to *feel* powerful. Where Bourdieu (1967) had seen *habitus* as a system for restricting the action of actors within culturally reproduced values and goals, and thereby expected their power to be a socially and culturally restricted commodity, for Foucault power is not total control by subjects, or by forces external to them, like the state. Power is relational and fluid; freedom is regulated not withheld (Dean 1999; Foucault 1977, 1988, 1991; Rose and Miller 1992).

Governmentality, then, can be understood as a way of describing how subjects are empowered by the freedom they are accorded by regimes of truth, and the patterns of actions such rationalizations produce, within strategies of governance (Dean 2010:37; Foucault 1991:78-80) as revealed by (for example) the language inherent to laws and policies regarding housing. Once again, governmentality studies ask *how* questions: how did a certain subjectivity come to be understood that way; how does an alcoholic come to see themselves as suffering a disease? Of particular interest to my research is how homeless people who fight for 1HC understand freedom and autonomy. For Dignity Village in particular, and for the many others 1 have met who fight for the right to build shacks, to self-govern in poverty, what does it mean to be free? If these are things that Ibrahim says we must work towards, then towards what, and against what impediments? Foucault has written,

> On the other hand, I do not think that there is anything that is func-
> tionally by its very nature absolutely liberating. Liberty is a practice.
> So there may, in fact, always be a certain number of projects whose
> aim is to modify some constraints, to loosen, or even to break them,
> but none of these projects can, simply by its nature, assure that peo-
> ple will have liberty automatically, that it will be established by the
> project itself. The liberty of men is never assured by the institutions
> and laws that are intended to guarantee them. This is why almost all
> of these laws and institutions are quite capable of being turned
> around. Not because they are ambiguous, but simply because "lib-
> erty" is what must be exercised (1984:245).

I take this to mean that there is ambiguity in the underlying values: liberty, freedom, or autonomy. And in this sense we are all free-lancing in ways, riding on and off the edge of liminality in pursuit of ourselves.

In this sense, Bevir argues that the two Foucaults, the *excitable* and the *composed*, use hostility towards the subject as an indictment of agency and as an endorsement, thus confounding what is already a difficult contemplation: the apposition to structure and agency. On the one hand, it seems reasonable that no subject stands outside of the social context, and on the other, rejecting autonomy does not necessarily spell a rejection of agency. "Different people adopt different beliefs and perform different actions against the background of the same social structure, so there must be at least an undecided space in front of these structures where individuals decide what beliefs to hold and what actions to perform" (Bevir 1999:68). In this ambiguous, unformed space we will locate the ideas of homeless people trying to change the tempo of their narrative inevitability by fighting for their rights to housing.

4.3 Critique, Resistance and Power

In certain ways, Foucault's governmentality project is about the limits self-governing imposes on actors, and therefore it is also equally about the condi-tions that make struggle and resistance possible for actors. For Foucault all these struggles revolve around the question, "Who are we? ... To sum up, the main objective of these struggles is to attack not so much 'such and such' an institution of power, or group, or elite, or class, but rather a technique, a form of power" (1982:82). While it is important to understand the previous transfor-mations of knowledge and power within historical circumstances that shape governance, it is also important to understand how actors come to understand themselves as beings, as subjects within a system that asserts its rationales upon them, and as subjects with power to comply or resist. It is the subject that exemplifies power, not the other way around. This understanding is summed up thusly by Foucault:

> This form of power applies itself to immediate everyday life which categorizes the individual, marks him by his own individuality, attaches him to his own identity, imposes a law of truth on him which he must recognize and which others have to recognize in him. It is a form of power that makes individuals subjects. There are two meanings of the word "subject": subject to someone else by control and dependence; and tied to his own identity by a conscience or self-knowledge. Both meanings suggest a form of power that subjugates and makes subject to (ibid).

What Foucault has instructed us to do in a way is to look at how the present state of power relations unites groups of individuals with the state through regimes of practice such as court or health care systems, and then to ideas about themselves that are linked in various ways through techniques that produce identities, or "subjectivities"—identities that are at once caught up in the power of others, and in their own sense of it, too. The procedures for gathering, formulating and disseminating knowledge therefore must be understood in order to understand how subjects understand themselves. Hence scientific discourses, juridical proclamations and political dogmas are examples of commonly accepted types of knowledge that critique must challenge.

It might be further argued from Foucault's position that knowledge creates a mental or analytic space in the realm of rationalities, but also in the body of the subject herself. Knowledge imbricates with the potential for action, compliance, and rejection of rules, codes or other persons, by undergirding this analytic space and underpinning such possibilities for power.

In the case of this book, this suggests understanding how homelessness has been problematized by dominant political and economic rationalities; but further—and this is where much of the literature is weakest—in how the homeless come to problematize themselves as relatively empowered and deserving identities, as "subject to someone else by control or dependence and tied to [their] own identity by self-conscience or self-knowledge" (ibid).

Wrapped up in this is the crucial separation of power from domination. Power is not destructive or restrictive. Power, out of its desire to know, creates objects. But it does not wish to subdue. Ideally, power is about understanding what freedom requires and approaching that ideal by constructing social, political and moral practices around that knowledge. Foucault tells us:

> When one defines the exercise of power as a mode of action upon the actions of others, when one characterizes these actions by the government of men by other men—in the broadest sense of the

term—one includes an important element: freedom. Power is exercised only over free subjects, and only insofar as they are free. By this we mean individual or collective subjects who are faced with a field of possibilities in which several ways of behaving, several reactions and diverse comportments, may be realized. Where the determining factors saturate the whole there is no relationship of power; slavery is not a power relationship when man is in chains (790).

Foucault cautions against notions of essential freedom and essential power. "Power exists only when it is put into action ... but it is not by nature the manifestation of consensus" (788). Power, unlike oppression through force or domination though violent means, works indirectly on subjects by creating possibilities, ranges of possible action that fall within its desires, and thereby suggest a certain freedom on the part of those engaged within a relation of power (789). For Foucault, it appears that freedom is better described as the perpetual antagonism between the will of the subject and the forces that would hem it in or steer it in a given direction. Freedom, therefore, is a value that exists within rather than outside relationships between people, as subjects

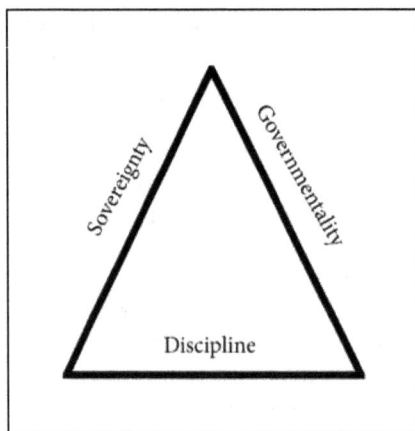

Foucault's triangle of power.

and "governments" charged with conducting their own affairs and well-being, and between people as subject to powerful regimes of knowledge promulgated through practice and governance, such as housing programs or other state programs and policies. Freedom is not an absolute value that exists outside of this relational probability (786). Hence in Foucault's genealogical history of the present, understanding a governmentality of poverty requires social critique to discern the probability of freedom within the historical conditions of possibility in which the subjects being examined are placed. That's what we will do in the next chapter.

Though we understand that societies defined by discipline have been usurped by neoliberal government, disciplinary capacity remains as a part of the triangle of power. In this light, we can look at the evictions enforced by the police of the activists leading up to the successful claim as examples of the sate demonstrating its sovereign domination of the poor. But under neoliberalism, such vulgar demonstrations of disciplinary power are not feasible to steer populations. Foucault said:

It must also master all the forces that are formed from the very constitution of an organized multiplicity; it must neutralize the effects of counter power that spring from them and which form a resistance to the power that wishes to dominate it: agitations, revolts, spontaneous organizations, coalitions-anything that may establish horizontal conjunctions. Hence the fact that the disciplines use procedures of partitioning and verticality; that they introduce, between the different elements at the same level, as solid separations as possible; that they define compact hierarchical networks; in short, that they oppose to the intrinsic, adverse force of multiplicity the technique of the continuous, individualizing pyramid . They must also increase the particular utility of each element of the multiplicity, but by means that are the most rapid and the least costly, that is to say, by using the multiplicity itself as an instrument of this growth (1984:207).

It is easier to help people govern in a way that is conducive to powerful narratives than to expend the resources to force people into roles they do not want. Part of this is helping people to choose to live in conventional homes in normal neighborhoods and to otherwise be as manageable as possible. Since space is not just physical but mental, too, it is possible to carry this sense of self-governance and reification of idealistic freedom into situations that most conventional citizens would fear.

The events in John Boy's life again underscore the complicated relationship between freedom and poverty. After being kicked out of the village in 2011, he had nowhere to live but his van. This is not an unusual case; there are no statistics, but it is well-known on the street and in food banks that tens of thousands of Americans are living in their cars. This descriptive passage from my monograph visualizes the experience of democratic denial, which is my way of saying that *democracy is broken.*

> I had been wondering about John Boy. I had heard rumors that he had come by and asked about me one day while I was out. But I hadn't seen him. Dave told me he wasn't looking good. "But you know John Boy. John Boy's John Boy!"
> "There he is now," Dave said....
> A little while later, I drove John Boy in my rental car, a Ford Fusion I had exchanged for the Subaru, so I could buy him some gas. We talked about the incident while I drove. The camera was mounted on my dash. He did hit the guy. He did think that TC was a deadbeat and a rat, and he would, if the situation presented itself again, do it over. "I miss the village, but I don't need it anymore," he said. "I have to make some moves, and it was time. It

wasn't right me being a leader, the Chair, and all that, and hitting a person, but there was two of us and he wasn't any angel, and he should be out too! That's what's gonna kill this place, anyway, all those little drug gangs and stuff. There's no balance. There was a fight. How can one person only be accused, be responsible for a fight? Violence of any kind is not tolerated! Fact is they wanted me out, so they could get their own people in council and I fucking blew it. Fuck them. Fuck this. And it's too bad because this place, the village, is really important." As I slowed to turn into the gas station, he looked at me and said, "I just hope I didn't fuck up your faith in the place."

Why would he worry about my opinion? I had enjoyed meeting him the year before and interviewing him, but who was I? For the first time since I'd got there, I realized that the villagers had distinct expectations from me. I pulled up in the queue to the pump. "Well, you're here," he said, "and the first thing you find out is I ain't here no more. And no one told you until you get here. That chokes me up. That ain't right. And it is really my fault for

John Boy in his van. Photo: Nigel Dickson.

fucking up in the first place, I guess." I tried to calm him. I told him it was all okay. "Everything happens for a reason" and other common phrases. "It all makes sense ten years later."

After a moment of silence, I told him what was really bothering me. "I just look at you and it worries me. You can't tell me you aren't doing meth." He said nothing for a moment. It was hot, sitting in the queue for the pump, and the smell of gasoline overtook us in the van as the guy on his motorcycle in front of the line overfilled his tank. John Boy took it in with a deep haul and laughed. I get that, I get that he liked the smell. (It is interesting how many of us addicts, in recovery or not, enjoy that biting, gaseous aroma. And skunk too.) "To tell ya the truth ..." he said, "... I prefer smack, but I don't do much of anything these days." The motorcyclist pulled away and I pulled up to the pump. I put the car in park. He asked, "Can you spot me ten bucks for gas?" John Boy filled up the small gas tank he had brought and I also bought a couple of sodas and ice cream bars for us.

On the drive back, we didn't say much. He asked me how long I was staying and he suggested we get out and see Portland together. It was a real shame to see John Boy like that. Even though he had been using substances when he'd lived at the village and when we had first met, at least he had been maintaining his structure. He had some order in his life, and was getting involved.

We drove past a stretch of riverside mansions, and one of the most exclusive golf courses in Portland. The villagers used to collect stray golf balls and sell them, but the golf course management had put an end to that when villagers started lingering around the course too often. With the car windows open, I could hear racing car engines off in the distance. He told me that they were coming from a track where he and some of the other villagers worked once a week, doing security and other odd jobs for cash. He didn't seem jumpy or edgy, he was smiling, and I wanted to believe that this was the real image of John Boy, driving down the open road in the sun, with the wind blowing in the window, arm crooked on the door, enjoying a haul off his cigarette. Was it possible, I asked myself, to be content with this lifestyle? So I had to ask him, based on the video shot back in 2010. "John Boy. Last year you said, and these are pretty close to your words, you said, 'This is America and I can be anyone I want to be.'"

"Yeah, I remember that, in my structure. I'd like to see that sometime."

I made the right turn onto Sunderland Ave., and I asked him if he didn't mind that I stop for a moment. We pulled over about 150 yards from the berm. A beat-up camper van we had not seen before was parked there. A young Afro-American man was cleaning stuff out of the back of the van.

"He'll learn pretty quick," John Boy said.

"What do you mean? Do you think the cops will roust him?" I asked.

John Boy looked at me like I was the greatest fool he had ever met. He propped his chin up and cocked his head back. "The cops? Not the cops. Eric. How many black guys have you seen in there?" he asked, pointing directly at the village.

"Well, I ..." I stumbled. I hadn't seen any, but the village did have a few native folks and a couple of gay people so I ... "What are you saying, the village is discriminating?" I asked.

"Naw, I ain't saying nothing. Nobody knows what to do in there...."

We watched the young man as he tried to unload a big box of old clothing. A cat leapt out of the van and he hustled after it, trapping it in the thick hedge next to the moving company yard. He picked up the cat and kissed it. Then scolded it. Returning to the van, he opened the side door and we could make out a couple of other cats.

John Boy smirked at the man. "Well, he might get in. He's perfect for that place. Ya never know. They're supposed to let anyone who needs it get in if there is room." John Boy kept his eyes on the man. I had to get out of the car. The aroma inside was beginning to sour from the gas, from his clothes. The sun was heating it up.

I asked, "Well, can you?"

He turned to me. "Can I what? I forget what we were talking about."

I tethered the conversation. "You still feel that way, you are free to do anything you—?"

He turned away from the man, who was, by then, fiddling with his headlight. He looked me deeply in the eyes. "This is America, Eric, and anyone can be anything they wanna be. I am doing what I want to do, for right now. I'm free."

If this was freedom, I wanted nothing to do with it.

A mentor of mine had told me. "Remember, governmentality is always bad. It is never really a good thing because it forces us into molds of ourselves that we think are good for us, but really all they do is stop us from seeking what is missing in our lives." For John Boy, it was true: he had no clock to punch, no job to be at, and no responsibilities, but he lived in his van and suffered horrible addictions. John Boy's story includes a lot of mistakes he made, but to see him in that van, decorated with stars and stripes seemed to me to be a desperate attempt to convince himself that he was the broken one, not the system, and this to me again, was indicative of a certain evil governmentality. It was domination of the mind, and after that what good would have been autonomy anyway?

4.4 Pragmatic Sociology of Critique

Another critical perspective that links critique and power is pragmatic sociology of critique. In early work, Boltanski and Thévenot ([1991] 2006) and then more recently Boltanski (2011) investigate the pragmatic understanding and experience of normative orders called "cités" that produce repertoires of justifications that actors use to critically navigate the world. In this perspective, social life, and society are about interruptions, conflicts, claims and change, not stable order. Pragmatic sociology is sometimes referred to as the "sociology of critical capacity" (Blokker and Brighenti 2011:1) or (the term I use here) the pragmatic sociology of critique (Boltanski 2011).

As a means to reunite social analysis with the moral political disposition that years of post-structuralism had all but stripped away, Boltanski has said, "Moral sociology should be understood as an attempt to reinsert, in the analysis of the action of persons in society, the reason for acting and the moral exigencies that these persons give themselves, or want to give themselves, if not by way of 'ideals'" (Boltanski 2005:20). Hence, its goals are essentially the same as mine, except I have used ethnographic storytelling as the driving mechanism for arriving at such knowledge.[85]

One of the key departures from critical sociology is that this newer approach invests the common actor with the capacity to be deluded or inspired, and hence to be understood as a locus for critique; whereas critical sociology, and much of the Marxist tradition, uses Engels' conception of a false consciousness to strip the actor of any self-contained potency, and to render him critically ineffective at the personal level (Marcuse 1964; Boltanski and Thévenot (2006).[86] Rather than looking for how the world is kept sane and ordered, this is a view of the world as a threatening place dominated by conflict between persons, groups and between persons and institutions. Critical moments happen all the time but are made more precarious by institutional and administrative failures, all which lead to Boltanski's "hermeneutic contradiction."

Hermeneutic contradiction is the critical moment in the space opened by the discontinuity between "the forms of domination in a certain social order from a position of exteriority ..." and "from within, by actors involved in disputes, and inserted into sequences of critique and justification, of highly variable levels of generality" (50). Boltanski discusses specific moments of social life that require the justification of action (Boltanski 2011 and also Boltanski and Thévenot 1999, 2006; Boltanski and Chiapello 2005). In situations of dispute, the need arises to examine the grounds of a complaint, to assign blame, or to address competencies out of which new agreements are reached (1999:359). The dispute hinges on the system of justifications that underlies this approach, and it is this moment that represents *moments critiques*, or "critical moments" (ibid). The moment is defined by the critical activity of persons in unusual moments of crisis. The crisis might emerge as a shift in a traditional occupational relationship, such as when a union and an employer begin to diverge on employment policies, or when a homeless community comes to realize that the promises of housing authorities will never be met. It is this process of realizing that most critiques, perched on foundational premises, have difficulty understanding.

Boltanski and Thévenot argued correctly that this is a very reflexive moment in which the actor, or a group of actors acting independently in terms of the reflexive process, engages antecedent narratives about the way things are done, or should be accomplished, and in this way provides a story that links past and present with a sense of the future that makes sense (1999:360). The critical moment where the critique becomes a critical action depends on when and how successfully the actor shares this discontent or fear with other actors who then, in an unanticipated result, in the sense that we have no way of predicting from outside how it might take effect, join within that narrative and a "scene" results (ibid). While it is understood that socialization, schools, experts, media and other agents of informing and nurturing are efficacious in creating the antecedent narratives, it is also understood that the distribution and range of such narratives is so diversely distributed across actors, that the potential for conflict and for critique is high. Such conflictual scenarios invoke various systems of justification, that is, that accusers, critics and defendants each have to reproduce acceptable narratives of justification, by which the critical claim is either refuted or recognized as legitimate by other actors. For Boltanski, there is no single measure of equivalence nor a universal basis on which to gauge justification. There is no external truth that can be imposed into every situation, nor a universal series of justifications that must be employed by groups produced in critiques of domination. Such universal explanations amount to nothing more than Utopias (365). As a bridge between universal formalism and unlimited pluralism, Boltanski and Thévenot (1991) offer the "possibility of a limited plurality of principles of equivalence." Instead of attributing the different systems of justifications to different groups, as traditional sociology would, or to powerful regimes of knowledge as would Foucault, Boltanski and Thévenot attribute the plurality to varied situations.

The implication for the actor is that one must be able to shift from situation to situation at various points during the day, week, year, career and lifetime. The critical experience is not simply a result of social or economic inequality. Justness is something which applies to the many social places people occupy as part of the complex nature of social life. One might find recourse to religious texts and criteria in planning a marriage or to business laws and ethics in forging a work relationship, but rarely are such systems of justification, or criteria interchangeable. Similarly, it means one must have the skills or knowledge of what types of justification are relevant in different situations and not impose justifications from one situation on another. Being legitimate in one situation means applying the relevant knowledge and actions to that experience, and in the case of dispute or negotiation, to invoke the logic of that regime of justice. We can revisit the concept of the Gray Zone. We can look at it now as a way of voiding the inherent truth of some situations, because we cannot find the means in our experience to justify or resolve them. There is a basic way to experience disagreements where pre-existing narratives of inevitability exist.

Boltanski and Thévenot ([1991] 2006) reviewed a spate of classical political philosophical texts to understand how notions of equivalence and humanity were incorporated over time into the practices of organizations, cities, people, and the like. They identified different principles of equivalence and suggested a model by which they can be said to support justifiable claims. In sum, they found that in cases of dispute (non-violent), there were common constraints that shape the behaviour of people involved; arguments must be based on strong evidence and demonstrate a serious desire to converge on resolution of the dispute (Boltanski and Thévenot 1999:366). The majority of the sources they reviewed were less concerned with force or power, than with understanding political and social equilibrium. Hence they found an important theme: that within these documents and codes, human beings are perceived of as sovereign and separated beings, yet they are united by the fundamental value of equality.

Boltanski and Thévenot regard persons as essentially equal. Yet principles of order of equivalence and worth do exist that tend to separate out exceptional persons and desires from the ordinary. Such exclusionary values, at the same time, provide a common measuring stick by which to provide actors with a sense of place in different situations. While the qualities that might define these standards shift, it is suggested that these qualitative measures of worth play a role in the justifications people employ in daily life. The critical moment is exactly the moment when these standards of worth are called into question (367). We have two choices in these moments—retreat into the Gray Zones of life, or enter a dispute with reality. Into these disputes enter reality tests, which enable judgments based on grounded and legitimate agreement and offer a resolution to disputes.

The justifications that one might need to call up in the course of a day are summed up as estimations of worth peculiar to "common worlds" or cités (Boltanski and Chiapello, [1999] 2005; Boltanski and Thévenot [1991] 2006). It is from the roles and narratives that each of these worlds prescribes or creates that individuals passing though these worldly identities at any given time can find recourse to justification arguments.

The first world is the world of inspiration, based on St. Augustine's City of God. Worth is based on one's relationship to the external source from which all worth is determined. It neither asks for rewards or recognition, nor requires such to provide worth. Recognition of others is completely unnecessary. Worth is measured by a sense of calm, transcendence, grace, and emotional stability. There is a sense that this world is governed by a universal sense of transcendent immaterialism; however, it is not dogmatic, nor foundational on other aspects of the lived world.

The second world is the domestic world. Worth is determined based on kinship, lineage, and estate. Having a family, and being recognized within that structure as fulfilling the duties of one's respective role, is vital. One is a good leader, a good reciprocator, delegator, or distinguished, and straightforward (371). The third world is the world of renown, which is based on Hobbes's Leviathan (371). In a domestic world, worth is based on one's value in a hierarchical chain of highly regarded commitments, but in the world of renown, worth is determined solely by other people's opinions. Conventional signs of public esteem secure stability; their absence or rejection become points of personal conflict.

Drawing on Rousseau's *The Social Contract*, in the fourth world, the civic world, people have worth to the degree that they are participants in the activities of membership in society. One is a good labourer, a good citizen, and a contributor to the general well-being of the group. Beings are perceived of here not in their role as individuals, but as collective beings and citizens. Important persons are members of federations, delegates, public communities, volunteers and the like (372). The fifth world is the market world. It is loosely based on Adam Smith's Wealth of Nations. Important persons here are buyers and sellers. They are worthy when they are rich, and connect to one another in competitive relationships aligned with the market (372). Lastly is the industrial world, where worth is measured by efficiency. Great persons are experts. Lowly persons are unskilled, poor or homeless. Worth is productive, efficient, calculating, effective. Relationships are said to be harmonious when they are in sync, measurable, and stabilized (Basaure 2011:373).

Because persons move in and out of these worlds, criticism can result when they participate in one world but import reality tests from another. In other words, in the case of the "shantytown" or IHC, no longer content with the tidbits tossed their way, the homeless strike and campaign and make an appeal to justice embodied in the constitutional laws that govern poverty. Emergency campground laws also exist in the civic world, and afford the poor an opportunity to justify their critique. Similarly, the same poor person cannot enter a business and demand money or support on the basis of being deserving under a civic sense of justification, because in the industrial world, they have no such claim. "The situation is then criticized as unfair because a kind of worth relevant inside one world has been carried into another" (373). The underlying principle on which the test is based remains unchallenged, and denunciation of the other, the critique or its rejoinder, is that the worth test has been inappropriately applied to conditions where it has no merit. So one source of conflict is assuming justification in one world based on a narrative of justice from another, when the opposing narratives are not interchangeable.

For that reason, claims resistant to IHC begin by calling them shantytowns in order to cast this form of community in anachronism and doubt. The counter-justification comes not from within, but from conventionally minded actors, who see it as an argument whose justifications in the civic world are outdated or incorrect altogether. Furthermore, when critics assail the image of Dignity Village and other camps as lawless dens of iniquity that are failing in their economic, transitional housing and social goals, they see a microcosm of many worlds that fails to justify itself on economic, domestic and other worths. The critique of which IHC is a part is very much one of proving the

worth of this kind of community to the justifications brought onto it by various worlds, but on the basis of new justifications it is fighting to implant into
them. This is the struggle that defined the early founders of Dignity Village.
This is the struggle that the founders of the new Rest Area movement are
engaged in. They are trying to justify themselves in terms of a new narrative
that has not yet been written, and so they find resistance.

Part of this means changing the perception of a shantytown to that of an
IHC, but this is hard to do because the name *intentional community* itself is
sufficiently vague. For conventional justification arguments, the village seems
radical or, worse, ambiguous. In this perception, it is a shantytown. Ambiguity
is more frightening and problematic to external critique because it is not clear
what criteria are to be used. At least a radical lawless den of iniquity can be
criticized and shuttered on the basis that it breaks laws or is a threat, but a
place that is poorly defined and therefore open to many positions is harder to
place.

A more crucial and radical critique occurs when from within the world,
one attempts to change the narrative on which justification based. In this case,
the critique emerges as a critical action where the aim is to replace a test with
an altogether new idea or one from another world. An example of this is when
environmentalists enter the industrial world and fight for greener industrial
practices, or when the homeless claim land and build housing regardless of
civic codes forbidding such use. Their claim is moral and civic, yet the argument is not coded in the dominant understandings of these worlds.

One of the very positive aspects of this approach is that though it posits six
ideal types, scholars also suggest that the types are rarely as pure as they
seem. The question of purity is important, for the more impure a world or a
situation or the more ambiguously it might be defined by elements of different
worlds, the more likely there are to be conflicts between reality tests and
worth. There is a veritable degree of ambiguity in these situations, or what
they call *situations troubles*. In the case of homeless persons making claims on
housing space, a claim within the civic world, one might see homeless people
with tents, placards, shopping carts, facing off against police with barricades,
bullhorns and city bylaw codes. The more objects from differing worlds enter a
situation, the more likely there is to be conflict of some kind. Once again we
get a sense that material things have efficacy if not agency in social critique.

There are many reasons why this seems an appropriate way to understand
the difficulty facing IHC in general, and Dignity Village and R2DToo in particular. In the sense that Boltanski et al. present objects, the tent camp or IHC as
a bounded parcel, a container of questionable social relations and a physical
"eyesore," creates the likelihood of conflict with other worlds. The way I am
trying to shape it, Dignity Village is a particularly ambiguous world of worlds
where liminality defines the justifications created by actors caught up in the

pragmatic navigation of extreme poverty. This concentrated spatialization of liminality that is the village, therefore, provokes critique of various kinds.

R2DToo, which I discuss at length later, is even more of a site of conflict because it remains fixed in the central business area. It is literally a tent camp with outhouses, homeless people lining up outside, and frequent media coverage; a space that combines the objects and performance of poverty that city councilors had wanted to avoid with Dignity Village. In the next chapter we will discuss how the emergence of Dignity Village was conditional on it being put out of sight to mitigate the impact of objects and ideas that confounded conventional views on urban space. So why is R2DToo allowed to remain in the city core? R2DToo provides an incontrovertible homage to the liminal space between conventional and poor worlds.

By way of indexing the intermixing of worlds and worth and tests, pragmatic sociology of critique suggests that by overlapping the six worlds one can see probable loci of conflict and critique. For example, the domestic world, where personal relationships and strong character are the keys to worth, finds as problematic the juridical and arbitrary nature of the civic world, where character and lineage are usurped by universalized laws and codes. The world of inspiration is going to have difficulty with the industrial since the latter is destructive and self-serving, mundane and material, and the former measures worth on the absence of such materialism. I am suggesting that the IHC is a liminal world, much as homelessness is, and insomuch as it is emerging, it is in the process of creating its own justifications. So when we look at where these models are, we can think of this argumentation as an extension or new point in the temporal experience of the social critique we started looking at in chapter two. It is very hard to pinpoint starts and ends in such critique. But it is possible by looking at the case studies to determine how power, now understood from Foucault as a form of resistance and as a measure of social relations, has been able to push and pull at opposition, leading to a shift in extant practices and the assertion of new kinds of justifications into housing paradigms.

Boltanski suggests that the outcome of disputes is not always the displacement of one justification over another. There can be compromise. Boltanski points out that compromises are often ridiculed because what they really do is subordinate the claim of each narrative to the power of an unseen external value that suggests the negotiation of positions. Hence, the homeless will feel vindicated if the city chooses not to evict them from a park one night in the name of a struggle for "justice," even if it means their rights to housing have not fully been met. Workers will accept a 2% pay increase as a compromise with the industrial powers that be, in a confrontation between the civic world, where citizens have rights, and the industrial world, where labour is a mere cost of production.

Where the radical criticism challenges a principle, the dispute becomes a competition between two reality tests (Boltanski and Thévenot 1999:374). Closure can come in the form of choosing one test over another. Or in the case of Dignity Village, closure will follow the period of justification creation in which it is engaged. I am arguing that the justifications in which it is imbricated are primarily dictated by a neoliberal sense of conduct, and it is here that pragmatic sociology of critique and governmentality join. IHCs must constantly prove to city and state governance that they comply with two essential reality tests. The first is the strictly codified rationalization of the living spaces and structures imposed by the city; the other is the role they play in regenerating self-conducting citizens. Regardless of worlds or justifications, this is primarily case of governmentality—that is, a case where the justification is to a discourse on what government means in the classic sense of self-conduct, and of conduct towards others.

Where pragmatic critique of sociology is strongest is in creating a series of interconnected worlds that correspond to the life events of actors and out of which emerge the potential for disputes or what we can think of as a call for critical action from an actor faced with a conundrum. Critique in the form of accusations and disputes are based on the description of the situation in terms of understandings of common good. Where the approach had suffered, in earlier forms, was from a lack of any critical mechanism to adjudicate the link between worlds and their worths, and the subtle nuanced behaviour of actors that could account for the substrate by which narratives and reality tests are forced to collide. That is, if critical action is real and lived, that does not mean all action is critical; in fact, it could not be so (Boltanski 2011:51). "The critical activity stands out against a background which, far from being critical, can on the contrary be characterized by a sort of tacit adherence to reality as it presents itself in the course of ordinary activities; or by a taken-for-granted world ... to account for the pregnancy of this background, we must return to the sociology of institutions"(51).

For Boltanski, institutions are foundational, operating within the worlds of worths, and in a sense presenting a structured means by which to suggest unbiased accounts of the world. Unlike actors who are grounded and embodied, the perception of an institution is largely that of an ethereal nexus for the locating of narratives in a bodiless state. Though they work through spokespersons, institutions present themselves as exterior proof of "whatness of what is" (55). They produce knowledge that might be called common sense but Boltanski argues there is nothing benevolent or gracious about their role; they frame order through narratives of justification that are almost always those of domination and exploitation.

Still, much of sociology has looked towards these common-sense constructions, ideology, conventional wisdom, symbolic imaginaries, "mainstream" attitudes, and narratives of inevitability as sorts of equalizing mechanisms in society, rather than as the points of discord that Boltanski, and Thévenot have examined. Surely it can be argued that the common sense produced by institutions has a moderating effect, but it is the often-rapid shifts from common sense to moments of rupture, such as a stock market crash, or witnessing the death of a poor addict on the streets, that call up narratives of justice and therefore are crucial for understanding critique (56). Reality, then, is an insufficient premise on which to base critique. It is necessary to study the imbrication of "what hangs together and what is stamped with uncertainty," if one is to understand critique. Dignity Village and homelessness in general are liminal modes of existence; liminality is uncertainty. So, critique is a process of discerning means to address uncertainty and is in pragmatic terms, a liminal event (Boland 2013; Szakolczai 2000).

Institutions and critique are set off against one another in pragmatic sociology; critique as a sort of countervailing force to the stabilizing role of institutions, which implies that their imbrication is a tantalization, a necessary codependence on which modern society is understood. Still, one must be able to address social change. Since critique and critical action are directed towards revealing or resolving conflicts in opposed ways of seeing and doing, then how does a pragmatic sociology of critique anticipate social change? If institutions do not have the totalizing effect of renewing and repeating systems of domination or maintaining the status quo, how does social change happen? Where most sociologies have attempted to understand how societies and cultures tend to reproduce themselves, they have looked at the stabilizing functions of social things like institutions. Boltanski's position is classical, but with a twist.

Change is the constant in the world, and it is against this fundamental dynamic that institutions struggle. It is not the problem of stability that institutions must face; that would not be problematic. It is instability and change that defines the real force behind worth worlds, institutions and actors. Assuming that all the worlds can be collapsed into hermeneutically simplified "world" where, under capitalism, political regimes can be said to be the designers and implementers of systems of domination, it would be possible to distinguish types of domination and the possibility for critique (change) they anticipate (125–27).

Domination changes, everything changes; simple domination is total, violent and constitutes oppression. Boltanski cites slavery as an example, but one could argue the case that poor houses and workfare (under neoliberalism) are equally oppressive. In any event, such extreme domination renders critique difficult or impossible. There are other kinds of simple domination, such as the tests used by officials to award merit or, more currently and pertinent to this book, the use of fundamental concepts of freedom and rights contained in constitutional frames to define the legal boundaries that housing critique and their manifestations in critical actions might take. Where simple domination seeks to control the world by use of police and force, modern neoliberalism seeks to do so through a system of complex, managerial capitalism, where experts are looked upon as avatars of authority and understanding (2011:136), and in which justifications for failure are increasingly bound to the failure of individuals.

Under the neologism, *dominant institutions* create the illusion that circumstances beyond their control explain the necessity of their actions, however dominating or liberating they might be constructed to appear (137). Disguised within this existential shill, institutions are occupied by groups of powerful people, not ideas or physical circumstances that, so hidden, are hard to identify within the critiques that would expose them. Hence, once again, Boltanski turns away from looking at structures and institutions as "building blocks" on which to place the mantle of responsibility for stability and injustice, to the people behind them who perpetuate, in their own (capitalist) interests and justifications, the injustices that confront people, and align worth worlds in a struggle with matters of humanity.

Institutions are not bad. Structure is not bad; it is actual. But the people that can be said to occupy these constructs need to be understood and held responsible for the injustices so often blamed on the institution or the structural condition. Critique, therefore, is not an opposition to institutions or to structure, but as a form of narrative and action that co-exists as a system of checks and balances that reveals the contradictions, injustices and other ways of doing established practices that might transcend the dominating and exploitative route of capitalism. Critique is the other side of the coin. As one housing activist in Portland remarked, "We are the remoras, picking off the parasites, keeping it all clean."

My last observation of pragmatic sociology of critique is that economies of worth are seen as complete worlds, and, though they overlap, the liminal space of homelessness is absorbed into the internal systems by which actors should become established in unique domains of, for example, the civic, political and religious worlds. A world of liminal potential of its own makes little sense in a model where established institutions and reality tests exist because neither can be in a "cité" of perpetually liminal experience. I am going to propose that the village is such a between-world, if only to get at how hard it is for critique to take hold there and how difficult it is going to be to convince planners that such spaces are relevant in the era of ten-year plans and rapid rehousing. After all, how do you package and get funding for ambiguous spaces that don't meet the justifications of a neoliberal civic world?

A major weakness of modern social critique, and therefore of our collective ability to overcome the convenience of narratives of inevitability, is that it has a hard time testing its criteria and methods in spaces that are hard to define.

Liminal or transitional subjectivities are seen as temporary and usually as epi-phenomenon of the critical action or the critique as it emerges over time. Rarely is the idea of perpetual liminality understood as a human condition that produces and is understandable by various forms of critique, because it is ambiguous and not wholly formed in a manner that is subject to external cri-tiques. Even deconstruction has difficulty in deconstructing what is not wholly present, but it offers the best shot. When we meet people with mental health issues, addictions and alternative lifestyles, we perceive of them in terms of their flaws or defects of character. Such traits are considered stigmas. We find it difficult to think of them as legitimate critical actors because, as Foucault demonstrated, we have already, by defining them as such—by stigmatizing them—placed them outside of legitimate government in the classic sense of the word. This kind of perception and targeting becomes even more of a conundrum when we find ourselves in communities defined by these ambigu-ous states of being, such as Dignity Village.

In the next chapter it will become clear that the irony is that as Western economies shrink, as traditional rituals and practices for transitioning through life fail, conventional mental and physical spaces are starting to be displaced by liminal experiences. The traits that used to stigmatize and marginalize minorities in our population are becoming more common. The liminal home-less person is no longer scattered to a space reserved for her by history—the streets, shelters, mental wards and prisons. They are becoming increasingly concentrated, creating new mental and physical spaces where life in the limi-nal realm challenges our conventional ways of understanding homeless-ness. As my experience on the streets during my early research demonstrated, the key to changing the narratives we hold about homelessness is opening our minds to the possibility of a socially organized and powerful homeless community. The stigma of being weak and homeless is a most powerful asset. Homeless people are organizing and this is power; this is threatening to the order of things. Without its ability to stigmatize poverty and the homeless per-son, the dominant conventional narrative about housing loses much of its force.

Chapter 5
INEVITABILITY AND PERCEPTIONS

5.1 Stigma, Power and Affiliation

In *Stigma* (1963), Erving Goffman discusses the way in which an individual's personal attributes can be discrediting and the various means by which one might attempt to overcome the deleterious social and political consequences of this self- and public perception. One method he discusses which has gained a great deal of discussion is "passing." Passing involves hiding the behavioral or obvious "signs" of a discrediting trait: a Satan worshipper wears a three-piece suit to the office, a gay hockey player flirts with girls in front of his teammates. Passing is easy if the stigmatized attribute is not visibly obvious. However, this is not always the case. For the cross-dresser or impoverished person wearing tattered clothes, establishing themselves in what the rest of us may feel are public spaces, passing is not possible. As Snow and Anderson (1993) tell us:

Homeless man. Photo: George Hodan.

> Their tattered and soiled clothes function as an ever-present and readily perceivable "role sign" (Banton 1965) or "stigma symbol" (Goffman 1963) that immediately draws attention to them and sets them apart from others. Actual or threatened proximity to them not only engenders fear and enmity in other citizens but also frequently invites the most visceral kinds of responses, ranging from shouts of invective to organized neighborhood opposition to proposed shelter locations to "troll-busting" campaigns aimed at terrorization.

171

I mention passing here because one of the biggest problems in the critique of social problems like homelessness is the need to identify those encumbered by the stigmatizing attributes. One of the keys to the narratives of inevitability that face the homeless people I work with, and that I faced when admitting to the world that I had become homeless, was the immediate categorization others make of the homeless based on assumptions about the human condition and how it is experienced. Earlier, I recounted the comment made to me by a publisher friend who had admonished me for claiming to be homeless. He suggested I hadn't been homeless because I did not live up to (or down to) his imagining of what homelessness looks like. He was, as I stated, incorrect. I had slept rough, sought shelter in unsavoury places, and so on. The difference between what he had seen of me and in me at that time and the later revelation that I was homeless called into question the very categories of experience and the expectations we hold of them that populate narratives of inevitability. I was able, as you will read later, to speak to the growing and complicated types of poverty that link people with the different kinds of homelessness we have discussed: chronic, literal, unsheltered, episodic, and so on. I am absolutely convinced that we need to understand the social problem in general, be it poverty or domestic violence or anything else, as a multifarious creature requiring far more inclusive language and imaginings, if the solutions we speak about are to be discovered and implemented. Returning to poverty and to homelessness, the social problems I am most concerned with, at the root of the stigma is our inability to deal with powerlessness, because powerlessness is hopelessness.

One aspect of stigma associated with poverty reflects the hopelessness and the irredeemability of the homeless condition. Helplessness embodies the antithesis of the capitalist ideal. This is an example of failed liminality. Inasmuch as capitalism absolutely requires economic and power inequalities, the absence of power altogether and the presence of its opposite—dependency—is ironically ridiculed, even though it is required of some members of the population for capitalism to be effective.[87] Under neoliberal governmentality, homelessness signifies a failed conduct of conduct (Foucault 1991; Rose 1999). Historically, social analysis has tended to study neoliberal hegemony as a model of the top-down flow of power, in which poor people are viewed in terms of their unequal power relations within capitalism. Street poverty confronts those who are desperately close to it as a warning of what could happen if, say, they gave up their low-paying job, or if the government did not fulfill its obligations to prop up the economy. Stigmas, then, are a negative valuation that dominant imaginaries oppose on those lesser and often difficult to manage human conditions such as abject poverty, disease and intemperance. But of all these conditions, the common experience of powerlessness is most feared. To not be in control of one's mental or physical faculties, to be denied the freedom that wealth provides: such is the powerlessness that we are led to see in these human conditions.

Massey's (1994) feminist cultural geography, Smith's institutional ethnography (1987, 2005), Wallerstein's (2004) core-periphery studies of globalization, Drache's (2008) "defiant publics" and others have validated studying the other end of the power continuum—that is, from the point of view of the less powerful. This book assumes a similar vantage point and looks to understand the ways that homelessness, odd as this may sound, creates certain under-recognized opportunities for empowerment among the Dignity Village poor and other IHCs. Conventional attitudes and marginalized ones do not separate along a clear dividing line. There are sympathies towards the less fortunate among the haves, or those with relatively more than the homeless, that can be mobilized to raise funds through charitable acts or to advocate for their needs in legislatures. In fact, the enormous non-profit housing sector exists because there is not only great need but a recognition that this is a deserving need. The stigma and marginality of the homeless become a sort of discursive rallying point for action around more widely held visions of social justice.

In the case of this fieldwork-based research, we are examining how activists making claims for their rights challenge the normative imaginings of the urban space of poverty. By fighting for the right to space, a number of issues that condition the homeless activist are concentrated into a neat bundle that fits into rationalized categories of governance. This rationalization is clearly defined by law and practice, such as zoning codes, constitutional laws and camping or sheltering traditions in local areas. In so much as the claim on space imbricates with indictments of the economy, partisan political rhetoric, and human rights discourses, fighting for space is a concrete and focused action where success or failure of the claim is easily understood by its result; rights to a space are granted or not. Such actions when they occur must be understood within the political and economic context that undergirds the claim and which created power relations that were available to the activist community at that time. While the poverty of the Village suggests a position of weakness, the poor people who participated in this research have powerful capacities that are under-realized because establishing conventional ties has been an historic problem for the poor, and part of that stigma.[88]

We have talked about power; it is variously described as the ability to motivate others to do action, to exercise influence in decision-making or to instigate processes, much as energy does in the "physical world" (Bahr 1973:29). Weber, who described power as the ability to make people *choose* to do things despite the cost to them, also speaks of the positive status attached to individuals who have power (1946:180). Foucault told us that power is not the same thing as domination, and Boltanski explained that power is often derived from the justifications we have recourse to in a number of variable social situations. But we have not isolated the absence of power in our discussion. The absence of power can at worst be valued as "none," but the negativity attached to the stigma of being powerless is considerably more than none (Goffman 1963; Liebow 1967; Snow and Anderson 1991; Moynihan 1967). Powerless is tolerated among the infirm and infants; however, for adults, the "incapacity to produce results" is rarely tolerated (Hawley 1963:423). Even, then, "tolerating" a human condition or an "other" is hardly the same thing as loving or caring for another. Tolerance implies a recognition of the other as less, and deviant from one's own values, and therefore, as "outside" (Fabian 1983; Brown 2006).

Bahr (1973) suggests that part of the mainstream's stigmatization of "skid row" men was the abhorrence of powerlessness, which is not measured in terms of a void, but in the language, and valuations of the social system of relations in which it is embedded (22). The powerless are persons without relations to others, or those lacking "office" (22). In the context of the street, then, the homeless I met were appraised through conventional symbolic imaginaries as powerless and *less than* because, following Bahr, the potential of their homeless affiliations remains undisclosed or underestimated.

Borrowing from Foucault (1991, 1994), personal empowerment through good government in a liberal democratic urban sense of good conduct produces experiences of dignity, freedom and self-worth. Furthermore, these values are culturally commoditized in the same way the economic and political individual is commoditized over time through participation in mainstream economic and political structures. Though a sense of being deserving is something "owned" by the individual, it is a tap turned on and off by performance of the lived and meaningful life, where meaning is derived from what others think of our roles, and fullness is measured by how much we produce, consume and accumulate. This includes having a home. The meaningful life narrative, of which stable housing is considered a part, thereby satisfies the regime's need for citizens to self-govern. In this sense, dignity and worth, two components of the *deserving* soul, and often understood by individuals as fulfilled by the rights to freedom and autonomy, are seen as rationalized outcomes of social practice and regimes of power, and their absence is the source rationalization for practices that stigmatize others (Bahr 1973; Caton 1990; Foucault 1994; Dean 2010; Weissman 2012). Powerlessness, then, is aberrant not only because it implies weakness, but because it defines the person so assessed as a failed citizen, as someone whose government is flawed; they are different, other, and less than—that is to say, undeserving. The undeserving nature of this powerlessness is distilled from the assumption by those with power that someone without it just doesn't care about themselves, so why should we? As Foucault suggests, it is not a question of a person's force in society but their seeming lack of care for the self. Foucault (1994) wrote:

Perhaps the equivocal nature of the term conduct is one of the best aids for coming to terms with the specificity of power relations. For to "conduct" is at the same time to "lead" others (according to mechanisms of coercion which are, to varying degrees, strict) and a way of behaving within a more or less open field of possibilities. The exercise of power consists in guiding the possibility of conduct and putting in order the possible outcome. Basically power is less a confrontation between two adversaries or the linking of one to the other than a question of government (1994:237).

In the social sciences the problem of power can be understood as the main vector in a continuum of debate over structure and agency. One might imagine structure and agency as points on a spectrum; a diversity of arguments on the one side of an imaginary center places structure over agency while on the other side are those arguments that place agency over structure. The imaginary center is where much of the literature tends to rest; positions such as *structuration* (Giddens 1984) see agency as the result of empirically observed and theoretically deduced basic structural "facts" like language, practices and ideological space, among many others. One might say that the debate really hinges over two opposing views. First are methodological holistic approaches which say that individuals are embedded in social structures and institutions (and spaces) that shape, constrain and determine their attempts at social action (Marx 1858; Marshall 1950; Durkheim 1964; Parsons 1968; Lefebvre 1974; Weber 1992). In opposition, a second position, that of the methodological individualist, says structures are really an epiphenomenon of the interplay of individuals bound up in structured relations but capable of choosing some things over others; hence the *subject* is at the center of social investigation (Goffman 1959, Garfinkel 1967; Bourdieu 1972; Giddens 1984; de Certeau 1999; Law 2004; Latour 2005).

On the streets of Toronto, and among the advocates I spoke to, talk was of obtaining for the homeless the same rights as any citizen—a home, a job, medical care and privacy. While everyone knew that capitalism had produced the conditions of their poverty—high rents, low-paying jobs, government cutbacks—few spoke of revolution or overturning extant power relations. They simply wanted what other people had, but were lost about how to obtain it. Later when we talk about how two activist factions in the struggle of Dignity Village split during negotiations with the city, this dual definition of emancipation will be important as well.

I remember sitting on a bench at the corner of Victoria Street and Queen East, with a half-dozen homeless men. They were all big, tough and experienced street men. In the park behind us were over 150 other homeless people, waiting for the church to open the doors to its soup kitchen. Around 5 p.m.

the doors opened and people queued up for soup and bread. There were only casual police drive-bys. Almost every night the robbery and fraud squads would set up surveillance since those were two activities for which some of the street men had been issued warrants. The "beat" cops were around the area, watching, 24 hours a day, and it became something of a sport to "watch back," taunting the cops with smirks and leers. At 7 p.m., after the soup kitchen was done serving, the park became very densely occupied. Two representatives from OCAP (the Ontario Coalition Against Poverty) had come to encourage people to join a protest march against police park sweeps to be held a few miles away at the Ontario legislature. The crowd became louder. I had remained, still seated on the bench, with one of the same fellows; we could hear the propaganda and the jeering. Within a few minutes there were a dozen police officers on foot, half-a-dozen squad cars, and four cops on horse-back. "Looks like we scared 'em again," Mike said. I had interviewed him several times. In the background we could hear one of the activists on a megaphone: "We can win housing, we can get off the streets, but we have to act together. We have the power." And the crowd howled. The cops looked really edgy, hands on their belts, a gesture to the crowd not to escalate, and the horse-riding cops moved out of sight towards a commotion in the church parking lot. Mike looked at me and he just laughed, spitting out, "Yeah, like *that* will ever happen." I could feel the energy, the force that was there in that angry group. It was pretty tense. The cops kept looking at each other as if ready to pounce on the group. And then a stream of perhaps 30 protesters left with the activists and marched up Victoria Street, followed by the four horse-men, and escorted by two squad cars, lights flashing. The event did not make headlines, or change anything, but there was power in their actions. It's quite fair to say that in the hour of the protest, and the time it took to march to Queen's Park, the protesters felt that they had some power—that emancipation needed to be understood as at least possible, though sometimes fleeting, at least in the moments we are fighting.

Boltanski (2011:1–3) has argued that all sociology can see is power, and therefore it has a hard time isolating the conditions of emancipation from rare instances of domination. In this book I take the problem of structure and agency as elements of understanding social critique. For the homeless, the same rules that structure their poverty also provide means by which to be empowered thorough critical action in pursuit of their rights. [89] The collective action of homeless people is interesting for another reason. It is one of the rare opportunities where the condition that stigmatizes them also grants them a way of participating in conventional power struggles that are essential to democratic participation under neoliberalism.

One must consider the following question: Is acting in protest marches or sleep-ins an *act of resistance* or a convergence on *practices of resistance*? I say conventional power struggles in the sense that protest and public marches are understandable in democratic imaginaries about how and where to resist as free (active) citizens. This minor protest was not a militant occupation, a kidnaping, or some other unusual form of resistance. It was quite regular and anticipated, and that is why the cops were always in the vicinity. This might not have been a huge march, but it was at least to a degree effective at mobilizing some actors and in garnering a measured response that, as far as we know, did not lead to oppression, although that was not always the case. Democracy as we understand it in the West includes the right to freely associate and to complain about political matters in public. In 2001, most Torontonians had difficulty understanding how "bums" could become mobilized and effective at influencing social change. We hadn't learned yet of the diversity of their composition, nor the strength and importance of social ties in their street groups. Most importantly, Torontonians thought of the homeless as idle and disorganized, and therefore as non-threats.

Bahr (1973) has pointed out that, when exploring homelessness as a human condition, the idea of disaffiliation is traditionally less primary a concern than power. This is because we "haves" have a good idea of what power is, but we generally do not understand disaffiliation in this concrete lived way. Disaffiliation implies something about how one's life is structured without others or with a limited few, and relates the size and form of assemblages with valuations of love or "belonging" and even power (31). Power is essential to the lived life, but in speaking in terms of the homeless it is prudent to construct these notions of power around assemblages, how they are constructed out of the places frequented, how durable they are over time, because power manifests through (social) organizations (31). It is for this reason that urban imaginaries resist congregations of the homeless. The shantytown, the tent camp, whatever they are called, even more poignantly than marches and churchyard protests, is if nothing else a superior example of the spatially concentrated power of the poor. As Bahr points out, the presumption is that "[a] homeless man lacks the power to influence others or to mold his own future. It is an unenviable, and at the same time, a threatening condition. Skid Row is reputed to be full of men in this state" (1973:31). I would add that the view of the streets and of poverty as depleted of power is one of the reasons conventional symbolic imaginaries and housed citizens fear it as they do.

Bahr and Lewis had succeeded in informing numerous debates about homelessness. Their influence is at least implicit in many works, including what follows. It was becoming clearer to me; the more I roamed the streets and met the new homeless, the more I learned that equating homelessness with absolute powerlessness was a mistake. It was really a question of relative power within a system of unequal distribution of resources and social ties that was of concern. And then again, it was unclear what kinds of power the home-less were seeking. Absolute notions of power, or of domination, seemed to be of little use other than as abstract ideals by which to provide an external meas-ure for a condition that is best understood as lived, from the inside, from within the social relation where it matters. On the streets, power resides in the guy who protects his lady and sticks up for his friends; with the one with a full bottle or a room where people can crash; with a person who earns street credit by never ratting out or ripping someone off (Bailey 1973; Wagner 1993; Cap-poni 1997; Bourgois 1995, 2010; Weissman 2012).

Interestingly, the homeless person in general, but the street man especially, is faced with a unique kind of perceptual dualism. His identity as "friend" or "foe" largely reflects mainstream symbolic norms about night and day, weak-ness and power, and space. Hence, we can see and value the very same street person in different ways depending not only on where but when and in what context we intercept him. One rarely takes notice of these street people beg-ging on a sidewalk during the daytime, because one is so used to seeing them on street corners in the capacity of a beggar in a normal state of weakness. The same group in a laneway becomes a potential threat.

Regardless of how one interprets the street person during waking hours, the same tolerance is quickly discarded upon nightfall. It is not normal for residents of the "mainstream" to skulk about in dark places. The same tragic beggar I gave a muffin to earlier today becomes Satan's handyman tonight as he shuffles in and about the parking lot as I unlock the car door. These are the people I was meeting in my early fieldwork. Though they may have resorted to hostels or fallen in and out of housing and welfare, they always ended up on the street, this intersection of laneways, bridges, parks and basements. The street came to define them, and under the shadow of night, they redefined the street as dangerous. Many of them had criminal records and blamed their homelessness on long periods of incarceration. Many of them broke into cars and went "boosting"—shoplifting—but highly organized and in packs. It was only in darkness that we in the mainstream saw that they had power, all bad, all dark, and all street. It is within the image of this dark power, this propensity to do harm perhaps, that urban planners and conventional citizens perceive street homeless. On their own, isolated at the fringes, they are not a threat to the mainstream in a physical or symbolic sense. Should they group together, put up tents and claim the right to land, the stigma and the fear attached to them by conventional imaginaries magnifies. The concentrated spatialization of poverty must also mean a concentration of crime, drugs, mental illness and all manner of depravity. An editorial comment in Portland's Street Roots maga-zine is a good reminder of how this power has generally unfortunate implica-tions and corresponds to notions of space that relate to the emplaced values of community. Wendy says:

Inevitability and Perceptions

May 31, 2008 at 6:51 p.m.—There's a small strip of city property next to my house where two homeless Vietnam vets lived for five years. The police explained a few times that they couldn't remove the men because the City of Portland wouldn't let them. My brother and I spoke to the vets and they seemed harmless enough and promised never to go onto my property—I was told this was all I could do.

Two days ago, I discovered that the vets were gone and I was stunned by just how happy and relieved I felt. I'm a single mother with two children. I'm also a caring person but I have an obligation and an instinct to protect my family. I am sorry for homeless people who want shelter and can't find it, but it has been very stressful to have men living so far outside social rules and mores living a few feet over my property line—I didn't realize how stressful until the stress was suddenly gone. It really did feel like a heavy weight had been physically lifted off my shoulders.

Not only was I periodically frightened (why is the tub inexplicably filthy on a day when the windows are left open? What happened to all the tomatoes in the garden? Did my daughter really see someone at the window?) but I was also very tense when it was freezing cold or pouring rain, even though our homeless guys were campers who didn't want a shelter bed or affordable housing. They had desks and a table and chairs as well as tents and sleeping bags and had been sent to us after living on the property of a Christian church for over 20 years. These men had defined their freedom and attained it. Does anyone have a plan for the campers?

This morning, after two days of this wonderful, free feeling and while I was mowing the city's property, I discovered that a new man has pitched his tent behind my house. He's a foot taller and two hundred pounds heavier than I am. I spoke with him (he's on my property so at the very least, he'll have to move twenty feet or so) and he's agreed to leave by this time next week, but I know another or others will come, if he leaves. It's a convenient spot to downtown and fairly hidden. The fellow said right away "I don't have to go; this is city property!" It isn't possible that the police are actually shuttling people to this space like realtors, is it?

I've been tense for five years and not even admitting it to myself because I wanted to be politically correct and think of myself as compassionate and liberal but I cannot live like this anymore. Should I sell my house? Who would buy it? I won't be able to send my children to college if I have to sell it at a deep discount—this collateral is my plan for tuition and I'm lucky to have it. Plus, we just love our little house; it's the first one I've owned.

Talking to and helping the homeless as part of a job—or just thinking about the homeless from behind a newspaper—is very different from seeing the homeless through the trees in your backyard every day and hearing the twigs snap as they visit their privy. "Fewer police sweeps" does not appeal to me. Each case ought to be considered individually—in some cases, it's appropriate to move the homeless; in other cases, it's not.

The old, dead ideas about fixing the problem are actually painful to hear. Section 8, shelters, low-income housing. All good ideas coming from people who never talked to the homeless people I've known. The new fellow has a beautiful, insulated tent, a boom box, furniture—even (apparently) a cell phone. His new home looks like a studio apartment, and we can see it from our living room window. Beyond it is a road and beyond that, nothing much. It is just him and me and my children.

I welcome advice but I hope any accusation that I am a "not in my back yard" sort of person will come only from people who have homeless people in their back yards.

Wendy, who is not a trained sociologist, offers up a very thorough rendition of her conventional analysis of the unconventional homeless folks living in her space. She quite clearly speaks to the problem of perception, one that is fuelled by narratives we tell ourselves about who should be in our backyards and what measures are appropriate to take when faced with the homeless. Popular and personal perceptions have much to do with how we understand not only the homeless but also the proper space for them to inhabit. When homeless people are not in the streets or shelters, they are rarely seen in positive terms. They are making a claim, taking something, some land, some fruit, they are occupiers and therefore powerful. However, some ethnography examines more positive, even communitarian perspectives amongst homeless street people. Bailey's (1973) *The Squatters* recounts the organizing efforts among Rethbridge, England's squatting community, focusing on how their success with local councils expanded to other locales throughout the country. Ward's (1979) *The Street Is Their Home: The Hobos' Manifesto* spoke to the unique and colorful culture of the streets and to the probability that the presence of hobos and "skids" was a benefit to the communities in which they lived. Of course, Ward, once a hobo himself, was biased. Ward pointed out that skid row men were consumers, even if only of cheap motel rooms and bar-room booze. He argued that they provided dispensable labor, undertaking "odd jobs" for locals; their presence on street corners and in parks wasn't encroachment or trespass necessarily, but added color and vibrancy to otherwise decaying neighborhoods. Though other "pro-skid" positions might exist, I did not come across this particularly positive portrayal often. Bahr's *Skid Row* (1973) provides an eloquent spatial and cultural interpretation set in an historical approach to understanding the vital "main stem" in North American cities where street poverty was most highly concentrated. Wagner's (1993) *Checker-*

board Square takes the opportunity to express the strides made by the homeless to build communities and to fight for their rights. Wagner explored alternative routes to homelessness: opting out, resistance to authoritative bosses, rejection of landlords, governments and spouses. He explains through the stories of the homeless themselves that homelessness is not just about a lack of housing or jobs but results from the very structure of dominant institutions, such as work and social welfare.

These views are a far cry from the moral high ground taken by Ferguson (1911) in *The Vagrant: What to Do with Him*, or Syme's (1904) *Honour All Men: A Plea for the Vagrant*. Each of these establishes a moral imperative that identifies the homeless (male) as an outcast and spiritually troubled figure in need of saving, either through moral or labor-intensive means.[90] As much as Lewis' *Culture of Poverty* is a departure from these early post-Victorian-era accounts, it too essentializes poverty as a "type" of human condition that confirms rather than rejects the hopelessness of poverty and sees the solution to the poverty as state, professional or otherwise exterior interventions into homeless subjectivities. As such it invites policies and interventions necessary to rectify a broken subjectivity into a self-governing one as the only means to redress poverty.

Despite some good attempts at understanding homelessness from the point of view of homeless persons, the dominant political framing of homelessness as a social problem affecting a troublesome population led to the bulk of statistical data obtained and discussed for the sole purpose of driving policies of containment. This led to an ideology of (ware)housing the poor on the basis of how they differed from conventionally employed and socialized groups. This is why we look at how different the homeless are rather than at how similar we all are. There are other points of contact between cultures and sub-cultures than merely housing or work.

Despite the numerous protests, legal claims and temporary occupations by homeless people and advocacy groups, the frame of understanding had until very recently been filtered through conflict theory, rather than taking seriously the power that homeless people might have within neoliberal governmentalities. A somewhat cynical explanation is offered by Wagner (1993) when he suggests that "the research methodologies used by several players, including social scientists; self-interested professionals in certain formulations of social problems; and the ideological pre-conceptions and political strategies of most advocates and researchers are the reasons for holding back progressive understanding of the "homeless" (7).[91] So, while one author might present a single valid ethnography of empowerment, many other studies point to the uniqueness of this quality and its incongruence with policy initiatives or goals on a much broader scale. More recently, as I discuss in my concluding chapter, the paradigm shift away from undeserving to deserving poor has begun to reframe these treatments of the homeless.

In early urban ethnography an emphasis on trying to discern what power might ideally mean tended to frame ethnographies in terms of classic binary positions. Social policy or laws governing the poor were interpreted in terms of how they fit into dominant perspectives within symbolic imaginaries about what ought to be. Under neoliberal governance, the homeless person's power was to be mitigated through continuum-of-care housing models, shelters, treatment and rehabs, diluted and scattered to dark places, which I discuss later as negative space. With masses of poor people congregating in parks, participating in sometimes violent protests against neoliberal policies targeting the poor, scholars and activists had no choice but to confront how devolution was creating new and diverse homeless subjectivities among a largely un-serviced poor population.

One of the ways that the power of the homeless was starting to manifest itself was through the actions of deliberate housing and homeless advocacy. Beric German of the TDRC had explained it many times: "It was no use, you see, to gather a group and make promises they expect you to keep. Mobilization and organization are about demonstrating ways that the poor person can have power. First you have to know who shares your policies and beliefs, who wants to participate, and then you lead by example. Protest, yell, scream, fight for your rights." Homeless activism was beginning to change how we thought of the poor; even if their power was limited, it was power nonetheless.[92]

While I was working in the streets of Toronto between 1999 and 2002, participating in sleep-ins at local parks or covering rallies in church yards, in Portland, unbeknownst to any of us, activists huddled under the Fremont Bridge in tents, toting shopping carts filled with their belongings, were organizing in a fight for the right to land on which to build homes. There was a new momentum among homeless activism. In Toronto, I had conversations with members of the homeless community about other parks, other cities, and other tent camps. A few even shared romantic stories of riding the freight trains out west. One had been to Seattle and Portland, and then to Sacramento. There were "unbelievable amounts of homeless people there" (Mike, homeless man at "St. Mike's," from *Street Beats* 2001 [2003]). We were not even aware of the tent camp taking root down by the lakeshore on Toronto's booming waterfront.

One of the homeless campers I met—I will call him Arthur—had travelled on five continents chasing the "spirit of alternative community." He had remarked many times that Canadians ought to give more graciously to the poor, because most of us had no idea how the rest of the world lived—he was referring to Davis' billion or so poor who live on this *Planet of Slums* (2006). He had just arrived from "Christiania," a large squatter community that started in deserted military barracks in Copenhagen. Fed up with the lack of housing for the poor, activists and the poor had squatted and successfully claimed the barracks for occupancy as long ago as 1971. Though the city recognizes it as a commune, the "Christiana Law" of 1989 transferred regulation of the commune to the state.[93] Although not a legally sanctioned city operation, and continuously steeped in controversy over its own dogmatic rules and codes, it remains one of the avatars of intentional squatting in the West.[94] Even Denmark had homelessness? He had been also in Kolkata, Karachi, Soweto, and he was in Toronto to help organizers build their own homeless camp, on the lakeshore, not far from my home, because he had heard rumours that homeless folks were organizing in Toronto. Apparently the beginnings of the camp had been there for over two years, but only a few of the park people knew of it, and certainly, even though it was next to a busy highway overpass (Toronto's famous Gardiner Expressway), few Torontonians had any idea what the six shacks on the empty lot had meant. There was no room in our urban imaginary for a shantytown. We failed to see the growing community, mistaking the new homes for deserted construction sheds.

Arthur took me there one day in late spring 2001. He was going to build shacks for folks to live in during the winter. He told me about how people from all over the world had come together to help local communities express themselves in a world where cities were increasingly displacing and marginalizing poor people. The homeless population of Toronto (including those on the streets, using shelters, and "doubling up") was less than it was elsewhere: the 2003 Street Health Report Card indicated there were approximately 5,000 to 6,000 people on the streets of Toronto on any given night, with some 32,000 accessing shelters in the previous twelve months.[95]

Assuming that this number excludes many others who eluded street counts and shelters, such numbers are significantly less than the 1.3 million who live in Rio's favelas[96] or the 1.5 million in Karachi's Orangi Town.[97] The 24-acre plot of land at the foot of Cherry Street looked like a deserted field with sporadic outbursts of trees, mostly sumacs and small poplars, large enough to barely conceal the structures in which homeless people were secretively living.

Next to abandoned grain elevators that remain something of a landmark on the lakeshore, by mid-summer the original settlement of six shacks had grown to fifteen, as well as several tents and a few trailers that been brought on site by the Toronto Disaster Relief Committee (TDRC) in 2000. The press began to refer to the settlement as "Tent City." The occupation at Tent City was very different than Dignity Village; here, squatters were on land owned by Home Depot, but land that could not be developed at that time because it was contaminated. The soil a few feet down contained dangerous levels of benzene from the Toronto dumps of 1908. Some of the squatters made good money digging in the toxic soil for antique bottles and other collectibles.[98] Home De-

183

pot had not bothered the squatters, and police had no cause to enter the site unless requested to do so by the property owners. And at first they did not. One of the most important distinctions from Dignity Village was that Dignity Village originated as a mobile caravan of homeless claimants seeking private land on which to live, while Tent City evolved organically and quickly. This growth was disturbing to Drei, Terry, Nancy and Yonish, four of the original squatters who had sneaked onto private property largely undetected as early as 1998. As a sparsely populated and almost undetectable community of discrete shacks, they had felt secure and safe there. But they knew that the attention the space was getting had led neighborhood associations to pressure the police and city councilors to police and shutter the community.

This period at Tent City was also my first real contact with community organizers; I became aware of their role, as well as the tension between organizers and those with competing views on how the community should evolve.

5.2 Community Organization: Some Basics

Community organizing is about mobilizing people, usually neighbors or members of a locality-based group. Unlike other forms of social movement, this work is primarily local, concentrated on the needs of a specific group of residents or inhabitants. While it might be tied to broader mobilizations, social movements link given localities into this broader experience. In some ways, the organized community is a locally-based building block for larger social movements. Tilly (1984) has said that a social movement is a "sustained series of actions between power holders and persons successfully claiming to speak on behalf of a constituency lacking formal representation, in the course of which those persons make publicly visible demands for changes in the distribution of exercise of power, and back those with public demonstrations of support." Shragge (2003), on the other hand, suggests that community organizing is more about people identifying problems with their living space and their community and desirable means around which to organize their power to pursue these ends:

> Community organizing at its best has created sites for the practice of opposition. Those interested in progressive social change and social justice were attracted to the community movement because it was a place to organize resistance to the system of global capitalism, patriarchy, racism, and other forms of socio-economic oppression and domination....I am not only talking about protest and confrontation, but the creation of democratic opportunities through which people can learn about their collective strengths and build social solidarity. In the community, there are a variety of practices that may not seem oppositional, but which do question relations of power, build alternative visions, and shift power to those

who usually do not have it (2003:11).

While Shragge also argues that organizers are outsiders (12), there is no way to distinguish the role of an organizer—nor the process of organizing—from its pragmatic connection to revealing unseen systems of power, domination and oppression to members of the community. Indeed, it is on the basis of how these revelations represent a disjuncture with values about justice that mobilization can take place. It is also clear that community organization suggests a different form of action from social movements. In the former, roles are clearly defined and individuals act in certain capacities as part of the critical action; in the latter, the action is decentralized around many such similar locales (25). Interestingly, Shragge points out that surprise, or "spontaneity" of action in unexpected places, creates the sense of movement (26). The two, then four, then six, then 15 shacks that were more or less hidden under the landfill and sumacs on the lakeshore went largely undetected until late summer of 2001 when they grew to 20, then 45. At this point, Torontonians became aware that the Toronto Disaster Relief Committee had been advocating for those residents, supplying them with a few DuraKit shacks, a trailer and other vital services as part of organizing this group into a community with power.

In Portland, tent camps were popping up under bridges and every few days they were moved by police. These were the early days of "Camp Dignity," which would become Dignity Village. This movement of homeless persons through the city in organized processions—people pushing shopping carts with all their belongings—continued for three years (1999–2001), eventually creating the image of a much larger movement. In fact, these "parades of poverty," as I call them, actually grew as they travelled, picking up supporters from within the homeless and conventionally housed community. They began as eight homeless people and ended with over a hundred. The emergence of Toronto's shanty community was insidious, even secretive, and those original campers were not happy that others had found their site. Curiosity grew.

This was the first shantytown of its kind in Toronto's modern history, even though shanties and shanty communities had been part of the fabric of settlement in the early twentieth century.[99] Over the next 12 months, I watched Tent City grow from an initial community of six well-concealed shacks into over 50 with a population of 115 people. It became clear that notions of basic freedom and rights were as important to questions of citizenship in Canada as they were in the US.

Having grown up in a Canada that most of us had thought quite skillfully ensured my generation's rights to health care, welfare and safety, the fact that a shantytown should emerge seemed prophetic and worrisome. The controversy surrounding Tent City and the incredible press it received were uneasy recognition that devolution had revealed the illusion of "welfare" and was questioning the meaning of freedom, even in Canada.

My first experiences at the village were of being in a surreal canvas of broken things: rough shacks made of tin siding and old lumber. One shack was built from discarded lumber and siding that had been tossed into the dumpsters at First Canadian Place, one of the city's tallest towers and perhaps the most noticeable of Toronto's phallic tributes to capital, to invoke Lefebvre (1974). Eventually, disposal companies, construction crews and many other businesses began dumping clothing, materials, and other garbage directly in the village, an illegal act but cloaking their actions in the dress of a good deed, a donation of sorts to the burgeoning community. I shot many hours of video with the man who lived in the southwest corner, set off the main drag and next to the lake; we dined on bok choy he grew in his garden, at a table he made out of old wood crates and that sat on the fine marble slabs he had recovered from the same dumpster. Surreal. Quaint. Six shacks that spring of 2001, then two more shelters closed. By July, 15 shacks and tents had been put up and the TDRC was organizing building and cleaning crews, seeking donations and fielding questions, sometimes angry and critical ones, from the mayor's office, the news media, and concerned citizens.

The TDRC included on its board of directors some wealthy business supporters, community organizations, concerned street medical specialists, and activists. Against the criticism of downtown businesses and residents, TDRC personnel made the observation that this site should be granted title to the land so they could organize and govern themselves. Furthermore, treating the site as a permanent location was tantamount to recognizing the absolutely fundamental relationship between housing and healthcare. I was not alone in wondering how healthcare could be well served living under *those* conditions. I understood, having been in both worlds, that these shacks were better than laneways; but they were not much better. In those few months after I saw Tent City for the first time, I shot over 40 hours of footage, and was spending three to five days a week there, building houses, getting to know people, and completely in awe of the effort to organize this modern day shantytown. I mentioned earlier why I called it a shantytown. In that period, the word shantytown seemed preferable to tent camp, and intentional community was an emergent concept we had not yet come to understand.

Shragge also suggests that the action can be thought of as occurring in stages: "Each new round of activity contributes positive and negative lessons about how to go forward to the next round of struggle" (26). A competition emerged between OCAP and the TDRC as external organizers from Toronto's activist community vied for the right to lead the community into a new permanent location, a proposed intentional community a few blocks away on city-owned land. While Tent City had "occupied" unusable land owned by Home Depot, the desire to move was generated neither from within the community itself, nor by Home Depot, which had tolerated their presence.[100] When the possibility of a permanent location arose, residents of Tent City were divided. Some wished to remain in charge of their own encampment; others argued over which community organizers should be in charge of the proposed site. The city would not even entertain the idea of a self-governed community and insisted on a board of directors that incorporated the interests of the city, advocates, the homeless community and representatives of the city ward.

As Tent City became more densely populated, as the war on camping in parks swept the city, Tent City suddenly found itself in the media, in the midst of debates between politicians and finally in conversations at dinner tables across the city, as part of a growing critique of housing policies. In short order, news of plans to build a permanent settlement of squatters on a larger piece of serviced land on Commissioner Street was in most newspapers.[101]

So contrary was the idea of a permanent squatter community to the conventional mindset that Tent City came under increasing surveillance, as well as becoming the subject of erroneous partisan articles, news reports and films. My own video interviews became part of the personal journeys of several of the residents, who hoped that through our participation in this project, the truth about their lives would get out.[102]

In the end, the new site did not happen. Downtown community and business groups would have no part of it, and it was not part of Housing First models from the U.S. that were beginning to be considered by cities in Canada. The fact that the city and other levels of government *had* considered building the planned community, however, meant that the homeless claimants who had aligned with various activist organizations to bid for their respective visions for the community had more power than most Torontonians had imagined. Power struggles do not always end in favor of the underdog, but the struggle itself is in some sense proof of agency.

Towards the winter of 2001, Arthur announced that he hoped to go to Oregon, to help build a community called Dignity Village in Portland. Tent City continued to grow to the point where as many as 200 people would be squatting at any given time, even though the official count of residents was pegged at 115. The TDRC remained heavily involved in the community, and what order there was resulted from their organizers being on site and advising residents. Beyond that, the community was chaos. With no concrete government or leadership, fear and drug use had grown to the point where Tent City was less safe than the shelters. Several members moved in with family or into slum-like lodgings paid for with their emergency welfare payments, with as many as 10 people living in a bachelor apartment outside the community. It was clear to most of us that its days were numbered.

My film *Subtext: Real Stories* is a thorough visual study of this transitional time. While Tent City was crumbling, "in Dignity," Arthur explained, "they were doing it right."[103] He wanted to be part of an initiative that confronted the problems of housing and community "head on." Tent City was not doing that. He had heard of this new city-sanctioned shantytown—what he described as an intentional community—from other homeless nomads and from activist sites online. I also went online and read the news stories and the comments on their developing web site. It was true; there was a legally sanctioned homeless shantytown in Portland called Dignity Village. It was at this point that I came to recognize that critics of such places embraced the word shantytown. I also realized that builders of such places preferred the word community, and, even today, most of us struggle with which kind of intentional community such places might represent. For legal purposes we will discuss, this so-called shantytown was designated an emergency transitional campground, a type of space anticipated in Oregon state law. My first question was, "How is *that* possible?" How did they go from shopping carts and tents to a real village?

In many ways that question shapes the spirit of this book. My point of inquiry was further tweaked by the astute comments made by Bonnie, one of the participants in my film. Bonnie was an activist and a resident of Tent City who had recognized that it was the establishment of an argument that made Dignity Village important. Dignity Village was always a political claim for space presented by organized individuals within the arena of the law. Tent City was a congregation but had no internal organization and no political strategy. The difference between Dignity Village and the doomed Tent City was that Dignity Village was better organized because its members were more willing to be activist citizens. Furthermore, state laws in Oregon gave the homeless a legal right to emergency shelter camps. Before Dignity, a homeless camp had never successfully made that claim. Dignity advocates exploited that loophole as a mobilizing resource. Those provisions did not exist in Toronto. Bonnie was quite convinced that "They aren't fighting to be different—well, I guess you could say that this fight for homes is different—but they don't want anything different than other so-called normal people have. They want homes, Eric. Just like other Canadians, or Americans. You know what I mean! They are willing to build their own." There was something about a loose aggregation of homeless people coming together, uniting over a definition of freedom and citizenship and making a concerted claim within the legal-political system that they were deserving of housing, and then winning, that represented an "impossible possibility" for Tent City.[104] In the film she discusses her conviction that if the city had allowed them to lease the land ("like in Dignity Village") they might have done better in Tent City.

Shragge also argues that extending democratic privileges to those often silenced in broader political actions through community organizing is essential to the initial success at meeting goals and then to the longevity of the community (19). In some ways community is locality-based, and in others, locale is meaningless. Not for Tent City. It was all about a place for emplaced community experience. It had been a perplexing problem for me; what was Tent City? Surely it wasn't a legitimate community, in the sense it was neither city-sanctioned nor legally tenured, but in appealing to my earlier discussion of community studies, it was an emplaced experience for residents who recognized each other as members, even though they rarely acted in unison towards political solutions for that community.

Tilly and Shorter (1974), Davis (1991), and Shragge (2003) each argued that it was important for social science to understand the conditions under which collective action occurs on a territorial basis. Tent City had a fence and areas that were defined by the residents: there was a "crack section," where dealers and crack whores did their business; the gate keepers, Brian and Hawk, lived by the front gate; and the back end, which Brian called "party central," was the location of a group of long-term residents who had established a sort of central core of die-hard partying and drugging. So it had physically and spatially definable characteristics that corresponded to how people spent time in that space. Since they had no sense of legal propriety over the land, or the community, it was hard to think of life there as emplaced. It seemed and was often described as not only temporary, but doomed.

As Davis (1991) points out, "place-bound communities" act for a variety of reasons, often because of infrastructural needs, tax battles, and for or against proposed zoning changes (5). Examining extant community, he has argued that locality-based action, which applies to neighborhoods and communities, is largely understandable and critiqued on the basis of the conflict and differentiation between domestic property interest groups (257). The implication of this statement is that the effectiveness of community organization and action will hinge on the degree to which actors are attached to their homes, and beyond that, to the interconnectedness of their propertied status to others who possess property. He suggests that the exercise of those democratic rights through protest and action is organized along the value of this action to their propertied status. This is not just about property value, but also the ancestral and aesthetic value of properties, understood as homes. When we discuss Dignity Village later, it will be important to understand that there, citizens are defined by their attachment to property, whereas in Tent City, they had no such entitlement, nor the identity of a citizen, even though they felt such attachments to the homes they had built and what goods they had gathered.

Both Shragge and Davis offer vantage points for understanding Tent City and Dignity Village. On the one hand, they both share the notion that communities are emplaced, and that territory is a basic way of defining the organizing efforts of activists. They also show that within the territory of the community there are other affinities and ties that go beyond the residence of the actor, but that "living" in the same community establishes a residential unity that underpins critical potential. They each acknowledge that on the basis of variable wealth and the status of members of the same territory, there is the potential for cleavages that community organizers must confront and mend. They also point out that in the face of a common enemy that threatens the territory or the community collectively, community organizing becomes more facile. At least that has been *their* experience.

Tent City confounded these community studies-based approaches because it was a struggle that tried to generate a community—a territory and a symbolic imaginary—out of garbage. The TDRC and other organizations such as Street Health[105] worked hard for the rights of the Tent City residents, but I witnessed the demise and fall of Tent City firsthand. Despite the efforts of the TDRC to organize and take it to the next level, most of the membership failed to rally in support. The residents of the community simply could not find the will to organize themselves because the image of what was happening in the community had been pirated by a negative press. They had no legal title to this privately owned space: theirs was an illegal occupation of someone else's land. How could illegal squatters legitimately organize rules of residency that restricted who settled there? This meant that drug dealers, prostitutes, criminals with warrants, underage runaways and legitimate homeless activists moved in and occupied the same place. What had started out as a reasonable demonstration of alternate IHC had soon turned into a lawless shantytown. A few of the activists who started the village found ways to get out by crashing with friends or returning to the streets, while others formed tight clusters of housing, which they defined as neighborhoods within the camp. Beyond this, there was no room in the symbolic imaginary of Torontonians for a massive 24-acre demonstration of how badly things had gone on, down there on the lakeshore next to the boardwalk, fine condominiums and business towers. If this was the work of activist citizens, Toronto was to have nothing to do with it. In the summer of 2002 we were all fairly certain that Tent City would be shuttered by the police. Our discussions turned to where and how to establish other squats and whether or not a legal squat like Dignity Village was possible in Toronto.

Bonnie and I debated whether the community model at Dignity Village constituted a true alternative or not. "You mean are the people free, is it c-o-m-m-u-n-i-s-m? I don't *know*, Eric. Geez, I've never been there. You go! You're the filmmaker," she said one day a few months before Tent City's residents were evicted in September 2002. Bonnie had moved out of the village and into an apartment in Hamilton. She had a domestic relationship that made that move possible. She stayed active in the metropolitan Toronto area as a harm reduction activist while Tent City began to overflow with ex-cons, drug dealers, and legit homeless folks with nowhere else to go. The population there was so unregulated that there were two shacks on the eastern border of the community that housed young people, just teenagers. Rumors of the underage residents and babies born in Tent City circulated in the news, including a story in the *New York Times*, and in conversation around town. In the autumn of 2002 these rumors inspired the mayor to evict the squatters.

As Drei, one of the first Tent City squatters iterates in the film, "Basically, it's an empty lot. How much damage can a bunch of hippies do to an empty lot?" The damage, it seems was not to the lot, but in the mindset of more conservative elements in charge of the city at that time: the damage was being done to the image of "Toronto the Good," a moniker we had all grown up with. The city was embarrassed. In three days, the site, consisting of dozens of structures and the accumulated belongings of 115 residents, was leveled. They had each been given two hours to gather essential belongings and depart.

As an illegal occupation they were not given prior notice, except that most people there knew the eviction was coming. Terry and Eddy, two key participants in my work, were scouting new squats by August in anticipation of the eviction. After the forced eviction in September, most of them were scattered once again to the streets. They literally had nowhere to sleep that same night or in the near future. There was significant public outcry against the evictions. If Tent City had looked bad, kicking 115 homeless people onto the streets looked worse in the eyes of the international press and among concerned Torontonians. Evictees linked with activists and legal counsel, and even concerned local politicians like Jack Layton and John Sewell campaigned in front of the press for compensation in the form of housing. As a temporary measure, some were placed in motels and low-rent apartments. They were scattered across the Greater Toronto Area (GTA), some as far away as 15 to 20 miles from the downtown core and the social services they required. Remarkably, as some disappeared from the radar altogether, others knew exactly where their friends were and how to contact them, and this without cellphones or the Internet. The TDRC held meetings with the evictees and advocates in order to strategize legal and political solutions to the eviction. What had seemed to most of us who studied the place to be a lawless homeless camp was finally coming together as a coordinated community. The tragedy or perhaps the irony is that this rallying around a cooperative came too late, and only after the community had been eradicated.

Responding to the combined physical efforts of evictees, the TDRC, Street Health, WoodGreen Community services and other concerned politicians and housing advocates advised the city of Toronto and the Ontario government, which introduced the Emergency Homelessness Pilot Project (EHPP).[106] This rent supplement program, the first of its kind in Canada, was based on an American model of housing called Housing First. The evictees were placed directly in mainstream rental units that, ironically, the condo boon had left vacant. This was different than programs I had been offered in rehab, where successfully graduating from rehab had been seen as evidence of my commitment to a new way of living and hence rendered me deserving of housing support, had it been available. The province of Ontario was willing to support outpatients from rehab at a time when welfare had been severely reduced *because* they had passed its courses and treatment program.

The idea behind the EHPP was that housing people first was essential to getting them to deal with other issues—addictions, community and so on. This landmark program has impacted the broader housing movement in Canada, as many other cities have introduced rental supplements and housing practices based on it. Cathy Crowe, author, street nurse and co-founder of the TDRC, called it the "Tent City housing win." And for many of us, it is still understood as that. Community organizers walked into Tent City, did their best to organize the community, and, later, kept the relational part of community alive by actively uniting them in their right to shelter. Though it was the organizational skills of the advocates and activists that orchestrated the success, it was the homeless person herself who provided the power. By speaking to the media, signing petitions, marching behind advocates and by acting like activists, the homeless ex-residents of Tent City were no longer addicts or ex-cons; they had reestablished themselves as legitimate claims makers.

Though the city of Toronto suggests that it acted immediately to find rental-supplemented units for the evictees, it took up to a year for many of those I knew to get housing. Regardless, it was clear to me that even the worst off *could be organized* and could fight for their rights and had power; it was exactly this kind of power that frightened conventional imaginaries.

In a candid interview three years after she instructed me to go to Dignity, Bonnie, who was still housed in the EHPP and by then was working in Toronto as a harm reduction worker and activist, referred to life in Dignity Village as cooperative, democratic and sustainable. We had learned more about the community on the web, in the news and among housing activist organizations in Toronto. At the same time, I had contacted Kwamba Productions, the video archivists of the Village, and they had sent me footage of the early days at Dignity to use in my films. In crafting the first cut of *Subtext*, I looked at the footage of Dignity. It seemed to be the homeless utopia that everyone had talked about. The first cut of *Subtext* was completed without the Dignity footage and I remember Jeff Mayhew, a photographer friend who had joined me in Tent City, asking me why I had edited the film as I had. He felt I had painted a rosier picture of Tent City than perhaps it really represented. Several cuts later, we agreed that to tell the story of Tent City meant showing both unfortunate and wonderful aspects of this community. Utopias are not supposed to be real, are they? How accurate was the footage that Kwamba sent me? I understood that as activists their early sharing of footage was motivated by the need to present an image of a viable alternative to the streets because Portland was literally overwhelmed by street-engaged poor, much as Toronto had been. Still, my scientific mind imagined that there must a certain darkness to Dignity Village, much as there was in Tent City, so how was it possible that they managed to organize and run a real village?

I continued to follow the lives of the Toronto participants in my film as they learned to adapt to housing or didn't. In its third year of having been the first and only city-sanctioned IHC in North America, Dignity Village represented to most ex-Tent City folks an example of what their community could have become, "if only...." These same people often described a sense of "not belonging," of having had a sense of place while in Tent City that EHCC housing did not provide. While they were grateful for having a roof over their heads, many of my informants had no idea how to live conventionally or how to feel engaged with their neighbors or communities. Thrust into conventional living arrangements and asked to unite in conventional affiliations, many struggled. Most who had addictions remained addicted. A few died as a result. Questions about the validity of Lewis' "culture of poverty" re-emerged in my notes, and in discussions with housing workers. One housing worker exclaimed that "We are always in crisis mode with them [ex-Tent City residents], so it's really hard for us—we're housing workers—to do our jobs." She also understood that many of the poor people she had met were from other countries, and had always lived modestly but had never been homeless. "The poor immigrants I see here at WoodGreen are not crackheads. They manage their poverty." The implicit argument here is that housing without supports for people off the streets is tantamount to warehousing the homeless. This becomes problematic.

Still, some ex-residents of Tent City have managed to use housing to root themselves in new and more conventional lifestyles. All of them who were aware of Dignity Village looked and continue to look at it as a statement about what could have been, once again "if only...." Brian Dodge, who remained a key informant, though I called him a "friend," who had been a crack addict, a bank robber and lived in Tent City in its heyday, was housed in a geared-to-income unit; he had three cats, a live-in friend and participated regularly in the Salvation Army. He wouldn't go back to the shantytown style of living because he had managed his liminality and passed from the mindset of a homeless man into a conventional imaginary. He died of cancer in a hospital having lived in his home for 10 years. Penny Marotte has also made a transition to housing and was working with a number of drug and psychological counselors. After selling her body for 20 years on the street for crack and cash, her housing had provided a stable enough space for her to address addiction and health issues, though she admitted she would never be fully clean. In speaking of Tent City, she said, "I'd never go back to that place. Fuck that."

Many others, who feel as though their conventional units were similar to prison cells, were largely isolated from the rest of the world, stigmatized for their history, their current poverty and their addictions. Terry Potts, who also remained a good friend, said often that at least "down there at Tent City I felt I was a part of something," but, after moving, "I dunno, I'm lost, buddy, I don't know what to do." He too wondered what his life would be like now if he were still struggling to build his life and contribute to the building of Tent City. I drove by the site of Tent City in January 2015. It was flattened. Various kinds of vehicles, trucks and trailers, are stored there. Construction crews were getting ready to blast the grain silos in advance of building a billion-dollar waterfront development, or so we are told—to date, nothing has changed. I called Terry to tell him. He laughed. As if on cue, he said, "If only, eh, bud? If only...."

"If only" suggests conditions of possibility—and the corollary of this is, of course, "what if?" My storytelling work with the street people of Toronto has led me to pursue both an analytical and personally satisfying rendition of the conditions of possibility and the meaning of that life for people who live in Dignity Village. In 2008, when I initially showed my film about Tent City at the Royal Ontario Museum, I was interested in understanding how spaces like Dignity Village come to be in the first place, and how living there is experienced by residents. What does living there do for people who are homeless, other than giving them a roof over their heads? How is that village different than Tent City, inasmuch as Dignity Village is considered a *legitimate* living space by the state?

In the beginning, then, roughly between 2002 and 2007, the stories I heard from homeless activists, the video I saw of the Village and the Village's website, painted a charming image of the place. If my experience at Tent City had taught me anything, it was to look beyond the appearances. Dignity Village was the icon; the symbolic center of the debate on intentional homeless camps for most of the 2000s. People from all over the world were visiting and talking about it. By 2007, I knew that someday I would have to go to Portland for a while in order to understand life in Dignity Village. Other forms of IHC, like the Emergency Rest Areas that are part of my current work, did not exist then. With every iteration of my film project, and with each year's successive arcs in the stories of the Brian and Terry and the rest, my interest became more oriented to understanding what it takes to become politically active as a claims maker and then to be successful at making claims.

5.3 Redemption

The single greatest regret I had from my active drug-using days was failing to reach my life-long dream of earning a Ph.D. In 2008, however, my research was going well, and it seemed to me that I had had a formidable participant experience on which to base a dissertation. So I applied to a number of universities with interests in homelessness and housing. For three years beginning in 2006 I applied. I was rejected each time.

In 2008 my documentary *Subtext: Real Stories* was incorporated into an exhibition at the Royal Ontario Museum called "House Paint Phase 2: Shelter." [107] The exhibition invited 25 of the country's most widely respected graffiti artists to paint on replica shacks modeled on the size and crudity of those at Tent City. The panels and roofs were sold later in auction as individual canvasses to raise money for Habitat for Humanity. In addition to the shacks, one artist was asked to paint a large model of a suburban home that was suspended from the walls. Over some weeks, visitors would come and check on his progress, and they would watch the film on a computer bank set off from the main exhibit. The idea behind the gallery was to use a multimedia exhibition to explore the history of such land claims in Toronto, the plight of the street person, and the different ways excluded voices are heard in cities. Graffiti and tagging, shack building and rough sleeping are examples; one of the shacks had a peephole that visitors could see through. In the dark interior, the names of 500 homeless people who had died on the streets of Toronto since 1985, over 95% of whom were men, scrolled on a perpetual film loop. [108] It was astonishing to watch visitors stare into that little hole while the ten-minute loop of names went by. Several reported that they had watched in amazement as they realized how many people had died in such a fashion. "Here, this city?" they asked.

Towards the end of the exhibition, *Subtext* was screened in the theatre at the museum. On stage with me were Brian Dodge, Terry Potts and Beric German of the TDRC and Rima Zavys of WoodGreen. She has since passed away, but she had been a major supporter of my work and a key player in the EHPP and subsequent programs for the poor. Many viewers were particularly interested in the short section that showed footage of the construction of Dignity Village.

A number of issues were raised by these questions. Some in the audience had argued that for residents, the EHPP program was superior to Tent City because Tent City was out of control. Rima and Beric argued that Tent City was preferable to the streets. In their view, however, housing with social supports should be the foundation. "Housing is healthcare," Beric said. In asking why the village didn't organize, Terry cited the drugs and the other criminal content of Tent City. He also they suggested that there was no real drive because they always felt they were doomed for eviction because they had no

Eric Weissman

lease. "We were occupiers after all," Terry said, so they "were always ready to boot it."

The laudable efforts of the TDC at community organizing did not reach their goal of establishing a community because the members had not acted like a community with a collective conscience, not really. "You can't organize an idea," Terry had said. Except he was wrong. Ideas are at the center of organizing. Ideas about freedom and rights. As we will see, these ideas were central to the organization and establishment of Dignity Village, and ideas also contribute to its current woes. Brian Dodge pointed out that every year they have a Tent City Christmas party at a local pub. WoodGreen held Tent City barbeques to help keep the memory alive, and the ex-residents who still have housing under EHPP have it because it was a program for folks *from* Tent City.

All these and other connections speak to the fluid nature of community I had been trying to conceptualize for some years by then. By fluid, I meant that community is emplaced as Edward Casey (1993) had suggested, but that the psychological attachment to a place that contributes to our identities travels with us wherever we go to live. What each of the residents of Tent City have, even today, more than a decade-and-a-half later, is the mental space that Foucault had talked about, that odd mixture of ideas and experiences about that doomed community that cannot be derided even by their eviction.

Beric spoke an important truth: No one wanted to live in Tent City, yet as utterly poor citizens abandoned by the state but still with civil rights, they had the duty to make that statement and to take land to build shelter, if society wouldn't do it for them.

By the time the exhibition had ended, I learned that I had been accepted into the individualized program at Concordia University. I had something to say and would do so while earning a Ph.D. in the social sciences. By then, based on all my research, Tent City had been described as a shantytown, a lawless community of addicts and criminals, and a statement of how Toronto had failed the poor. However, beyond these opinions, very little theorizing about the community had taken place. In Portland, Dignity Village was touted as an alternative community: it was green, sustainable, and described by housing activists from around the world as a successful claim by worthy citizens. How different was the claim in Portland, if it was considered legitimate under the rule of law?

What do rejection of accepted practices and a "break with habitus" mean in the context of people fighting for basic rights denied to them by the state? Why should two similar solutions to the problem of access to housing lead to such different results? What is critical activity? It seemed to me that the EHPP resolution to the Tent City closure was evidence of each—that is, that structural forces and the power of critical groups create new structures and new types of agents when claims are successfully involved. So there is structure but also agency. So what did a legitimate homeless camp mean to the discussion of structure and agency? To begin to answer these questions, I wanted to understand how an act which leads to absorption into existing legal frames could be considered activist? My understanding had always been that activists challenged not only the ways things were done, but also the very legal principles, some very antiquated, that continued to hold people down.

Isin, Nielsen and other contributors to *Acts of Citizenship* (2008) offer the concept of *acts of citizenship* as an innovation in the way social sciences can study *citizenship*. In this work, the idea of the citizen is expressed in a variety of performative contexts that go beyond the traditional notion of a state with borders, which imposes obligations and rights on individuals, thus creating a citizen, or *ascribing citizenship*. What separates the concept of *acts of citizenship* most importantly from many mainstream citizenship studies is its insistence on showing how citizens occupy a dichotomous position within the legal-rational state (*structure*) and in their "own" constitutive state (their Being), and hence are not merely subject to *containment* (Isin 2008:15). There is an individuated performative quality to the "actors" in acts of citizenship that transcends points of view that proffer abstract ideals.

Isin (2008), once again, points out that the citizen is involuntarily caught up in a web of rights and responsibilities which overlap such things as the environment, rules of copyright, traffic rules, and so on. Such accords cross objective-subjective interstices of social and political choice and are clearly related to the structural mechanisms of the state, so that the state is "implicated in varying degrees of influence and autonomy" (2008: 15). Still, a further complication in the current context of the political world is that citizens now carry these "webs of obligation" with them and are affected by those of other citizens well beyond local contexts into the global arena. "The intensification of social relations through movements and (global) flows has generated new affinities, identifications, loyalties, animosities and hostilities across borders" (16). It has become difficult to locate citizens within their local belief systems or to isolate the origins of a trend that makes its way onto the local scene. Drache (2008) similarly dresses the citizen in a coat of many colours, explaining that the boom in information technology has provided new modes of action, new modes of interaction across borders without the need for spatial demands on citizenship, so that the citizen now comprises the citizen of the nation and world simultaneously. The act of citizenship then can be retooled slightly to include acts, which may require no more than writing a protest letter and hitting the "send" button.

The most influential element of Isin's construction, and one that propels this book to inquire into the nature of critique, is the distinction I made earlier between *activist citizens* and *active citizens*. In the former, actors are created by engagement in writing new scripts about how to approach just and critical aims; in the latter, citizens act out according to or within the limits set out by pre-existing critical scripts (38). Isin argues that acts of citizenship do not need to originate in the name of anything, but are interpreted in how they orient themselves towards justice.

Tent City had never really oriented itself towards anything coherent. Some residents, from time to time, acted cooperatively, or went to protests, usually at the request of TDRC or other organizers. And these were Canadian citizens. For some, that was entitlement enough to what they mistakenly thought was an inalienable right to housing. So they did nothing, because as citizens they possessed but did not have to fight for rights. I would also suggest that in the context of extreme drug use, mental illness and lack of any real tenure on the property that they occupied, fighting for community seemed unreasonable. So one way I interrogated the matter of acts and citizenship was by asking, "Why don't people act when they really must in order to preserve their way of life or for their rights?"

I had a number of discussions with housing activists about how Dignity Village in 2001 had represented a group of people motivated to produce positive living conditions for themselves, as a tribute to the self-help ethos of neoliberal governance. This was Bonni and Drei's position, as well as that of Beric German and Cathy Crowe from TDRC, all of whom understood the idea of people gathering together and helping themselves form a community as a necessary and positive response to the lack of services in the age of devolution. Clearly, in the 1990s, addicts, alcoholics, the poor and the mentally challenged, together with the communities in which they lived, had been left to find solutions to their problems. By the 2000s, this abandonment was yielding to widespread adoption of the self-help era.

A number of articles examine the spaces occupied by the homeless as evidence of the self-help ethos (Marin and Vacha

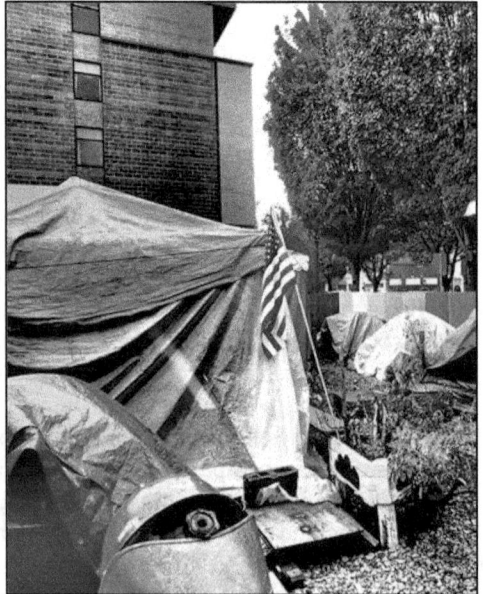

R2DToo. Photo: Eric Weissman.

1994; Rivlin and 2001; Rivlin and Imbimbo 1989; Swithinbank 1997; Mental Help Net 2002; Fairbanks Jr. 2004; Kwamba 2005). The U.S. National Coalition for the Homeless supports a "self-help and empowerment web site" that supplies web site and email addresses to establish a self-help network for the homeless and community organizers. Kwamba, who had been working with Dignity since 2001, had produced the "Tent City Tolls Kit," a video that shows would-be village builders how to do it. The spirit of the self-help ethos is the same one that drives those ethnographies that understand IHC as a noble actioning of needs by disadvantaged persons. Having witnessed the utter decay of Tent City, having learned more about Dignity Village, I had been left with something of a conceptual conundrum. If these places were evidence if not spatializations of poor people "self-helping," building homes and trying to recover from homelessness, wasn't this a type of governmentality? No doubt the squatting and fighting for community was unusual, but was it the break with habitus that I had been trying to imagine?

In a conversation with Dr. Nielsen (who had agreed to be my dissertation supervisor), I learned about the importance of understanding how critical actors come to be and what the real critical act looks like. By this he meant something that inverts, twists, tries on, abandons and settles into a new way of approaching a matter of social justice. We agreed that governmentality was a powerful and persuasive tool for understanding the tension between acts and practices, especially in the self-help era, where "we are constantly being told to fix some thing or another" but that in order to understand the act as something that stands outside of governmentality, one needs to understand how critical actors come to the point in their deliberative and performative capacities to act beyond those constraining tendencies to which both Foucault and Boltanski had spoken.

In some ways, it might be that the distinction between active and activist citizens is close to the two kinds of emancipation I have spoken to earlier. The former seeks to improve a citizen's outcome in the world through political acts that are acceptable. The latter seeks a transformation in the way social justice is looked at and realized through the performance of unanticipated acts that rupture conventional practices. So what kind of action do IHCs represent? Are we talking about places that threaten the dominant powers that create the narratives that undergird the status quo? Are they radical places that threaten to erode the social system and pose a threat to conventionally housed people? What are the provisions that make an IHC viable?

These are important deliberations for me, and constitute the aim of my pragmatic ethnography. To begin to understand the potential for current IHCs to be included in official state language to end homelessness requires that one understands the degree to which the action that created Dignity Village confirms the activist citizen's role to invert and reinvent, or the active citizen's role to follow scripts about how to be critical. For many of us, it is more comfortable to reside in the narratives we have learned along the way, and to condemn places like IHC and the rest areas for their poverty and because people die there sometimes from drug overdoses. We leave little room for the kind of understanding we have embarked upon in the last chapters, an understanding that will never be completely accurate, but even this provisional accuracy, this reflexive narrative where you can read how my critical position emerged out of the melding of my life and intuitive experiences, challenges the blind conviction most of us have to powerful narratives of inevitability. The inevitability of people like E. to die from a mix-up of medication on the streets requires that we look far more critically at how individual lives imbricate with structural conditions of possibility, and then to find a way to help people see where they are in this constellation of contextual factors. If we do this, using the critical and pragmatic ethnographic approach I have discussed, I know we can change our own narratives, and identify others that are fixed, however unfortunate this might seem. For me, with my focus on housing and poverty, this suggests that we need to know how it is that a homeless and struggling subject finds empowerment and becomes a political subject.

So now we can turn fully to our case studies, Dignity Village and, later, R2DTOO. We will look at some theory about space and contests over its use. Then we will look at how Dignity Village came to be the first city-sanctioned emergency campground in U.S. history. The inevitability of Dignity's failure was built into it by the way power used justifications to rationalize the Village in a devastating compromise that 14 years later holds the Village in a death grip. Changing the narratives that govern these spaces, though, means that other IHCs can transcend these weaknesses and improve the social problem we call homelessness. Is the world ready to accept IHCs as a legitimate form of housing? If we yield to the inevitability of these spaces, one that is historically pervasive, what are we saying about the society we live in and the narratives we use to understand our world?

Chapter 6
A History of Spaces, Places and States of Mind

6.1 Spaces and States of Mind

There simply are too many people on the streets of all major North American cities; the criminalization of squatting and camping does nothing to remedy the need for shelter (National Law Center on Homelessness and Poverty 2009, 2011).[109] According to the U.S. Western Regional Advocacy Project, or WRAP, the assault on urban homelessness arises in part because of the inertia of attitudes expressed and formalized by UNESCO and UN-HABITAT conventions on "The Right to the City." These human rights groups draw on Lefebvre's famous (1968) call towards "a transformed and renewed access to urban life" (WRAP [Roy] 2008; Lefebvre 1974:158). Accordingly, the human-rights based social justice critiques look at the claims of homeless activists as based on the very real need for physical spaces to house poor people. This is an often Marxist lens that indicts capitalist tendencies to appraise the value of city space as a commodity more precious than the well-being of the worst off.

As David Harvey suggests, "We live in a world in which the rights of private property and the profit rate trump all other notions of rights" (2008:13). In conveying an epistemic and moral shift in the dominant narratives governing spatial justice from civil to human rights, accumulation and transformative social processes, he argues:

> The right to the city is far more than the individual liberty to access urban resources: it is a right to change ourselves by changing the city. It is, moreover, a common rather than an individual right since this transformation inevitably depends upon the exercise of a collective power to reshape the processes of urbanization. The freedom to make and remake our cities and ourselves is, I want to argue, one of the most precious yet most neglected of our human rights (ibid).

Shifting public and state attitudes towards tent camps and IHCs recognize that shelter is a human right, even if such a right is limited by laws and regulations. But there is an exception. Combined with the shift from rights-based to needs-based approaches in international, national and local grassroots activist communities like WRAP is the expectation that the state understands the destabilizing effects of large marginalized populations, defined by what has been called "an absence of belonging" (Hopper and Baumhol 1996:3).

Eric Weissman

Elsewhere I have described this as perpetual liminality. The danger is not just the cost of policing and emergency services, but also the moral and political weight of sustaining a large population on the margins of economic and social structures. The amount of effort invested in debating, studying, proposing solutions and testing them has given rise to a vast, de facto service industry (Leginski 2007). Beyond this is the negative symbolic value that poor populations offer, calling into the question the ability of the individual or the system.

Wright (1997, 2003) has suggested that control over urban space is a highly political creation, a means by which the powerful render the poor invisible: out of sight, out of mind. Capitalism works (1997:40). Municipal government ensures that the homeless are installed in shelters, "in their place." This kind of spatial discourse is part of the symbolic imaginary of the neocapitalist city. The patriarchal gaze, the framing of the "unhousable" as "outcast," is a symbolic mediation of the limits of material wealth with the contradictions of the moral that at once underpin and are reproduced by the hegemonic social imaginary in the capitalist city. Some might call it a vicious cycle of capitalist accumulation. The wealthy get wealthier and the poorer get poorer, while at the same time the rich make basic needs like housing and food more difficult to secure for the poor and, making things even worse, those interested in accumulating wealth must increasingly speculate in real estate investments, driving even more people into precariousness. I have discussed the streets and various other programs like emergency shelters for the poor as the conventional imaginary's depots for failure. Conventional imaginaries have traditionally had less the difficulty with these spaces than accepting the kinds of unstable housing I had experienced as legitimate forms of homelessness.

Castoriadis (1987) suggests that the symbolic value of "outcasting" the poor or sending the police in to evict squatters has some cohesive value for the powers that govern the city as a "system of signifieds." Recall Derrida and other deconstructionists. Here the suggestion is that parts of the urban social world are meaningless except in reference to others. The meaning of the actions taken by housing protestors or the police, as examples, have symbolic value that is rarely arbitrary, but "fixed through *social practice* which serves to reinforce economic, political and cultural power operating through daily life" (Wright 1997:43). Relationships that generate domination and submission of the homeless person come to be tolerated, if not normalized, in western cities. In chapter five, I suggested that it is this perception of powerlessness that stigmatizes the homeless perhaps more than other defining characteristic. Conventional citizens come not to embrace the homeless as lovable souls but to tolerate their condition as a necessary aspect of capitalist wealth production.

Tolerance, following Wendy Brown (2009), is something learned; the tolerance expressed under western neoliberalism results from clear mediations over time of religious moral and ethical considerations anchored in the western patriarchal anticipation of the problem of the "other." As such, tolerance and other guiding civic principles are implanted in symbolic imaginaries through powerful institutions over time. Foucault refers to these as regimes of knowledge and power. Where many urbanites look at tolerance as a gift, as a sign of "progress" and civilized society, Brown has shown that tolerance falls short of embracing the difference of the other because the fundamental categorization between an "us" and a "them" is essential to make tolerance possible. Accepting the perpetually excluded other from us perpetuates the systemic conditions that create their demise in the first place.[110] Wright (1997) reminds us that the way we think about life and what is tolerable in it is learned, and so then are our basic categories of deserving or worthy uses of public space and resources:

> Therefore the organization of societies, of race, ethnic, gender, and class configurations, of social-physical space and temporal organization, is not conducted strictly along biological or chemical lines, or by the logic of reason, or by the materialist logic of capital development, but are the byproducts of the organization of fantasies, of the working of the social imaginary in a dialectical relationship with the material world. A social world comprised of vast social inequalities will produce different fantasies of "normality," struggle, resistance, and domination than a world in which social inequality is abolished (1997:44).

The historical record will show how the social world of the homeless is linked to conventional systems of signification which neoliberal hegemony uses to discredit and marginalize them. The dominant urban imaginaries transform this linkage into an apparently natural state of affairs, as well as a proviso to citizens to not fail. Wright suggests that it is in the operation of the dominant social imaginary on usually unknowing participants (citizens, members of the mainstream and even the homeless) that questions such as "Who are we?" arise, and also that identification of the *other* takes place. The formation of imaginary categories of *deserving* and *undeserving*, such as the "undeserving poor," must be understood as resulting from social practices within a social and physical space. This social space, to recall Bourdieu (1958, 1972), is the lived field in which policy and law work to shape the conduct of individuals through culturally and scientifically approved modes of behaviour or *habitus* that manifest in the somatic experience of social practices and cultural symbols.

Capital has abandoned North America. Much manufacturing is moving to Asia. Capitalists have forced North American urban economies to endure a decline in manufacturing, with little need for labour. Not only are ex-labourers entering the ranks of the homeless, but those homeless poor who served as casual labour no longer fit into the economy. As part of its self-protective tendency, neoliberal regimes of power have placed the onus on individuals to recover from this abandonment. For anyone who fails to succeed, the primary problem has been reframed as an inability to self-govern, rather than as a reflection of economic dysfunction made possible by states that do very little to protect low income individuals.

In a Lefebvrian city, hegemony (or perhaps "the state" under neoliberalism) intentionally creates spaces for failed classes as well. These include the tenements and cheap motel units where many of the working poor reside. And then there are the spaces for those without work that the literally homeless must occupy. Gary McDonogh (1993:13) argues that lots, fields left fallow, underdeveloped areas or buildings awaiting use are signs of the ambiguous presence of power in the city. These liminal *no man's lands* become poorly defined as types of space, and the relations they are meant to support do not situate easily in conventional housing narratives.

Empty urban space is generally given a negative twist and comes to be feared as the source of potential conflict. The laneway, the bridge, the derelict building all become the sites of negative discourse. So too do their inhabitants, victims of economic narratives of inevitability. As negative as such places are, the repetition of this ambiguity through successive generations of experience normalizes them for both those who must seek shelter there, and to a conventional symbolic imaginary that has come to expect such usage by flawed poor people. Capitalism produces this narrative: it wants extreme poverty to be understood as clandestine and dangerous. It wants citizens to fight for work even when work is scarce.

Lefebvre (1974) asserts that each kind of economic regime creates a space of its own. Cities with skyscrapers and freeways are testaments to the power and pervasiveness of the capitalist regime and the wealth it produces. Since inequality and poverty are also universal to capitalism, analysis of capitalist hegemonic space must include the negative places such as the rundown ramshackle abodes where the poorest and worst-off cases live. [III]

The street is that part of that place, a nondescript, largely un-built place, absent of feasibility, lacking functional structures, dilapidated, broken and unusable to most; the street is not finite or bounded in the sense that a room or a building might be. Most often the street is described as the unused, discarded and unintended places within the city (my definition but see also Wagner 1993; Bourgois 2002, 2009; Weissman 2012). The street also has come to include all places that a homeless person who has no address might use in the course of their homelessness. When I use the term "the street" it is with regard to this continuum of impermanent, ambiguously formed and described, and often-illegal shelter.

It is only when homeless people group together to make a claim on these spaces that the attenuated ambiguity of street life—what Lefebvre would call its existence as a loosely wrapped parcel with unidentifiable contents, *people* in extreme poverty—can be seen as part of a discourse on citizenship. In this case, the narrative produced by the claim on space by unworthy types shifts to an indictment of conventional social relations that unites homeless people in a community of others. But such a gathering is understood here as emplaced lived experience, and is a community in the liminal stage of becoming conventionalized. As such, it threatens hegemonic values.

For a shantytown to be accepted as an IHC means demonstrating its potential to be more than a "parcel with various contents"; instead, it is envisioned as something different than life on the streets (Lefebvre 1971:27). This means that to be seen as a legitimate community by more powerful groups, the way life is lived there must conform to certain conventional ideas about how to live in urban spaces.

Abstract notions of space impose critical qualities onto types or categories of space and eliminate the key factor to understanding what the social implications of space are—its lived and social qualities. By conceptually taking the actor out of the imagining, abstractions would predict what humans should do rather than what they might do. For example, the assumption that a park should only be used for temporary visits and leisure activities because our hegemonic abstraction of it sees it that way does not change the fact that people with different ideas and needs live and sleep in parks and have done that since recorded history began. This is not simply to say that most people would rather not see homeless people sleeping in a park. The point is that homeless people are not the only ones who sleep, have sex and do other things associated with home in parks. Furthermore, Mitchell (1991), Ward (1975) and numerous others have established that the public imaginary is a difficult one to pin down. Even courts in some Canadian cities are at a loss how to interpret such spaces. In Victoria, B.C.,people are allowed to camp overnight in parks, while in most other cities this is forbidden.

The negative interpretation of IHC as a shantytown—a slum, in other words—is a means of "transferring the etymological sequences" out of the hands of people who need and create that space and delivering them once again into abstract ideals about appropriate relations. Lefebvre would argue that neoliberal, neocapitalist imaginaries want us to see the shantytown as a negative place in order to protect the integrity of their capitalist imaginary (4–5). This means very simply that more powerful groups can use laws and media to restrict how people interpret the use of urban spaces.

In this sense, the street one encounters today is an historically conditioned version of how capitalism abstracts idealized space through the implementation of welfare and housing policy over long periods of time. In the span of four centuries in the U.S., federal, state and municipal governments have governed city spaces with a very clear eye to making it difficult for the marginalized to find a sense of place by establishing viable social affiliations. A way to do this is to make the spaces occupied by the weak and marginalized more dangerous, less permanent and very inhospitable. If not explicitly constructed for the purpose of warehousing the villains and failures, the street fulfills those expectations. A series of historical mediations of representational spaces that go back to the first cities, mediations which have confronted the symbolic with the rational, have made this so (Lefebvre 1991:231).

Beyond the streets, therefore, hegemony countenances certain constructed spaces such as hostels, shelters, prisons, and housing programs for the management of the very poor. The myth of an undeserving, flawed homeless person, or the underlying mental and physical conditions that correlate strongly with this, serve to deflect attention away from inequitable relations of production. Hegemony eschews responsibility for the root cause by legalizing spaces and places for the care of the failed; we build hospitals, rehabs and prisons so that neoliberal government can appear as a reflexive and capable way of shaping the social world. Suspended in marginality, somewhere between the streets, a course of spaces notoriously understood as sites of death, disease, and starvation, and the impossibility of finding conventional housing, are millions of people in North American cities who struggle with the exigencies of daily life, and who fear ending up on the streets. I noted at the beginning of this book that there are 146 million people in the United States living between insecure housing and literal homelessness. At times in the history of the U.S., especially during economic collapses, such people were granted the privilege of living in intentional communities of squalor called shantytowns.

In the case of late capitalism under neoliberalism the politics of shifting economic fortunes create certain acceptable imaginings of how poverty should be experienced and where the homeless should endure. Following Foucault's work on power and Lefebvre's attention to the social construction of space, I will argue that beyond creating economic inequality, power concentrated in ideological and knowledge centers creates ideas about spatial imaginaries— attitudes towards and narratives about the proper space for the performance of poverty, commerce, public events and private life.

We will also see that the cases we are going to look at appeal to activists' sense of fighting for rights. These, however, can also be interpreted as those "rare instances of domination" to which Foucault spoke. The current state of affairs to which Harvey speaks did not just happen as the result of some sudden political shift or unforeseen massive structural upheaval. It must be understood in terms of how it came to be thought of in this way over time. The case of Dignity Village, the precedent-setting and first legally city sanctioned IHC in U.S. history, is not explainable simply by describing the village as it is today. We need to examine how the problem of homelessness has been rationalized and conditioned by government since the American colonies emerged in the seventeenth century in order to understand how a village like Dignity could come to exist in a history that has done much to quell the activism of the homeless. By doing this, we can see why new visions of IHC are taking the shape they do, and we can ask what provisions are necessary to change the narrative on housing.

6.2 History Per Se

Snow and Andersen (1993) argue that street poverty is the most visible example of chronic homelessness, and as such it is a sort of historical and cultural universal. Even Biblical references to the beggar and the poor are common. A cursory search of references to poverty and homelessness returned over 2000 verses that reflect on the condition of poverty and the advocacy of neighbors in the care of the poor (LAMPA website; the Official King James Bible Online; Democratic Underground.com). [112] Most literature reviews of ancient attitudes towards poverty link to concerns over fasting, a ritual common to ancient and modern Judeo-Christian and Islamic practices. Some scholars have approached the issue by looking at how ancient cities (in this case, in ancient Greece) managed their homeless populations (Ault 2001:278). These references can be seen as evidence of poverty at least in the value systems of early civilizations, if not as some kind of empirical evidence of the scope of the problem throughout all recorded time. More importantly, these citations give evidence of the linkage between ethical treatment of the poor as the essence of charity, public policy and civic morality. Furthermore, in Europe during the Middle Ages and well into the nineteenth century, attitudes towards the poor were influenced by the central role of churches and parishes. European attitudes are particularly germane to our discussion since the colonies that became "America" were the result of European colonialism.

As Snow and Anderson suggest, English folk traditions steeped in this religious ferment had two mitigating effects on the experience of poverty in preindustrial Europe. First, tradition was to offer assistance to the needy. Second was esteem for the poor; a sense of noble deprivation in which poverty was idealized and the liminality of the poor understood as a morally transcendental experience (1993:10–11). Under the influence of the Franciscans, "It was an age of considerable charity towards the destitute" (ibid). Rather than being devalued on the basis of marginality or failure, the poor were reified in ways that rarely distinguished between deserving or undeserving, except in cases of criminality or intemperance.

Snow and Anderson suggest that during the Renaissance, growing interest among humanists in mundane activity and material success undermined the

Eric Weissman

valuation of poverty. The casting out of the poor was catalyzed by the Black Death in 1348, which imposed a sense of urgency to control "floating populations" and unhygienic masses of poor people flocking to towns and villages. England's first vagrancy law appears in 1349. From this time on, according to Chambliss (1964) and Foote (1956), vagrancy would be associated with homelessness, and henceforth laws referred to "a lack of housing and no means of support"; this becomes an important distinction later in our discussion of hobos and modern homelessness (in Snow and Anderson 1997).

In 1388, English law required that homeless wanderers—meaning un-housed, un-propertied laborers, scholars and religious figures—secure a letter from town officials permitting their travel; otherwise, they could be imprisoned for vagrancy (Wallace 1985:4 in Caton 1990:4). These measures were designed to ensure that feudal enclosures had sufficient labor at sufficiently low cost to remain solvent. As such, the laws were designed strictly to control the emigration of the vagabond from one locale to another in search of better wages or working conditions (Caton 1990; Snow and Anderson 1997:11). DePastino (2003) and Dean (1991) understand this tradition as an essential means of controlling the wages of poor laborer to ensure the competitiveness of producers.

Tudor laws towards the homeless were less generous. Whereas vagabonds and poverty had previously been associated with a certain condonable idleness, under the Tudors the vagabond was reinvented as a criminal type (Snow and Anderson 1993:11). By 1495, Henry VII imposed the Vagabond Act, outlawing wandering and loitering in places other than a home village.[113] During the Protestant Reformation, Henry VIII separated from the Catholic Church and formed the Church of England. This action led to the closure of monasteries, the retention of church lands by the sovereign for his own use, and the loss of that charitable support base for the poor (ibid). At the same time, large numbers of returning soldiers and agricultural laborers displaced by the enclosures flocked to the burgeoning cities seeking charity and alms no longer available in their rural home communities (Slack 1988).

By the mid-1500s the monarchy and parliament were aligned over measures designed to deter subjects from entering homelessness. In 1547, Edward VI ordered that vagabonds were subject to imprisonment or servitude as slaves and could be branded with the mark of a "V." Such undesirables would be taken to a local magistrate and placed with a master to work. Failure to comply resulted in banishment to colonies as slave labor or even in execution (Caton 1990:4; Snow and Anderson 1997:11–12).[114] Though the act was not rigidly enforced, the tendency to mark the poor person in terms of deserving and undeserving was by then also a determining factor in whether a given homeless person was tolerable or not. In this case, the aged and the infirm were considered legitimate recipients of alms, charity and tolerance, whereas

208

all others fell into the category of undeserving on the basis of their unwilling-ness to work.[115]

By 1572, the poor were increasingly categorized by the monarchy, the state and local parish authorities on the bases of deserving or undeserving. Poverty, then, is not restricted to advanced capitalism. The problem has increasingly been associated with an ideological shift among powerful interest groups con-comitant with restrictions on land use, agricultural compartmentalization and other socio-economic changes associated with a shift towards capital-ism. These transformations restrict the solvency of the very poor and reflect an ideological shift in which the moral virtue of abject poverty is replaced with its civic criminality.[116]

It was the Elizabethan Poor Law of 1601 that most directly impacted the tradition of categorizing communities' responses to the homeless on the basis of deserving and undeserving. By 1601, a legacy of laws that defined the rights and duties of the homeless poor increasingly became framed in terms of whether the individual was perceived as mentally or physically deprived of the requisite ability to care for themselves or whether they were able but not will-ing to participate in the economic functions of the community in order to se-cure food, shelter and clothing for themselves (Caton 1987; Slack 1988; Dean 1991). The Poor Law, which remained in effect in England until 1834, down-loaded the responsibility for caring for deserving poor onto local parishes. While the law required the taxation of wealthier citizens to pay for this care, it imposed no levy on them for care outside of their own parish. The law was brought to the American colonies, where local landowners and businessmen often responded by making it uncomfortable for the homeless poor to settle in their communities, or ensured that immigrants were solvent before settling (5). As Caton points out, when the first wave of English immigrants came to what is now the United States in the early 1600s, they came with indentured vagrants and criminals exiled by the English government.

Caton surmises that these indentured persons were probably constituents of the first homeless populations in the New World, ill-equipped as they were to cope with the "harsh demands of Colonial life" (1990:5). In either case, com-munities developed means by which to determine the value of certain individuals based on their usefulness to the community. Hence the religiously and morally inscribed obligation to care for the poor and the old through acts of charity transforms into a basic problem of dealing with economic liabilities that is effectively a civic problem involving members of the community who do not fit in.

In cases where large agricultural or resource projects were underway, such transients became a vital element of the casual labor force. Their well-being and care was irregular, dependent on the ebbs and tides of production, and while they may have been provided shelter and food in exchange for their

Eric Weissman

labor, when production ceased they were most often left to begging in order to survive. Almost immediately, then, vagrancy and poverty accompanied the commercialization of agriculture, the rise of mercantilism and the high price of accommodation in towns and cities in the New World, as had been the case in England, and "a cadre of homeless wanderers emerged among the destitute and disabled in the American colonies" (Deutsch 1937:39–54 in Caton 1987:5). This marks the beginning of the first "wave" of homelessness in the United States and also the beginning of policies of various kinds to control homeless populations and to determine the social worth of the poor, understood as deserving or undeserving on the basis of their capacity to self-govern.

Early colonialists had incorporated English poor laws, which simultaneously created the local parish as the authority for dispensing with care for the poor and forced communities to find discursive and practical means for casting out the needy. With the growth of cities, increased commercial agriculture and rising industrialism in the late eighteenth century, the poorest once again become disparaged for being ineffective. In larger towns and urban centers, correctional work and almshouses begin to appear (Caton 1990). As Dean (1991) points out, it was during the late 1700s in Europe that debates about pauperism become the basis for discussions of the constitution of poverty (1991:7), and when also we can see a direct connection between the pauper as constituent of a class of labor necessary to emerging capitalism. Hence, paupers and vagabonds in the new world were increasingly jailed for their vagrancy and for trespass, and set to work side by side with the disabled, the mentally handicapped and the convicted felon in mills, commercial cultivation and other forms of essentially slave labor (Caton 1990:7; Dean 1991). In what seems like a vulgar reflection of present-day workfare propositions, at the end of the colonial wave, the pauper, the able-bodied mentally insane and other dependent persons were bid upon at auction and put to work in return for shelter and food (Deutsch 1937 in Caton 1987:6). Marshall (1972) argued that the treatment of pauperism inhered the incorrect and usurious belief that poverty was necessary to progress in the economy and the state and that work programs offered emancipation.

Dean (1991) suggests that the particular treatment of paupers in a given regime is emblematic of the general tendency of liberalism to infuse the economy with the will of a strong centralized state that works though individuals and collectives to ensure the health of the economy (6). Paupers thereby become the subject of laws governing their freedom and their movement. Hence, from roughly 1800 onward, poverty is increasingly constituted in liberal democracies as a central problem for governance and for governmentality (Foucault 1991, 1975; Dean 1991, 2010). Poverty emerges out of the eighteenth century as a discursive and practical consideration for states, one which ultimately rests on the implanting of normatively accepted beliefs about being deserving or undeserving in the minds of the poor themselves. While the colonies became independent of English rule, the poor were not freed from the draconian measures that undergirded treatment of the homeless in poor laws. In 1819 and 1837, economic crises in the U.S. displaced able-bodied men on a massive scale. While soup kitchens and other institutional responses to the poor had been developing in New York and other major cities since 1802, it was the combination of these two crises and then the massive displacement of men after the Civil War that created a widely held notion of a national homeless problem (Caton 1990:7; DePastino 2003; Leginski 2007). With large numbers of able-bodied men who were willing to work but had to seek assistance, cities became increasingly intolerant of vagrants who became understood as idle and were represented by politicians and newspapers as alcoholic, law breakers and troublesome, and hence undeserving. The attack on the homeless character manifested itself in attacks on the places the homeless would use for refuge: doorways, tunnels, forests, and abandoned structures. Many of these unemployed men travelled from city to city looking for work.

It is from this tradition that the image of the American hobo is crafted (Anderson 1923; 1975; Ward 1979; DePastino 2003). The word appears in nineteenth-century literature but is of unknown origins. What we know of hobos is very much the result of how their experience has been told, and therefore the hobo identity crafted, by writers, often hobos themselves. John Riis and Nels Andersen are two examples of men with experience in that way of life. They speak and write directly to the types of spaces lived in by nomadic men in search of work in the U.S. Unlike vagrants and tramps who were penniless and idle wanderers, hobos are understood as a form of migrant worker often not just poor but also intemperate in nature (Anderson 1923, 1975; Ward 1979; DePastino 2003). In the west, they had sought employment in the resource industries of California, Washington and Oregon. When unemployed, they camped rough near the forests and mills waiting for work. In Washington, they had occupied Seattle's Skid Road, a run-down section of downtown Seattle where lodgings and drink were cheap (Caton 1990; Rossi 1989). By 1872, the term "Skid Row" had been synthesized from this former usage, and was used extensively in other cities, starting with New York City, to define the area of the city, sometimes also referred to as the "main stem," where vagrants and hoboes sought refuge and association (Bahr 1968, 1973; Rossi 1989).[117] It should be noted that skid rows have been commonly associated with densely populated urban cores (Bahr 1968, 1973; Ward 1979; Rossi 1989; Caton 1990). This is a misconception. Skid rows began as outlying communities established in unused public lands between cities and wealthy estates.

It was the expansion of the city that in most cases brought skid rows into the core urban space; as cities expanded, skid rows, flop houses and cheap bars increasingly became associated with downtown cores (ibid). In the expanding cities of an industrializing America, skid rows become difficult to tolerate within mainstream imaginaries. Isolated by poverty and the need to form alliances with other transient men, by 1873 (during yet another economic reversal) tens of thousands of homeless men took up residence in various skid rows, the only space where they enjoyed social and economic ties (Bahr 1973; Caton 1990). If not an actual threat to conventional citizens, skid rows burgeoning with troubled and often desperate men gave the impression of danger. With unemployment as high as 40%, no national homeless policy emerged, but the Young Men's Christian Association and the Salvation Army did build hotels for the poor and encouraged their repatriation into a growing resource economy in the Western United States (Caton 1990). While police stations were increasingly used as temporary night shelters for vagrants, the majority of displaced men found themselves secreted away in abandoned or unused buildings, in the flops along skid rows or in the streets, and in the various city shelter spaces made available by municipal housing authorities, while many more rode the trains in search of casual work (Riis 1902; Anderson 1923, 1975; DePastino 2003; Caton 1990; Leginski 2007).

Whereas the homeless might ideally have looked for work, in the absence of employment they resorted to begging. In 1877 the New York Board of Charities advocated outlawing begging and posited jailing vagrants in work camps (Caton 1990). The Rhode Island Tramps Act of 1880 is emblematic of such an official law prohibiting camping, sleeping in parks or vagrancy of any kind (ibid). Such laws opposing the settlement of hobos and vagrants were common and underscore the ban on camping in many U.S. cities today. Another law, the Kansas Vagrancy Statute of 1889, attacked vagrants on the basis that jobs were always available and that vagrancy was tantamount to idleness. A brief economic upswing occurred between 1888 and 1892 only to be dramatically reversed on May 5, 1893, on what is now known as "Industrial Black Friday" or the Panic of 1893. As many as three million men suddenly found themselves unemployed during yet another dramatic failure of the economy (Caton 1990:8). The U.S. economy—not character—is far more closely connected to the numbers of persons who suffer from housing security.

Marcuse (1990) points out that there has always been a difficulty in defining homelessness, given the variance of definitions across local, state and federal jurisdictions, not to mention across periods of history. The definitions tend to reflect several important differences, including those who voluntarily abandon their roles in the economy, those who eschew the virtues of the model home, and those who are forced against their own will to abandon traditional roles either through calamity or illness (141). Furthermore, there is a tendency to define homelessness for the purposes of policy making. *Shelterless, homeless in shelters, housed but imminently shelterless, housed but not in homes* and, finally, *at risk of being homeless* are categories which Marcuse (1990:140-42) suggests follow a sort of continuum in which the *shelterless* is a person living on the streets, and the *at risk* category includes anyone who might be adequately housed but is at risk of losing their residence due to illness, financial worries, or loss of employment. These "types" continue to complicate definitions of homelessness. The degree to which the definition of homeless is inclusive of some or all of these definitions will therefore inflate or deflate the numbers. Furthermore, there is some sense that the degree to which an individual can be blamed for their own poverty justifies their treatment as deserving or not.

By 1913, a new recession had led to an increase in demands on city shelters and church alms houses and had swelled the numbers of men living on skid rows. New York's famous Bowery had as many as 75,000 men living there in the first half of 1915 alone (Caton 1990:9). [118] While the majority of the homeless lived in rundown rooms or in shelters, Anderson's famous study of "hobohemia" revealed the marginal life of the hobo in urban "jungles" or shanty camps on the outskirts of town near railway junctions, where they could hop freight trains and search for work as migrant laborers. Anderson found that these men started out in search of work, often with families to attend to back home, but ended up jobless and lost because they were industrially inadequate or had personality defects (Anderson 1923, 1975; also Caton 1990:10). With the skids infested with homeless men, and with a scarcity of employment, the social ties and cliques that hobos tended to establish were best addressed in their own social organization. For this reason hobo camps became fairly common in the outlying regions of cities, even if they were frequently routed by the police in the service of expanding city cores.

Reliable data on homelessness are scarce, but it is suggested that by the mid-point of the Great Depression, as many as five million Americans were homeless (Caton 1990; Reed 2008). The jungles of Hobohemia, as DePastino reminds us, were not lawless and without order. Beginning with Nels Anderson's (1923) study of the *American Hobo*, we understand the culture of the hobo as one of ritually reinforced rites of passage and camaraderie, invested with symbols and a lexicon and regarded with high esteem by those who had come to be defined by that manner of living.

While mainstream society had looked upon hobos as dangerous and ambiguous characters, they were cautiously recognized by the state and by industrialists for the important migrant and casual labor function they provided. By the time of the Great Depression, the hobo camps that had been seen as dens of iniquity and as potentially dangerous places by most of the conventional population (along with the politicians who represented them) were on the decline. In the meantime, there was a wider understanding of these camps as problems associated with the location of employment.

The Depression extended this need to millions of others. With nowhere else to live, hundreds of thousands of newly homeless persons slept in cars, abandoned lots, under bridges and in ad hoc shantytowns frequently referred to as Hoovervilles.[119] Under such conditions of massive economic decline, federal and state governments understood shantytowns as a legitimate but temporary response by deserving citizens to the need for shelter that had been stripped from them by circumstances beyond their control. Between 1927 and 1941, shantytowns were grudgingly embraced as inevitable manifestations of massive poverty.[120]

Without a well-funded housing or welfare sector, tens of thousands of families became literally homeless, that is, unsheltered and with no place to sleep. For the first time in U.S. history, the majority of the homeless were no longer intemperate transient men, but included able-bodied and motivated men, women, and children of all ages and from all ethnicities. Whereas most studies of skid row had revealed a population of mostly white men, the new poor comprised blacks, whites, families, children, and single women (Bahr 1968, 1973; Caton 1990; Snow and Anderson 1993). The social structure of the homeless shifted dramatically from small groups of randomly affiliated men to mobile collectives comprised of families and friends, and, in some cases, entire communities.[121] When Hoover left office in 1933, unemployment was at 25%, millions of Americans were living outside of the normal housing market, and more than 100,000 businesses had failed (Best 1991, 1993; Reed 2008).

Shantytowns popped up near churches and missions and along city access routes along which family members could more easily travel to find handouts of food, clothing and fuel, and perhaps day labor. The structures were crude, usually fabricated from any discarded building material, but included items like old car seats, chassis, road ductwork and culverts and even cardboard. Many people were forced to live in their cars, the image of which is indelibly recalled in Steinbeck's *The Grapes of Wrath* (1939). Hoover lost the election of 1932 to the Democratic candidate, Franklin D. Roosevelt. In several places, states set up large work camps to house workers in the infrastructural work programs introduced by FDR.[122]

Shelter was only one part of the problem facing the government; others included jump-starting a dead economy, providing jobs, and guaranteeing the income and safety of those for whom a return into employment or strong family lives was unlikely. As a result, Roosevelt introduced two New Deals. The first in 1933 included economic regulatory measures while the second in 1935 introduced various measures to stimulate bottom-up solvency.[123] While some support was offered to homeowners to avoid foreclosure, the only national shelter-related policy measure was to create emergency camps and shelters for displaced persons. By the end of World War II, under a resurgent economy, most New Deal incentives were abandoned.[124] Today the securities regulations and Social Security are all that remain of the New Deals, but the Great Depression and the intervention of the state in economic and social areas of governance are often referenced when considering homelessness today.

By 1941, the economy had revived and the homeless population declined, as many unemployed were swept up into service in the army and the laws against shantytowns that had been ignored in the previous decade were vigorously enforced. In cases where shantytown residents did not disband willingly, the federal government went about dismantling the shantytowns with the help of the army. The attack on shantytowns was especially damaging to the culture of the American hobo, which was largely eradicated as an historical form as a result of the sweeping of shantytowns and the participation of their members in the war effort (Ward 1979; Rossi 1989; Caton 1990; DePastino 2003).

The boom in the U.S. economy continued from the end of World War II until the early 1970s, when rising oil prices and high inflation destabilized growth. In the intervening 30 years, suburbia became the norm for middle-class America, and the outlying regions of towns where shantytowns had once rooted were aggressively rezoned and developed into the now familiar suburban communities. At the same time, downtown cores increasingly became the targets of urban renewal initiatives; the chronically homeless population, which had tended to remain in skid rows and slums, was left with few places to call home (Jackson 1985:220–225; Rossi 1989:32–44; Gans 1991). By the mid-1960s their numbers had increased, while their housing options had all but disappeared. The homeless, deserving or not, were painfully visible (Rossi 1989:33–35; Caton 1990; Marcuse 1990).[125]

In 1949, President Harry Truman signed the Housing Act, which gave federal, state, and local governments "unprecedented power to shape residential life" (Jackson 1985; Rossi 1989). This act, designed to encourage what was termed "urban redevelopment"—later to be known as "urban renewal"—gave private housing contractors the right to build and manage low-income housing. An interesting blog sums up the main criticism of urban renewal, which "destroyed about 2,000 communities in the 1950s and '60s and forced more than 300,000 families from their homes. Overall, about half of urban renewal's victims were Black, a reality that led to James Baldwin's famous quip that 'urban renewal means Negro removal' (Jim Rongstad, "Preserving Freedom Blog," October 3, 2011). Jackson (1985) reviews the intent of laws and housing policy since the New Deals, and concludes that "the result, if not the intent, of the public housing program of the United States was to segregate the races, to concentrate the disadvantaged in inner cities, and to reinforce the image of suburbia as a place of refuge for the problems of race, crime, and poverty" (218–219).

Jackson's (1985) *Crabgrass Frontier: The Suburbanization of the United States* traces the roots of the suburban tradition in the United States back to the nineteenth century. The allocation of a privileged, clean and separate zone for wealthy living had created a uniquely American sense of what I refer to as the "home myth"; the belief that a detached single-family dwelling was a step in the right direction; in other words, it is "normal."[126] Emigration of middle and upper classes to the outskirts of increasingly run-down and congested cities left city cores to the poor, blue-collar laborers and the homeless. Where incentives and housing policy were directed towards building new homes for single nuclear families and expanding suburban areas, creating effective transit and road systems, fixing bridges and improving communication systems, affordable housing for the very poor as a policy consideration remained mired in the practice of letting charitable organizations and communities manage their poor, or relocating the poor into slummed-out ghettoes sometimes called "projects". Official housing strategies entering the mid-1960s supported the practice of building high-density housing for the poor under the label "affordable housing."[127] For the poor, housing projects emerge as a sort of "counter" space to the single family suburban home. As for the homeless themselves, urban renewal had begun to eliminate the cheap hotel, the rooming houses and the flops where they might previously have found shelter. The attack on skid row entered a new phase, as vagrancy laws began to be more vigilantly imposed. The poor, displaced and increasingly without shelter or alms, become far more visible. In the wake of redevelopment, under the towering shadows of the projects, homelessness is lost in outcries against racism and the black/white divide.

An influential volume was Michael Harrington's *The Other America* (1962). This book exposed the widespread failure of the American way of life to meet the needs of the nation. Over 25% of the population was considered poor and this despite great national wealth. Today it is easy to see that the perverse dichotomy between wealth and poverty is an epidemic of sorts. In the 1960s, American society largely operated under the delusion that poverty was isolated to the neat little pockets cities had created for it in the mostly black ghettoes. Harrington's work exposed the broader reality of poverty, alluded to the future implications of an uneducated and unattended large citizenry, and argued that the state had to assume a central role in redressing social needs on moral and practical economic grounds. Harrington influenced both President Kennedy's and President Johnson's concern for social welfare, by suggesting a relationship between normative values for housing and security and the utter impossibility of either in poor, slummed out neighborhoods.

In pointing out that America's preoccupation with its technological and urban mastery had misdirected attention to the 40 or 50 million persons who were living in squalor, Harrington shook up the image of a morally and scientifically superior America and challenged Americans to explain how it was that the poor who were poor in 1950 were still poor: "They were poor. They still are" (1962:1). It's a challenge that could be reiterated today.[128] By 1964, the poverty rate in the U.S. stood at almost 20 percent of the population, in spite of sustained economic growth. Civil unrest was on the increase, and important social research and activist actions shed light on an increasingly difficult problem. If social welfare was not a direct boon to economic growth, then it was arguably a preventive measure inasmuch as it addressed the constitutionally guaranteed rights of Americans against their growing discontent. And by the mid-1960s, the extent to which housing policies had discriminated against the very poor became difficult to ignore. With poverty at 24 percent, Lyndon Johnson examined the role of state intervention through education and improved health care as a means to address poverty. The discussion was never framed in terms of the relationship between labor, and exploitative work relations, even though criticism of Johnson's vision of the Great Society by economists like Milton Freidman characterized these interventions as harmful to the economy.[129]

In his 1964 inaugural address, Lyndon Johnson announced an (un)official War on Poverty. Johnson's vision of the Great Society hinged on poverty reduction strategies that required expanding the government's role in education and health care.[130] Extension of programs aimed at helping the poor, of whom blacks were disproportionately represented, came under fire after the Watts Riots. The increasingly visible Black Power movement enabled conservative critics of welfare to argue against what was essentialized as a problem of ghettoized blacks (Moynihan 1966; Liebow 1967). Support for the war on poverty turned to outright rejection in the Congress. As it regards housing, however, Johnson's platform was extremely important. In addition to setting up extensions of funding to locally based community projects, the Department of Housing and Urban Development (HUD) was created under Johnson's watch. It is within this federal department that national strategies are designed and implemented today. And it is within the limitations of this system that we will understand how Dignity Village and other emergency camps find relevance.

Opponents of welfarist positions assumed that the economy should be attended to combat poverty. Influenced by Oscar Lewis (1961, 1962, 1963), Daniel Moynihan's (1965) *The Negro Family: The Case for National Action*, concentrated on the culture of black poverty that was not unique simply for its lack of real or social capital, but for its unique appearance and role within the context of capitalist relations and segregated modes of urban development. Colloquially entitled the "Moynihan Report," the plan suggested finding jobs for the male heads of black households. Lewis' famous framing of the "culture of poverty" is incorrectly summarized as 70 traits that can be said to be true of all the poor. While Lewis describes these traits as "guidelines," he makes the important point that a difference between poverty and a "subculture of poverty" must be understood to include the contextual conditions that define some types of poverty in terms different from others: "the meaning and the consequences of poverty vary considerably in different contexts.... [T]he subculture of poverty is part of the larger culture of capitalism, whose social and economic system channels wealth into the hands of a relatively small group and thereby makes for the growth of sharp class distinctions" (1968:20). Despite my earlier critique of his work (in particular his interventionist-determinist proxy), the concentration of wealth he spoke of is now well understood now.

As Lefebvre (1974) has suggested, capitalist cities recreate spaces that repro-duce the social relations necessary to the dominant mode of production com-mensurate with urban imaginaries on proper use of space. Bringing the idea of the culture of poverty to bear on Lefebvre's interpretation of the socially created value of space, it could be argued that urban renewal and housing poli-cies that propped up the independent home myth by creating slummed-out projects were means by which the worst-off were and continue to be subjected to domination. The demise of those of us who fall in to homelessness is, there-fore, not just about given choices or problems, but also about the way capital-ist urban imaginaries choose to construct solutions that include or exclude the very poor from the equation of spaces. In the long run, Johnson's war did little to redress poverty or to create a Great Society.[131] Small decreases in the num-bers of homeless during the 1960s were to be quickly erased with the eco-nomic and state contractions of the 1970s (Rossi 1989:37).

By the 1970s, as Caton (1990) argues, it became impossible to ignore the homeless, who were becoming ever more visible. They were sleeping in door-ways, wandering streets aimlessly, dressed in torn and tattered clothes (12). Rossi (1989) explains that despite a short period between 1970 and 1973, when subsidized housing for the elderly actually reduced the numbers of homeless, by the mid-1970s downtown cores seemed to be filled with home-less people. Among these were numbers of unemployed, mainly men of various colors, who had joined the ranks of the homeless on skid row (Bahr 1968, 1973; Ward 1979; Cuomo 1983). Skid rows increasingly stood in the way of redevelopment projects. Displaced as they were, the homeless became far more visible in parks, lanes, scrambling in the night, begging on street corners, or seeking refuge in any public space with night time access (Rossi 1989:34).

The sluggish economy and rising inflation of the 1970s, combined with the relaxation of public inebriation and vagrancy laws and the loss of skid row territories, resulted in the homeless increasing not only in real numbers but also in terms of their visibility within the urban mainstream imaginary. The inadequacy of measures introduced to redress the problem in the 1960s became clear. Many scholars note that the 1970s were noticeably different from the 1950s and 1960s, when homelessness (as distinct from vagrancy or transience) first came to be discussed in the media and the social sciences as a unique category of poverty (Bahr 1973; Rossi 1989; Caton 1990; Hulchanski 2009). Among these differences was the emergence on the streets of families and single mothers with children, seeking assistance. This changes in the demographics of poverty caught the attention of the media and the state, a trend that continues today (Rossi 1989). As Rossi suggests, whereas rundown and slummed-out housing had sufficed in the mainstream imaginary for the very worst-off poor in the previous decades, even this affordable but decrepit form was disappearing, and something new that remains most disturbing today—literal homelessness—began to increase, becoming a highly public phenomenon (1989:34; Caton 1990). There was no place in the urban symbolic imaginaries for women and children on the streets (Wright 1997, 2000).

One response to this literally homeless population was the emergency shelter system that many cities currently employ. While shelters and almshouses have existed in various forms since the mid-nineteenth century, the emergency shelter presents itself as an evolution of sorts, as well as a response to the very real presence of large numbers of homeless persons on city streets. While there are no accurate figures of this national population, New York City doubled shelter capacity from 3,000 to 6,000 units over the five years from the end of the 1970s into early 1984. The number of families housed in emergency welfare hotels (hotel rooms secured by federally funded vouchers to homeless families) increased from a few hundred to over 3,500 per month (37).

The current system in many cities of emergency shelter spaces for the poor is rooted in the landmark 1979 court case, Callahan vs. Carey. In this case, the director of New York Coalition for the Homeless successfully sued the city on the grounds that the city was constitutionally required to provide emergency shelter for those deemed in need. Following an injunction requiring the expansion of the city's shelter system, the city settled the suit with a promise to increase shelter space as demanded. Since then, emergency shelter systems have emerged from city to city on the premise that the worst-off *deserve* emergency protection under the law, but the conditions therein are often worse than on the streets, and, as Rossi points out, were even in the beginning not much better than the cubicle rooms found on skid row (35).

Rossi cites a study by Crystal and Goldstein (1982) in which shelter clients rate prisons above shelters in terms of safety cleanliness and food quality" (35). [132] In any event, emergency shelters are designed to offer temporary relief from the exigencies of street life and are not permanent solutions to homelessness. In my way of understanding, shelters are no more than an extension of street life: every person I have interviewed on the street or in homeless communities has some personal knowledge of shelters. The requirements for getting into shelter often include lining up early, curfews, restrictions on co-habitation, daytime closures, regulations on inebriation, limits on goods and belongings—this last may have the effect of restricting the homeless person from seeking work, taking on part-time or shift work, or gathering resources that might otherwise be useful (Crystal and Goldstein 1984; Rossi 1989; Weissman, 2005, 2012).

While the previous discussion suggests that homelessness has been a recognized issue for scholars and government for over three centuries in the U.S., it is only since the 1980s that the bulk of work has been done in scholarly activist circles. Interestingly, Hulchanski's (2009) study showed that 87% of the 4,744 articles found between 1851 to 2005 that contained the word "homelessness" appeared in the 20 years between 1985 and 2005 (2009:1). The 1980s represented a particularly difficult time for the poor in North American cities. In terms of actual numbers, using New York again as an example[133] in the absence of reliable national statistics, the number of persons accessing shelter beds per night was conservatively estimated to have increased from 5,000 in 1983 to 9,000 in 1988 (Caton 1990:12). Part of the rise in numbers was related to an economic recession that had in due course led to the highest national unemployment since the Great Depression, reaching 10.7% in 1982 before settling back to around 6% by late 1988 (ibid). In early 2017, the U.S. national unemployment rate had fallen to less than 5%, its lowest level in nearly a decade, but because of the increasing unaffordability of housing, the number of the precariously housed has increased.

Many accounts of the Reagan years look upon his presidency as one of the grimmest periods in American history for working people and the underclass. Reagan's administration is often placed side by side with that of Margaret Thatcher as emblematic of conservative neoliberalism (Rose 1999; Gordon 1991; Dean 1999, 2010). The mandate of government under neoliberalism was to reduce government expenditure. Under Reagan, increases in military and defense budgets occurred at the expense of national welfare and housing programs. In the online journal *Shelterforce*, Peter Dreier (2004, #135) makes many interesting observations that correlate the Reagan administration's policies with rising numbers of homeless people. While overall economic stability was restored, the gap between the wealthy and the poor continued to widen, as it does today. As far as the phenomenon of the shantytown is concerned, the withdrawal of funding to cities was perhaps most dramatic. Other than maintaining high amounts of funding for the highways that connected suburbs to cities, federal funding of urban centers declined; before 1980, federal transfers represented 22% of city budgets, but afterward only 6%. On a national scale, this led to closure of fire stations, hospitals, outpatient psychiatric services, schools and various programs for the needy, many of whom were homeless. In this environment of reduced spending, in which cities and communities were increasingly expected to bear the weight of social programs, it seems unsurprising that the visibility of the poor would increase, and it did. At the same time, urban spaces set aside for the homeless declined in number due to incentive-driven urban renewal projects by private contractors, or were converted into undesirable shelters. To his critics, Reagan was robbing from the poor to give to the rich.

Boltanski (2010) has noted that while institutions such as the government, bureaucracies, and religious, educational or employment organizations are administrative and policy-driven, they are also comprised of individuals with particular values and abilities that contribute to the creation of knowledge and decision-making inside the institution.[134] The critique of institutions must therefore include the critique of individuals. In cases such as Roosevelt's New Deal initiatives, the critique is often framed within the debate between liberalism and emerging neoliberalism in the U.S., as I have done. In Reagan's case, any critique must take into account not only his political conservatism, but also his uncanny ability to convert ignorance into policy.

As a gifted communicator, however, Reagan convinced much of the nation that what was good for the economy and for business was good for America. Under the imperative of economic recovery, slashing social welfare programs seemed necessary. Reagan and those who supported him employed a deceptive form of communication to paint the homeless in negative terms. "In early 1984 on *Good Morning America*, Reagan defended himself against charges of callousness toward the poor in a classic blaming-the-victim statement: 'people who are sleeping on the grates ... the homeless ... are homeless, you might say, by choice'" (Dreier 2004).

According to *The Eighties in America* (2005: "Homelessness"), the actual number of homeless in the early 1980s ranged from 250,000 (according to HUD) to 3 million (according to activists). The discrepancy is indicative of the tendency of the former to downplay the failure of the state to redress poverty and of the latter to dramatize big problems with big numbers. While Reagan's critique reflected a longstanding sentiment towards the undeserving poor, a great deal of attention began to be paid to revealing the actual causes of homelessness.

The theories of causation rotated on two axes. The first was the characteristics of homeless individuals and the structural conditions that contributed to homelessness. With some variation, most studies noted the dramatic increase in families that were increasingly falling into chronic homelessness and the fact that many homeless people had jobs but could not afford shelter. Simply put, when compared to the homeless of previous decades, the new homeless were younger, more racially diverse, and despite continuing trends of addiction and mental incapacitation, they were notably able-bodied and willing to work (ibid).[135]

Among researchers, it was concluded that no single axis, or any single category of infliction or experience, was responsible for what was emerging as an increasingly diverse expression of homelessness. Among structural variables, research considered the following:

1. Closure of mental hospitals. Since almost 33% of the homeless were determined to have mental illness, a reduction in total psychiatric beds from 550,000 in 1955, to 120,000 in 1984 had some effect but could not be wholly to blame for the dramatic increases, nor the range of types of homelessness.
2. The introduction of crack cocaine (similarly to meth-amphetamine today). Drug testing in some New York shelters suggested that over 83% of homeless tested positive for cocaine use. While cocaine use did increase, the overall measure of drug use in the homeless population did not change in the 1980s, so cocaine could not be the cause of the increase, nor overall drug use.
3. Policy changes that occurred just before the spike in numbers. These are associated with Reagan's policy towards the undeserving poor. Cutbacks to low-income housing, long-term care facilities and other programs for the very poor must played a contributing role in the rise of homelessness.
4. Gentrification of urban cores. The elimination of low-income housing was made worse by the gentrification of city centers, which hinged on the elimination of single room occupancy units and overcrowding in cheap motels that were increasingly becoming occupied by families forced out of the housing market.
5. Reliance on shelters. Faced with the choice of food and clothing or accommodation for their children, many families chose the former and were forced into shelters or the streets in order to satisfy the latter need.[136]

The implication of these general observations is that in some cases of chronic street homelessness, certain people are rendered incapable of working and caring for themselves because of addiction or mental health issues. It also suggests that others are willing to work but are unable to find the type of employment that pays well enough to support a family. Homelessness, then, is a manifestation of working poverty; jobs simply did not pay enough for a family to survive. By the late 1980s, the fallacy of Reagan's ridiculous comments about poor people choosing to be homeless had been exposed. As the economy showed signs of recovery, the persistence of advocates such as the National Alliance to End Homelessness,[137] the media representation of homeless children and parents on the streets, and the academic attention paid to urban social problems pressured the federal government to introduce the first large-scale housing program.

Under Reagan, the federal McKinney-Vento Homeless Assistance Act (1987) was passed with much ceremony, including a sleep-in on Capitol Hill in which congressmen, advocates and the homeless demonstrated their unity over the issue. The act allocated close to $2 billion, spread over two years, into housing programs, subsidies for existing emergency shelters, rehabs and other medical services (Rossi 1989:37; also USICH 2010). When added to existing social programs for the poor at federal, state, and local levels, it was expected that these monies would buttress efforts to stem new cases of homelessness. It was also expected that they would extend services beyond their normal reach to existing homeless clients. Today, however, the prevailing view is that these monies were too few, spread too thinly, and often too misused to effect meaningful change.[138] Since then, the Act has been re-written and invigilated by the United States Interagency Council on Homelessness (USICH), which was created in the same act.

The purpose of USICH is to "coordinate the federal response to homelessness and to create a national partnership at every level of government and with the private sector to reduce and end homelessness in the nation while maximizing the effectiveness of the federal Government in contributing to the end of homelessness" (USICH 2010). By the beginning of the 1990s the failure of this spending to effect real change had created a strong conservative opposition to the program (Rossi 1989). Caton suggested at the beginning of the 1990s that the following factors contributed to increased numbers of homeless:

1. Economic recession coupled with high inflation and lowered benefits for the unemployed.
2. Lack of affordable housing based on the gentrification of city cores and money spent on temporary shelter measures.
3. Reforms in social security that steered funding away from able-bodied persons to those with known disabilities.
4. Deinstitutionalization of mental health, health and welfare services which had seen the increased downloading of services once provided by state and federal hospitals and agencies to local providers or none at all. This is especially true of state mental institutions, state child welfare services and prison systems (15–17). The result was the beginning of the exposure of a massive problem of widely distributed homelessness "ripped from its customary habitat" (Hopper 2003: 176).

As Rossi pointed out in 1989, the actual numbers of the homeless are difficult to ascertain and largely unimportant in the sense that homelessness is clearly a major social problem (38). Of the forty or so "reasonably well-conducted" studies on the homeless during the first half of the 1980s, Rossi suggests that information has been collected with a particular eye to influence policy directions. Out of this research came some substantive, useful information. First, the old versions of the "homeless" (prior to 1980) were able to find shelter either legally or by trespassing indoors; by the end of the 1980s, this had become far more difficult to do.

Early studies had also shown that the institutional solution—the shelter— proved less hospitable than squats or the street or the run-down motels of skid row (Levinson 2004). Perhaps most importantly, these factors had combined to make homelessness extremely visible in cities. With this transparency, the presence of women and children on the streets became alarming. Between 1976 and 1986 the number of women on the streets rose from less than 3% to over 25% of the street population (this number is a composite based on partial data from New York and Chicago in Rossi 1989:39). An interesting change noted was that old-age pensioners were largely underrepresented in street counts during the 1980s, whereas the mean age of the homeless in 1989 was 39 (40). Social Security and affordable senior residences had served that demographic well. Rossi also points out that while 25% of respondents in Bogue's well-known 1963 study of skid rows were employed at some point during the week, in 1989 a survey in Chicago demonstrated that only 3% worked. Rossi calculated that in terms of absolute poverty, the homeless in 1989 were worse off than their 1958 counterparts; the actual spending power of the average street person in 1989 was less than one-third that of his counterpart in 1958 (ibid).

The final contrast is something that today we find unsurprising. In 1958, Chicago's skid row and New York's Bowery were primarily white: 82% and 70% respectively. By 1989, the ethnic composition had shifted toward black Americans: 54% and 74% respectively. These rates started increasing in the 1980s and homelessness, like poverty, is now more likely among black Americans (Rossi 1989; Caton 1990; Marcuse 1990; Wright 2000; State Of Oregon 2011). Rossi adds that disabilities, alcoholism and drug abuse are still significant factors amongst the homeless. However, it is cautioned that all these variables are additive and conditioning (42–43). It is unlikely that any single factor can explain the kind of abject poverty and street-engaged homelessness on which these observations were based.

Yet despite the various studies and programs, the U.S. was left with a growing and ever-more-entrenched form of homelessness in 2012, when I first wrote my dissertation and my first book. And a dozen years after the announcement of the first "ten-year plans" to end homelessness, none has been successful. The current dilemma with homelessness in the U.S. is in part due to the same type of underfunding of programs that hampered the McKinney Act, and to a loosely structured, largely uncoordinated housing services and care sector (Leginski 2007). Homelessness also spread into new categories of deserving poor, such as middle-class families struck by illness or unemployment. In other words, since the 1980s, homelessness has mutated even further.

One of the main differences noted by Wright (2000) is that by 1990, home-lessness had become understood as episodic and therefore difficult to under-stand, given a wide variance in terms of how long a poor person might be without shelter, or why. Whereas hobos and vagabonds had come to define a sort of lifestyle, individuals who experienced the new poverty were of new conventionally minded types who fell in and out of housing with the ebbs and tides of their irregular work opportunities (2000:28). Most if asked would explain they desired a conventional home, but that was impossible to find given the job market. It was not so much that homelessness "was you might say a choice"—many homeless worked or sought gainful employment—but the experience of employment and relative value of wages had changed. They were insufficient relative to the cost of living. And then there were those, too, who were mentally or physically ill and needed care, those who were incarcerated frequently, and those addicts who had nowhere else to go. My own story from chapter three falls into these categories. This diverse composition makes it difficult to ascertain the actual numbers of homeless people because they are hard to locate and harder still to define.

Wright looks at shelter usage as an indicator of the dimension of the prob-lem, a practice carried out by most agencies today looking for street counts of the homeless.[139] Between 1985 and 1991, he estimated that 5.7 million Ameri-cans had experienced episodes of homelessness (28). Between 1997 and 1998 alone, the number increased annually by as much as 11%. In 1999 participants at the U.S. conference of mayors identified a lack of affordable housing as the major cause of homelessness in their jurisdictions (ibid). Wright makes an interesting survey of several countries, arguing that increases in the number of people who were literally homeless or inadequately sheltered increased glob-ally between 1980 and 1996 as a result of the increasingly neoliberal policies in the West which promoted devolution, and, in the case of the former Soviet Union, after the rise of the market economy had made housing unaffordable.

Based on figures released at the Habitat II Conference in Istanbul, by 1996 the number of people living in inadequate shelter had reached one billion (ibid.; also see Davis 2006). While the U.S. followed the model of other countries, including Canada, for quick and temporary fixes to dire circum-stances and increased spending on emergency shelters and food banks, the numbers of homeless continued to rise and policy began to reflect more punitive attitudes. I have discussed Wright's discussion of enforcement earlier but it should be noted that many of the laws and regulations criminalizing homelessness are articulated by the National Law Center on Homelessness and Poverty (1999). Mitchell (1991) and others, including Stoner (1995) and Barak (1992), sketch some of these general measures: anti-camping, anti-sit-ting and staying laws, anti-panhandling and loitering regulations, and laws regarding sexual indecency (such as urinating in public). Wright has discussed

Eric Weissman

these as attempts to isolate the very poor in institutional spaces created by capital such as shelters and prisons, or to discard them into the invisible margins—the dark places I have referred to as negative space (Wright 1997, 2000; Weissman 2012). For Wright, such policies are very much directed towards the attitudes of mainstream imaginaries and tourists. Sweeping the streets and parks is just that, an attempt to present a cleaned-up version of the city to the opinion of the world.

Wright follows Headley (1990–91) in framing the modern penal system as a branch of housing policy. With as many as 1.63 million people incarcerated in the U.S. in 1996, and 54% of them poor and black, Wright frames the lack of real effort in the realm of housing as indicative of the disinterest of neoliberal regimes to effect programs that would cost money to benefit people of no use to capital, which was engaged in a process of relocating to cheaper low wage regions of the world (2000:29). Today, according to "The Sentencing Project,"[140] as many as 2.2 million Americans are imprisoned annually. Since 1925, the incarcerated population has grown tenfold, making prisons the largest single housing project in the US.

Implicit in this statement is the widely held belief that deserving and underserving categories of poor, or of the homeless, inhere the traditional expectation of personal solvency or of usefulness to others in economic performance. We saw above that this was an early condition of residency in the colonies, a system imported from England, and iterated in poor laws. It remains essential to neoliberal constructions of "deserving" moral character.

Under neoliberal policies, there is some recognition that people have rights to shelter and food, but little recognition of the state's direct and explicit role in providing this. Underlying this difficulty is the inherent complexity of the types of homelessness encountered. As Wright suggests, there is a tendency to look at homelessness in terms of fanciful causal narratives about personal limitations (Baumhol 1996 in Wright 2000:30). Conservatives tend to view the homeless within a religious/moral framework, "to invite homeless people to repent for their sins." They react to homeless people as crazy and/or dangerous, in need of social control (30). On the other hand, liberals often see individuals as flawed or incapable of any economic or normal function. As such, they are either useless in the context of capitalism, undeserving of any real measures to improve their lives (unless they are willing to enter a rehab program of some sort, and better themselves). This liberal position assumes that people can be fixed through rehabs and other programs, supported housing and/or medical interventions (30). The push is for more shelters, more rehabs, more money to "fix" people and their social condition of despair. Much research on the homeless has been done in shelters, rehabs, and treatment centers, and hence my earlier interrogation of the limits of governmentality. It is within this latter context that categories of deserving and undeserving, such as looking for work in order to obtain welfare or unemployment, impose conditional worth on individuals.

Both positions are misguided and simplistic. Each perceives homeless people as either characters in need of a spiritual awakening, or as constitutionally flawed and in need of "treatment." As such, they fail to emphasize that these possibilities result from weaknesses in broader political and economic contexts. Wright therefore suggests looking at the imbrication of so-called "causes": social-structural, individual causes within the wider politico-economic struggle for capital accumulation and racial privilege (ibid). The major problem with poverty and housing policies under the neoliberalism of the 1990s was that they reflected an overemphasis on addressing the symptoms of troubled or addicted individuals in order to access shelter without addressing the basic issues of social structural poverty; housing and income are not (sufficiently) addressed. The way that the homeless had been studied by academics, researchers, foundations and the media tended to support a taxonomic representation of the poor by identifying special needs, such as homeless veterans, HIV drug users, single mothers, teenagers, the mentally ill, and so on. In espousing the prevalence of special needs, a new category of deserving poor people emerged (31). Wright points out that out of 354 articles on homelessness studied by Blasi (1994), two-thirds were in journals devoted to psychiatry, medicine, and psychology (Wright 2000:3; Blasi 1995:580). The implication of this finding, according to Blasi, was that the way American social science looked at social life, especially as it related to poverty, was through the highly individualized personalities and life choices made by individuals (581, in Wright 2000, ibid).

Without addressing all the laws and policies of the U.S. federal government, welfare reform is one area worth mentioning in advance of our discussion of specific cases. All studies attest to the fact that the numbers of homeless increased steadily between 1980 and 2000 (Caton 1990; Marcuse 1990; Wright, Rubin and Devine 1998; Wright 2000; Leginski 2007). Wright remarks that attention to poverty rates tell us very little about real numbers of those experiencing poverty. Between 1980 and 1996, the number of Americans entering poverty increased by over 7%, or 7.3 million people, while poverty rates fluctuated. At the same time, despite short periods of economic decline, the overall economy grew faster than ever before. The top one-fifth of the population became wealthier than it had ever been. This trend continues today. This accumulation of great wealth occurred at a time when the incomes of the other four-fifths of the country began to decline. The bottom fifth of the population saw its share of wealth decline from 5.4% to 4.7% as a result of declining incomes and the loss of low-paying jobs (Wright 2000:31). It is into this steady decline of the worst-off that the retraction of welfare placed the unrealistic burden of maintaining housing.

It is important to note that during the 1990s a number of business improvement districts (BIDS) were introduced in U.S. cities. I mentioned earlier that such districts of capitalization used the press, sit-and-stay laws enforced by the police, and other means to discourage homeless people from remaining in city cores. With urban economies thirsty for recovery, capital enjoyed a certain freedom in effecting policy towards the homeless in most cities. Under this "rule," shelters, hostels and rehabs are understood as well-organized, disciplinary institutions geared towards restoring homeless people to some useful capacity (for capital).

Wright and Leginski share contempt for the intake policies of municipal shelters and the ethos of the Temporary Assistance for Needy Families (TANF) program. TANF[141] was an essential element of the 1996 welfare reform law. It shifted cash assistance away from aid to children in low-income families to temporary aid conditional on work. The effectiveness of this program is disputed. TANF caseloads have dropped by as much as 60%, which has prompted claims that many welfare moms have made their way into the labor market (Leginski 2007:23). There is little data on what these jobs might be or how satisfactory their housing is as a result. Furthermore, other studies suggest that in the first ten years since its inception, many former TANF recipients failed to pay their rent and entered homelessness. The number, inaccurate as usual, is between 7% and 44% (Leginski 2007). Wright (2000) finds the assessment, sanctions, and punitive structures and practices of the shelter system equally troubling and self-serving. Where HUD tends to represent the rules of TANF in a progressive policy frame, and asserts that its weaknesses have been addressed by more flexible language in subsequent versions (2005), critics see the rules as setting restrictions on people in need, especially regarding housing (Leginski 2007:23). For Wright such policies serve only to accentuate the bias of the federal government to seek solutions that benefit policy makers and institutions before those they serve, a criticism Boltanski would find sensible.

Taking TANF as an example, policies introduced in the late 1990s were designed to instill a sense of purpose in poor single mothers and their families that those who were not poor were presumed to enjoy. Similarly, homeless men were expected to pursue the activities and freedoms of a normalized population. Work was worth. This sentiment is 400 years old. But what work was there? It is hard to separate the ethos of this policy from the debates over worth couched in the deserving–undeserving continuum that I have alluded to many times. In this case, the distinction excludes all able-bodied persons without dependents, and casts the worst-off poor, the street-engaged homeless, into an un-serviced category of undeserving poor, whose only recourse is to occupy physically accessible but usually legally prohibited space, beg, become jailed, institutionalized or die.

Wright suggested that, by the end of the 1990s, both the Republican and

Democratic parties in the U.S. subscribed to the same "cultural ideology," one predicated on the "assumptions that spending on social welfare increases dependency and that 'excessive' government intervention in markets and state regulation makes it difficult for businesses to stay competitive in a global marketplace." Such an ideology, combined with the "'no new taxes' rebellion of the 1980s, undercut[s] attempts to use government for social good" (34). He went on to argue that

> [a]t the level of appearance, homelessness is about poverty and ill health. However, these conditions are created by the normal capitalist production of low-wage jobs, high housing costs, coupled with a reduction in social welfare benefits from states attempting to compete with one another over the price of labor and the costs of benefits.... These policy shifts have increased the vulnerability of the poor, with the abolishment of the safety net, medicalization and criminalization of the homeless, and the shifting of funds from the civil welfare state to the corporate welfare state" (34–35).

It should be noted that in this passage, even Wright considers homelessness to be a largely uniform experience. My research and fieldwork, however, found a great diversity in homelessness, a mixture of literal, chronic and periodic episodes of homelessness; with origins in diverse socio-economic backgrounds, a mixture of women and men and of different races, they come to be associated with various categories that reflect the mandates of various acts and plans at different times. What unites these people, at least in part, is their co-residence in a modern shantytown. We recognize this place as an intentional homeless community for its collective orientation to transcend the limits of poverty by building a community to provide emergency housing. At least we will soon be able to decide if the goal of transitioning people away from poverty is a fair claim, or more precisely, under what provisions such a claim is feasible. As a measure not discussed in official plans to end homelessness, nor as a model of alternative housing that meets the expectations of capital in a privatized service sector, the IHC then must be understood as related to (but not resulting from)—perhaps even a response to—this legacy of plans and attitudes towards deserving and undeserving poor.

The history I have summarized here provides a clear context for critiquing the current official competition between supportive housing models such as Housing First, shelter models like the emergency shelters provided by many cities, and the emergent intentional homeless communities, which only now are finding meaning and definition in the narrative on housing. This history also explains why many persons are left to the streets as a function of hegemonic narratives about who deserves help. While tent camps and squats were

Eric Weissman

historically accepted as temporary measures to house sudden bursts of nation-wide homeless, they were not recognized as governable extensions of policies on homelessness, not until Dignity Village became city-sanctioned in 2001. Currently, some U.S. and Canadian cities are publicly and officially exploring the temporary and adjunct roles such IHC can play in short term goals to help the homeless. There is some discussion that these places will become part of official plans to end homelessness. In order to understand the conditions that make this narrative shift possible, we need to look at Dignity Village's legal sanction as an eventalization in the Foucauldian sense; an important discursive event that changed the way a certain social problem (in this case) came to be thought of. In the next chapter we will look at the precise conditions that led to that event.

It is worth taking a moment here to understand the current Housing First model praised by HUD and USICH. It is not commonly understood that the principles of housing people quickly and addressing ancillary conditions secondarily that characterizes current visions of Housing First started as early as 1977 in Canada and not in the U.S. According to Waegemakers-Schiff and Schiff (2014), "housing first is both a housing philosophy and paradigm." It is connected to the Houselink program in Toronto in 1977, which provided "housing without treatment or abstinence requirements for persons with mental illness and dual disorders (Houselink 2011). It is based on the values that housing is a right, and also that individuals have a right to participate in the organization as partners in housing. It was recognized as a best-practice by the Ontario Non-Profit Housing Association in 2001" (5).

This model moves persons in need into housing immediately with social supports available to them 24/7. The authors point out that the earliest use of the term "housing first" was by the organization Beyond Shelter in Los Angeles in 1988, which informally borrowed the term from the emergent Pathways to Housing Model. Pathways is commonly credited with being the initiator of the Housing First philosophy and paradigm (4). Regardless of the origin or the de-bate over the roots, suffice to say that Housing First is the dominant state-funded housing paradigm in the U.S. and Canada today.

Since our emphasis is on U.S. IHC and that nation's housing paradigms, let us briefly look at Pathways. In 1992, Pathways to Housing had emerged as a local response to street homelessness in New York. Though limited in scope, this model recognized that the influence of variables on homelessness was additive and often co-dependent, especially amongst the chronically home-less. As an evidence-based model, it identified that among the street population a combination of psychiatric disorder and addiction confounded responses to chronic street-engaged homelessness, and that periods of incarceration or other traumas contributed to the difficulty of remaining housed (Koegel and Beck 2004:284; Tsemberis 2004:277). Prior to this recognition, shelters, housing programs and rehabilitation models had demanded sobriety as a condition of housing as part of the continuum of housing model.[142] Under the continuum of housing, potential recipients of housing were expected to get sober, learn how to maintain housing in transitional or sheltered spaces while maintaining sobriety, and then would be placed into housing, if it were available (279). Advocates of Pathways recognized that not only was sobriety unlikely or sustainable for most people who suffered addictions, but when presented with other symptoms such as mental illness, the idea that "only through treatment could a consumer become housing ready" was (liuterally) as likely as a phoenix rising from the ashes (278). The Pathways to Housing model views housing as a right for all people, and claims that housing and treatment are not inherently linked domains.

Beric German (2005) of the Toronto Disaster Relief Committee said that we must think of housing as health care,[143] suggesting a link between stable shelter and the ancillary likelihood of dealing with mental health and addictions subsequent to this. This is the position that grew out of the Pathways initiative. The Emergency Housing and Homelessness Pilot Project that housed ex-residents of Toronto's Tent City in 2003 also used rent supplement programs to rapidly re-house homeless folks. Initial reports in 2005 cited improved physical health as one of the benefits of the housing, while my film *Subtext* used ethnography to show that the transition to housing from the streets was very difficult for some recipients without assistance and social supports (WoodGreen 2005; Weissman 2005). Hence, the argument is that housing ought to be provided and that the choice to pursue treatment of substance or other issues should rest with the individual. Tsemberis (2004:277-281), citing Rowe (1999:85), argues that denying the individual this voice is tantamount to oppression. Within the Pathways model, homeless persons are placed in self-contained apartments, usually found in the regular housing market. Assertive Community Treatment (or ACT) teams comprised of social workers, housing workers and medical officers provide the necessary social and other supports as requested by individuals in rental units and on the streets, as yet unhoused. By the late 1990s, the model was successful in New York, Philadelphia and Burlington, Vermont. Success in this case is understood as most recipients of assistance maintaining their housing and, in some cases, achieving the goal of overcoming addictions and other complicating issues.

In the Pathways model, residents spent more time in stable housing than control groups in continuum of care models (Tsemberis 2004:282). Entering the 2000s, a Pathways to Housing paradigm was being more widely experienced and was incorporated into Housing First, a national-scale model of supportive housing initiated by President George W. Bush in 2003. While it seemed as if housing was finally receiving the attention it deserved, the extension of supportive housing was slow. Shelters in North American cities continued to overflow, families on the streets increased in number, and the numbers of homeless continued to rise as tent camps hidden along our cities' riverbanks and forested areas became noticeable. This brings us to the historically important emergence of Dignity Village. At the same time that Tent City was under siege by its critics and eventually erased in Toronto, Dignity Village was emerging as an activist-led expression of a very real need for housing.

As this chapter has shown, history reveals that not only is homelessness as old as urban civilization, many different responses to it are equally enduring. States and charities have offered up shelters, soup kitchens, conditional housing based on overcoming addictions, a prison system to house the "worst of the worst," and as a last resort there is "the street," that repository for failed narratives. From the actioning of needs by homeless people we see squatting, rough sleeping and establishing camps as part of U.S. and Canadian histories. But over time, Canada has not embraced these actor-driven solutions. We tend to move in the direction of emergency shelters and creating housing, although not successfully. In the southern and western U.S., while Tent City was being leveled, a number of campgrounds were arguing for the right to be part of the solution to homelessness. One such camp, Camp Dignity, was to become the first city-sanctioned homeless campground in U.S. history. It presents a lesson in how the critical outcomes of social actors are not isolated from the powers of other groups often opposed to new narratives. We can also look at the terms of the city-sanction as the imposition of a compromise on a critical actor-driven moment. Given the built-in provisions that do not work in Dignity Village, as well as those that do, we can then ask what it would take to change the narrative about the role of IHC in plans to end homelessness.

Chapter 7
Enter the Shantytown

The tents at R2DToo, 2016. Photo: Eric Weissman.

> Tent Cities are America's de facto waiting room for affordable and accessible housing. The idea of someone living in a tent (or other encampment) in this country says little about the decisions made by those who dwell within and so much more about our nation's inability to adequately respond to those in need.
>
> —*Neil Donovan, director, National Coalition of the Homeless, 2010*

7.1 The Fight

Tent camps, temporary squats and overnight sleeping in parks and empty buildings remain fairly constant spatializations of the need for shelter in North American cities. I want to distinguish between these places and Dignity Village on the grounds that the former are regarded as impermanent aspects of street life and the latter is a recognized community. In cities, temporary shelters like squats and camps are not often tolerated but when they are, it is on the basis of this impermanence. In Victoria, B.C., for example, the courts have recently decided to allow homeless camping overnight in public parks, but *only* overnight: the tents must be removed by 7 a.m. Most cities have no-sit-no-stay laws, which we have discussed. If loitering and merely being seated in a park for more than 20 minutes is illegal in many U.S. cities for homeless persons, then squatting and camping remain a serious crapshoot. All cities in the U.S. maintain anti-panhandling, anti-sleeping, anti-camping laws that are exercised at the discretion of the police (NCH 2006, 2010, 2014; Conner 2006). In many cities it is illegal to feed the homeless. Whereas the squatting or occupation of vacant buildings usually results in the eviction and arrest of homeless trespassers on private property, camping in public parks or setting up tents on state lands tend to become legal and political statements about the constitutionality of the right to shelter that draw activists and opponents into legal discourses that play out in courts or in council chambers and certainly in the press and across dining tables in housed communities.

As we saw in the previous chapter, in the 1990s Pathways models enjoyed some success and proved they could help even tough homeless cases maintain their housing; Pathways was (and remains) cost-efficient and humane. Rapid rehousing has been understood in this sense since 1977, yet 40 years later, it is still not a universal system for housing the homeless. By the end of the 1990s, we also saw that a diversification of the varieties of homelessness was becoming more common. There were more of every category—women, women with kids, men, young people, gay, trans and so on—and the numbers continued to climb. While cities were redeveloping urban wastelands and derelict factories into lofts and condos, negative urban spaces were in greater demand by poor people. Access to these sites was becoming ever more restricted because of laws enforced by the police and private security companies.

By 2000, all over the U.S., this contest between the will of homeless people and city governments had led to a more or less consistent response by cities to move illegal homeless campers from site to site, delivering them to jails, even transporting them other jurisdictions, in keeping with laws governing trespass, loitering and public mischief (NCH 2010: National Center for Law and Economic Justice, National Law Center on Poverty and Homelessness).[144]

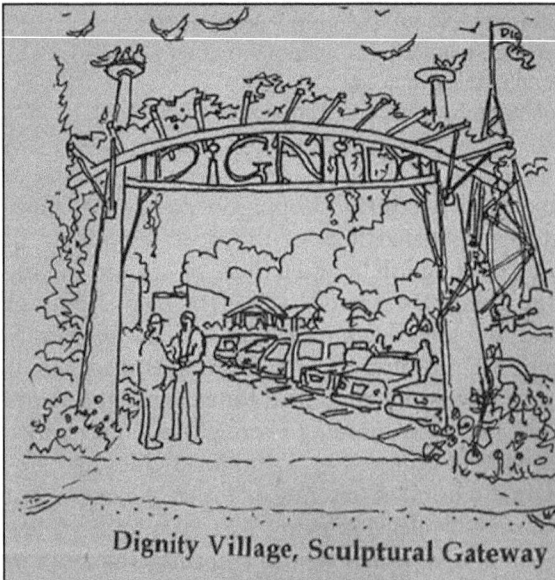

Dignity Village, Sculptural Gateway

Early imaginings of Dignity Village, c. 2004.

In Seattle, Tent City 3, a camp spearheaded by a non-profit organization, was moved as many as 134 times in less than five years.[145] Still, the camps and occupations were a consistent response to a ubiquitous shortage of shelter beds, deplorable shelter conditions, and a lack of affordable housing. In 2000, the core group responsible for the formation of Dignity Village was a group of eight homeless folks who had banded together on the streets of Portland, Oregon, and who were subsequently evicted, moving from park to park, bridge underpass to bridge underpass. They were moved no less than seven times in one year. The numbers of poor on the streets of Portland were swelling because almost every other region of Oregon was suffering from economic decline while Portland offered social services and a supportive homeless community.

Between December 2000 and September 2001, these occupations and subsequent evictions were designed by the city to create the impression of a weak and impermanent group of troublemakers. With each humiliating eviction, and as their numbers grew, the arduous parade of wheelchairs, shopping carts and bicycles helped the nomadic community gain sympathetic attention in the press and with activists elsewhere in the country. As a group growing in number, some organizational changes had to be made. They organized as a handful of radical housing warriors known as the Housing Liberation Front (HLF). As Jack Tafari, an early member, recounted recently, "We were soldiers, soldiers, and that was their front, the streets" (Mosher 2010: DS DISC 1, part 1, "Kwamba" at 00:09:30). When they started gathering new members and squatting in parks, they became known as "Out of the Doorways," and then a few stops later, as a nomadic tent squat called "Camp Dignity." The changing names are not indicative of a group that had no vision, but rather reflected the changing nature of their vision as the movement grew. One of the keys to making the Dignity Village movement successful was that its members did not pedantically cling to a certain vision of themselves that all would-be members had to adopt. New members brought ideas and values into a group united by the need for housing. Now, this does not mean that there was an easy consensus. In fact, the critique that started the movement was about to be co-opted in important ways.

Camp Dignity had come to a final squat under the Fremont Bridge; their number, perhaps as high as 150. Eventually inspired by the savvy of activists and professional legal counsel, these homeless activists challenged in court the city ban on emergency campgrounds on the grounds that it violated the Oregon State Constitution, which provided each municipality with the right to two emergency camps. Local environmental activists, such as Jack Tafari, celebrated the shopping-cart parades as a critique of capitalism and an indictment of the structural violence enacted towards the poor (Mosher 2010). The cart migrations became the mobile discursive site for "good old-fashioned" politicking. According to Tafari and later Ibrahim Mubarak, another founder of the village, the media loved the image of the homeless frontiersmen—defiant in the face of oppression, standing up for their rights—because it made sense in Oregon to do things this way. I argued earlier that Oregon has a history of rough camping and sleeping because of its rugged terrain, resource economy and the place of hobos and adventurers in local folklore. It is not unfair to say that Oregonians might not have liked poor folks camping in their parks, but they could see how it might make sense.

Even the police recognized that the group was involved in complex constitutional matters of "redress of grievance and deferred the political issue to the local political authority" (NCH 2010:11). The position of the police, the romantic nostalgia of the activists' links with a very simple argument steeped in local history, the use of signs, placards, t-shirts, and news media, were specific circumstances that served the emerging claim. Recall Boltanski's suggestion that the more physical presence a critique has, the more likely it is to succeed; or Latour, telling us to give agency to the things in our assemblages. These activists used images, photographs, shopping carts, occupations of land, signs (literally, hand- painted signs), and inverted American flags (the symbol of distress) to very effective ends.

One of the most impactful conditions, however, was that the claim emerged within a symbolic imaginary that had room for alternative notions about how to live in urban space. Portland itself is rather unique, for despite the wealthy and conservative elements in the population, it fosters a variety of environmentally friendly and community-oriented groups such as "City Repair," "The Village Building Convergence,"[146] Columbia Eco Village[147] and other alternative housing groups, the actions of which lend credibility to the self-housing efforts of the very poor.

Starting in 1996, City Repair[148] has inspired many Portland neighborhoods to claim their community streets and to occupy them with their own interpretation of safety and utility. Many Portlanders take part in collective actions to recover unused lots as parks and playgrounds. They close off intersections with creative sculpted and painted installations that slow or inhibit vehicles in order to produce safety zones for children. Embedded in this movement is a desire to provide an ideological, behavioral and experiential buffer between the urban complex and the peaceful community; these zones represent thresholds between the two vectors of city space (business and living) as means of creating a safe liminal passage from one to the other; cars are forced to slow or not enter; people are offered free tea from communal tea stands that stand unguarded; wildflowers and interactive sculptures invite passersby to take a break and relax—you can pick a flower if you want.

These are *heterotopias*, the term Foucault (1967) used to describe temporary and fluid spaces that invert and twist around common practices associated with spaces and lived experiences therein. It is not unimportant to think of these city spaces this way, for they are, in vital ways, types of resistance to capital and the power of state controls over space. They are sites of resistance, even though they are not the least bit violent. And it is this spirit of resistance and community well-being that is perhaps the value system that lets Oregonians understand claims like Dignity Village, even if they disagree with them on other grounds.

The sites are clearly defined. When you look at those features—the painted sidewalks, the free tea dispensers, the no-car zones built on intersections in the middle of city neighborhoods—you can also see that they seem out of place in the middle of a busy city. How can an intersection be a playground? These ludic (playful) places are, once again, legalized, so they are not outside of the purview of the state. Portland City Council passed ordinance #172207, an "Intersection Repair" ordinance, allowing neighborhoods to develop public gathering places in certain street intersections in 2000. It is fair to say, then, that the social critique of poverty in places like Portland was entering a sense of spatial justice already tilted in favour of alternative interpretations.

In these reimagined urban places, such as the one I visited in 2011, there are passive solar greenhouses, rain recycling systems that conserve water, completely organic composting—in fact, neighbors are encouraged to bring their organic waste to the site. Neighbors dress up in costumes, children play out fantasies, people share resources and help each other out. In understanding these spaces as thresholds between urban and communitarian values, one must appreciate that they are, as Van Gennep (1908) suggested, symbolic of rites of actual passage in a territorial sense; they are markers and liminal spaces that define and separate the activities of city governance and ludic activity from one area to another. In this sense, the annual ten-day Village Building Convergence (VBC) celebration and festival ritualizes the liminal mental space of alternatives to urban space. Each year, during the annual celebration, housing and community activists unite with artists and environmentalists to re-dress parts of the city in a mass performance.

Turner (1964), whose work on rites of passage and rituals transitions is rooted in Van Gennep, reworked the essential problem of liminality within the context of complex societies and cultures. He offers a secondary critical mental space for human social relations that occurs in rituals and festivals and affords access to and expression of critiques of extant processes, a ritualized liminal space called *communitas*. Since society is constantly in a state of becoming, its movement forward intact in a structural sense required places for the periodic playing out of shifting categories of experience.[149]

Turner sees beings in this ludic second model, communitas, as apolitical or, at best, ineffective politically, since the purpose or function of communitas is to provide this cohesion through often festive and not insurgent events. And so at this important juncture, it is not unreasonable to understand these places as evidence of communitas, even as they are evidence of a certain activist symbolic and ludic frivolity being managed through spatial practice. These were (are) evidence or manifestations of the political actions of communities out of which city ordinances were challenged and changed; they in fact were politically motivating for actors, and had been effective in changing extant practices in a permanent and symbolic sense. The alteration of city space for grassroots and permanent uses is historically common to Portland, so if a legally sanctioned shantytown were to happen anywhere, it would be in Portland.

By 2000, the VBC had emerged as an ongoing competitive urban imaginary and as a ten-day festival celebration of these alternatives, so the VBC can be considered heterotopic in the classic sense. These zones are regarded henceforth as symbolic and functional representations of this alternative way of approaching community. In general, between 1996 and 2000 the idea that urban space was public space and its use could be interpreted in myriad ways by local groups had won over the city council. In January 2000, the city passed an ordinance allowing neighborhoods to interpret these spaces for themselves. In many ways, it was the manipulation of the symbolic imagining of the use of space that preconditioned the representational possibilities of Dignity Village.

In 2000, Dignity Village amounted to little more than a few dozen tents under a bridge in downtown Portland. In the process of successfully claiming

Dignity Village Main Drag, 2010. Photo: Eric Weissman.

urban space, they used a variety of tactics, including occupations of city spaces, media events, press coverage and appeals to constitutional law. The spatialization of the claim made at that time—occupation of the land under the bridge in the city—was deemed illegal. Furthermore, the occupation had grown in size, was no longer festive in spirit like the VBC events, and, most importantly, was presented to the public by opponents as a threatening and unstable liminal population. As in all power struggles, the engaged parties use legal and other resources to effect a response in opponents and competitors. In this case, because the camp was on state land adjacent to a state highway, the city urged the state to impose a 48-hour eviction order on the camp. This happened during negotiations between the city and the campers and must be understood as a device to speed along negotiations—that is, they wanted to use fear to drive the campers into a decision. On the other end of the tactical spectrum, Camp Dignity used emotional pleas on TV and in the press to establish the moral validity of its claim. Faced with the state eviction notice, the campers' advocates recognized a legal opportunity to challenge the eviction. Since the state constitution grants them the right to shelter and allows cities to build emergency camps under precisely these conditions, the activists challenged the eviction and their claim to a camp in the courts.

And they won. But the city had the right to decide where to place the emergency campground. So they put it as far from downtown Portland as possible, out by the airport a quarter-mile from the Columbia River. While some of the city's population supported the intentional community, there was still a large entrenched conservative element, especially developers of the city core near the bridge occupation who were solidly against homeless camps. However, as Mosher (2010) points out, as the community gained support among the public, activists and other supporters, they gained power within the regional political structure. Mosher's argument and the one I entertain in this book is that the involvement of the homeless, and perhaps of all exploited and under-represented people under neoliberal governmentality, even in resistance, helps them understand that they have a place and roles within the power structure. Being involved in these processes provides a sense of the viability of the choices we can make to redress situations or to make claims.

Michel De Certeau has suggested such choices appear as tactics and strategies that are essential to making the "practice of everyday life" possible, even desirable (1984).[150] Always understood in his way as a means to redress the domination of people by powerful interest groups and regimes, the practice of resistance amounts to a way to see one's own performance in the shadow of these powerful strategies of domination (ibid).

There was also a great deal of resistance to the campers' critique. Jim Francisconi, a wealthy Portlander and city council member, vocally opposed the claim from within the council:

> You need professional help. That's my opinion, you can agree or disagree. What if I had come to that camp in November or December? Now I could go, that could be [me] or that could be my kids. That's never going to be me—that's never going to be my kids! Because I've got money! [The crowd of activists heckles.] ... I've got assets," he says over the noise. (Mosher 2010: DS DISC 1, part 1).

Far from stemming the action, such vulgar acclamations galvanized support among the housing activists. As part of the claim process, local environmental activist Mark Lakeman declared:

> For these people their highest need has to do with not just shelter, but dignity. Who even knows what that really consists of when you don't really know what it's like not to have it?" (Mosher 2010 DS DISC 1, "Kwamba" at 00:18:24).

By reviewing the video shot by Kwamba Productions during this time, it is clear that at first, many of the campers did not fully understand themselves as claimants. As the protest, the occupation, the court case and the community discussions evolved, campers became critically aware of themselves and envisioned the action and the direction this would take. It was not an easy period and there were many competing points of view. This direction, expressed in critical communicative action, takes fundamental values such as dignity and freedom, which are indescribable absent of ways to signify their meaning, and gives them meaning in a transcendent context of critical action. The action, the fight for the land was an expression of freedom and the dignity was in having those rights recognized. Still, campers disagreed with each other about what freedom meant to them as individuals and had to ask themselves how to collectively stay on point—the goal was to obtain space to build a camp. While acts of resistance are not always successful in achieving concrete collective ends, it might be that resistance in itself is dignifying. Despite the uncertainty of their actions and the competition between visions of what the claim should be for, 150 broke, broken and traumatized street folks carried the battle to the city. As much as the Dignity activists resisted their poverty, government resisted the claim, too.

It is essential to remember that city governance plays a role in what the outcome of such resistance looks like. Habermas (1971, 1987) suggested that the transcendent communicative action employs a fairly stable vision of an ultimate truth in the ethical debate about the course of moral action. Certainly Jim Francisconi believed in democracy and freedom, yet his vision of these things was very different than the campers'. In the ranks of Camp Dignity, there was also some question about how this claim should have manifested, and the answer was clearly not understood by each party in the same way. A majority of the campers wanted to stay put near the downtown world that was socially vital to them. A location further away from the core would have impaired their ability to find casual work, seek social services, connect socially with other street people and access the shelters, soup kitchens and other places that were part of their lives. Business and capital wanted to cleanse the core of the campers, so if Camp Dignity were to get land, it would have had to be as far away from their investment properties as possible. And the city had its own objectives: it wanted to contain a hazardous liminal population and to find a place where their poverty could be managed without damaging other conventional values, such as the prosperity of the downtown core and urban redevelopment. The activists themselves were divided on what they would accept as a dignified response. Was it dignified to accept anything less than the right to build a camp downtown? As the activists clung to the idea of a solid community rooted in the downtown space that was their world, they embraced housing at any cost as a collective goal and incorporated under the name Dignity Village, a 501C(3) charitable corporation.

In the case of claims-making by Dignity Village, there was little consensus about how to dignify the aim or what the limits on freedom really meant among the homeless claims makers nor among the politicians. Divisions within each group destabilized the force of resistance exerted by city councillors opposed to the village, and also threatened to weaken the village's claim to be competent enough to be self-managed. Activists such as Mosher and her partner Wendy Kohn as well as the homeless people who started the village sought a structural reformation that saw "truly equal access to jobs and housing" as a result of the critical action, at least somewhere down the road (Mosher 2010: DS DISC, part 1, "Kwamba," various). This did little to solidify divergent versions of the truth within the activist collective.

In open-air protests leading up to the settlement with the city, an Out of the Doorways spokesperson (recall that the hard-core activists who started the Dignity movement were called the Housing Liberation Front [HLF] and then Out of the Doorways) said:

> Americans are willing to embrace the fact that racism is wrong, Americans are willing to embrace the fact that homophobia is wrong, that sexism is wrong—it's time to embrace the fact that classism is wrong. It's discrimination. We will not stand for it. We will stand united and we will die with dignity. If you will try and sweep us I promise on my grave that there will be more tent cities, if you sweep us we will come back, if you sweep us we will come back, and back and back [the crowd joins in] and back and back....

At the city council meeting in 2001 where the decision to place Dignity activists on a piece of distant city land was announced, the mayor said that the decision to try this intentional community (defined as an emergency campground) was an appeal to the desire to "provide a sense of place that we always talk about, and a sense of community to residents of our community that never experienced it before" (ibid). The conditions of the claim can be understood as a new discursive normalization of a liminal space within poverty governance (Dean 1991). This means the city was ordaining an experimental way to house literally homeless people. In this way, the lives of Dignity Villagers and their stories are to be understood as expressions of how their liminality is inscribed in a deliberately fabricated culture of poverty peculiar to a certain neoliberal governmentality, one that unites a sense of place with legitimacy within the broader community. Presently we will look at how this inscription is served in the contracts and codes that restrain the village.

In the five-member city council executive, a division had emerged between those who understood the claim as fundamental to the rights of all citizens to make shelter, and others who felt that the drugs, characterological defects and appearance of idleness amongst Portland's homeless rendered them undeserving. Beyond this basic debate there was, too, the problem of scale and the willingness to adopt such a space to accommodate the vastly larger representation of chronically homeless people. Boltanski (2010) has suggested that in the justifications produced by coterminous worth economies or worlds that tend to structure modern social life, there resides the possibility for arguments both to resolve or to append conflict. The moral claim made by village activists on the grounds of a greater sense of dignity and justice, a *greater good,* one might say, did not resonate well with the standard arguments about cost-effectiveness and deserving-vs.-undeserving individuals that were presented by some of the opponents.

In a city hall hearing to adjudicate the lease for Dignity Village on August 30, 2001, Portland city commissioner, Jim Francisconi said:

> My own prior experience, which is not in the area of homelessness, but based on conversations with people I truly respect, based on some of the testimony here today, based on my own experience in community organizing—Folks! You need some professional help to crack the issue of homelessness [someone heckles in the audience, a homeless spectator]— and you can disagree with me, and that is fine, that is my belief, and I have that strong belief. So for the reasons, and the last one, let me tell you, just the practicalities—we have such a homeless issue in this city—we're talking about 60 people. So are we providing campsites for 2,000 people? We're not folks. It isn't going to happen.

Portland city commissioner Dan Saltzman echoed the sentiment:

> I am not prepared to accept the idea of camping as a permanent element of our homeless shelter system. We need housing. We need roofs over people's heads, and while I think that a particular constellation of people have aligned themselves with Dignity Village—you've sort of enamored a lot of people ... and it may

work ... for Dignity Village. But I am not prepared to take the next step and say the next camp that comes along no matter how well organized should become a permanent fixture of the system. That is to me, not the way the system needs to go.

Other members of the council, buoyed by the positive spin in some media outlets and by the support of local politicians and religious groups, took another path. A year after it opened, Erik Sten, Portland city commissioner (interviewed in 2002 for *Doorways to Dignity*, Mosher 2010, DS DISC 1) said of the emergence of Dignity Village:

> It's a hundred percent driven by the individuals that made it happen ... and to my opinion, zero percent driven by the city ... You can say we did a little to make it possible: probably better, you can say, "we didn't stop it"... is a better description of what we did.

Later he added:

> We have an immense amount of activists in this community who have supported Dignity Village. There's a lot of churches, individuals, businesses that have been helping Dignity for years ... and then we tend to have, you know, very independent activists—the people who live at Dignity Village, I mean, so I don't know if it's unique for Portland, but I mean, you've got a tolerant government, you know, we're a supportive government, a very active community that was willing to lend a hand, and then you've got the right kind of activists. And those seem to me to be the three things that have to be in place. And I don't think those things are unique to Portland, but if you were lacking any one of those three things, I don't think Dignity would have survived—without all the volunteer support it got; obviously the people drove it and if the city wanted to shut it down, we would of. I mean, yeah, it would get some bad press for two or three days, but it would be over (Mosher 2011).

In the case of the Village, Boltanski would say that a "compromise" was reached that bridged two worlds, the emerging liminal world of homeless activists and the other a political world of governance. However, he would also argue that compromises are rarely as powerful as the principles that comprise them. Compromises lead to conflict down the road as they unravel and their contradictions become apparent. Revealing the contradiction requires deconstructing the narratives of domination or control produced by the compromise. The critical point in this kind of approach, then, is what do we do with information that points out weaknesses in the structure or modes of domination that need to be resolved to help the community? In chapter two, we used the term aporias to describe these points where we can no longer understand situations based on our prior knowledge of them—when we need to think of things anew.

One such aporia appeared even before the official site was settled. The impossibility of transcendental and stable truths is the aporia that lies at the heart of their deconstruction. No value is inherently understandable or expressible without a signifier to give it sensibility. Above I posed the question, "Was it dignified to accept anything less than the right to build downtown?" The hard-core activists from Out of the Doorways who were the original movers in this claim process rejected the city's offer. They correctly recognized the re-settling of the camp to a suburban tarmac as co-opting of the claim through the power of the city—a type of domination.

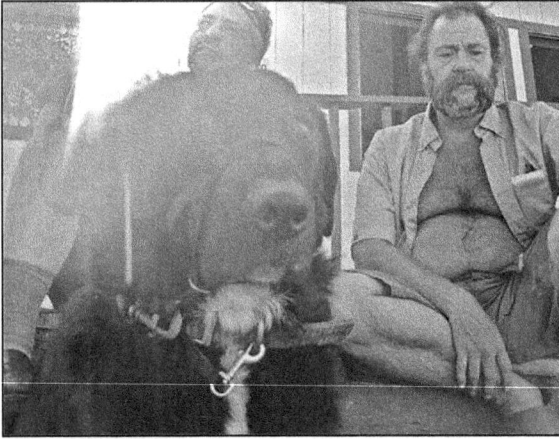

The look of liminality: Mitch, Samson and the "barking" dog, July 2011. Photo: Eric Weissman.

This led to an emotional split between activists who had fought together for three years. People who had been battling for years on the streets for the right to land on which to build a community became divided on the very issue that united them. In seeking the sanction of the city, some activists had invited the rationalization techniques of housing and urban governance to dictate the terms, at least insofar as the space of the settlement was concerned. HLF radicals recognized the impossibility of being truly self-determined or self-governing if the ultimate authority over village life was the city through its codes, inspectors and laws. They fragmented from the larger collective action and occupied a field near downtown known affectionately at the time as the Field of Dreams (comments by Jack Tafari, from Mosher 2010, DS DISC 1, "Kwamba" at 00:19:00).

In short order, even dreams fade; the HLF was evicted and scattered to the streets again. For the HLF, understanding the claim meant understanding that the right of the individual to pursue freedom on her own terms was the essence of dignity, and that no other body or institution should have a say in that definition or where that freedom should take place, literally understood as the space of freedom. They had felt freedom and dignity meant the right to choose where and how to live. It was not a question of what democracy looked like to them. Derrida said earlier in this book that democracy is always in the process of becoming—as yet to become—and is never finished. For the HLF, if democracy meant being forced to live many miles from their social world, then they wanted nothing to do with that political process. They were looking for an altogether different type of government. To invoke Foucault, the problem of self-conduct and thereby conduct towards the collectivity is very much a choice about how to be governed in a certain way rather than not to be governed at all. The HLF were choosing to be governed on terms they had yet to define, but which they knew had nothing to do with a city contract and a swept-off tarmac.

The HLF were the real radical faction, even if many conventional Portlanders saw the whole group as one big problem. Once again the issue came down to the two key views of emancipation I began with. The HLF wanted to govern themselves in a way they hadn't seen as yet. Emancipation meant spatial and political detachment from what they doubted was a true democracy. The compromise made clear the discursive and moral split between hard-core activists who embraced the claim as a chance to embrace a new model of community, and the other activists, who, beaten down by years of street life and feeling disengaged from the world, wanted back in. For them, freedom meant the chance to regain their vision of the American dream by being housed again and participating more fully in democracy, because they understood democracy to *mean* freedom. They understood freedom as an attachment to the right to pursue your dreams and to have stable housing—they wanted a base on which to live and from which to begin to participate again. The right to housing for other homeless people would be served by their actions because they had a role in setting a precedent. The precedent was in establishing intentional camps as part of a neoliberal narrative on self-conduct. It is in this sense that I have always found right-wing resistance to these communities troubling, because at the heart of such actions is the desire not to reject conventional attitudes and principles but to conform, and to do so at little or no cost to taxpayers.

For some people, participating lawfully is more just than being forced to live on the margins. Membership in Dignity Village then is appealing not simply because it provides housing, but because the housing is legal and sanctioned—it is lawful, which, based on my conversations, appeals to the villagers' sense of morality. This is not because the law is just, but because their membership is just, because there *is* law (Derrida 1996). The less radical group led by Tafari and Ibrahim Mubarak went along with the city proposal to relocate the protesters to a site of the city's choosing because, after all is said and done, people die on the streets more easily without shelter. Not everyone who is poor or homeless blames democracy for their problems. In my experience, and in the testimony of Dignity activists, most homeless people want to participate more in the system we have, but they feel they need a leg up to do so. And that leg up they had hoped would be Dignity Village, located at 9401 NE Sunderland Avenue in Portland, next to a prison, a composting facility and an airport.

Hence, Saltzman's proviso is noteworthy as more than a footnote to the scenario. The proviso that no other camps be investigated made the claim more precious and rare. The uniqueness compelled those who were offered a chance to live there a sense of urgency to comply with the city, since there was this proviso that symbolized the city's ultimate authority over the claim. It is noteworthy as well because it laid down certain preconditions that continued to limit the actions of activists from Dignity Village who were fighting for the village and for new camps in 2010–2011 when I was there. Much as the movement by VBC and other members of the "constellation" around Dignity had conditioned its possibility in 2000, this proviso by Saltzman— that no further camps should be allowed—echoes within current debates about the rights of homeless activists who struggle to open camps in Portland in the age of Housing First models announced first by the Bush administration in 2003, and reiterated with amendments by the Obama administration.

I want to explain one more important facet that contributes to the analytics of space we will turn to next in this chapter. Other programs that were favoured by the federal government conditioned the restrictions placed on Dignity Village and continue to impact life there today. The first decade of the twenty-first century was the decade of ten-year plans to end homelessness. When George W. Bush was elected president in 2000, homelessness had come to be understood as pervasive and of myriad kinds. Among those kinds, chronic homelessness associated with street persons and often with the undeserving poor had come to be understood as the most troublesome and expensive form. [151] The National Alliance to End Homelessness, which had grown from a group of 2,000 or so community-based providers to over 10,000, promoted the idea of a ten-year plan to end homelessness in 2000. [152] The secretary of the Department of Housing and Urban Development (HUD) viewed this initiative favorably, and in Bush's 2003 budget the plan was officially sanctioned and embraced as a major policy directive to encourage local communities and municipalities to find creative ways of addressing homelessness, especially chronic homelessness, and to end it at last.

Under the new directive, the Ulnited States Interagency Council on Homelessness (USICH) was re-endowed with significant discretionary power in allotting funds and incentives based on its adjudication of local ten-year plans. Part of the plan was to encourage a better structural arrangement between different agencies. So, ten-year plans appear in the form of federal, state, county and municipal packages, each of which defines a certain level of potential HUD funding and other incentives. By 2005, 48 of 50 states had adopted the plans. Close to $40 million was slated for the new programs, while HUD financing of other homelessness projects remained close to $1.3 billion.

USICH encourages the participation of many individuals and groups in the process of developing these plans, including the heads of municipalities and agencies, charitable foundations, non-profits, hospital administrators, chronically homeless persons, the general public, developers and industry specialists and researchers. Since the turn of the millennium, a sense that some of the worst-off homeless deserved assistance appears to have taken root in governments at all levels. But one must ask how far this recognition really went. In a simple mathematical sense, the United States has enough money to build the 250,000 to 400,000 units of new housing (including family dwellings) that it is conservatively argued the country requires to satisfy national requirements.[153] Unfortunately, the goal has not been reached. Within the context of local governments struggling to manage growing populations of homeless persons, a variety of institutional models play off against one another.

In 2000, with less than $50 million available nationwide for inventive plans to help the chronically homeless, cities such as Portland were unlikely to resolve the problem of chronic street-engaged homelessness through government funding or official housing models. The housing strategies under various neoliberal regimes, therefore, identify the problem—chronic homelessness, among various other types—and suggest the implementation of policies interpreted and executed at local levels. However, Leginski (2007) points out that despite such national goals, a diverse and decentralized system exists in which the competitive framing of granting programs perpetuates the disjointed efforts of myriad service providers. It is within this de facto system of service and programs that past and present efforts and programs are invigilated rather wastefully.

There was and remains so much overlap, repetition and competition between different models of housing strategy that while cities scrambled to design and implement ten-year plans in order to avail themselves of HUD and USICH dollars, the next wave of new poor cast into the streets by the 2007–08 recession proved once again that homelessness was, in its simplest, most symptomatic expression, a problem with space; that is, cities did not provide adequate space for poor people to live. They needed affordable housing.

Since HUD distributes funds on a competitive basis between jurisdictions, the articulation of ten-year plans is vital to securing those funds and standardization is sought across the various service providers. Shantytowns, IHC or whatever we choose to call them had not been included in any of these federally sanctioned ten-year plans. So why would a city want to invest in such a place unless they could finance it? Since those days, financing has become more inventive, and later we will discuss how reframing these camps as IHC

Eric Weissman

and Housing First projects (and in the context of the tiny and micro housing paradigm) helps cities finance them. In fact, as just one example, in 2015, the city of Dallas entered into a similar arrangement with a non-profit organization to build "The Cottages at Hickory Crossing," a professionally managed Housing First IHC, and profiled the project as part of the city's plans to end homelessness[154]. We will discuss what this means in the last chapter. This is a very different animal than Dignity Village, borne out of very different conditions of possibility. In 2000, the city of Portland was to be commended for allowing this experimentation with space when most of the country was in denial about the gross dimensions of literal homelessness. But when we review the language of the contract in the next section, we will see how this experimentation has always been controlled by the city and mitigated by the logical tensions inherent to democratic self-rule

While Dignity Village was being built out on Sunderland yard between 2002 and 2004, municipalities in Oregon were studying the ten-year-plan model. The first of these studies was published in 2004 (PHA(B) 2004). In 2006, Oregon's first ten-year-plan deliberations created the Ending Homelessness Advisory Council (EHAC) to inform and implement measures included in the plan (Executive Order: 06–05). EHAC's 2009 report on the first year of implementation (i.e., 2008) showed that homelessness in Oregon had increased by 37% over the year previous. This was blamed on the economic crisis, including widespread mortgage foreclosures. EHAC reported that Oregon had the highest number of homelessness per capita in the nation in 2008–09 (this was when I began preliminary research for my fieldwork). More than 17,000 people, or 43% of the total, were in families with children, of whom more than 4,300 were younger than 18 (ibid). The number of veterans in homelessness had doubled. In all, 59% of the vulnerable households surveyed included family members suffering from mental health or addiction issues.

The report is somewhat vague, but it claims that despite these horrifying numbers, it had managed to create 200 units of permanent supportive housing and also to have preserved housing for very low-income earners though no figures are offered in relation to the latter. Framed as progress in the direction of solving homelessness, these measures were touted as evidence of the capacity to "end and prevent the cycle of homelessness affecting families, children and youth, and single adults" (Oregon, EHAC 2009:3). This claim was laughed at when I showed it to members of the Village in 2011. One villager said, "Well then, they only need to provide 16,800 or so more spaces I guess. At this rate, let's see, that'll be 17,000 divided by 200 ... well, you see where I am going with this" (David Samson 2012). If nothing else, their skepticism underscored the fact that ten-year plans as currently understood are not effective at ending homelessness. And so we can ask: "Why not include IHC as official parts of our narrative on ending homelessness?" The answer has two parts. First, whether officially recognized or not as part of the formal housing system, when we analyze the way IHC is contracted and encoded, it *is* a de facto part of that system because it is encoded by it. Second, when we consider Dignity Village as a cautionary tale about the limits of membership-run self-governed IHC, we can discern certain provisions that will improve the performance of such spaces and make these communities parts of ten-year plans.

In exploring these two issues, we must first analyze how the compromise encoded governmentality into the social critique that began the claim. Second, the villagers must be asked what they can do to overcome the contradictions that stem from this compromise. We will do that in the next chapter. First, however, let's make use of Mitchell Dean's analytics of government to understand just how limited the freedom of Dignity Villagers really is.

7.2 An Analytics of Government

In this section I am going to look at how Dean's (1999, 2010) analytics of government addresses the "how" questions posed by governmentality studies. I am going to show you some of the many pages that accompanied the Dignity Village claim, or, rather, that *encoded* the claim into the language of conventional governance. (It should be noted that some items were dated retroactively and inaccurately, and some of the forms contain typos and other formatting glitches.) The point behind this section is to show that at least from the point of view of those who govern other people, governmentality is a desirable state of affairs. For we who self-govern—well, we need to question the degree to which our freedom is really ours.

Just as the village is governed by rules and codes, villagers are required to act according to the self-directed governing principles of the village. Much of what is written in codes and mission statements for the villager is idealistic and never happens, nor did it ever happen. The problem with governmentality studies, such as Dean's analytics and also Boltanski's pragmatic sociology, is that they each use such codes and manuals as guides from which rational results are expected to occur or by which the failure of consignees is measured. In other words, the codes, manuals and scripts, which are part of the institutional aspect of the organization, say one thing, while the ethnographic experience of the place shows another.

In his two versions of *Governmentality: Power and Rule in Modern Society*, (1999, 2010) Mitchell Dean introduces a formal analytics of power in order to bridge the gap between Foucault and methods. "An analytics of government thus views practices of government in their complex and variable relations to the different ways in which 'truth' is produced in social, cultural and political practices" (Dean 2010:27). Action is a reflection of governing; we do things according to what we take to be true of ourselves, who we are, who others are, and what areas of the our world need improvement. [155]

An important step in an analytics of government is to identify the specific conditions under which the activity of governing is called into question. "Problematizations" of this nature are relatively rare and are circumstance specific (39). So it is necessary to avoid looking at broad or global expressions of the "same" problem. An analytics of government looks at very specific situations where the "conduct of conduct" becomes difficult. The problematization often unites both the governor and the governed in questions about how each conducts itself. An example is a services contract that was issued in 2007, but had been formulated in 2003–04:

> **AGREEMENT FOR SERVICES CONTRACT NO. 53015**
> This Agreement is between the City of Portland, acting by and through the City Council (the City), and Dignity Village, an Oregon non-profit corporation (the Contractor).
> RECITALS:
> 1.   Homelessness is an ongoing national dilemma with an esti-mated three million people sleeping outside at some time during any given year. Portland's publicly funded year-round homeless shelters have permanent waiting lists. Due to limited shelter space and a lack of affordable housing, many people in Portland have no practical alternative to homelessness.... [In] January 2007, a study of the homeless within Portland counted over 1400 homeless people in Portland sleeping outside on one night.
> 2.   In Resolution No. 36200, passed February 26, 2004, the Port-land City Council designated a specific portion of property owned by the City, commonly known as Sunderland Recycling Facility, located at 9325 NE Sunderland Road, Tax Lot 100 1N1E12B (Tax Account R-315196), as a campground under the terms of ORS 446.265 (the "Designated Campground"). The intent of the City of Portland in contracting with Dignity Village is for the contractor to provide temporary housing for otherwise homeless individuals and to help its temporary residents find permanent housing.
> 3.   Dignity Village is incorporated in Oregon as a non-profit corpo-ration. Dignity Village has independently developed a proposal to provide an alternative to sleeping outside for the homeless within Portland. Local religious organizations, schools, philanthropists, architects, and others have combined to help Dignity Village develop a community approach to addressing homelessness. Due to on-going shortages of adequate shelter space and affordable permanent hous-ing, the transitional housing accommodations provided by Dignity Village would be used by persons who lack permanent shelter, and who have not been placed into low-income housing.
> 4.   The model for Dignity Village functions upon a democratically elected governance model for the administration of day-to-day operations and regulation. Dignity Village strives to generally provide

some group services such as a kitchen, bathrooms and community telephones. Dignity Village, with the assistance of donated materials, equipment and labor, builds transitional housing structures that are capable of being transported from location to location. Dignity Village is the owner of these structures. Representatives from Dignity Village, including architects, have worked with the Bureau of Development Services in developing plans for transitional housing structures that will comply with the requirements of ORS 446.265. Dignity Village provides residents with job training opportunities, continuing education opportunities, healthcare, and access to housing placement assistance and a supportive environment in which homeless people are able to address the issues that led to them becoming homeless.

5. The City of Portland desires to have someone serve as manager for the Designated Campground. Dignity Village is willing to provide this management service as a steward of the property. Dignity Village will provide a unique and coordinated services program developed by Dignity Village....

By 2002, Dignity Village was undergoing a construction boom and proving itself capable of growth and government. While the village abandoned any grandiose community structural goals such as the large archway and the decorative flower gardens that the VBC had envisioned, they were organizing and building and creating a physical and social community. They had no permanent contract yet but were complying with codes and local laws, and defending themselves against opposition in *The Oregonian* newspaper. Most importantly, their articles of incorporation were commensurate with the original operating agreement they had with the city. Between 2002 and 2005, the village's reputation grew widely and globally. Their list of supporters grew, including local businesspeople, religious orders and scores of Portlanders who came to the village to build and paint structures, and to purchase recycled donations.

The following document is the village intake committee's mandate. It lists the obligations and duties of a small elected group of village residents who adjudicate who gets into the village. This process is not like getting into a condominium building. Not getting into the village means a return to the streets. So the stakes are high, and in that sense the role of VIC is more important to social justice than a condominium board. Being on the committee gives one considerable power and influence in the village and it often places committee members in heated arguments with other villagers. Often these arguments are over who to let in. I was surprised by how homeless people—that is, the villagers—would say anything to anyone to prevent some other homeless person from getting into the village on the grounds of personality differences and other subjective prejudices, when the bottom line uniting them was homelessness. But they did it frequently. Villagers had in mind what the ideal villager-neighbor looked like, how they would act, and what they would bring to the village. This intake process is a would-be villager's first experience with the village governmentality:

> The purpose of the Village Intake Committee (VIC) is to review potential residents, to see if the Village can fit an individual in question's needs or if they may, perhaps, be better served by other options. VIC also works to meld individuals in question to the general planning needs and mission statement of Dignity Village Inc., as well as to assign and coordinate space allotment and monitor new additions to Dignity Village Inc., for a period of 30 days.
>
> VIC is a formally recognized standing committee of Dignity Village, Inc., that comes under the auspices of the Secretary of the Board of Dignity Village. The committee shall consist of not less than 4 or more than 7 Villagers. All such Villagers shall be members in good standing for not less than 90 days.
>
> The Chairman of the Board shall appoint the Chairman of the VIC committee the first two weeks after his/her election and work with the Chairman of VIC to appoint the balance of the committee. This committee shall need to be ratified by the Council of Dignity Village. In the event new members are needed or existing members either drop out or are not fulfilling their obligations, all additional members shall be voted on to the committee by the existing members, presented to the Council, and ratified at that time. If the VIC committee feels that one of its members is not fulfilling his/her obligations to the rest of the committee they may decide to remove that person or persons by a majority vote of the committee. No one person shall have more input or "power" than any other member of the committee....
>
> [The] Inspector ... shall faithfully attend all weekly held VIC meetings to the best of their abilities....
>
> [The Inspector shall] Inspect all structures before and after all individual's leave and provide a written report to the VIC committee. A copy of this report is to go to the Secretary of Dignity Village Inc. for their personal file, and a copy to the Secretary of the VIC committee.
>
> [The Inspector shall] Identify and inventory all property left behind by former residents and guests, as well as protecting and coordinating its storage on an extremely short-term basis.... The Inspector will ensure that all property is removed within 30 days of a written statement being issued [and] not less than 14 days unless an individual in question contacts the Inspector or any member of the VIC Committee. A list of inventory shall be kept in the individual's personal file and a copy with the Secretary of VIC.

A second problematization requires going beyond merely listing all the "actors" and all the programs. "It is an attempt to understand how [such things have] to be *thought*" (39). This step invites a deconstructionist lens. Of special interest is how, for example, political parties, ideological groups and activist organizations bundle elements of such things into policy or into "mission statements"—how a set of guiding principles come to be associated with a particular party, interest group, and indeed with an individual subject. This is an excerpt from the mission statement and proposal from 2001:

> OVERVIEW: OUR VISION FOR DIGNITY VILLAGE
> At a May 16, 2001 meeting with staff from City Commissioner Eric Stern's office and the Bureau of Housing and Community Development, Dignity Village representatives presented a letter of concern to City Comissioner Eric Stern about their current situation. In response, city officials asked the Dignity contingent to assemble a comprehensive outline for "taking Dignity to its next level of development." This is a working document prepared in response to that request, developed over several weeks, which will continue to be further developed over time. We feel the innovative collaboration outlined here represents a truly win/win strategy that, given a chance, will provide important benefits both to homeless residents and to the City of Portland.
> Dignity Village has evolved and thrived over the past 6 months due in large part to its uniquely organic process. In this manner, we have efficiently implemented programs (such as the self-management structure and cooperative farm) that more rigid organizations might have taken years to get off the ground. This creative energy, motivated by basic human needs for shelter, food and water, is a key ingredient to our success thus far. As we plan for the future, it is imperative to retain this organic organizational dynamic, in order to insure that such creativity is allowed to flourish into the future.
> Any organization— including Dignity Village—requires a structure, a clear vision, and detailed plans in order to navigate confidently into the future. This proposal assembles the shared ideas and dreams of our current residents and supporters into an organized planning document. In preparing this document, particular attention is given to addressing the kinds of "due diligence" issues that the City of Portland routinely poses to emerging organizations or new programs. Beyond such basic threshold requirements, however, this also provides narrative, site design, architectural, social and organizational components reflecting what Dignity Village has already achieved and can become in the future.[156]

Dean suggests that an analytics of government stands out from other theories of government by paying less attention to questions of who governs and on what legitimate grounds, and the form such rule takes. Rather, an analytics is conditioned by a desire to understand how unique locales, authorities and actors are constructed and interrelated and how governable domains are constructed and administered (40). It is essentially an ethnographic approach, in the sense of writing culture. An analytics of power benefits from the destabilization of the locus of power at the apex of political and civic relationships and anticipates the shifting, complex and unpredictable actual networks, connections and assemblages that unite regimes of practice and subjects in social and material ways.

The articles of incorporation and the mission statement of the village, the contract from the city and various legal notices between both parties, provide a mapping of the ideas and the agencies responsible for negotiating their outcome. In effect, Dean suggests, an analytics asks: "What happens when we are governed or govern?" What does it look like when we try to imagine the relations of influence and tension that governing produces? The question of how agents with particular abilities and identities are formed leads one to ask how practices and techniques, rationalities and knowledge contribute to governing.[157]

Within an analytics of government, there are four basic dimensions to the "how questions." The first element suggests looking at how regimes of practice encode and visualize the tasks and subjects of their tasks. I argue that these are best understood as the housing policies and ten-year plans that currently shape the dominant strategies. In Dignity Village this includes such artifacts as conceptual planning drawings, flow charts, blueprints, contracts and by-laws. Such documentations are ways of visualizing the "fields" to be managed, making it possible to see "who and what is to be governed" (41), as in this excerpt from the original city contract with Dignity Village. Note that a time frame is not specified in the early contract:

> **Scope of Services.** The Subrecipient shall provide the following services:
>
> I.   *Transitional campground.* Subrecipient shall provide management services for the Designated Campground at Sunderland Recycling Facility. Subrecipient will, under the Agreement, have authority to administer, manage, and operate the Designated Campground, and to control the use, maintenance, services or other matters relating to the Designated Campground, subject to the provisions and limitations of the Agreement. Specifically, Subrecipient shall:
>> 1)   Operate the campground for the specific and sole purpose of providing temporary shelter to persons who cannot locate safe, decent affordable permanent housing and are otherwise homeless.

2) To the extent practicable, assist residents of the campground with locating and transitioning to safe, decent, affordable permanent housing. Assistance shall include, but not be limited to, permitting access to the campground by programs that assist homeless persons with locating and accessing permanent affordable housing....

From the perspective of government, visualizing and mapping a field are connected practices (Dean 2012:41). Clinical medical practices visualize the body as the site of a disease model for addictions; it is health care services that isolate the infected, the street homeless, the junkies, in political and special spaces by discerning who they are and keeping track of their whereabouts (41). Hence a key component of governmentality studies is to discern the way objects of governance are imagined, visualized as good, bad, deserving or undeserving, and placed within the strategies of government. In this sense, we need to understand how the spatialization of the village represents power values that are part of the rational practices of government external to the village but inculcated with its own legal rights. The following excerpt from the original contract indicates some of these concerns:

Minors shall not be allowed to remain as residents at the Designated Campground, but minors may enter as guests for periods of not longer than twelve (12) hours and
(a) Minor children must be supervised at all times by a designated parent/guardian or caregiver.
(b) If minor children are staying with parent/guardian, there may be no other guests staying within the household's structure when children are present.
(c) Parents/guardians must show proof of guardianship (i.e. this does not apply to "street families")....

A second element concerns the technical aspect of government (42). Dean refers to this as the *techne*. This requires looking at "the mechanisms, procedures, instruments, tactics, techniques, technologies, and vocabularies" that constitute the authority and the means by which rule is achieved (42). Consider, for example, the first page of the Articles of Incorporation of Dignity Village Inc.:

The undersigned natural persons of the age of eighteen years or more, acting as an Incorporate under the Oregon Nonprofit Corporation Law, adopt the following Articles of Incorporation:
The name of this corporation is Dignity Village, Inc. and its duration shall be perpetual.

The purposes for which this Corporation is organized are exclusively charitable and educational and consist of the following:
(A) The specific and primary purposes are:
(1) To create a safe, clean, self-governed community environment for economically distressed residents of the State of Oregon, through establishment of an open-air place where people living on the streets can have their basic needs met in a stable, sanitary environment, until they are able to access another form of housing more in keeping with said resident's personal goals and aspirations.
(2) To promote community wide interest and concern for homeless and other economically distressed residents of the State of Oregon, to the end that:
(a) their quality of life may be improved,
(b) their educational and economic opportunities may be improved,
(c) sickness, poverty and crime may be lessened,
(d) all constitutional and human rights of all people are respected and protected,
(e) mutual interdependence of all people may be recognized, and
(f) the mutual aid among, by and for poor people may be facilitated.

The third element is what he refers to as the *episteme*, or the forms of knowledge that inform government activity (42). Governmentality studies explore how governments create knowledge and, in so doing, produce "truth." The use of statistics to analyze a population's characteristics, debates between experts and politicians, all forms of rationalizing the conditions said to be true of given governable task or population relate to the episteme. Such knowledge is concrete; it appears in graphs, maps, contracts, assessments and the like.

Newspaper articles, chat forums about poverty, public protests, research papers and self-reporting requirements from the village are ways that external governance understands Dignity Village and also how it comes to understand itself. Artifacts such as these are also fixed in time and exist as a record of thought at a given time providing the link between "govern" and "mentality" mentioned earlier; it produces the "hybrid" *governmentality*. On the next page is an excerpt from the contract that indicates the reporting requirements of the village to the city. Even though these records were rarely filled out adequately in the past, they reflect the obvious role the village is supposed to play in keeping tabs on Portland's homeless.

Dean points out that the "welfare state" was less a concrete arrangement of institutions than it was the reflection of thought about how to arrange certain institutions, personnel and incentives around an ideal of government. An important part of episteme is the intentional organization of institutional spaces, the rituals and routines associated with them, and the conduct of actors in specific ways to produce programmes of conduct, which are in short, attempts to regulate and improve what occurs in specific regimes of practice and in those places built around such principles.

CONTRACT EXCERPT: REPORTING REQUIREMENTS

Reasons for leaving. Of those residents who <u>left</u> during the quarter, how many left for the following reasons? If a person left for multiple reasons, include only the primary reason.

Reason for Departure:	7/01/12-9/30/12	10/1/12-12/31/12	1/1/13-3/31/13	4/1/13-6/30/13	YTD
Total # of individuals who departed in quarter					
# who departed voluntarily	6				
# who departed for rules violations	1				
# who departed – unknown reason	7				

7a. Length of stay. For those residents who <u>left</u> during the quarter, how many were there for the following lengths of time?

	7/01/12-9/30/12	10/1/12-12/31/12	1/1/13-3/31/13	4/1/13-6/30/13	YTD
Less than 1 month	1				
1 to 2 months	1				
3–6 months					
7 months–12 months	1				
13 months–24 months	2				
25 months—3 years					
4 years–5 years	1				
6–7 years	1				
8–10 years					

So drug rehabs have a fairly understandable program; they are designed to help people get off and stay off drugs. They don't always succeed, or have limited success, but they must live up to rigorous standards in order to be considered valid institutions. The same is true of emergency shelters, emergency campgrounds and other intentional communities. Since the latest assessment in 2010, the city has demanded these forms be filled out each month and submitted. This renewed demand reflects the growing *desire* of the city to rationalize the effectiveness of the village to new critics and in the response to new claims being made by Right 2 Dream Too and other homeless activists. We cannot think of Dignity Village in isolation from the newer claims that are entering the critique. These "other spaces" reflect meaning onto and against DV and other sites. And all these sites achieve their meaning in relation to the other elements in the housing spectrum, such as Housing First. As newer sites, which we will discuss in the following chapters, gain momentum, Dignity's incapacities to meet the sanctions of the city become more urgent. The fear among village leadership is that the data is rarely good. As Brad Gibson, CEO in 2012-13, suggested, "It can't look good that every month we lose people back to the streets." The 2010 assessment shows that, in fact, of the people who left the village at that time, only about 18% found housing of some kind.

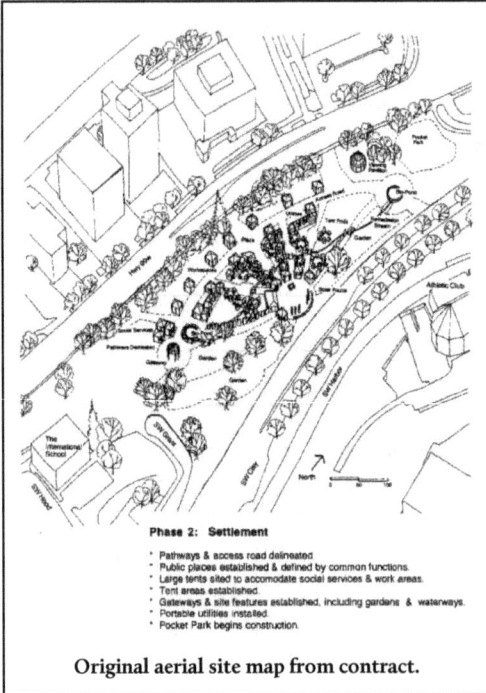

Phase 2: Settlement

* Pathways & access road delineated.
* Public places established & defined by common functions.
* Large tents sited to accomodate social services & work areas.
* Tent areas established.
* Gateways & site features established, including gardens & waterways.
* Portable utilities installed.
* Pocket Park begins construction.

Original aerial site map from contract.

As it attends to the spatial rules on the village, the site plan is very important. Any unlicensed variance and the city can shutter the village. Land use, emergency shelter allotments, fire zones and codes, waste removal, physical appearance, liability and corporate insurance, site inspections and site maps updated yearly are all means by which external governance ensures that the village is a good corporate citizen. This drawing is not accurate. It was produced in the planning documents in 2000 before the split, before the activists learned they were to live out by the airport. The current camp looks nothing like this.

The final dimension involves how specific programs of government seek to transform, moderate or identify specific ideas about the self and identity. What attributes come to be attached to authoritative or citizen identities? What duties and obligations are produced for those who govern and those who are governed? Far from locking an individual into a specific identity, governmentality assumes that individuals can occupy many subjective positions relative to these various rights and obligations. Care of the self entails understanding the myriad dimensions of subjectivity that intersect one's real life. This approach is especially amenable to understanding the homeless. Whereas critical theory and theories of state tend to imply a complicit overpowered person defined by their poverty, this Foucauldian approach suggests understanding how multiple facets of identity and experience combine to produce what are arguably unique conditions of possibility. Sexuality, philosophical knowledge, religion, citizenship, imagination, innovation, complacency as examples, meth addiction, pot-addiction, are dimensions of subjectivity that vary across persons and fields. So one might ask, "How is someone who buys goods at a supermarket to be made to identify as a consumer?" (Maffesoli (1991, in Dean 2010:44). For the purposes of this book, how might a marginalized, traumatized homeless person be made to become a consumer of the shelter system, or on the other hand, directed towards fighting for housing as an activist citizen? How does the ethnographic arrangement of homeless persons inform their sense of deserving or undeserving freedoms? Once again, Dean asks, for example, "How are we all to become good citizens?"(44). Today, villagers and critics of these IHC spaces are asking themselves "What does it mean to be a Dignity Villager or to live in a rest area? What does homelessness really mean?"

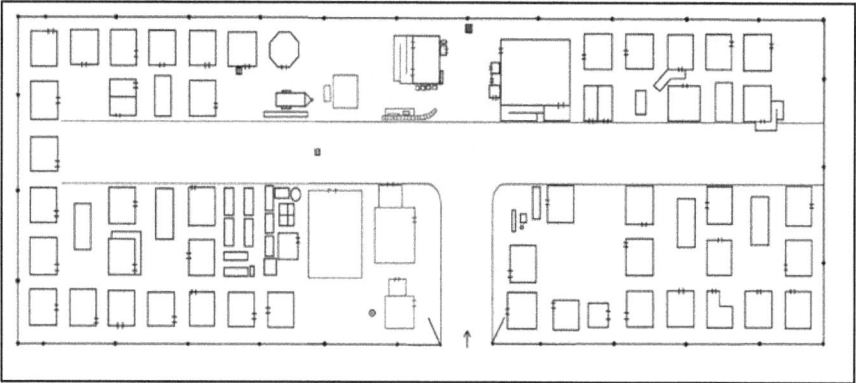

Schematic view of Village.

In the case of Dignity Village the combination of available land, activist, church, and popular support and a sympathetic regime aligned to create the conditions of its possibility. In 2012, it was presented with a revised contract that was meant to emphasize its transitional role in a changing governmentality of housing. Villagers were expected to accommodate themselves to this change. The bolded sections in the passage below indicate where language was changed to reflect the city's changed attitude. Section A, subsection 3 was especially troublesome; it established transition as a requirement of residence, but offered no guarantee of transition. Though the city wanted people to transition into housing, there was in fact very little secure and supportive housing available to them. This perpetual incapacity for transition is at the root of the problem with liminality in the village, and constitutes a certain institutionalization of limbo as a human condition of living there. The revised contract represented a strategically worded ideological shift in the city, a shift that occurred concomitantly with the federal incentives for Housing First, and cast the reality of Dignity Village in a different light within the constellation of possibility in Oregon.

> *1. By the end of November 2012, Dignity Village will be required to submit a completed, revised site plan that lays out structure, pathways, etc. This will be added as Exhibit D to the contract and must be approved/initialed by the Dignity Village Board Chair, and authorized staff from BDS, Fire, and PHB....*
> A. For the purposes of Portland City Code 5.36.115, Contractor is designated as a "person in charge" for excluding persons from the Designated Campground for violations of the written rules. As a designated "person in charge," Contractor may lawfully direct persons to leave the Designated Campground.
> *3. It is expected that Dignity Village residents will remain at the Campground for as short a period of time as possible while they seek out community services and affordable permanent housing. The City holds the discretion to either shorten or lengthen a maximum time that residents may remain at the Campground. Contractor must establish written rules that residents may not live at the Campground for longer than 24 months after the date of November 1, 2012. If a person became a resident on November 1, 2012 they would need to find other housing arrangements by October 31, 2014. If an individual is in an active housing search and/or active in Village leadership, Dignity Village may request an extension and the City Contract Manager can make individual exceptions to this.*

Make note of the above bolded clause. It is the ticking clock, the supreme outing of democracy's attachment to sovereignty and the impossibility of a generalized sense of freedom that does not require the suppression of (some) others. Finally, Dean's analytics tenders the proposition that conditions of freedom and domination coexist within regimes of government. Furthermore, Dean says that an analytics of government does not have as its goal the ideal that all human subjects should be emancipated from governing. Avoiding this radical position is essential because an analytics of government seeks to understand how subjects are both dominated and liberated within systems of governing.

During 2009–10, the city hired an outside agency to assess the village. The

2010 Village Assessment notes that despite the praiseworthy goals expressed in the mission statement, even villagers debate the village's ability to deliver such lofty and idyllic promises. The assessment also notes many ways that the city can help the village achieve its goals. To this day, that has not happened. They have achieved few if any of them, as we will discuss. Indeed, current residents tell me nothing has changed, though the contracts still loom over them. Some even contend this is exactly what the city wants. If DV is lulled into a complacent state of inadequate performance, a new regime at City Hall could evict them all the more easily. For its part, the city, in a 2011 interview, claimed that the village had not reached out for help, while the villagers argued they had reached out many times but had not been heard. Israel Bayer, publisher of *Street Roots*, a popular Oregonian homeless newspaper and activist, said in 2016, "No one needs to hear them stuck way out here, on a tarmac." This speaks to the out-of-sight, out-of-mind proposition I began with. So the village must find its voice and a way to deliver it.

Nonetheless, the 2009–10 assessment was surprisingly favourable to the village. The following excerpt is noteworthy:

> In contrast to traditional Transitional Housing programs, however, residents and supporters emphasize that one of the Village's strengths is that it allows residents the flexibility to stabilize on their own time-lines and on their own terms. For some people, this can happen in a month, for others it takes much longer. An essay on Dignity Village's website explains, "So now that I have this home, will I stay forever? No. The Village is my home until I am able to move on with my life, and soon, I hope. The average stay in Dignity Village is 18 months. Many stay for less, and a few stay longer. For now, this is the only home we know."
>
> The majority of the residents and stakeholders interviewed for this report described the Village as transitional or temporary. But for a small number of residents, the very notion of the Village as "transitional housing" is offensive. From their perspective, the Village is about having a home and a community. They view Dignity Village as an autonomous, semi-permanent "village", similar to co-housing. As one long-time resident put it, "For people who have been here for a while, this is home. . . If you come here and decide to stay, nobody should be able to tell you to leave. This is not transitional housing, and not a campground. It's a village. This is our home."
>
> These divergent views of the Village's mission shape the way residents and stakeholders evaluate the Village's outcomes. The differences in their perspectives make it difficult to know how to measure the Village's success. If we are comparing it to emergency shelter or the streets, the yardstick is very different than if we are comparing it to Transitional Housing programs or co-housing (PHB 2010:7).

Since I have been speaking of liminality and transitional housing from a theoretical point of view, it is worth noting the definition of transitional housing under Oregon law:

> Transitional housing accommodations described under subsection (1) of this section shall be limited to persons who lack permanent shelter and cannot be placed in other low income housing. A municipality may limit the maximum amount of time that an individual or a family may use the accommodations.
>
> Campgrounds providing transitional housing accommodations described under this section may be operated by private persons or nonprofit organizations. The shared facilities of the campgrounds are subject to regulation under the recreation park specialty code described under ORS 446.310....
>
> To the extent deemed relevant by the Department of Consumer and Business Services, the construction and installation of yurts on campgrounds used for providing transitional housing accommodations established under this section is subject to the manufactured structures specialty code described in ORS 446.155.... Transitional housing accommodations not appurtenant to a yurt are subject to regulation as provided under subsection (3) of this section.

The assessment provided other data as well. Unlike the streets, the village is over 90% white; as on the streets, most of the residents are men, aged 31 to 50, but there are more women and couples. The village is safer for single women and is couple-friendly, unlike the shelters, and in fact, it is safer, statistically, than all other parts of Portland, because villagers constantly monitor each other's behavior (PHB 2010:8–10, also from my notes 2011). The assessment also speaks to the deficiencies in the village, many of which I have addressed: poor location, poor service infrastructure, lack of supports and toxicity from the compost facilities, to name but a few. But by the time the assessment was completed, the village was delighted at the recommendation for a contract extension, and also for support for the move to a greener permanent location.

When I entered the village for the first time in 2010, then, as it prepared for a city inspection, I experienced the place as alive and vibrant, partly because they understood themselves as part of a viable strategy with real potential within the broader strategies to end homelessness. There was no real need to fight for their collective rights anymore. No reason to stay united with other homeless communities. They thought they were going to get a long-term contract together with a new and safer permanent location. They were doing everything they could to bring the village up to code and, to me, it looked like the utopia they had been claiming it was over the prior ten years. Dignity Village had been officially assessed and placed within an imaginary orbit of housing strategies without having been inscribed in official public planning language. Despite the wealth of forms and regulations governing and licensing the space, in no official plans will you find Dignity Village or any other IHC as I have described them because they are incongruent with current ten-year plans, even if they are vital to the survival of homeless people. We will discuss shortly how changing the brand of IHC creates official recognition.

As a result of being taken for granted, the villagers themselves take the site for granted and do little to push for other homeless camps in order to help people. "Why poke a snake?" Samson once asked me. In 2010, when I first went to Dignity Village, no one mentioned activism or homeless rights unless I asked them about it. They were convinced they were a community, a village called Dignity, and that they had earned their future place in the broader community experience of Portland.

I say "imaginary orbit" because despite the contract, despite the promissory language in the assessment, Dignity Village is not recognized or alluded to in any of the actual EHAC planning strategies or language. EHAC announced its first ten-year plan in 2007, the same year Dignity was officially contracted, but the village is not part of that plan. This is because, I want to argue, it is not Housing First, but a shelter in the imaginary of housing governance, and shelters are not part of the long-term ideology embedded in the rapid rehousing concepts of ten-year plans. Dignity Village is legal. It is contractual. It is transitional, emergency housing, even with the complicated understandings of what it represents to villagers and which I referred to previously. As to governance, as Israel Bayer said on August 12, 2013, in a telephone interview, "It is unlikely that the city is ever going to officially recognize the village because they can't explain the village to their critics. It's not just out there [by the airport] ... no one can say what it is or what's going on in there."

While the original EHAC (2007, 2008)[158] documents include images and plans for several supportive housing projects in line with the needs of the medically or psychiatrically affected homeless, the elderly, and families, intentional communities are not even referred to as possibilities. This lack of recognition did not go unnoticed and contributed to a growing anxiety over the possibility of eviction from Dignity Village in 2011–14 when the new contract, excerpts of which were presented above, was proposed. It is also very important to note that during that time, despite increases in funding for homeless projects, the dimension of the problem became even greater: "Despite the influx of American Recovery and Reinvestment Act (ARRA) dollars, Oregon witnessed an increase in the number of people experiencing homelessness, rising from 17,122 in 2009 to 22,111 individuals in January 2011" (EHAC 2011). This means that during the period in which I did my advance field trip and extended fieldwork, homelessness was on the rise all over Oregon, and Portland, much as any major city in a period of economic decline, became a hub for those seeking assistance and solidarity on the streets. On a walk through Portland in late July 2011, with a writer named Tyler, 1 commented on how 1 had not seen so many homeless people on the streets, sleeping on benches and in parks, since my days on the streets in Toronto. He had travelled from the east to the west coast, stopping in 15 cities, as part of research for a master's thesis: a blog about the streets in these cities. He explained to me that everywhere, from New York to Portland, he had seen alarming numbers of people on the streets, living in their cars and overflowing at shelters. We had met at Dignity Village because in each of the places he visited he had heard of this legal camp on the west coast. He had remarked after visiting the village that the people there seemed lost, as lost as the street poor. "Worse," he said. "At least on the streets, people want to get out of there. No one seems to know what they want out here [at the village]."

Chapter Eight
Spaces and Liminality

Jay's new home. In 2011, Jay had been 86'd from Dignity Village and forced to live under the adjacent side road. Photo: Nigel Dickson.

8.1 Liminality and Paralytic Community

It might be that Tyler was correct: no one knew what he or she wanted out of village life. Or perhaps, more correctly, it might be said that no one expected much to come out of life at the village. Expectations are not moot. It is one thing to expect conventionally housed and resourced people to navigate their roles and social statuses in more or less the same manner, given to the same sense of the imaginary. IHC activists are in the strange place of having none of the conventional materials or social assets, yet occupying space with conventional expectations built into it. Those expectations seemed a million miles away from that tarmac on the outskirts of town.

Of the people I interviewed, most simply wanted a safe place to sleep and live: safe from the oppressive police, protected from street diseases like pneumonia and scabies, freed to rest and heal from the extreme survival anxieties that street life produced. Earlier, Ibrahim pointed out, however, that soon after entering Dignity Village, people became greedy and complacent; they tended to horde donated goods and to covet their neighbors' material goods; the villagers disassociated from the street networks that were once important to them.

By the time Tyler and I had taken our walk, the meaning of transitional experience for the Dignity villagers had become obscured by structural conditions that made a return to normal society unlikely and by internal self-governing contradictions that created a place where villagers could live out their addictions, mental health problems and poverty, free from the exigencies of the street. The village had emerged out of the prosperous and upbeat days of early community building, to those of paralytic community—a community caught up in limbo and struggling to act collectively.

It seems unrealistic to expect very poor and often damaged people to transition from that state to a better role when such opportunities just don't exist. One has to ask: "Viewed from within the gates of Dignity Village, just what opportunities actually exist on the other side?" There really is not much to transition to. Does anyone really want to toil at minimum-wage labour to pay most of his or her income for rent in a rundown tenement? In the U.S., tens of thousands of people with jobs are on the streets or living in camps. So if by transitional one means "moving toward socially supported housing and jobs training," one might as well talk of unicorns. By the mid-2000s, after the main body of buildings had been built at Dignity, the community collapsed into its most minimally sustainable form. Despite its own claims of doing outreach to communities, I would argue that, rather than work outwardly to achieve the mission statement's community-oriented networks, it has instead produced a space where if people play the game properly, they can stay, virtually forever. And why shouldn't they, when they don't have faith that moving out into the real world will be better than their last go at it?

So much of the pressure imposed on IHC by outsiders is just such a transitional expectation. We will examine it here in more detail because of the way narratives of inevitability are inflected by conventional expectations about progressive self-care into what it is reasonable to expect from homelessness. We will also consider whether such expectations are viable any longer in a North American culture where it may be the case that we cannot do anything successfully about addiction and homelessness within these traditional narratives. In fact, successfully dealing with homelessness and ending it might require looking at the lived and spatial measures of success in new ways, asking these experiences to inform rather than conform to social policy.

8.2 Emerging Popular Narratives

There are two key popular narratives that are beginning to impact the way we see IHC. The first is a care or harm reduction paradigm. Harm reduction paradigms accept that drug use, mental health issues and extreme poverty are high among the homeless and support efforts to reduce the impact of these problems on community health. The best way to reduce the harm produced by addictions is not by forcing people into drug rehab programs that often don't work. Instead, best practice is to provide free needle and pipe exchanges, free injections sites (and smoking sites), free birth control and contraception, and even free drugs for addicts in order to curtail violent and non-violent crimes directed towards securing drugs.

In this paradigm, IHC—especially emergency rest areas—is popular because it is a form of harm reduction, ameliorating the effects of sleep deprivation and poor hygiene. IHCs are not zones that tolerate drug use or promote it. Rest areas such as Right to Dream Too and legal camps such as Dignity Village are intended to be drug-free zones, though it is safe to say that drugs are part of the lives of many of the people that use these spaces. These places, however, reduce the harm caused by street life by providing a place to sleep, be fed and to cleanse.

The main bent of this paradigm is pragmatic and immediate: reduce the harm to individuals and communities by limiting the negative health impacts of addictions and poverty. There is no emphasis on transitioning people away from the problem as a condition of receiving assistance. But the paradigm opens up urban space to uses that many citizens disagree with. Its most salient impact on housing has been the resurgence of supportive Housing First models, which provide housing for people first, and then offer them opportunities to work on related issues later if they so choose. In a sense, Dignity Village is a kind of Housing First model, though the necessary network and proper funding for social supports to make it more effective than a shelter do not actually exist.

The other paradigm that has emerged as something of a social movement is the Tiny Home Movement (THM). The origins of the movement are difficult to trace but the THM is strongly linked with the IHC movement that Dignity Village helped to produce. Instead of poor people building small shacks out of recycled and discarded materials, in the tiny home movement people of varying degrees of wealth, who are employed or retired, sell their large homes and downsize their carbon footprint by building tiny homes resembling cottages. These homes are not the shacks at Dignity Village or the tents at R2DTOO; they are well-built, fully serviced small homes, but at a price of $15,000 to $100,000, they represent an affordability and sustainability that have wide appeal.

These two paradigms produce powerful narratives about popular living that make the IHCs we are discussing more understandable to policy-makers and conventionally minded citizens. We now have a continuum of housing alternatives that includes both very poor people and people with significant assets, living in structures and communities that resemble each other. One could argue that the THM makes the general narrative on housing friendlier to camps, villages and new ways of thinking about housing and urban space. With these two paradigms increasing the degree of diversity in discourses on urban space and raising questions about existing social policy, IHC activists

have found a narrative bridge between the marginal narratives on homelessness and a new conventionalism in how to deal with social and environmental
needs. Cities are beginning to see a convergence between these practices.

8.3 The New Continuum

But these two paradigms are not in themselves sufficient to explain the
current ascendancy of IHC within city planning circles. The undeniable truth
is that in the U.S. and Canada, the numbers of people living without shelter
continues to be problematic for most cities. As I noted earlier, reliable data are
difficult to come by, but let us accept as valid for the sake of argument the
earlier numbers I presented: 146 million Americans in precarious financial
situations and 52 million living below the poverty line. While some cities have
managed to curb certain types of homelessness (veterans and families, for
example, receive a great deal of attention in most ten-year plans), not a single
ten-year plan has resolved the overall problem of homelessness since they
began to be implemented in 2003 (although, as noted earlier, Medicine Hat,
Alberta claimed to have done so in 2016). Indeed, the problem seems more
urgent because of the number of people living below the poverty line. And in
some cities where the numbers are extreme, such as Portland, with close to
4,000 people literally living on the streets and in shelters, politicians and
planners have had to recognize that IHC will be part of short- and long-term
strategies to manage homelessness.

In this chapter and the next, we are going to consider why in February
2016, six candidates for mayor in Portland unanimously agreed about the need
for IHC as part of the city's strategies for managing homelessness. Portland,
like many other cities, is finally admitting the danger of having large populations living in inter-structural roles, lacking assets or any viable means of
moving forward within the popular narrative of self-government. The cities
are also admitting that they do not want to spend money to help these
people. So when we read about some of the proposed ways to house people,
you might find it sounding rather like science fiction. Critical to this book is
my attempt to reinforce the awareness that "granting" homeless non-profits
the right to build rest areas and tent camps in dismal conditions is *not* a win
for the worst-off poor, but a cleverly disguised policy measure designed to
make it look as though politicians are doing something about social problems,
when in fact they really are not doing anything at all.

This critique is based once again on a continuum of IHC types, with tent
camps at one end, Dignity Village in the middle, and more advanced versions
such as Opportunity Village at the other, more desirable pole, very close to the
THM. From this perspective, we can begin to understand what it takes to
make Dignity Village and other grassroots IHC compatible with official housing and planning objectives and morally acceptable to people who care about

other people. The new narratives introduced in this book position housing security as a necessary aspect of managing liminal transitions for members of our society at a time when traditional experts and institutions are failing to do so.

Hopper and Baumohl (2004) argue that "[i]n America in the late twentieth century, life-course transitions in general have become more individualized, less bound to strategic family decisions, less subject to custom's scripting. As liminality become[s] riskier and more easily derailed, its casualties may find their way into the ranks of the *officially* homeless" (2004:356 [my emphasis]). In fact, I would argue that they have arrived. They *are* among the ranks; homelessness *is* a type of liminality. This is vitally important; liminality applies to us all as we experience our own rites of passage. University educations no longer guarantee jobs. Seniority no longer guarantees one's pension. College grads are living at home. Homes are becoming more difficult to hold onto, and illness or mental breakdowns are on the rise across all categories.

We can abridge my use of liminality to extend to people who are not homeless. However—and my own case provides a good example—liminal portions of life can be mediated if one has the proper supports. My life story, which you have read in part, is replete with disastrous choices and dangerous circumstances that disrupted my transitional experiences to the point of my becoming insecurely housed, periodically homeless, addicted, mentally unwell, and unemployable. Depending on the narratives employed by the many observers such as psychiatrists, drug counsellors, social workers and physicians who had opportunity to analyze me, my problems were "too vast," "too entrenched," and "statistically among the most difficult to overcome." One psychiatrist, well-known in the addictions field, was so overwhelmed by my life history that he told me that there was nothing psychiatry could do for me unless I was prepared to work with him five days a week for several years. Because that was neither financially nor practically possible, I remember staggering—quite literally staggering—out of his office to a pay phone, where I called my sister. (We didn't have cell phones in 1994.) I told her: "Andrea, he told me there was no help for me, none ..."—and I sobbed. I sobbed so hard that an elderly woman passing by tapped on the glass of the phone booth and asked if I was okay. A bizarre mélange of fear and titillation ran through me as I said, if memory serves correctly, "No, I am going to die," and I remember running off into the busy streets, hell-bent on getting really high—because I knew of no other way to die. The idea of getting *that high* turned me on.

The implication of the twisted diagnosis of inevitable failure made by this key specialist was, as I saw it, an indictment of my capacity to fulfill the role of the neoliberal citizen. Not only did I not want to self-govern, I was not going to regain this facility, and so what hope was there, really? It is very hard to blame the victims when they try to heal themselves but are left stranded in that strange psychic space between the old self-narratives they want to change and the healed, more progressive narratives they wish to join but which are forbidden by powerful opposing narratives. In my case, addictions had created a strange sense of limbo, and it would take me two more years to find a way to heal myself—two years during which I began using drugs at a level even I had thought impossible to maintain, in order to numb myself into abstraction and dissolution so as not to feel pain, not to feel *anything* at that inevitable moment when life would cease. Instead of putting a bullet in my head, I drugged heavier than ever before, suffered a sense of loss for a self suspended in a dubious history of failure, and waited for death to take me. After all, that was my inevitability. And so on that morning when not death but my sister found me, I had no other narrative left, and I started a journey of transitions back into the world. Very few people who need this help get it. And I will remind you once again that not all homeless people are homeless because of addiction; a great many work and have families but cannot afford a home.

The experience of becoming an addict and mentally unwell, of searching for help but being discarded as useless, seemed like a death blow at the time, but knowing how easy it is to self-medicate failure was very useful for me when I later did my work in Dignity Village and other camps. When people told me there was no help for them, no medical, psychiatric, housing or other help that was actually effective, I understood; I understood they had spent years suspended in the false promise of a transitional experience from their mental health or addiction issues, from abusive husbands and family, or from their low-paying jobs, but that their stories were permeated by despair and hopelessness. The pervasive whine of the blame-the-victim discourse, which is the core of neoliberal and neo-conservative attacks on the homeless, uses exactly this despair to motivate people to fight against liminality and to reject the idea of inter-structural roles. When people finally get to Dignity Village, or any other IHC, they are coming from a world made untenable because of an always uniquely proportioned mélange of personal defects of character and structural impossibilities, false hopes and poor systemic provisions.

8.4 Other Spaces

So living spaces like Dignity Village remain noteworthy for the unique way they bundle all the hope and insecurity into a single bounded spatialization. I describe this as a sort of idealized community model, which in a way is a between-world, a sort of hybridized space that combines Foucault's (failed) governmentality with a range of ill-formed and liminal forms of justification for resolving conflict that combine to create this perpetually liminal space. By now, it should be clear that in the sense that it is populated by homeless people who live in a social structure that reflects conventional ideals but interprets broader legal and political processes in its own convenient and irregular self-governing system, the space is both real and unreal: real in the Cartesian sense of being bounded by thresholds, unreal in the sense that it is largely a place of fantasies about how members are successfully performing conventional ways of living.

Foucault (1984) had ideas about how to understand places that invert, twist, resist and reject. If the village could learn to re-imagine itself for these other qualities, twisting, inverting, resisting, would we see the re-emergence of the village activist citizen? Would people transcend the liminal horizons of village life? I want to re-enter the earlier brief discussion of spatial heterotopias because they have had some popularity in recent years as models for spaces of resistance and alternate living. But as such they impose a narrative of otherness—of being outside and therefore of being suspect to conventional narratives of inevitability. I want to demonstrate that resistance is only one of many possible ways to look at IHC, which represents not a rejection of government but a desire to self-govern, to re-engage with the very narratives of inevitability that have marginalized the weak and the poor under capitalism. Using Dignity Village as our main case study, we will try to determine what role IHC is coming to play in shifting narratives on ending homelessness.

According to Foucault (2007), resistance is a way to question how we are governed, not a rejection of government. Questions about how to be governed can result in "counter-conducts" that reflect the choice of actors and groups of actors in the pursuit of alternative ways to achieve the same ends, through new leaders, new political alliances, new rationales and new strategies *vis à vis* political, economic and social areas of living:

> Yes. Space is fundamental in any form of communal life; space is fundamental in any exercise of power. To make a parenthetical remark, I recall having been invited, in 1966, by a group of architects to do a study of space, of something that I called at that time "heterotopias," those singular spaces to be found in some given social spaces whose functions are different or even opposite others (Foucault, 1984:252).

Recall that in a 1967 lecture entitled "Des Espace Autres," Foucault presents heterotopias as zones of contestations and resistance. I would argue that in cases such as the IHC, they are in fact sites of a reordering of extant relations of power that delineate the bounds of freedom and autonomy for actors pursuing alternative avenues towards these ends. They cannot find autonomy and freedom in the conventional social structure and capitalist culture so they inhabit these other zones. But these zones are not anarchist— their attraction to the marginalized is an *opportunity* to reclaim their *dignity*, which is a value inherent to all people. Hence we have Portland's Dignity

Village and Eugene's Opportunity Village. They are zones where one critique of dominant power displaces that power and fills space with its own version of order. In effect, the heterotopia is most useful for understanding resistance, not as an outright rejection of power, but as a means by which actors try to realign themselves in order to have more of it, even if in a ludic, event-based or highly temporary and concentrated spatialization.

There are places, too, in every culture, where the other sites of normal living are simultaneously represented, contested, and inverted. We might think of theatre, sports, funerals and carnivals, the tea gardens in downtown Portland, the tent in a city park. They are outside these other normal places, but are real, they have context in space, the same space, but as places of counter-ideas and actions. These are heterotopias. Bakhtin (1941) wrote of the "carnivalesque" to refer to literary modes and festivals that subverted or shed the dominant conventions of a time or style and were, in that way, liberating if not comical or chaotic. Today sociologists study the degree to which online communities and multi-user games provide heterotopic experiences (Haider and Sundin 2010).[159]

Between the utopia and the heterotopia, Foucault gives us another site, which he calls the *mirror*:

> In the mirror, I see myself there where I am not, in an unreal, virtual space that opens up behind the surface; I am over there, there, where I am not, a sort of shadow that gives my own visibility to myself, that enables me to see myself there where I am absent: such is the utopia of the mirror. But it is also a heterotopia in so far as the mirror does exist in reality, where it exerts a sort of counteraction on the position I occupy (Foucault 1984:5–6).

The mirror functions as a heterotopia in the sense that it makes the place from which the reflection originates, the place of the viewer, absolutely real and connected to all points in space around him, yet it is also absolutely unreal since this spatialization of inverted reality must be reflected through a virtual point that exists outside the viewer. The mirror is a reflector of numerous powerful discourses about identity, self-worth, freedom, rights and dignity: perhaps any value or idea for which narratives exist and in which a person might find implication. In many ways, living at Dignity embodies this self-reflection in other people's narratives—they look at themselves in the critiques of the village that appear in media, research, conversations and political statements from city governance, that see the village in unique ways that villagers must reconcile with their own self-perceptions. It is also partly the place (or the space, if you will) of my fieldwork, the book, *Dignity in Exile*, Mosher's "Doorways to Dignity" and "Tent City Toolkit," my videos for the village, and hundreds of other articles and essays about the village, all these combining to create a certain kind of composite mirror that gives villagers and IHC activists something to think about. It was against the weird eddies and twisted currents of these many interpretations, and the whitewashed tours that the village outreach team offered visitors, that I did my research.

For Foucault, heterotopias, like Turner's communitas, are effective at the personal level of the actor and at a social-structural level, as sites in which to play out the fantasies of rejection and of unrestrained freedom, to imagine one's life as more empowered, more pagan, more wealthy, less confined or managed (these are only examples), contesting and rejecting in a critical and, at the same time, ludic manner, the status quo.

Topinka (2010) and St. John (2001) employ the idea of *alternative cultural heterotopias* to events such as Burning Man, a pagan festival in the U.S. desert, and it might be argued the actions of Portland's urban re-claimers, which we discussed earlier, could be framed in this light. Inasmuch as heterotopias suggest a destabilization of how actors look at fixed perceptions of social and spatial reality, they suggest that, beginning with a shift in ideas, things can then change.

In Foucault's view, heterotopias are linked to all other spaces even though they are isolated. When St. John and Hetherington (1997:41), for example, assert that heterotopias exist "apart from central spaces that are seen to represent social order," the emphasis seems to be on this physical firstspace that *Of Other Places* suggests, the parkette or the shantytown on the outskirts of town, and not on the secondspace, that of knowledge creation and experience, that imbricates not only with the formation of spaces, but with the actions of actors within them. In this sense, the claim that became Dignity Village through collective action presented alternative ideas about how to use space, which suggests a certain mental or ideological space, and then secured an actual physical space as the spatialization of new knowledge. The parkette is understood as a fun place for recreation and relaxation within an arrangement of various other spaces, but the village is not so clearly separate.

The very effectiveness of heterotopias rests in the fact that they are not utopias. As an unreal space, utopias exist as fantasy worlds outside of extant power and systems of order. The mission statement we have looked at—the designs and goals of Dignity Village—presented a democratic utopia, and so the goals were never really attainable. In fact, the village, as Israel Bayer noted, had fit so uneasily into conventional narratives about housing that "they were out there." The village and, more recently, these other emergency camps could not officially challenge order since they were not implicated in the official scripts and laws that cities used to address poverty. They were experiments, test cases, liminal cases in the process of becoming. The city and the IHCs had to find a way to fit these new models into the discursive containers that cities used to form policy.

The key to making the IHC model integral rather than marginal is not by demonstrating its otherness, but proving its narrative proximity to conventional symbolic imaginaries. Even the most elaborate heterotopias, such as Burning Man, offer alternate versions of order, not anti-order. They may be counter-hegemonic, but they are tied to hegemony—they are a rejoinder to its weight—and it is out of this necessary relational tension that the heterotopia first finds its existence rationalized and then constructs its actions that define it as resistance or as a counter-site. Recall that Foucault argues that heterotopias "function in relation to all other sites that remain" (1967:7). Topinka astutely points out that what such counter-sites do is to make visible the "formations of received knowledge"; the resulting "confrontation with knowledge production ... promises new information. Yet these formulations will not shed the dominant order" (60).

Foucault claimed that "To analyze 'regimes of practices' mean to analyze programmes of conduct which have both prescriptive effects regarding what is to be done and codifying effects regarding what is to be known" (1991a [1980]: 75). So in my work, which is both theoretical and practical, there is a need to demonstrate the degree to which efforts such as Dignity Village help save lives by providing housing, but also how their appearance of resistance is really a buy-in to broader conventional imaginings of how people should live. In 2012, after the book had been repatriated to the village and I was finishing my dissertation, events occurred that had the villagers and me, as well as other activists in the region, asking how it would be possible to refresh the village's public image to help it get more support. Other cities were toying with the idea of using camps and IHC to alleviate the strain of homelessness. Urban planners, graduate students in architecture and a number of non-profits were actively carving out test communities and prototypical structures for the emergent Tiny Home Movement. While the village struggled to find relevance by figuring out how to follow the codes forced upon it, it had become fairly obvious that life in the camp took on a nature that had little to do with the rules. In our many discussions, there was a constant tension between the way villagers described the village on the basis of the mission statement and the bylaws (the way they wanted to be seen), and the actual way people experienced life in that space (what one sees if one stays there long enough). The easiest and most appropriate thing for the village to do, it seemed to me and most of the others, was to shed the unrealistic mantle of responsibility imposed by the rules and the city, and to establish the camp's relevance to other popular narratives: but how to do that became a central problem.

8.5 Thirding Spaces

Understanding space then, and life in space, as a certain way that people become socially oriented towards their own meaning, cannot be achieved by fitting space into narrow containers. Life should create, not conform to narratives. Once again, we need to see diversity. There are ways. Recall that Soja (1996) described thirdspace as a means of uniting Lefebvrian and Foucauldian spatial modes into a flexible and progressive way of looking at matters of spatial justice, which overcomes the firstspace-secondspace myopia:

> I define Thirdspace as an-Other [sic] way of understanding and acting to change the spatiality of human life, a distinct mode of critical spatial awareness that is appropriate to the new scope and significance being brought about in the rebalanced trialectices of spatiality-historicality-sociality (1996:57).

Thirdspace is meant to engage, critique and synthesize cultural and spatial boundaries into inclusive spatializations of experience. The application of the concept to understand spaces means that one can look at the same community, but from differing points of interpretation. Soja called this approach "thirding," and it is exactly the kind of critique that undergirds the diverse positions taken by opposing points of views in the debates over Dignity Village's right to be:

> I just want to address briefly the notion of heterotopia.... I am often asked, "does place X or site Y fit your definition of a Thirdspace?" There is no direct answer here, for all spaces can be seen as Thirdspaces or heterotopias depending on the scope of one's critical geographical imagination, the perspective one has on how far one can reach with a critical spatial perspective. Heterotopias are what you open up to view when you look at space heterotopologically, whether you are looking at an asylum, a garden, a boat, or Los Angeles (2011:114).

If we look at IHC as shelters we can see the way they conform to our visions of how a shelter works. If we look at IHC as communities we see those qualities. If we force the language of a transitional campground on the village, we cannot but see its failures. So what would be a better way of seeing the village? Or perhaps: What are the ways that *villagers* see their village? That was how I began to think about the village in researching and writing this book. What does living in the village tell us about helping people overcome the range of conditions we associate with homelessness?

In this sense, what we are wanting to do is a queering of space and of life in spaces. Since the 1970s the notion of *queer space* and *queering* has been used for the most part to destabilize colonial and patriarchal narratives of the other based on an heteronormative gender binary with the ideal masculine and feminine identity residing at polar ends of a hierarchical plane. In brief, without digressing into the vast field of queer studies or of queer theory, the idea of queering space is similar to that of thirding space, in the sense that each describes opening up space to recognize an inclusive discussion of what really goes on there, regardless of how such life conforms or diverges from dominant narratives about how life should take place. We can queer medicine, science, languages, politics and so on by emphasizing the place of excluded and marginalized categorizations of experience in the narratives that populate the dominant forces in those areas of social life. When we queer space, beyond the pseudo-traditional goal of neutralizing how hetero-normative discourses produce the basic values of patriarchy, capitalism and spatial justice, we are then "thirding space." We are letting the space do the telling.

Soja clarifies what he means by thirdspace in the following passage:

> All three of the spaces I discuss in Thirdspace are perspectives, different ways in which observers look at and interpret space. The main historical observation I make is that until recently most observers/scholars looked at space in only two broad ways, either as material forms (things in space) or as imagined representations about material space (thoughts about space). What I argue, following Lefebvre and Foucault's lead, is that there is another, different perspective that sees space as fully lived, as things in and thoughts about space and more. The arguments against the privileging of time over space, history over geography, are not very convincing (114).

Here we have an interesting way of understanding narrative inevitability. Arguments which privilege any idea over another are socially constructed visions of reality, not social truths constructed by reality. Inevitability is socially constructed over time into the narratives we use to justify social order and social policy, especially regarding poverty and the use of space. This is key: the narratives we tell ourselves about ourselves (e.g., the way I condemned myself because of the psychiatrist's misgivings), the way we understand ourselves as good Americans or Canadians (for instance, by virtue of having or not having self-contained housing), the way we tolerate or embrace other uses of time and space (like tent camps), are pre-conditioned narratives made sensible by historically powerful institutions like medicine and education, for our consumption as would-be self-governed citizens.

Soja wants our spatiality—the geography of how our lives are carried out—to have equal weight in this trialectic of spatial, social and historical narratives. If we look at spaces through the lens of firstspace we are forced to measure the space and place a monetary value on it. In that case, tent camps should only be located on the least valuable land in the city. If we look through the lens of secondspace, we are asked to evaluate what is done in a space: a park is for playing, not sleeping. But if we use Soja's notion of thirdspace, then we can eschew these powerful imaginaries and look at "fully lived space." And fully lived space, as a mediation of firstspace and secondspace ideal expectations, will almost always look heterotopic and resistant because total conformity to spatial rules never happens, anywhere, not in rigorously enforced spaces like prisons, not in "normal" homes.

We are aware these days of the crises facing penal and domestic institutions because we have come to recognize the ways that they fail to live up to the inevitabilities that have been built into our expectations. The same goes for the streets. We rarely seem shocked that homeless people are on the street. But when homeless people staking a claim to the streets shake up these narrative expectations, we feel confusion, resort to othering, and experience a lack of tolerance. In 2012, as I wrote my dissertation, I entertained the disappointing feelings I had had about the village. And I came to realize that the disappointment lay not in the village nor in the villagers and their collective failure to live up to the mission and rules, but in the failure of the mission and the rules to live up to the lives of the residents. Worse, the failure was that I had clung to the notion that people in this place ought to live up to these expectations. It is a notion that I abandoned that fateful day when E. died, when the cops and EMS guys joked over her corpse; when life, or death perhaps, said, "This is what happens—this is the narrative, abandon your preconceptions."

Since then, I have come to think that we were witnessing the creation of a new urban space devoted to a spatialization of broadly based liminality, similar to what happened after the Civil War and the Great Depression with hobo camps and shantytowns. In those cases, tolerance of these communities was short-lived, and as soon as the state could eliminate them, it did. However, Dignity Village and the emerging villages that were popping up in Eugene, Seattle and other places were not temporary reactions to nationwide poverty; they were enduring spatializations that were fighting for the rights of poor people to live in transcendence of conventional expectations of secondspace. They were creating new justifications, new Boltanskian *citées*; they were fighting for living space. So the real problem for the village was to either conform to the unrealistic expectations of the contract and bylaws, or otherwise make a powerful argument by demonstrating how the village satisfied the less popular but equally necessary need of some homeless people to find life—to live.

We will address whether this fully lived space defined by their actual needs is enough to ask of people, or to ask them to fight for—we will revisit the question of whether or not self-governing in poverty is a "good" thing at the end of this book. But self-governing in poverty is a *necessary* thing in the cities I study. As we will see, as other sites began to emerge successfully in the broader

IHC debates, Dignity Village had to begin to think about ways it could seem more relevant and attach itself to the critical tide. To me, and to some of the villagers, the real problem facing Dignity Village was how to rebrand itself in the emerging social critique of housing, and to regain the power discussed in earlier chapters. It had to put itself back on that continuum of debate.

8.6 Tick, Tick Tick …

Let me rewind the clock a little. In the months that followed my departure from Dignity Village in 2011, participants and I had dozens of conversations about what the word "transitional" means; what their rights as a nonprofit corporation were. We also talked about what they might want to do to be heard. At the top of the list was to avail themselves of legal aid and advice to manage the contract language that was being forced on them by the city. The city imposed the new version of the contract by insisting it be signed by a certain deadline, or else it would be withdrawn. Had the contract been withdrawn, the village could have been shuttered, and this tactic-threat had been used consistently during the village's by then 11-year history. In screenwriting and storytelling, the contract is called the ticking clock. It is the detective tracking down the hero, the virus spiraling out of control while the hero tests his vaccine. In Dignity Village in 2012, it was the contract hanging like the sword of Damocles over the community's head.

They had six months to come up with a contract of their own design and to enter negotiations with the city. This seems simple enough to some of us, for that is how business is done. It's a power struggle, a compromise and a renewed contract. But this was Dignity Village, and it was member-run and member-managed. They lacked the skills and wherewithal to address the negotiated order of policy processes (Strauss 1978).

Mitch Grubic had been elected CEO for the 2012 session, and though a capable leader, was too authoritarian for some people. Rocky had said he had "that God thing." He tried to start enforcing rules in the village. In his own words, some months later, it proved "impossible to do this because I would have had to kick everyone out." Because the village was so poorly organized, they did very little in the six months they had to write a response to the contract. That was the way things are done or, perhaps more correctly, not done in the village. Mitch could not do everything. His fellow council members were guessing at how to do their jobs. There was no guidebook or instructor's manual for how to bookkeep or do the monthly and quarterly reports. There was never a formally organized procedure for teaching these skills, yet self-government demands these skills.

Such skill sets came to the village originally in the natural abilities of its founders; the skills they naturally possessed were built into how they imagined the administrative system. Leaders were supposed to share with new members these skills, so that each year, with the election of a new council, residents would progressively transition into leadership roles. But once again there was no institutionalized structure for helping people transition into roles, even if the electoral process afforded residents new statuses. The roles were taken by residents before they could learn what those roles really meant by interacting with skilled leaders and practitioners. Over the course of two years, two secretaries and three treasurers were asked to leave the village because their incapacity to do their job well had appeared to be malfeasance.

Church et al. (2008) suggest that informal learning is any process by which learning occurs outside of formal school or educational settings. But in the village, there was an absence of such a process; there was the need to learn, and there were people who could help, including Ibrahim, Wendy, Heather and me; a number of local activist supporters offered and even tried to force the villagers to "learn"; but there the desire on the part of the village as a group to do so was clearly absent. Then there was, too, the debilitating effect of having the majority of villagers stoned, drunk or high most of the time. Many of them also suffered from learning disabilities and psychiatric issues that contributed to an inability to learn. Mitch, Brad Gibson and Ptery were the only ones who ventured out to learn how to lead, going to leadership meetings at R2DTOO and other housing activist groups. As a result, they appeared to have the knowledge to carry the village into a new phase of critical engagement and power within the city's strategic plan. But with a 30-day grace period expended, and a promise from the city not to move anyone who had been there for at least three years, in early December 2012 Mitch in his final act as CEO of the village signed the new contact without fighting for any changes to the transitional language.

At the end of Mitch's term, Brad Gibson was elected as CEO, Ptery was elected as treasurer, Scot and Lisa were elected as secretary and outreach officer, and Dave Samson was elected as security officer. During this transition, it was revealed that several of the older members were under suspicion of malfeasance and other wrongdoing while they had been in charge of donations and other administrative positions. The city was dubious about the village's viability given such improprieties. As a way to reassure the city, these folks were asked to leave the village. Some went to family, most to the streets.

Over the next six months, a dozen new members came in, several of whom had been there before and were anxious to get involved in outreach and activist activities. They were enthusiastic, feeding off the general fervor amongst the ranks of the student and homeless protesters who were now identifying as the "houseless" and gearing up for Occupy Portland, which had established itself in the city. In 2012–13, while Occupy camps were disappearing elsewhere, its influence in Portland was still salient and contributed to the power of housing activists in the downtown core, including Ibrahim's rest area. While

Dignity Villagers anchored themselves in a struggle to maintain the status quo, their participation in direct housing actions elsewhere dropped off; they stopped doing community service and so began the village's quiet exit from the discourse on lHC.

Recall that I had discussed how I met Ibrahim and learned of his plans to fight for a rest area in downtown Portland. When I left Portland in 2011, he had asked me not to write about the details of his plans until it was realized. One of the reasons for that request was to make sure that the deal actually went through. Ibrahim and fellow founders Trillium Shannon, Leo Rhodes and Lisa Fay, along with others, had started a non-profit called Right to Survive. They planned to build emergency rest camps for people, as Portland's unsheltered population kept growing and the city was doing little to remedy the situation. But activists like Ib are not simply radicals looking to transform society. They recognize that a complete social transformation of society is an idealistic vision that does little to help people who are dying on the streets right now. Sure, they want to build a world free of social inequality, but they also want to save lives. They are savvy business people with expertise in health, law, direct action, lobbying and impression management. And they have street "cred." Ib was a gang-banger, crackhead and "all around serious punk back in Chicago, back in the day." He wears his Chicago Bears football jerseys over his traditional Muslim dress on Sundays during football season. He also attended four different colleges, studying electronics, technology, real estate and business. Nothing is black and white in this world of homelessness and activism. The group found a disgruntled landowner in downtown Portland who agreed to lease them land for a dollar a year. Their camp, what came to be known as R2DTOO, initiated a series of legal debates about how to define such alternative shelters. As their website explained:

> Right 2 Dream Too (R2DToo) was established on World Homeless Action Day, Oct. 10, 2011. We are a nonprofit organization operating a space that provides refuge and a safe space to rest or sleep undisturbed for Portland's unhoused community who cannot access affordable housing or shelter. We exist to awaken social and political groups to the importance of safe undisturbed sleep. Our purpose is to create a place where unhoused people can rest or sleep without being rousted by police or private security and without being under the threat of violence (http://right2dreamtoo.blogspot.ca/p/our-history-past-and-present.html).

Moments after the group began moving onto the property, city officials and concerned Portlanders began the debate about the right of the poor to house themselves on city spaces not directly managed by the city as shelters.

To underscore the role of narratives in understanding lHC, the case of

R2DToo is very useful. The city of Portland had imposed a ban on camping in the city other than under the emergency provisions in the state constitution. That meant that, in public parks and other city spaces, no one could sleep overnight. The city, under pressure from local businesses, tried to ticket R2DToo for being an illegal campground. Ticketing and inspections went on for two years in a typical power play between firstspace governmentality with specific secondspace expectations, and a new kind of space trying to define itself. Spaces that define themselves are not easily understood, and are the essential liminal spaces.

The city had become so worried, in fact, that it offered the group an entire 10,000-square-foot building for a year to operate as a shelter, paid for and serviced, as a compromise. The city wanted to enforce its own shelter codes through the use of the building. Ibrahim rejected that. There were only certain conditions under which he would give up the visibility that R2DToo had. "They all must be smoking some of the village drugs, man," he declared. "We ain't givin' up our space and our fight so they can tell us how long and how to run ourselves."

8.7 The Mirror or the Magnifying Glass

I will return to the story of R2DToo shortly, but we must not ignore how important its emergence was to Dignity Village, which entered 2012 with the newly revised, city-favored contract in place. More than the mirror that Foucault had spoken of, this site served the heterotopic function of re-ordering life within the structures of domination it threatened to shed, but, somehow, it was able to surpass the temporary nature suggested by heterotopias. To this day, and here, in this book, we are asking what the performances of R2DToo or Dignity Village tell us about that space which is always a site of contestation and which, ironically, is also supposed to be a safe harbor for troubled souls. And it seemed that R2DToo had begun to attract so much attention to the number and condition of the street poor in Portland that by the autumn of 2012, Dignity Village itself had fallen under a very critical magnifying glass.

And then there was my book, *Dignity in Exile*, some excerpts from which are included in this book. I had sent several copies to the village in order to ask villagers how seeing themselves in Nigel Dickson's photos, how reading the very critical stories the villagers and I collaborated on, might change the way they saw the village. I was using these responses in my dissertation research, and as a way to start conversations between villagers about practical needs. Some local activists and advocates read the book, and not everyone was pleased by the representation I had made; many people who had vested inter-ests in the village and wanted to promote safe places for people to live felt that the stories in the book confirmed the negative press the village had always received. But there were many others who were astonished by the residents' stories and how they had overcome certain obstacles to live in the community. And there was the fact that, despite all its struggles, Dignity Village had at that point managed to stay open for 11 years. Not all the villagers participated or were interested in the book or my research. But those who did tended to have some tenure at the village and to move in and out of leadership roles. The book came out close to the time that the latest contract had to be signed, and villagers were struggling to reconcile the meaning they brought with them into the camp—how they saw their world—and the meaning that the contract, if finally lived out as written, would impose on them.

Bogged down by the city's rewording of the contract, villagers began to ask themselves what a transitional experience might have meant to them as individuals. They were reaching a certain sense of desperation where they knew what was wanted from them as an endgame but had neither the rituals nor the leaders in place to get them there. They understood that in the discourse of the contract and the views of governance embodied in it they were liminal personae, expected to move on after a suitable period in the village (two years).

There were several strategies available to them. They could do nothing and get high all the time, and if the past was a good indicator of the future, nothing would happen. They could go on to live in relative obscurity because the city had often threatened but never acted on this transitional language. They could put their names on waiting lists and hopefully get housing before the contract expired, but that usually took more than three years if it happened at all. One man, White Cloud, could not get housing because he had killed someone years ago, done his time, and was on a housing "no-fly list," as it were. I mentioned earlier that sex offenders and serious felons have a hard time getting housing, and that includes a lot of people we are talking about in the spatial contexts of the camps.

Another option for villagers was that they could organize and start to fight for the health and longevity of the community— they could do the hard work of fixing what was broken and prove themselves worthy once again of what the founders had earned so long ago. In so doing, they might once again infuse the very active housing critique in Portland with their own concerns. They could offer up a thirding of their lives and fight for that reality.

By all accounts this was a difficult period and very clear cleavages formed. The most dramatic cleavage was between those villagers who were willing to "activate" and those who, through drug alliances and their status as old-timers, were empowered by the village and were either too shortsighted or too optimistic to realize the serious conditions this contract placed on their future. They argued that the contracts had always been there to keep them in line, and this was "just another. There would be more."

In the depths of a certain crisis of community, villagers made inquiries to Kwamba and to me about the direction the village might take. And as this was happening, the Oregon cities of Eugene and Ashland were seeking the advice of village members Dave Samson, Brad Gibson, Ibrahim, Ptery and a few others in order to inform these cities' own plans to build intentional homeless camps in 2012 and 2013. (We will discuss these later, too.) At the request of the leadership at the village and, as a way to help finalize my own research, we agreed to have a series of conversations about Dignity Village and what the future might hold. I asked: "What is going on there now, and what would you do to fix it?" As Shorty, the last remaining original member of the village, said:

> You know, this place has been many things. It was a camp, then a shantytown. They called us transitional to fit into the language of their laws, but they never enforced it. So, people are used to living here. It's our homes. And even last year, when the contract came up for renewal, they suggested taking out the word transitional because, for sure, it wasn't working like, to get folks back into houses. So they was content to keep it as was. They even wanted to take 'transitional' out. And this is what is really scary to us... you know, they have the power. They can tell us what we are and how we are, uh, how we should be. Someone somewhere doesn't like what we are doing here, and maybe they are afraid that too many of us, places like this are popping up, or will. But now they are gonna tell us that we are nothing more than a shelter. They are turning us into a part of their shelter system. Not only are they telling us we have to be transitional, they told us it has to be in two years. It's scary. Scary, you know. Most of us won't be able to find a place, and the few that do will end up in shit holes. [Shorty left in June 2013 to live with a friend because the drug gangs and emotional violence in the village were too much for him.]

Ken, 2011. Photo: Nigel Dickson.

Most of the immediate replies I received from villagers reiterated what I had been told in 2011 by Ken, a long-term member:

JULY 2011

Ken has been at the village for four years. He's a big unkempt man. He walks with a cane. Seven years earlier, he came to Oregon to work with his brother, but the job fell through. He ended up living under the Burnside Bridge and various parks. The cops used to come by usually around three in the morning to roust the sleepers. There were a lot of them he says. "It was crazy, chaos." He came to the village because he got tired of being rousted.

"So what was the vibe like in the village then?" I asked.

"Phew. A lot better than it is now."

"How would you describe the vibe now?"

He looks down. Shakes his head. A deep sigh. "The politics are outta control. I don't go to the meetings unless I absolutely have to."

"Do you feel like it's futile to go to the meetings?"

Quietly. Reserved. "Yeah ..."

"What makes it so futile?" I ask.

"People constantly at each other's throats. Just the politics are getting outta hand."

"Do you think it would be better if more people were involved in the council. If the council was bigger than as small as it is?" He looks around to see who's listening. No one was around.

"Yeah, but ... the biggest thing I've noticed is the drug problem. There's too many people using that stuff in here ... it's a violation of rule 3."

I interrupt him. "But don't you drink beer?"

He looks at me like I should know everyone does. "Sometimes but I can safely say that in 34 years I have been alive, I have never used drugs."

I look at him away from the lens of my camera. "But it's not a secret that people here are doing drugs—people admit it then deny and admit it and—how do you think it translates into a political problem, the drug problem?"

"It's not so much it's a political problem as it affects people's judgment. You know. Everybody's got their own little cliques around here. Everyone that's on the council with the exception of a couple is in their own little clique."

I offer, "And the cliques are based on support related to certain resources like drugs or something?"

"Some of them, yeah."

I agree with him that hard drugs are a real problem for the village. "But the bylaw that says 'you can't have any beer or drugs' is a little unrealistic, because everyone smokes dope or drinks beer here, right?"

"Almost everyone," he adds.

He sounds to me like he is trying to convince himself, as if it is important that not everyone does drugs. "Not everyone, but close."

"Can you tell me a bit about the IR system?"

He cuts me off—with an instructive outstretched hand.

"I've written one IR since I got here, I don't like them."

"And can you tell me what's an IR?"

"It's an incident report. People write up IRs on other people for violating rules around the village. Pet rules ... ah, violating the five basic rules, you know ... stuff like that"

I ask him, "But isn't the fact that they have IRs a good way to stop people from conflicting directly—"

"Yeah, well, a lot of the time those IRs are frivolous—they write 'em just to be pain in the ass."

I ask, "So they are not really used to mediate conflict, which is what they were for ..."

"Right. See, what we're trying to do is set up a committee to investigate the IRs once they're written before they actually go up in front of the council. Because a lot of these IRs are like I said, frivolous. They write 'em just to be MEAN. I've had IRs written on me because people didn't like me.

"A couple of months back I had my house broken into. They took almost a thousand dollars' worth of my electronics. They took my netbook, my PSB, and my Internet modem.... I just called the police and gave them the serial numbers. Which means if they try and sell it a pawn shop the serial numbers will be flagged."

"How common is that sort of thing around here?"

Unfortunately it's pretty common as of late.

"It wasn't that way before," I said.

"No, it ... you know, when I first got here you could walk out of the village all day long and leave your door standing wide open and come back and everything would be right where it was. But now you know if I leave my house even for a second, I'll lock it up.

"So let me ask you a question. Do you think we should have more Dignity Villages ... here, now, this place, should there be more?"

"Well, they could actually set another one up in Portland because the city's zoned for two of these."

"Well, do you think they should? Knowing what you know about this place now, and the way it runs and all the crap that's going on these days, do you think it's a good idea?"

"Well, I think if they could take 8 to 12 individuals from here that are really committed to the village itself and set up another site somewhere, I think it could happen."

I agree: "Right, that way, they could start and invigilate the rules properly, it could happen ... because it's kind of hard to go backwards. This place kinda feels like it's imploding."

He is nodding his head pensively but agreeably the whole time. "Well, it's a lot better than when it started ... you know they started out underneath the Morrison Bridge (they moved shortly after to the Fremont)."

"No, that's not what I mean. I mean it was functioning like a community far better four years ago, three years ago, two years ago ... in the last two years it hasn't really been much of a community. And a lot of people are saying that's when the meth started."

He is not sure it has anything to do with the drugs. He is pretty sure the drug use is because of a certain hopelessness that people have about the possibility of leaving there and finding anything better.

"I think with the economy, the jobs and everything, it's affecting everyone's judgment."

I ask him, "So it's a question of judgment? People are making poor decisions?"

"Yeah. But that's just my opinion, and you know what they say about opinions ..."

If Ken's words sound familiar, it is because they *are all too familiar*. Addiction is partly a psychological and somatic dependence on substances, but in this case is symptomatic of an underlying and fundamental disconnect that people have with their surroundings. At the beginning of the chapter, I called it paralytic community.

I talked earlier about my own addictions and those of others, and it should be clear that having a beer or smoking marijuana on a Sunday afternoon with no responsibilities, for fun, what we call recreational use, is not what Ken or the others refer to as the drug problem in the village. They are talking primarily of a meth-amphetamine epidemic. When he refers to the village being a better place in the past, it was because during that time they had goals. They were building a community, helping each other build structures and figure out ways to get food; they were helping other homeless people who came to the village or they went out into the community and offered help. They were active in the sense their mission statement had demanded. But by 2011, they were lost and unimportant. Perhaps worse than that, they developed a local culture that rested on its laurels and accepted limbo as normal. No one really wanted to leave because staying was easier and understandable.

Again, the image problem comes down to the contract and the rights and freedoms it encodes—and, too, to the willingness of either the city or the villagers to fight for those values they respectively hold dear. While Brad Gibson was CEO, city representatives had inspected the village and asked residents to sign up for housing wait lists. They stressed the transitional definition of how life was *supposed to be lived there*. As I jotted on a note after a phone call with Samson and then Brad:

> Villagers were being asked, perhaps told, to think of the village in alternate terms. The group was pretty nervous and everything they

say is all about the village, all about the contract, all about what to do. I told Brad it was time to think pragmatically and he said, "It was a pretty God-pragdammic time, for the village, a real challenge to his emotions." [We talked about the contract, and Brad said:] "They hold this up to us like a threat, as a way to remind us who's ultimately in charge. But they wouldn't dare kick someone else out. No way. They couldn't handle the repercussions in the press. The village. Now that's a different matter. The village has got five more years. They want us off of here and moved, or gone in five years [the contract said three years; he was being optimistic]. If we don't find a place for the community, they can say we failed because we as a group had ample notice, and maybe we weren't viable as a community anymore. But no way they can pick on people like they are black sheep and force them out of here. Even if it is in writing. All that section of the contract does is make people walk around in a dirge, so they got no motivation to do nuthin'. And so now when we try to get them motivated, it's like zapping a sleeping dog with a prod, it just gits up, shuffles over to another corner and goes back to sleep. They don't know or want to believe that they have rights and this contract doesn't mean the end of anything. We have paper, see. We're a 501-C3 non-profit and even if they wiped us out tomorrow, that paper is in good standing, so the village goes on, just as long as there is people willing to fight for it and to support it. Maybe not here. Maybe somewhere else."

If the state does manage to "make people walk around in a dirge," as Brad put it, the first thing critique must do is expose that fact, and make villagers aware of their need to resist it. Critique, then, at least in this sense, is what we were trying to produce. I was consciously trying to get the villagers to think critically about the "dirge" and to establish means of redress. Recall that governments work "through practices of freedom and states of domination, forms of subjection and subjectification" (Dean 1999:46). Brad and Ptery, who had spent considerable time with Ibrahim and other community activists, were trying to introduce policies and practices that got "people thinking." They introduced conversations about rehabilitation, psychiatric supports and cleaning up the village, in addition to reiterating the village's commitment to community service as a basic requirement of membership. If it isn't obvious, it should be: the drug-based factions rejected progressive and health conscious measures, and the few residents who wanted the village to perform well and in line with its mission were at loggerheads with these other groups.

Brad, a technician by trade, took charge of the computers and other communal devices making sure they were working properly and not misused. *Things* often went missing, and when sponsors were giving the village 52-inch TVs and remote controls, iPads and other devices to share, and these things broke from misuse or disappeared, it was a problem. Supporters stopped donating valuable assets to the village and began eyeing the upstart camp at R2DToo and other prospects in Oregon. Dignity felt the impact of supporters abandoning them. The largest single supporter they had, Leland Larson, had spent thousands of dollars on the village and was beginning to field criticism for supporting a place where drugs and theft were common.

The village was getting a reputation for complacency and theft, and, of course, drug use. Some people when they heard of this said things like, "So what, they are just people," or "Sounds like any other community, what's the big deal?" But these were not "just" people—they were discursive characters living in space with implications for the future of intentional homeless communities. And it wasn't going unnoticed. A number of activists from other cities visited Dignity to take note of what was not working. Word was spreading. The ticking clock was getting louder, with different parties holding opposing views on how to silence it.

So Brad started organizing tools, machines, electronics and other community property. Organizing, to him, meant storing things in his office or at home so they weren't misused. He spent a lot of time working at the R2DToo campsite, going to local community meetings, and even helped plan the actions of R2DToo as a means to keep alive the link between Dignity Village and other actions. To their credit, a few of the other faction leaders participated. Scot and Lisa, for example, attended a couple of meetings to symbolically support the movement. They didn't stick it out, appearing at two protests only, but even this was an improvement. While Brad was trying to run things like a business, Ptery was spending most of his time working in a local wellness center and advocating for various groups, especially R2DToo and City Repair.

There had been a transition in membership, too. I mentioned that several residents were removed from council positions. Two died. Three others left to get into city housing spaces. And several others left simply to escape the "dirge." By January 2013, 23 new members had joined the village. Of course, because the village keeps terrible records, this number is hard to verify, but I did a head count by video at a membership meeting, and it seemed accurate.

Most of these new members were fresh from the streets, and all had addiction or mental health issues of one kind or another. Though I was not there to witness it, each week I would talk to different villagers who described how new alliances were forming in the village, around drugs and other promises. A big issue was favouritism—granting new residents membership or shacks of their own, letting them jump the queue, as it were: patronage, village style. While Brad was out trying to "activate," fulfilling the role of the leader as set out by Ibrahim, addicted factions in the village rallied against his discussions and invitations to bring outside medical and rehabilitative help into the village, including a joint effort by him, Ptery and a few community activists, and supported by all of us who advised the community, to request a community health agency to undertake a village-wide drug intervention.

One can see from the few stories I have told that Brad was acting in ways that broke with the unfortunate habitus of the village. What was he doing? He was trying to clean up the village, including his own addictions; he was trying to manage the affairs of the village by actually taking control over resources and management procedures; he was trying to reactivate the village's promise to be a part of the community. In a sort of anti- Bourdieusen break with habitus, he was trying to get villagers to be activists in their own affairs and the affairs of the village, because he recognized just how mired in this liminal dirge (dirge as habitus?) they had become as a result of long-term structural conditions that held no promise of emancipation from poverty or homelessness. Most importantly, Brad and the other activists, Samson, Ptery, and most of us who supported the village, had suggested bringing in outside advisors to help handle things such as bookkeeping and general maintenance, and also to sit on council as a way to rebalance the way decisions were made.

But most of the villagers who were mired in the dirge also were in denial about that fact. This structural liminality, the threat of the new contract, the drug epidemic, the loss of supporters, this dirge, in short, was a product of the city's long-term control over the village, the lack of any real supports or "after-care" plan for villagers, except the long-shot prospect of finding housing. And then there was its isolation at the margins that gave villagers a reason not to go downtown and activate. Most importantly, strong leadership and legitimate authority had come to mean little in the village; in their place was the perpetual angst of conflict between uncooperative factions who seeded council with their members.

All of these impediments to developing fully participative political subjects were, as I have shown, built into the city's strategy for experimenting with intentional community, even if this capacity was merely immanent. To be an active citizen in the village, to follow that habitus, if you will, had come to mean locking yourself into a limited political role and contributing only minimal sweat equity as a measure of good conduct. If one thinks of the amount of time that it takes to sit in on village meetings (four hours per month), or how much sweat equity was exchanged for rent (40 hours per month), it is clear a great deal of time is left to do other things, such as picking up garbage or tending the gardens, or generally "picking up the slack."

I wrote in my notes several times that the village "was like a summer camp for troubled teens" whose members "acted like spoiled children." Even Ibrahim said that in the village, they have "silver spoons in they mouths." If governmentality is real, then why did some of the villagers exercise the critical attitude that Foucault says is part of the care of the self, and therefore integral

to conduct towards others, while others did not? Surely some of this diver-
gence was because they were, as Dave said, a heterogeneous group, some new
to homelessness or the village and thereby infected with intense survival
anxieties, and others longer-term residents, able to see beyond the fog of the
street mentality. Unfortunately, even long-term villagers were not looking
after themselves very well. The only villagers I knew who were overcoming the
dirge were those who were actively fighting to wipe it out, to open the village
up to new possibilities: Dave Samson, Mitch Grubic, Ptery and Brad Gibson, all
of whom had become key council members.

With the new members in 2012 and 2013 came a few who joined in calling
for an alternative path for the village. "New Larry," as he called himself, "Dog
Dave," and a man named "Chuck" joined with Brad and the others in discussions about how to kill the dirge. Dog Dave had been at the village years earlier
when it was still under construction. He wanted to get that vibe back. Like
Samson, he had returned to the village a second time. It was with this group
that I held a series of conversations about what direction they wanted to take
the village. It was essentially a pragmatic exercise—we shared ideas on how we
understood the village, and how it might work differently. We confronted the
implications for lived experience contained in competing first- and
secondspace values.

JANUARY 22, 2013. SKYPE CONFERENCE. *Participants: Brad Gibson, Ptery, Jeff,
"Dog Dave", Dave Samson, Lisa, Scot, and a few other unnamed participants.
It's midday. They are talking to me from the commons room at Dignity Village.*

I begin: "Well, you have a had a new election and from my point of view it
seems to have worked out really well for you. From my point of view it
seems to be a really great mix of people."

Lisa says, in a humorous tone, "A motley crew?" But she is participating
on camera with them, as a part of that team. That in itself is noteworthy
since when I was there, she and Scot both had a great deal of distrust for
Ptery and Brad's activism. Now, Brad was the CEO and Ptery was treasurer
and Lisa was secretary, and they were working together on cleaning up the
village's affairs and image.

Brad says, "The first council meeting went off without a hitch. It was a
pleasurable meeting. The first one I had here actually. There was more
communication, everyone worked it out; we were doing our human
resources stuff, assigning jobs, making sure everyone got in the right place.
And it went off without a hitch!"

Samson pipes up, "We do still have the torches and pitchforks on the
ready just in case things do go."

I expressed my concerns. "Okay, so I am concerned for a bunch of reasons. One is the contract automatically puts limits on your freedom and autonomy, so I question the degree to whether you can fulfill this idyllic mandate that the founders had 11 years ago.... There are two questions; one is how realistic is it for you guys to consider yourselves an alternative housing project, when the city is trying to impose all these standards on you? The other one: ... you seem to recognize that in order to carry this project forward you need to kind of leave the village and take it elsewhere and start fresh and I am wondering what you would do in the new project that you would do differently than now?

Brad pipes up very directly, "NOT HAVE A CONTRACT WITH THE CITY!"

They all laughed, and Dog Dave, lurking in the background, added, "On private land there is no need for a private contract with the city."

"He was one of the original founders," Ptery added in the background. I recalled Dave's voice from the tapes Kwamba had made. He confirmed that it was a different place in those early years, a period when building community, literally, also had meant building community, spiritually, and that had become the "dead zone" the village had had to fight in 2012. He rightly pointed out that in the early years, they were expected to fail at certain things because no one had done this kind of thing before, but after so many years, the public and other homeless people had watched the place rise and then simply "kind of stagnate." The way he described it, as a temporary place but permanent fixture in the activist mentality, rang true. "It's impossible to define this place. It pisses me off you ask us what it means," a villager had once said to me. At some point later, off Skype, we had discussed, Brad, me, Jeff and Dave, how the village had to "try on a bunch of hats," that it was a place where people had to try on many hats because "homelessness kind of rips that stuff you know about yourself, out of you, and ya gotta put it back in somehow, from the whole world, you know out there, you're in here, and you have to stick that toe in the water and get wet a little to see if you wanna swim." I suggested that the original plan wouldn't work there because it had gone so far in the other direction that you just couldn't step back.

Several times in this book I have spoken about the goals and desires of planners. A closer review of the planning documents in chapter seven revealed that they used terms such as "stability," "safety" and "self-governed," which city councillors had even doubted possible in populations of long-term homeless people. The ethnographic excerpts presented here tend to support these doubts. When I reiterated to Dog Dave that it would be impossible to create the conditions of stability and harmony they had envisioned because the village dynamic was irreversible, he seemed to be speaking in different terms, as if the size or location of the place would have implications on the factions and lack of communicative action in the village. While I disagreed with him about the focus of his analysis, I agreed with him, Soja, Foucault, and Lefebvre, that space is not some cold, abject, lifeless material, but is meaningful in its imbrication with time. Dave had felt that the village space needed to be bigger, in spatial terms, more land, whereas I felt to improve things they could expand performative experiences on the same space.

"Well it's partly that," he says, "and it's partly that there just is no room to grow, to develop that vision."

I ask, "And so when you guys talk to the city now, is that the image you are presenting them to now?"

Brad tells me that they were just trying to avoid contacting the city too much right then—they just want to get everything in order in the village so the city doesn't invoke its punitive measures and restrictions, so they don't clamp down hard on the village. The new leadership wants to get the village "in line" with the demands of the contract so the members know where they will be sleeping for the next couple of years. "I imagine we will have further conversations, at some point down the line pertaining to this, but at present we have no plans," says Brad.

"And what happened with Eugene and Ashland?" I ask. During our last conversation, just around the time of the book launch in October 2012, they had invited me to come live with them when they moved to a proposed camp in Ashland slated for 2013. Ptery answered my query by telling me that Ashland had decided to build an emergency day-shelter program instead of a permanent camp. Eugene was still in the market for a new intentional site on which to house homeless people. The camp would be run for the city through intermediate agencies and NPOs. It would be self-managed by the residents but steered by a joint board. The permits had been passed and it was at that time located on church property while the city, the church and other NPOs tried to implement a management plan.

"Sounds like a shelter to me." I said. I added, "But at least they are moving forward."

I had wanted the villagers to understand that, based on my observation of Portlanders, the city council, the advocates and the village, all that was required to get more support was good will and a willingness to make critique—to show up and state your position with some regularity. Good will, through acts of community well-being and good corporate citizenship, not just direct resistance through protest, were the keys to displacing opposing power. If the city had been unwilling to take the village seriously as a good member of the Portland community, then the village had to change that knowledge.

I summed it up thus later in that conversation: "I understand that the city wants to treat you as part of the shelter system, but that's not what you want, that's what you want to overcome, correct?"

Absolutely, correct, they all agree.

Brad confirms, "And we don't get any of the VSGs [village support grants] or any of the other monies that other shelters get, we are totally separate from them. And they stick us out there on our own, and they want to pin their name on us ... and that is not right."

"Right, so I thought. You know, I had a chat with Ptery about this before I left. That I thought the payoff for people at the village wasn't just that they were finding a place that was safer than living off the streets—it worked at a whole other level. You know, for Lisa it was the kind of place she could come and find her voice—and for you, Brad, you know you came there, and you have been there for three years now, and now you have a top managerial position and that's pretty cool; and Ptery found a place where he could bring information from the outside to people who needed to know, you found a safe home—so it's the kind of place that works at these personal levels ... it doesn't help if I write my book and I write my dissertation and you guys aren't out there carrying your own personal message. I mean, personally going out and getting to know guys on the street—and I am not talking about recruiting, I am just talking about doing outreach—you know, like how the Three Amigos [a Christian group] come and bring dinner to you guys? I'm not saying their [religious] motives are cool, but I think if Dignity Village was known amongst the community as giving back, that it would be easier for you to ask and to get zoning."

Ptery adds, "There was good will in the beginning ... but that had changed because out there on the present site, there is no local community in which to demonstrate good will. That whole function was lost ... by being out here."

"So the village has to find something else to give back," I add. "It doesn't matter if you write your own articles and post them, or if one of the papers does it, once a week a bunch of you goes out with sacks on your back to give back to some of the poorest still suffering in Portland—and I am going to tell you that if you guys keep doing that for four or five months, you're gonna have more support than you ever dreamed of. And that's what critical action is all about. You are not doing this to buy a new car. You are doing this to get support to provide a new village for more housing for more people."

Brad asserts, "And that's what I did. Me and Ptery went out and help to start a new organization (in Eugene) ... and it has ..."

Ptery interrupts him. I think he is getting the point at least. He says to

Brad: "But they don't have our story on it, they don't know it's us (the village) doing it.... We are not known for doing that—we are not known for that. We need to correct that."

I suggest that if they want to brand the village, they need to brand it as future-looking and as gracious, "because out there they want to know that you guys are working hard and grateful for the opportunities that you do have."

Dog Dave pipes in. "It's hard to move ahead with a noose around your neck."

I agree with him, but I suggest the contract is the real noose. He disagrees. He thinks the noose is the location. "We can't move forward with anything we are talking about from here."

So I agree with that also, but that is not what stops the action.

"So I think part of critical action is acting strategically and having tactics—the strategy is to get new land, and now you have to employ tactics to help get it. So one of the tactics is to get out there as Dignity Village, not one or two guys from Dignity Village, representatives of Dignity Village going out and helping the community and helping it on your own, a completely unilateral effort."

Dave seems to missing this point. He goes on about how they have found locations and are looking at tactics for getting pieces of land, but he is not willing to entertain that the village still needs to unite with the critical action of other homeless in Portland. He is fixated on the schematic drawings and design of the green sustainable village envisioned back in 2001.

Attempting a group conference from a tent at R2DToo, 2014. Photo: Eric Weissman.

Caught up in that utopian imagery, it is easy to not to see the hard, dirty work that ensures that the village generates the critique to continuously displace power. But Brad understands. So do Ptery and the few others who remained for the duration of this conversation. I can see them nodding their heads and making notes on pads and on scraps of cardboard, over the screen, over Skype.

Brad says, "Right, they gotta be more behind the Movement. It's there." There is a brief pause. I see a few of the villagers shuffle through the door.

Spaces and Liminality

Mitch, Lisa and Scot, and a new member named Nancy. I could sense they did not like what we were talking about or where this discussion was going. They say they need a break—"It's been a long and heated discussion"—but I knew them. I wrote about them. We hung out together for two months. Scott especially did not get this "whole activism thing."

On May 28, 2013, just five months later, the clock stopped. Brad's colleagues on council approached me by phone, text, email and Skype to participate as an advisor in the impeachment proceedings against the current chief executive officer, the same Brad Gibson. Along with me, video archivists, community-based researchers and organizers, Kwamba Productions, and a few other supporters of the village were asked to "be critical" and to offer advice regarding the procedural validity of the impeachment. They asked us whether or not the villagers were adhering to strict codes embedded in its articles of incorporation as a democratic membership-run community, but also to gauge whether the accusations had real merit. "Is it consistent?" asked one accuser. "What do you think the implications will be?" asked another. "You should know, you lived here, you know what people are like you know what we are supposed to be about, do you think we are justified?"

They were grappling with new and old visions of what the village means; Brad's traditionally rooted, activist "take-charge of the drugs and sloth fervor" (as he put it), and the do-little-or-nothing attitude of the drug factions. They had created fantasies about Brad stealing tools and the iPad. There were other accusations, other defenses, all moot. In the village, if a faction wants you out, they will get a majority of the village to vote you out. It is that simple. For my own part, I reiterated that I had a right to share my opinion on the poor image these constant political fights in the village were casting outside the village.

In the end, one faction created illegitimate accusations against Brad, managed to get a majority of their followers to vote against him, and, against all of the experts' advice, they impeached him. He was the fourth CEO to be removed prematurely in the past six years. Not too many democracies could survive that in the real world. Mitch Grubic, Lisa Larson, Scot and the new person, Nancy, the same group who had abandoned our Skype conversation, led the impeachment. They were to become the leadership of the council in 2013. Since then, the village has remained more or less mired in a certain stillness, trading on the popular misbelief that it is a green, sustainable and progressive community, but doing very little to prove that to more critical eyes.

I should reiterate that Dignity Village does not revolve in its own orbit. The sovereign power here is not the village but the city, and even Portland City Council must answer to popular opinion. There is a question about how many of these "other spaces" a city can support before it comes to be seen as a slum-lord. After all, Toronto abandoned Tent City when the world starting hearing about babies born in shantytowns. The city of Portland is quite aware of its need to do something about its street homeless, or to at least *appear* to be doing something, but can the Portland symbolic imaginary comprehend rest areas like R2DToo or emergency campgrounds like Dignity Village as permanent fixtures? Are these spaces in a thirdspace sense, solutions to homelessness?

While Dignity Village was firing its CEO and the next faction was taking power, R2DToo was gaining actual strategic weight by legally occupying a visually compelling and valuable piece of city land. As R2DToo's claim played out in the courts, the city leaders became nervous. At the end of the first 30-day judicial review, the judge ordered a second 30-day period to review the constitutionality of the claim. A few hours after that, the city invited Ibrahim to look at several parcels of city land, away from the thriving core. The sites had less critical visibility but they did have basic electrical and water service and were reasonably close (within long walking distance) of missions, soup kitchens and the core. The city promoted the spaces as safe places to build a larger, permanent emergency sleep station. Ibrahim and I talked about the potential for this, and he sent the following email on August 12, 2013:

> Salaam Board,
> I[,] Ibrahim, am sending out this E-mail to inform you-all that an ultimatum was put tom us this morning by Commissioner Amanda Fritz. The Space next to the Bud Clark Commons was taken off the agenda from us and under the Broadway bridge was introduce[d] as the new possible area for Right2Dreamtoo. We have until Noon tomorrow to tentative[ly] accept this offer. A few of us went to view this site. [I]t has great potential, however it takes away from our visibility.
> I thought on this offer and I have to take my direct Action Right2Survive mentality away. THAT is R2DToo['s] mission statement. Do we want R2DToo to be publicity Action or an [sic] Rest Area to help Houseless People get sleep? This is my biggest question. I also remember when Dignity Village was under the bridges. Do we have control around the Bridge like we did when were at Dignity. [W]ill people sleep down around us when we have No more room? [W]ill we pull the drugs and other negative that we will have to tell them WHAT leave, when we are fighting for people a place to sleep? These are some of the things that is [sic] going thru my mind.
> Ma Salaam
> Ib

He called me to talk about this decision. Ibrahim says there are two levels to social critique:

The first is the ideas what you all about. See that's how people know what you angry about. Like us, we are "Right to Survive," and R2DToo is our camp. Like Dignity Village is two things too, it's the fight that Jack and us made a long time ago, on paper, an activist corporation, and then it's also the camp, like it is also where they is at and how they live. But didn't forget who we are, we don't go acting like cuz we got a spot to sleep, that we don't have a message to fight for. We are looking into taking this spot, because we have to be clear. I got to be clear with myself, like you said to me, we are really about two things, helping people live and sleep and not die on the street, and also we's about carrying this fight. I was worried that by givin' up the spot in downtown we would lose that visibility, like they done to Dignity. They try to put it out of sight, out the way—out of mind, I guess you would say, but we have to work at the message harder, because we are about saving people that's gonna die on the street of we don't. See none of is afraid to work hard to carry the fight. This ain't been easy here. It's not meant to be easy. Na aha. The village, they gone and forgot that. It's like Jack Tafari said, "Once you win your rights, you have to keep fighting for you rights." They all asleep up there." (Telephone conversation, August 19, 2013)

The courts finally agreed that the city had no grounds to shutter the R2DToo because it was a private enterprise for which there were neither sanctions nor prohibitions. It was a new type of space—no narrative existed to determine its legitimacy. R2DToo had used its own critique of housing policy *to make an argument* and to create a new narrative. At the same time, the courts acknowledged the rest area was doing a service to the local area and to people who had no other options for finding a place to rest. So Ibrahim's group was able to stave off the city's attempts by arguing it was not a camp nor a shelter, but an "emergency rest area," something no one had heard of. And to this day, referring to it as anything other than that is immediately rebuked by Right to Survive, because that would invite other critiques into its own discursive space. They know that language is everything in understanding narratives, and they have to fight for their otherness, for the uniqueness of their project, or else fall victim to the language of domination the city has imposed on the homeless in the past. In fact, Ibrahim and the others now describe themselves as *houseless*, not homeless, a theme we will discuss later. Ibrahim and his fellow activists are well aware that because of its resources the city is the sovereign power, but also that transcendent laws can trump instrumental force.

It was a tough choice for Ibrahim and the group. Would they give up a location that simply by its visibility empowered them? Would they get more land to help more people? Could they even trust what the city was offering? They had made the choice to accept new, larger, permanent locations, if offered, on the moral grounds that more people needed a place to sleep. But we all recalled that such spatial and visual marginalization was exactly what the HLF and Dignity Villagers had found disagreeable in 2001, when the compromise was made to place Dignity on that remote tarmac.

Ibrahim at a mayor's meeting, 2016. Activism is like a shark: it needs to keep moving. Photo: Eric Weissman.

And so one might ask, where are they now? We are going to get into that in detail in the next chapter. The short answer is that so far, despite six potential sites being selected, they have not moved because of resistance from local ratepayers' associations and business improvement districts, and also because R2DToo did not like the terms being imposed on them. They are sticking to the belief that they are reinventing space that fulfills both the moral need to help people and the discursive need to push the critique of housing.

The above discussion underscores the importance of language, or perhaps even more the importance of an *absence* of language, in determining social outcomes. We can do things differently; we can create new alternatives and ways of imagining solutions to social problems, if we are willing to eschew the narratives of dominant paradigms, carve out our own spaces and fight like hell for them. Inevitability exists only in the buy-in to powerful narratives, where lived experience must and can only be measured in terms of those discourses. But presenting a new discourse, and resisting other dominant forms, destabilizes inevitability. In storytelling and novel writing, such instability makes a story hard to read, since there is no way to anticipate and to strategize against what seems to be a plot or series of plots leading towards a certain conclusion. Editors call this a problem with structure. So do social planners. And this is what throws symbolic imaginaries, which I think we now recognize as broad communities sharing the same stories about reality, into a panic-driven chaos of sorts. Fairly subtly, Ibrahim and his group made the deal, loaded the site with their tents, and quietly introduced a plot change to the way things were going to take place in Portland, while Dignity Village struggled against its own reality to conform to the city's plot line for it.

R2DToo went up under the yawning gates of Old Chinatown, and was estimated to last about six months. Five and a half years later, it has never given up its claim and has created a certain narrative counterpoint to the stagnation

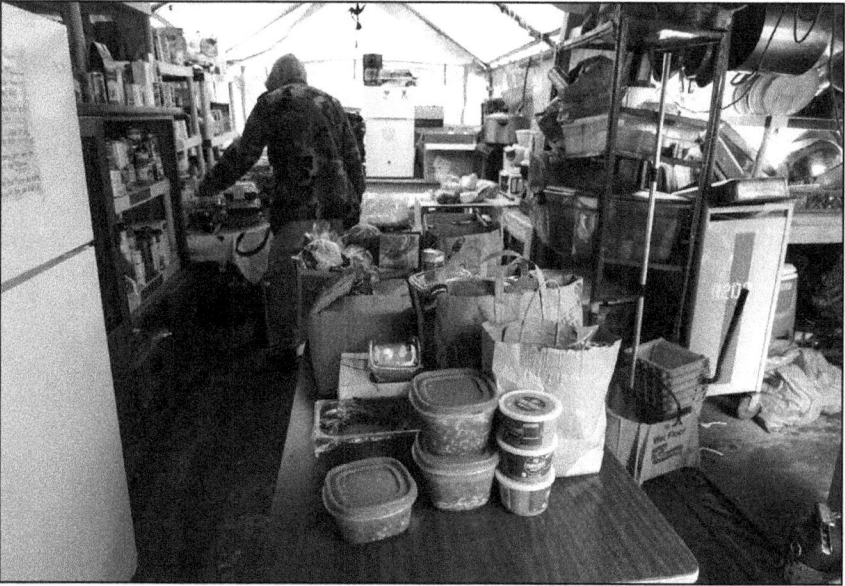

Kitchen area at R2DToo, 2016. Photo: Eric Weissman.

at Dignity Village. The attention that R2DToo brought to the plight of the street poor resulted in renewed scrutiny of Dignity Village, raising questions within the village about how it resonated with or fell short of its mission statement. People, not activists or citizens, but actual souls were being asked what they really wanted from life in the village and how far they were willing to go to get it.

Portland was engaged in a constant battle on the streets with small encampments and trying to manage over 2,000 literally homeless people. IHC models in other cities like Eugene were emerging that held greater promise of achieving transitional and other requirements for emergency municipal campgrounds. In this context, the city had a need to poke Dignity Village with a stick in order to gauge its ability to comply. In the field of choices left open to the city, the most resistant and therefore powerful groups would be granted space, and others might be shuttered.

Chapter 9
FROM AMERICAN DREAMS TO STRATEGIC
MANAGEMENT: THE REAL INEVITABILITY

9.1 Critical Waves

By the summer of 2013, activity around the Tiny House Movement had picked up in the U.S., especially in Oregon. It is worth noting that since then, the definition of tiny homes has been contested, too. Because the tiny house or tiny home movement had so clearly been linked to the self-housing efforts of the homeless, entrepreneurs promoting small homes and small home communities have found the term "micro-housing" more palatable. But the fact that small cottage-like structures are now part of mainstream and conventional narratives on how to house people has provided a discursive bridge between the goals of homeless housing activists and the broader social critique of urban space.

In 2012, housing activists from Eugene and Ashland had visited Dignity Village. They paid close attention to both the strengths and weaknesses of that kind of tiny home community. Strengths included the self-governing capacity of people often thought of as "undeserving" and "incapable," and the ability to build a community for very little money using recycled and discarded materials. Weaknesses included drug problems, faction-led power structures and a failure to provide adequate transitional experiences for people wishing to reclaim their roles in society.

Andrew Heben was one of these activists. For his master's degree at the University of Cincinnati's College of Design, Architecture, Art, and Planning he designed and co-founded an IHC project called Opportunity Village in Eugene ("OVE" for short). The project was situated on city land, fuelled by $100,000 in donations and looked to improve on the experience of Dignity Village and other camps he had studied. To the untrained eye, OVE is just another IHC but in fact it is noteworthy as a new way of imagining IHC.

> Opportunity Village Eugene (OVE) opened in August 2013 as a "transitional micro-housing" pilot project. The vision was to create a collaboration between the housed and unhoused that provides stable and safe places to be through cost-effective, human-scale approaches for transitioning the unhoused to more sustainable living situations It accommodates around 30 otherwise homeless individuals and couples at a time in simple, micro-housing (60–80sf) that provides residents with security, stability, and privacy. By consolidating utilities to common cooking, gathering, restroom, and laundry facili-

ties we were able to keep costs very low, providing an intermediate solution between the street and traditional housing (OVE website).

The key difference between OVE and DV is that OVE actually asks for and utilizes the participation of external, non-resident advisors. OVE cooperated with the city and with professionals whose skill sets augmented the values and ideas of OVE membership in designing policy and solving village problems. At the point that OVE was established, DV leadership had sometimes sought advice on village affairs, but only members had any say in the political and administrative concerns of the village, and good advice was often ignored. Furthermore, very often, outside advisors of DV felt ignored. Because other non-profit IHC (like OVE) were innovating their governance structures, the Portland Housing Bureau and supporting advocates on the DV advisory board continued to lobby the village's leadership to recognize the necessity of opening up management and governance to external, non-member participants. If nothing else, reference to DV by the press, by other municipal jurisdictions and by other IHC planners was evidence that DV was still part of the social critique of housing, even if the villagers did not participate in actions and conversations outside their own gates.

Other events had occurred in the housing critique, too. In the summer of 2011, while I was at Dignity Village, there was much talk of the city's building a large Supportive Housing First project in downtown Portland. That August, the city of Portland finished building the Bud Clark Commons, a $47 million Housing First community. This project is part of the rapid rehousing paradigm, similar to the one in Canada we discussed earlier, At Home/Chez Soi (CMHC 2014).[160] The difference is that in the latter project people were housed in regular market apartments while in the former a building was constructed for them. But the Supportive Housing First model is very popular among federal policy-makers in Canada and the U.S. because it reduces the costs associated with managing people living in dire poverty and homelessness, especially on the streets (ibid). However, there is little reliable evidence to suggest that the ancillary and demonized conditions—addictions, poor mental health, and criminal behaviour, which are often part of the blame-the-victim discourse—are better handled in these state-driven and expensive HF models than in IHC. Clearly both types of space reduce the cost to society of people living poorly on the streets (Weissman 2012). That day when E. died, the EMTs had just come from Bud Clark following another overdose. Clearly people use drugs (and OD on them) in Bud Clark Commons as well as Dignity Village and R2DToo.

HF might be worthwhile but supportive housing structures like the Bud Clark Commons are not being built in sufficient numbers to keep everyone who needs housing off the streets. So the need for IHC remains high. That said, by 2013, if an IHC had wanted to start up in Oregon, it was going to have to argue that it would be more supportive of its residents than Dignity Village. That same year, despite several drug-related deaths and over 260 pre-eviction complaints being issued to residents for drug dealing and other alleged criminal activity,[161] Bud Clark Commons was touted by the city as a great success. How could it not be? How could the city admit that a $47 million project with operating costs of over $200,000 per year produced similar results to an IHC that cost about .0025% of that figure?

The BC Commons is situated in a mixed-use neighborhood near the fancy Pearl District and also adjacent to historic Union Station, part of the very efficient rapid MAX light-rail system. On my most recent visit there in February 2016 I stopped at the Union Station platform. On the platform a dozen or so BCC residents and their friends were actively using crack and other drugs. In conversations with MAX riders, I learned that seeing people doing these things worried other pedestrians and commuters who used the nearby rapid transit hub, but that they felt they simply had to "grin and bear it." It was no secret that people with mental health issues and drug addictions used the light rail platform to meet and sometimes to get high. Whatever the Commons (or city) might claim, many Portlanders found the Commons a problematic project.

Then again, the same kinds of drug abuse and dealing occur far more often in private homes and market rental units. The angst felt by critics was that these HF models run counter to people's sense of wise public spending. Israel Bayer refers to these HF models as "one-stop housing"—places where, ideally at least, addicts, mental health survivors and other poor folks can get everything they need: housing, supports and stability. But there is no system for ensuring, or rules insisting, that these supports are pursued or effective. With such a hefty price tag, there is good reason to wonder if it wouldn't make sense to build more shelters or finance more camps, because at least that way, more people would have a place to sleep and the impact of supports might be similar.

Now it is important to gather up a few ideas here so as not to let this all get away from us. Alternative housing spaces had been part of the narrative on extreme homelessness in Oregon since 2000, but the key to their relevance from 2012 onward seemed to be the degree to which they fit into the emerging THM and Harm Reduction paradigms. IHC initiatives that could not be understood in terms of these emerging narratives were at risk.

In August 2013, it was a local activist's ravings about Dignity Village that brought the Village unwanted attention. The activist had been staying as a guest at DV, but was asked to leave because she was constantly stirring up trouble, which in the village's bylaws is an infraction ("no constant disruption to others"). In response, she went to the city, the police and the media to complain about drugs in the camp. Most of the villagers dismissed the matter as being of little importance because that aspect of the village's reputation was not new. The same day in 2013 that Ibrahim announced his success in court, and two days after the activist's threat to "out" the village, the city of Portland notified Dignity Village of a new inspection. The city representatives came out to the site and did a walk-through. They pointed out 11 requirements in the new contract that were not being met. These were items that had seemed moot, the sort of stuff that was ignored by the village and by city inspectors for more than 13 years. But with R2DToo and Opportunity Village demonstrating a willingness to work with their cities, and these new complaints about the village being raised, some villagers were sure that the inspection would be a prelude to something pivotal.

In brief, the city inspection led to three primary concerns for villagers. First, the city observed that "[t]he contract states that: 'Residents may not use, possess or share alcoholic beverages, or illegal drugs, controlled substances or prescription drugs without a medical prescription, on or at the Designated Campground or within the Sunderland Recycling facility," and then asked: "How is the board maintaining this rule?" Second, the city called the camp on violating its transitional campground status: "I would like to see your written rules that residents may not live at the campground for longer than 24 months after the date of December 1st, 2012." Finally, and this speaks directly to progress made in other camps, the city asked: "What progress has been made toward demonstrating a sustainable board structure, such as broadening board membership to include adding former residents, donors or community supporters? As we've discussed, this would be very useful in assisting the village in long-term sustainability."

The first item (sanctions against drug and alcohol use) was the oldest problem in the village and the least easy to fix. It was just part of life—normal, housed, unhoused—and its presence in the contract seems almost surreal. It was the one unfixable problem that drove the ticking clock. After that violation, all the others were redundant, since drug use in such spaces is indefensible according to the mission-statement narratives that support IHC initiatives like OVE and DV. Opponents of IHC often cite the drug use, as they did in Toronto's Tent City, as a rationalization for clamping down on these spaces. As then-CEO Mitch Grubic said, the only thing preventing the city from invoking that rule during all the years the village had existed was how poorly it would look in the press if the city cast 50 drug addicts back onto the streets.

The second item relates to how transitional housing is defined. "Transitional" means preparing people for and finding mainstream housing. Even if the city enforced its two-year limitation on residency, it could not force people out of the village onto the streets; there would have to be housing for them. And there really wasn't much housing for people. According to DV leadership, in 2013 only four out of 19 applications for housing —less than 18%—actually led to a transition into housing.

The final item is very important to the way I understand narrative inevitability. The city was telling the village that the neoliberal critique of housing has room for such places if they open up their self-governance to more effective hybrid modes of governing. The village was being told straight-out what Councillor Francisconi said in 2001: "You need professional help." Villagers were literally being asked to consider being governed another way. Foucault was in part correct when he said that resistance has come to mean asking how much we want to be governed and in what way, rather than how we can do without government altogether.

Insomuch as the concentrated and concerted activist spatializations of other housing critiques such as R2DToo were being sanctioned and would save lives, the village needed to recognize that there was a body of critique that it helped to create, and which it could have rejoined. In other words, there was considerable power in the narratives being driven by OVE and R2DToo, and all DV had to do to fortify its place in relation to the city's power was to earnestly reattach to this activism by joining these groups in court battles, city hall meetings, community actions and so on.

There was no way to predict what would happen. I had argued that if past trends were good indicators of future events, then nothing would happen; the village would continue to fester, and the city would watch to see if public opinion was for or against the village. In the end, if the city sent in the police and did what they call a "dog search," for drugs and drug dealers, it was likely that the village would experience a shut-down and eviction, just as had happened to Tent City. In Toronto, because of a high rental vacancy rate, the city found apartments for the evictees. In Portland, with a vacancy rate of less than 1% and rising rents, the average number of homeless people in street counts was likely to rise if the village was closed.

9.2 Right 2 Dream Too

In October 2013, I attended the annual conference for the Association of Applied and Clinical Sociology (AACS) in Portland. I had been busy finishing up my final draft of my dissertation and had been very busy on Skype and in correspondence with Ibrahim's group at R2DToo and with Dignity Villagers. At the AACS, I was given a full session to present my film *Subtext: Real Stories* about Toronto's Tent City and to show some footage of Dignity Village. For that session I had invited Ibrahim and some of the Dignity Villagers. Brad and Ptery, who had each been estranged from the village following unfounded accusations of malfeasance after Brad's impeachment, attended as well. For those interested in how sociology could be applied to solving practical issues like housing, this was a rare opportunity for academics to sit with homeless people and activists and critically discuss each other's ideas. Many of the people at the AACS had never heard of these camps and so for those who attended, it was a good chance to recognize that grassroots housing activism was far more advanced and homeless people far savvier than they had imagined. The best part was that we could visit the camps at the heart of this discursive battle because they were in Portland.

A few of us went on a tour of Right 2 Dream Too. For all my work with Ibrahim over the phone and on Skype, I hadn't been there yet. I did not have big hopes for it. I had seen images of it online, and R2DToo had sent me self-shot video installments of the progress at the camp. But there is always a gap between our expectations and the reality of a new place. The first sight of R2DToo is frightening and surreal. For my colleagues and me it was impossible to immediately transcend the clearly tragic nature of such a place. It would be hard for anyone to accept the gravel tarmac, the odorous outhouses, the damp and dirty tent grounds and grimy common areas as acceptable housing. This is not to blame R2DToo. This site resembles a modern day urban MASH unit: emergency shelter space in a war zone. But the demand for this place is not their doing. They fill a niche, sad as it is.

R2DToo is on a street corner below the Paifang gates of old Chinatown. The city required the rest area to be fenced and gated for security reasons. To save money they sought and received donations of old used doors. Their perimeter along West Burnside is a six-foot-high fence completely fabricated out of used doors. Each door in turn has been auctioned off to donors who are permitted, in exchange for cash donations, to decorate the door space with a logo, message or design of their choosing.

The front of the rest area is a simple fence and small gate. A person can be a member or a guest of the camp. Members follow certain rules, attend regular meetings, must do chores and must be actively seeking work or working. Members act as security officers whose duties are to monitor the comings and goings of day/night users, who are called guests, and other members. The camp is a general rest area for men and for women; by definition it is not a village or a permanent IHC, and people are not allowed to live there, at least not technically. This cannot be their permanent address per se. Unlike DV, where residents often ignore the rules, at R2DToo members *must* follow the same rules (there is a conscious effort to avoid factions) and they must participate in the organization's activist and community services.

At R2DToo, like DV, when you enter, you must have permission, you must sign in, and you must be escorted by a member when moving around the camp. One must remember that these folks are street folks, and there are many struggles with mental health and addictions, as well as a salient and recognizable street anxiety— many of the people you meet look like they are about to crash hard from no sleep, too much dope and not enough nourishment. You might think that the members have to work at keeping order, but this is not really a problem. The services that the camp provides are so vital and the people who come there so torn up by street life, that inside the rest area there is a real sense of cooperation and peace.

Providing food is a central concern. There is a large kitchen tent with all the necessary utensils and cutlery. A number of different charitable groups, markets and restaurants from around Portland donate food. While some food is prepared onsite, the majority of food donations are dry or canned goods and products from local markets.

Hygiene and sanitation are two heavily disputed zoning issues in the downtown core. Homeless people do not have public access to restrooms or showers except under very restricted conditions. A few churches and drop-ins provide such services. Homeless folks have few places to relieve themselves. I mentioned earlier that if caught, a person who urinates on the street can be charged with sexual indecency, which is a felony. R2DToo attracts people looking for food or shelter or to use the outhouses. On site there are three Portalets supplied by a local company. R2DToo pays for their maintenance. Opponents of the camp had argued that R2DToo would lead to the local area becoming putrefied with human waste. In fact, the block that surrounds R2DToo is one of the cleanest and safest in downtown Portland because the members make a point of keeping clean and safe.

One of the big attractions had been the mobile showers that a local sponsor used to bring with his modified truck. But the city, wishing to hamper the group's efforts, targeted his vehicle for ticketing and made it impossible for him to provide this service any longer. Staying clean in the damp, rainy and grimy city space is difficult to do and is made much harder because the rest area does not have running water, proper sanitation or drainage. Suffice to say that my colleagues and I were astonished by how much humanity was crammed into a 60-by-100-foot area. Ibrahim led our tour of the site. It was quite amazing to see the donations tent full of blankets and sleeping bags, clothes and raincoats. Even in the damp and cramped space they managed to organize and keep their stores relatively orderly. One of the tents was a community communications tent with a computer and WiFi. They hoped to add more computers soon to help people find work and housing. We talked about the difficulties of providing for people when the terminology "rest area" actually restricted the breadth of service they were allowed to provide.

When I was doing my fieldwork two years earlier at Dignity Village, I had met many activists and supporters of the IHC movement. That day we visited, they had come by as well, testifying to the site's second but equally important purpose—it was a nexus, a discursive site where the houseless community and its supporters found common ground. Despite the shadows of business towers, building cranes and rezoning notices around us, all of which reinforced the inevitability of R2DToo's own ticking clock, in that small quarter-acre space houseless people got served. As unusual as the site was/is, it was difficult not to be half-heartedly optimistic about its existence. Each of us academics tried to be supportive and encouraging. Yet it was very hard to understand how such a place could be so necessary in a city of such wealth.

We walked quietly on the tour. We were each of us caught up in the surreality of the emergency rest area. As interesting a discursive site as this rest area might have been, the space itself was a bleak statement about the housing priorities of American cities. We took photos. We smiled. We bought R2DToo T-shirts to help them raise money. I had thought Dignity Village was an evil expression of governmentality, but this space was homage to desperation. I couldn't help but feel anger at the city and the state for tearing down and not replacing the shelter and affordable housing space needed so badly. But I also felt that people who were able to live this way had fundamental problems as I once did, and they needed to be told about, perhaps even forced to buy in to a program of self-help. That such programs were unavailable only added to the desperateness of the streets and reinforced the absolutely vital nature of camps like this. After a jaunt over a few city blocks, it became apparent to me that such spaces were actually necessary. Within a thousand yards of the camp, there were over 200 people huddled in doorways, laneways and other spaces, and my own informal PIT street count of the two-mile square area along the Willamette River and downtown core came to over 500. In other words, there were large numbers of people living in dire conditions.

Earlier in this book I quoted Beric German, who had asked if all we wanted from people was if they were an addict or they were straight. He suggested we needed to deal with emotional pain and suffering and that if we did, there would be less street poverty. I agreed with him then, but seeing people living in these conditions, and recognizing the absolute unsustainability of that life, I have come to think that we might have to have unpopular conversations; we might have to employ very unpopular narratives, bordering on interfering with other people's free will. It may be that we need to build spaces for people to live out their addictions and in which to die unfortunate deaths; it may be that we must abandon the call to "end homelessness," because there will always be people who find themselves outside of housing. I stood in strange silence look-ing at the camp from across the road. All these crazy notions muddled up my head and I must have looked stressed, because Ibrahim came over to me and asked me what was wrong. I looked at my watch and suggested it was time for us to go to Dignity Village.

After R2DToo, we took a very silent cab ride up to Dignity Village. It's a long ride, about 25 minutes and eight miles or so through interesting neighborhoods, up along Martin Luther King Drive, Rosa Parks graffiti here and there— a city that touts such homages to African American culture yet is considered one of the most racist places in America. Consistently dotting the landscape were Hispanic eateries and stores. The neighborhoods were remodeling and along Alberta Street, trendy shops stretched from end to end, culminating in a New Seasons Organic Foods Supermarket. For all intents and purposes, this neighborhood was a pleasant, clean and mod part of town in the midst of a transition from yuppie to hipster motifs and cuisine.

And then a few blocks away, the world changed to industrial parks and overgrown sloughs. Snow-capped Mount Hood, 100 miles away, towered over northeastern Portland, as if in a cheap motel painting. A very swanky golf course was hidden behind 20-foot cedar hedges. Next to it was the Columbia Correctional Institute and next to that, on a swept-off acre beside a compost facility reeking of methane, Dignity Village. I had to yell at the cabbie three or four times to turn because he had no idea there was a camp there, and seemed not to want to believe me. He shared with my colleagues the same kind of eye-opening, jaw-dropping amazement that others had shown when I resided there—a sense of utter befuddlement at what exactly a place like that meant. Was it a homeless camp, or a poor community? Was it for real? Why did they call it Dignity? Why the hell was it out here, surrounded by nothing but a prison and compost? How do people live all the way out here? An F-16 fighter screamed only a few hundred yards above our heads. Several times a day, fighters from the Air National Guard took off and made their landing approaches right over the camp. A person could smell the expended jet fuel as it rained down on the camp. I have no idea what the cabbie thought or how he later described the place, but I imagine he probably wanted to forget about it as soon as he could.

The village is well organized now. In the beginning years it was very rough, but they have come a long way to meet fire codes and other bylaws. There is a parking area big enough for six vehicles right in front. The camp is fenced on all sides with chain link, and two larger chain-link security gates protect the village. It is, in every sense of the word, a gated community. We parked and hesitantly got out of the car. I wondered what it would be like to see my friends again. No doubt my colleagues wondered all sorts of things.

We walked by the big yellow fiberglass cow up to the security shack and signed in. A number of residents came over to say hello and greet my friends, especially Dr. Sandra Joy from Rowan University. Sandra is a human rights activist who has been fighting for the rights of death-row inmates across the U.S. Her work is well known among African Americans. None of the people at DV knew of her. There were no black people at the camp. She has a lovely smile and is well aware that people look to our faces for approval and acceptance. So she put on a pleasant expression but I could see in the slight frown after her courteous smile that she could see the mess, could smell the air, could see the archaeology of a community approaching its due date. We walked around the camp, escorted by a couple of villagers, then three, and then a few other supporters joined in and we had a reunion of sorts. It was an almost festive moment; after all, not every second of our time spent together in 2011 was bleak. The camp had its humor and its darkness. And I needed it. Steve Wilson, a photographer who has taken thousands of pictures of the village and who has supported it for many years, asked if I had seen Dave Samson. He looked very discouraged. I had heard rumours that my dear friend Dave, who had given up his bed for me, who had been the voice of reason and calm, had been stricken by a powerful methamphetamine addiction.

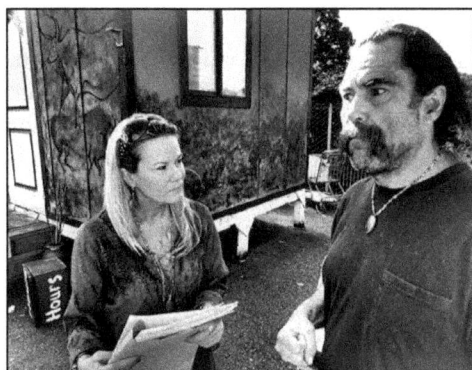

Sandra and Dave Samson, 2013. Photo: Eric Weissman.

I yelled out to Dave as we approached his structure, yelled again and again, and then rapped on his door. It was 2:00 in the afternoon, but he was crashed hard. Still, he managed to open his door and come outside. I felt my heart sink. You have to understand that when I see someone in this position, it is not some altruistic or charitable bent that gives me cause to sigh, but a swift kick-in-the-ass remember-when, as they say in 12-step meetings—a clear recollection of myself, caught up in the narrative of inevitability that had trapped me.

Dave had lost 30 pounds, his teeth were brownish, his eyes bloodshot and skin yellowed from liver stress. He was five days into a methamphetamine binge. On the phone, people had told me he had fallen victim to the dirge and succumbed to meth and crack. The drugs did not just medicate away pain and mental anguish; they also fuelled the economy of the village. Following Michels and Lipset, selling, buying and using drugs constituted the economic underpinnings of the village's social and political system. Drugs became a sacred resource for building alliances and making friends.

Seeing Dave so encumbered was a shock to me. He took me into his shack. It was crammed to the rafters with books and ornate curios; artifacts of his dead mother, which he had inherited. Thousands of rock shards, waiting to be carved or polished were organized randomly in Rubbermaid and Tupperware containers, remnants of his younger days as a mineralogy enthusiast. His room was dirty, filled with glass pipes and empty baggies, residue thick on the glass, tiny shavings of ash and glass on his sheets and bed frame—evidence of his crazed attempts to stave off the jones by scraping out another hit from the emptiness. My heart sank again, deeper. I know these spaces. I know that desperation. I had spent hours sweating over a pipe or two, gingerly scraping the last essence of a high so as to not mix any glass into the residue. I had been so high and become so paranoid that I spent hours staring through my peephole because I lived next to an elevator. I did that for nine years, and wore out the carpet at my door.

I was David.

I interviewed him, a once lucid and clear-minded man, now victim to streams of rambling unconsciousness and given to delusional outbursts. That was me, too. I cannot deny that. Sandra senses it too. She knows my story. She senses the hopelessness of David's situation. But she is a very hopeful person. How could she not be? Her work saves people's lives; she has seen justice happen on those occasions where death-row sentences have been revoked. Death row and these other spaces are not dissimilar. Dave had once told me "life is a death sentence." I knew he had seen the phrase on social media and was being clever, but seeing him in that state, I wanted to find an eleventh-hour reprieve that he would buy into. I told him how I felt seeing him that way.

We read some of his poetry and talked with him. I wanted to turn the video camera off because I felt ashamed for him. But I left it on, and he encouraged me to do so. He wanted people to hear and see him in this state. Part of me felt this unethical and another part felt it was important for people who had followed this research to see what can happen to people when they fall victim to paralytic communities. At one point in his rambling, I literally felt a pain in my head and could not muster up the emotional strength to distance myself from his suffering. I told him so, straight out, that I was worried that I would not be around to save him, and he needed to stop.

The day had grown late, or maybe it just felt that way because I was very stressed. We had to return to the hotel. I was so aghast at the events that had taken place at the village that year—the impeachment, the sloth, the witch-hunt against Brad, Ptery and others—that seeing Dave in this state put me over the edge. The only bright spot, if one can call it that, was that Ibrahim and his group were really giving it to the city, punching holes in the narratives that powerful groups had always used to hold down the poor.

I had to stop dwelling on Dignity Village. There was not a great deal going on there that hadn't gone on before. As I was friendly with some of the people there, I was beginning to lose that complex exteriority that Boltanski had spoken of. I was not being professional. I am not suggesting I needed to be objective. But clearly my emotional ties to people made me feel guilty about being angry at their continual addiction and unwillingness to work towards a sustainable future for the village. In Malinowski's *Diary* (1967), he reveals himself to have experienced similar emotions that coloured his sometimes judg-mental and critical observations of Tobriand Islanders. When we read this diary, almost 100 years later, we have to face the fact that an objective exteriority is not just complex: it is in part farcical. But still, I had reached a certain point where more information was not good information. At some point I had to decide that the research was over, didn't I? I had to submit my dissertation and get on with my own future. But as life would have it, closure would not be forthcoming.

When I returned to Montreal, I had a course to teach and a dissertation to finish. I did both. I submitted the final draft in November and defended it in early December 2013. I completed my dissertation with high distinction, as they say. My mom and stepdad were there. Of all the people who had watched me crash and burn, they had been my closest mentors and advisors; he a well-known academic, she a great artist and my confidant. But they perhaps knew best what that defense had meant to my life narrative. Everyone who had been part of my dissertation, my committee, the people in the Department of Sociology and Anthropology, even some of the Concordia leadership were familiar with my own rites of passage and the great lengths I had gone to pursue this research with a certain fidelity to the unfinished and emerging narratives, the blurred genres of a pragmatic approach to social prob-lems. Four years of work came down that single moment when I looked at my mom wiping a tear from her eye. And there were laughter and smiles and an invitation to lunch. And then someone asked if I really thought we could not end homelessness. We went to lunch, the question unanswered, but seeded well in the fertile matter in my brain.

I thought I might be done with DV and IHC for a bit, but I got a call from Mitch a couple of days later. Nancy, one of the key complainants in Brad's impeachment, was elected as the new CEO, and Mitch became her Assistant CEO. On that same day I packed up my belongings and drove back home to Toronto. There were no jobs for a freshly minted Ph.D. There are not too many now. But I did manage to land an interesting visiting scholarship at the University of Texas in Galveston in their Institute for the Medical Humani-ties. I was going to teach grad students about doing visual and critical ethno-graphy and about visual narratives. My research would continue but in a new area using an online visual elicitation tool called VWIRE to help communities publicly address pervasive social issues.

In early January 2014, after camping in a friend's house during the ice storm that left much of Toronto without power for eight days, I got in my car and drove to Texas. I want to tell you that I was freed of the obsession that Dignity and Portland had become. But I cannot say that was true. All the way to Texas I wondered whether or not we could use the online tools we were going to develop to help people in camps and rest areas get help and fight for their rights. And what about Dave? I remember calling the village one night from Little Rock and asking for Dave, but the person who answered the phone said they hadn't seen him for days.

Dave's addictions became so bad that he crossed a certain line. Meth is one of those drugs, like cocaine, that has a strong cross-addictive tendency towards sexual aggression. When high, Dave had started becoming verbally and physically flirtatious with women in the camp. A few members had written him up in incident reports. He began to fail to carry out his insurance and sweat equity duties. There were many there who did these things or failed in these ways, but Dave had hit on the wrong woman and offended the wrong council members. So as is the way with the village, he became undesirable and was 86'd – forced to leave. He went to live with his father on the outskirts of Portland. I haven't seen him since, though he sends me strange psychedelic artworks on Facebook.

9.3 Texas

Texas is as big as they say. And driving through Texas was, for me, like driving through my favourite memories of the '60s and '70s. Glen Campbell on the radio, wild plains and rolling hills, oil rigs and cattle ranches, big shiny trucks and wide open spaces. Then I got to Houston. And it is just another massive city with too many cars. Over two million people live in the city of Houston, and over 6.4 million in the greater metro area. I stayed in downtown Houston before driving to Galveston and the UTMB. There are the massive steel and glass pillars of capital that stand guard over a very clean downtown core. Much of the shopping and other services are underground because in the summer it gets extremely hot, the air very still. It is quite literally unbearable. And then on the streets, just as in every major city I have visited, there are homeless people. Without denying the urgency of their lives, I recognize them as being interchangeable with other homeless people in other cities. Their personal stories are inflected with their own unique constellations of events, but the root causes of their being on the street are buried in the same muddled narratives of addictions, mental health, domestic abuse, unemployment, incarceration, military service, and a lack of services and affordable housing.

Many of Houston's homeless are war vets, both male and female. In the U.S. in 2014, there were as many as 250,000 homeless veterans. In Houston the number was estimated to be close to 4,000, almost half of the total number of homeless in the city's official count. The federal government defined Houston as a priority community for addressing homelessness because of the large number of homeless vets. There are obvious reasons why the number of people literally living on the streets is so high. Like all cities its size, Houston generates homelessness. Also, despite cold snaps in the winter months, Houston has a climate that is suitable for year-round rough sleeping and living. There are numerous green belts and bijous, underpasses and derelict buildings, a great deal of empty and negative space that people can inhabit at least temporarily. With the priority designation, Texas was ambitiously addressing veteran homelessness when I got there,[162] but it seemed to matter little; homeless folks were everywhere in the downtown area. In 2013, the three poorest metropolitan areas in the U.S. were in Texas.[163] Houston had a poverty rate of almost 20%, 4 percentage points higher than the national average. And so for me, having travelled from Toronto to Houston, witnessing homeless men and women in every city I passed through, it was impossible to think that, to date, any efforts to "end" homelessness were effective. I stayed at a fancy Holiday Inn near the football stadium overnight, and the concierge reminded me not to worry about the belongings in my car because the parking lot, like those of all the good hotels, "had a fence and 24 hour security. You need that here." The next day, I made my way to the University of Texas in Galveston.

Galveston City is built on an island on the Gulf coast. It was an important immigration station at the start of the twentieth century. By some accounts as many as 50,000 people entered the U.S. through the Pelican Island station between 1906 and 1914. So it has seen its share of hard luck cases. In fact it had been the capital of Texas in the mid-1800s and the world's largest distribution center for cotton. In 1900 the city and much of the island was wiped out by the worst hurricane in U.S. history and the city began a process of rebuilding. By the 1930s it had become a resort and gambling hub, the "Sin City of the Gulf." By 1950 most of the illegal gambling and prostitution venues were shuttered and Galveston entered a steep economic decline. Today it serves as an important port city for the oil and gas industry. Two branches of the University of Texas and Texas A& M are there. But mainly it is a resort and vacation town. Hurricanes have much to do with the demographics of Galveston, which has close to 50,000 residents; the number had been higher before 2008 when Hurricane Ike eradicated much of the poorly constructed low-income housing. The population is approximately 46% white, 26% Latino, and 25 black.[164]

I became good friends with Robert, a third-generation Jewish Galvestonian. In the early 1900s, some 10,000 Jews landed in Galveston. He was descended from them. He showed me around Galveston. I didn't expect to see synagogues in Glenn Campbell's favourite town, but there they were—two of them! Robert became a good friend of mine; he often drove me around town to talk about growing up in a city where prosperity and decline tend to change with the weather. In central parts of the city there were many run-down or abandoned homes and buildings that had been scoured by Hurricane Ike. In large empty fields where social housing projects had once stood, construction companies had begun staking out new housing projects. FEMA had promised

Galveston some $89 million for post-Ike rebuilding but was holding back the funds until the city committed to social housing provisions. There was a growing debate, mostly among the established white gentry, about whether or not to accept the money, if it meant rebuilding social housing into the fabric of downtown Galveston.

In my early days there, many people rumbled about the mythic FEMA money and suggested that the city might be better off if it just sold all those properties and developed the gambling industry. The feeling was that many Galvestonians were happy that an undesirable population had been swept away and that crime rates had dropped significantly. Robert explained to me that during Ike, more than 10,000 low-income earners and people on social assistance had been forced to move elsewhere. When they did, the crime rate fell by (it was claimed) as much as 35%. No one really wanted them back.

This claim forced me to confront an unfriendly narrative. This was not simply the Not in My Backyard (NIMBY) discourse that we have talked about earlier in the book. This was a narrative about hospitality towards others who were as much a part of the history and landscape of the city as anyone else. These were the field hands and cotton labourers, the dockhands and other labourers who were an integral part of the region's history. It is also true that at least two generations of disenfranchised black folks had grown up in Galveston, knowing nothing but poverty and welfare dependence. It was unfortunate that their economic roles had been displaced by technology and lack of opportunity, and that an entire generation of people had become dependent on social assistance. But that did not change the fact that they lived in Galveston. Their homes had been washed away by tragic circumstances and I found myself wondering what southern hospitality had really meant.

"Why bring them back?" Robert asked. "They went somewhere." Robert, like most of the longtime white residents of Galveston, did not want them back and was dubious about FEMA's plan to rebuild social housing. His argument was in part quite sound. These people were not really economically necessary. There were no jobs for them, they were housed (obviously) somewhere, perhaps with friends or family in other cities or states, the crime rate was down, and all these prime locations could be redeveloped into casinos and other resort attractions. But such a narrative did not consider the poor as people who had lived in Galveston all their lives. The city was as legitimately their home as anyone else's.

It is also important to note that poverty in Galveston is higher than in the rest of the state. In 2013, the poverty rate was 22.3%, eight percentage points higher than the state average. Black and Latino poverty rates were two to three times those of whites, and Native Americans experienced the most poverty of all.[165] The number of children living in poverty is twice the state average. For native-born Galvestonians, poor or rich, this extreme disparity between wealthy and poor people is an historic reality and one which seems natural to them.

Now you must understand that Robert is a good friend and a very decent and kind man. He does not want people to suffer. His opinion is not unique. It is common.

One of my side missions while there was to get a handle on Texas gun culture. I made some friends in Galveston who were gun enthusiasts.

The first time I held a handgun was a surreal experience. It was on the fairway at a local golf course. I had been paired off with a middle-aged brother and sister who were aghast that we did not have the right to carry handguns in Canada. On the eighth fairway at the Moody Gardens Golf Course, the sister opened her purse, slapped a 9-mm Berretta in my hand, and said, "I never go anywhere without it." I had seen guns before, in my using days. A few of the guys I ran with carried pistols and small-caliber handguns, nothing automatic. One guy shot his own hand while cleaning his .25 Derringer.

I handed the gun back to her pretty quickly. When they asked me about my work, I explained that I was trying to develop ideas about how to solve homelessness. She asked me, "What kind? Do you mean deadbeats and bums, or folks who deserve help?" In the background, her brother joked "Shoot 'em." The brother had been fairly quiet till then. He said, "One thing that chokes me up is all them vets without houses. That ain't right."

I mentioned the chat I'd had with Robert. They took some offense when I explained that while I understood they felt justified in defending themselves and their homes with firearms—many U.S. states have "stand your ground" laws that allow you to shoot someone if you feel that you are threatened—I did not think that meant you should be able to kill people. Long story short: I did not enter a debate with them on the golf course because they had guns. But I did suggest that we could all agree that a sense of home and belonging was something pretty much everyone deserved, and that poor people could have that sense, too. I managed to finish the round rather peacefully and, of course, by the end of the round I had been "outed" as a socialist because I believed in universal healthcare and housing. They told me I should go to a range and learn how to shoot.

So I did. My shooting guide ended up being a dread-locked, tattooed, motorcycle-driving coffee barista named Coffee. I met him at the MOD Café in downtown Galveston, the only cool meeting spot in the entire city core. He was really nice and about 25 years old. He made his own weapons, everything from pistols to modified semi-automatic AR-15 machine guns. He took me to his gun club where there were several fellows shooting the breeze and their targets. They were looking at each other's guns and ammunition. It reminded me of my fly-fishing club where we gathered to talk about fishing, build rods and tie flies, and fish together.

Many of the shooters had done service in the armed forces and had a soft spot for homeless vets, but not much tolerance for deadbeats and welfare bums. And all of them were happy that most of that riff-raff had been washed off the island. I fired several handguns, a couple of machine guns, and while it was interesting, it was incredibly easy, and I recall thinking (I get a chill writing this now) that tens of millions of Americans with opposing views on life have weapons and dubious propositions about their legitimate use, and wouldn't it be easy for absolute chaos to break out.

Forget what you see in movies. When you see a dozen shooters with fully automatic weapons firing and missing from 30 feet, it is a lie designed to fill air time. No one misses that many times. When a cop fatally shoots a kid holding a submarine sandwich, it is also a lie. You can fire a weapon to injure or put down an assailant with great ease. Even I could do that without killing someone. So when the police shoot a kid holding a knife nine times and kill him, they are either completely incompetent or vilely malevolent. With these modern weapons, a child could pick up a pistol, point it and not miss their target. And just a few months later, in December 2014, one did just that in a Wal-Mart in Idaho: the child picked up his parent's gun, which had been placed on a counter because, apparently, you need to carry a gun while shopping, pointed it and shot the parent, dead.

Another gunsmith named Jeff took me skeet-shooting. He was in a 12-step program with me in Galveston, and so he understood addictions and recovery. We had some frank conversations. He was a very kind and humble man. He understood that even homeless people who got that way because of addictions had a disease, and he figured they could get sober as he and I had done and could therefore cure their poverty, too. It was hard for him to imagine anyone being poor and then homeless because the economic system was just too hard on people and housing too expensive.

His argument was one I have heard a great deal in the last two years since HF has really taken off. He said—I am a paraphrasing—"Yeah, it's okay to give them housing and support, but I don't think they should get as much as we have." When I showed him the photos of DV and R2DToo, he felt they were legitimate. They appealed to his sense of freedom and the American Dream. They were places, in his thinking, where people were working, were earning their keep, and they were not getting "fat," meaning they were not getting showered with things other really hard-working people did not have. It was that day that I really understood the kind of compromise these IHCs had meant to the American popular ethos and why they were starting to have so much appeal to cities.

The appeal was not just because they were necessary, but because they appeared to be sites where people made a public demonstration of their willingness *to settle for less*. I cannot quantify it, but of the dozens of conversations I had all over Texas and Oregon, conservatives who supported (or, shall we say, did not reject) these IHC did so because they recognized there was a large problem with housing availability and because these were sites where people earned the right to have less than they did. I am sorry if this sounds harsh, but it is true. That said, because Jeff and I shared an addiction and a path of recovery, just before we parted ways he reiterated the view that if people were going to get housing and social assistance, they should be forced to address conditions that might be "messing them up." It seemed reasonable, and it might be, except that it excludes what we now know to be true: most people do not recover from addictions or mental health conditions, but must live with them; more importantly, any attempt at recovery (redemption) requires stable housing.

9.4 Paralytic Communities Southern Style

The Institute for the Medical Humanities at UTMB Galveston was concerned with using the humanities to address ethical and other debates in medicine and community health. My program of research was to use the critical and visual ethnographic methods you have read about in this book to look at local social problems and to get a cross-cultural sense of the values impacting housing policies.

I visited Houston often and began working with local community organizers on Galveston Island. Each of my colleagues had suggested one man as central to my research. His name was Reverend Michael Jackson. On the day I went to meet him at the St. Vincent Community Center, the radio played singer Michael Jackson's "Thriller" as I parked my car. I never listen to MJ. I took that as a sign.

This Michael Jackson was close to 70. He wore a small Kufi hat and beautifully woven traditional West African blouse. He is brilliant. Went to Rutgers. Hung out with real radicals in the late '60s and '70s. He had collected so many mementos and curios, thank-you notes and gifts for his services to the community that his desk—his office—was almost completely filled with them. And he was a well-spoken man. Smooth: a southern inflected paternal voice that was strict but playful, cautious but not judgmental. Michael took me all over Galveston and showed me how the poorest were living. We visited a couple of the projects that remained overpopulated and relatively intact despite the devastation caused by Ike. We attended community barbeques at schools and I even went to his son's Eagle Scout Ceremony. We shot hoops in the playground and he took me to a few good restaurants on the island. He had begun calling me his "white, Jewish, Canadian son."

If Michael was a gatekeeper in the sense I used earlier—a key informant—he was also someone who introduced me to the "black experience" in Galveston. He was very critical of the way his people had bought into the double veil portrayed by W.E. Du Bois in his *The Souls of Black Folk* and had become self-consumers of the culture of poverty. Michael did not blame whites for the demise of the African American family or for the poverty of his flocks. He had argued rather astutely that 100 years of welfare and social assistance had painted black families into the poorest corners of the American portrait, solidifying their place in the foundations of social inequality. From this raw anchorage in dependency and uselessness there was very little chance of escape. But this was not simply because of systemic racism exacted on his people, but because of a certain internalized self-racism that took the easy way out in life. He argued that in Galveston and most of the south, Latinos were now taking on the jobs that blacks should have been doing, work that could lift communities into prosperity.

We know that poverty is highest among blacks and Latinos in the U.S., and that was true in Galveston, too; white folks were all but absent in the city's ghettoes. The dispersed poor people who had been washed away into the northern headwaters of the Mississippi, there to be taken in by families and loved ones already barely surviving in poverty, were mostly black and Latino. The hurricane had not scattered them to better places but to even worse housing insecurity, even deeper into the hopelessness of homelessness.

Clever wordsmiths like to emphasize the "unity" in words like "comm*unity*" or "opport*unity*." But Michael understood that community is (as Casey had argued) only possible when human actors share values and beliefs to a degree sufficient to live and *work* together. There is little hope of community when so many people are disenfranchised, unemployed, unhoused and therefore unable to live and work together. A century of waiting for the government to bring jobs and education had not elevated the poor black families of the south, and Michael wanted to encourage, perhaps even inspire younger members of his flock to think beyond the poverty that welfare and social assistance seemingly encouraged. He believed in the culture of poverty argument, and, in part, he *did* blame the victim for not digging in and fighting for a better life.

It was hard for me to decide if, having been educated in the heyday of the culture of poverty argument in the 1960s and '70s, he had adopted the position then or if he had, over the years, come to it on his own. Regardless, he made the case that the narrative of poverty also made great moments of satisfaction and salvation possible. If one was freed of the need to attend to excessive material needs, then surely a person would have the time and freedom to care for and nurture others, and tend to their spiritual community. Jackson saw the struggle for community as paramount and he took me to many community events to prove that, despite poverty, community spirit was possible.

Michael argued that a strong commitment to God and to one's fellow human beings is its own great reward. The downside of poverty was not the loss of community, for in poverty there was in fact great freedom to invest, especially in community. The real problem was that young people growing up in poverty looked at themselves through a mirror, the same mirror as did the Dignity Villagers, and, I would argue, the same mirror through which all poor people must look, the one that tantalizes them with fame, fortune and material gratification, but which makes such things all but unattainable.

I showed Michael the photos of Dignity Village and he said, "I am not going

Michael Jackson at his desk, 2014. Photo: Eric Weissman.

to say a word, just go where I tell you." He took me to a part of town I had been told by my colleagues to avoid, the neighborhood north of the main road bordered by the causeway and the factories. Here were homes which, partly because the climate permitted, were of a quality similar to the structures found in Dignity Village or in many struggling northern native communities in Canada. These places were broken and needed fixing. Michael reminded me that the key to understanding homelessness was not the quality of a home's construction but whether the individual or family was able to own that experience—to invest that place with their own personal or familial culture. That was when a house became a home. Brad Powell was not simply being metaphorical when he had said, "Home is where the heart is, so you are never without a home." Even a tenement could become home if one had to live there, and I think that realism had troubled Michael. He told me that this kind of housing was not homelessness—it was a tragedy, and if I wanted to see real homelessness I should look further into Houston's "enormous problem." I still speak and correspond by email with Michael, who has since retired and moved to eastern Texas.

9.5 Urban Wilderness

Between 2012 and 2014 some conservative estimates put the number of home-less people on the streets or seeking shelter in Houston as high as 9,500. I met social workers who argued the number was much higher and politicians who argued it was far less. Such estimates are unreliable because of subtle changes in definitions and categories. Those definitions suit the interests of policy-makers. Although official Point in Time (PIT) counts indicated that the num-ber of homeless in Houston had fallen by nearly half between 2011 and 2016, other data cited by the Coalition for the Homeless painted a different picture:

> HUD's rules and regulations dictate the definition of homelessness that was used for the count, and these figures were reported to HUD in the Homeless Data Exchange. However, a more complete picture of homelessness in the region can be obtained by widening the definition of homeless to include individuals in the Harris County Jail the night of the count that indicated that they were homeless before arrest (and therefore likely to be so after release). When these numbers are added to the 2015 PIT Count ... the total number of homeless individuals in the region is 6,690 with the largest percent-age sheltered (34%). School districts in the area report data for stu-dents who are considered homeless although the education definition is broader than the HUD PIT definition. Of the 969,624 students enrolled, 20,613 (2.1%) were considered homeless by the edu-cation definition, which includes students doubled up or living in unstable housing. Only 425 students in area school districts were determined to be unsheltered homeless. This determination is done at the beginning of the school year and so numbers may have changed by January. Therefore, they are not included in the expanded homelessness numbers (2015:6).

So let's abandon contested numbers for the moment in favour of actuality. There are thousands of people in Houston who have nowhere to sleep, or who sleep in shelters but spend the rest of their time on the streets. The Houston Police have a special unit called the Houston Outreach Team, or HOT, which is specially trained to help locate and advocate for people living on the streets who suffer addiction or mental health issues. One supervisor, four officers and three caseworkers from the Mental Health and Mental Retardation Authority (MHMRA—we don't use that term in Canada) make up the unit. It was Michael Jackson who suggested I visit Sergeant Steve Wick, who had started the unit.

Sgt. Wick took me for a tour on one of the unit's special all-terrain vehicles deigned for getting in and out of the empty, very dark spaces where these people lived. Houston is a large city with numerous skyscrapers. It has no zoning laws so five separate business cores have emerged, which, if consolidated, would be the third-largest central business district in the U.S. Urban growth has spread outward from the main downtown area, not too far from the museum and hospital districts, and has given rise to sprawling housing developments, crisscrossed and intersected by huge highways and threaded by four slow-moving bayous and sloughs. The Interstate 610 freeway forms a loop around central Houston and it was within this loop that most of my footwork took place. With numerous parks, lanes, roadways and underpasses, empty space is plentiful.

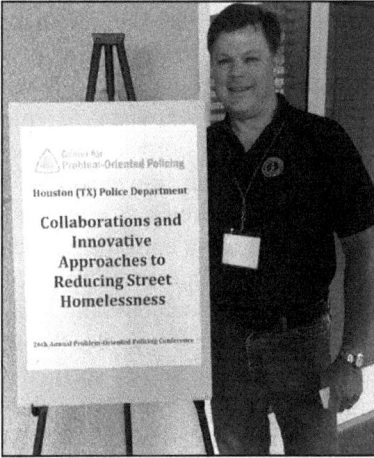

Steve Wick. (Courtesy Sgt. Wick.)

Sgt. Wick has taken thousands of photos of the people who live in these spaces. The goal of HOT is not to arrest homeless people but to help people who slip through the cracks, who don't use shelters and who probably never end up on any of the official counts we have mentioned. HOT enforces the law when necessary but it also helps those who want to access medical, psychiatric and housing services. HOT members are human contacts for people who are often wary of strangers. They are a form of outreach.

Departing the HOT headquarters, we drove a few minutes towards one of the city bayous and Interstate 69 underpass systems adjacent to James Bute Park. The heat is unbearable in the summer. Insects and snakes are everywhere. The brush grows thickly wherever the concrete stops, so there are many places where camps and other types of shelter can be hidden from public view. The rampart of the underpass we visited was littered with needles, crack pipes, human waste and discarded clothes. But it was not the filth that concerned me. The most disconcerting experience for me was the incessant screaming and pounding of tires and engines above our heads, a constant mind-blowing roar, deafening and maddening. Yet people lived under there, some as long as four years. They had nowhere else to go. They mostly suffered from mental illness. And all day long they sat there in the darkness listening to the deafening roar of cars and trucks. "Imagine getting used to that," I said to Sgt. Wick. "To what, exactly?" he replied sarcastically. It hadn't occurred to me that for many of the people out here in this negative space, such sounds are just part of the cacophony of voices and noises that rage in their minds. And there is the fact that all of us who live in cities filter out frequently heard sounds. But this roaring noise—how could anyone get used to it? Still, under each rampart and support anchor of that section of bridge, homeless people had set up homes.

Many of the homeless people we met had jobs: mechanics, nurses, sales people, street vendors. Some were unemployed: junkies, addicts, PTSD survivors of Iraq and Afghanistan, recent ex-cons. The camps we visited were their homes, the only shelter they could find.

According to Sgt. Wick, the PIT counts indicating reduced numbers of homeless "are all fed into the narrative that something great has been done about homelessness." But the narrative has not really changed: "I started in 1994. They were here then. They are here now in 2016," he said to me. That is a fact. But while street homelessness is the most visible reminder of what extreme poverty looks like, it is not the only one. Recall the typology of homelessness I introduced earlier in the book, the one I used to describe my own episodic periods of homelessness, the spectrum that includes literally homeless people (no shelter), sheltered homeless people (those who access shelters or couch surf), the chronically homeless (those who experience either of these situations more than twice in 18 months), the episodically homeless (those who experience these problems for short periods over a number of years), and precariously housed people (those in jeopardy of losing their homes).

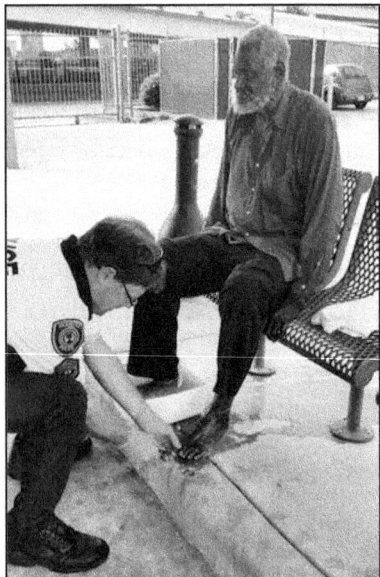

Steve Wick helps out Quintus Moore. Police forces have manpower and willingness to help in ways we don't normally expect. Photo courtesy Sgt. Wick.

Instead of actually reducing rates of homelessness to justify the "ending homelessness" mantra, definitions of this complex social problem get shifted around. Parts of the problem appear to be impacted by policy measures. We may pick off some scabs, or heal a few tumors of a particular kind. But the underlying condition is not cured. In many cases, the mental and physical diseases that afflict people are so complex and pervasive that to remedy them would require an interventionist narrative in which police, doctors, social workers, advocates and others would have to intentionally influence the choices made by people. We might have to tell someone, "Hey look, you need help," or "You need *this kind* of help." We might have to force more people to get medical and psychiatric help (assuming it was available) in order to get them off the streets, and to make real progress towards ending homelessness. Are we ready to bring back invasive interventionist narratives? This interventionist narrative is a tough sell in a Western neoliberal framework emphasizing freedom and individual rights. Interventionist narratives tend to suppress the rights and freedoms of people deemed dangerous or failures in order to uphold the values of others who are more powerful. But moving forward, we may need to consider new modes of intervention. A common misperception is that intervention only requires short-term treatment in order to establish a potentially long-term result. My own story tends to support the argument that a properly orchestrated intervention and treatment can be effective. But since only two of us from my cohort in rehab remained sober after ten years, it is not necessarily reasonable to expect such results of everyone. Furthermore, the mechanisms I learned in my intervention and the support offered to me by family and doctors are ongoing. Intervention, even a humane and considerate one like mine, is a process and can be life-long. If we are going to talk about intervention, we must recognize that the measures needed to help someone overcome medical or psychi-

Shacks wiped out by Hurricane Ike, 2014. Photo: Eric Weissman.

atric problems will likely require long-term commitment by all parties. It is the long-term nature of intervention that scares off cost-wary governments and individuals whose prior experience with long-term care has been less than dignified.

Interventionist narratives hinge on a perception of the social contract in which accepting housing (or any other social assistance, for that matter) means accepting the responsibility to better one's self. This sounds foreign if not antiquated to us: beyond the pleas and words of friends and families, therapists and doctors, our culture does not accept more dramatic interventions in other people's lives except under extreme conditions, and even then only in matters of life and death. Conversations I have had with a wide variety of people suggest there is overwhelming support in lay communities for conditional Housing First programs: most people think housing poor people is fine *if poor people are forced to make an effort to improve their lot in life, whatever that might be.* Publicly, however, Housing First and the emerging harm reduction ethos do not make such requirements.

And perhaps even more peculiar is the fact that most people turn a blind eye to the illogical aspects of liberal democracies and neoliberal market mentalities. The idea of intervening in the economy or in the actions of capital is supposedly as alien to the neoliberal ethos as direct, uninvited intervention in the personal life of a sovereign individual. But we *do* see economic interventions—bailing out banks and automakers, subsidizing public works and health care. Intervention is *not* actually alien to neoliberal political or social culture. In the context of extreme situations, the sorts of things we see in reality TV programs—famous drug addicts losing their homes, obese humans who cannot lift themselves out of bed, hoarders buried in their own purchases—there is even a robust market for such narratives. The popularity of such shows demonstrates that viewers buy into the narrative that people who fail but want a leg up deserve an intervention. Popular culture wants to see people redeem themselves. My own story has been of interest because, as a reporter said to me, "everyone loves a redemption story."

But people who are failing or troubled do not always want such interventions or understand themselves as deserving of them. The key to framing intervention narratives is to convince people that they need an intervention, and that they deserve and can have a better life. The key to making interventions work is to ensure the supports and personnel needed to help people are in place. That is how I was helped. Even in Housing First models which do not require people to seek help for addictions or other problems, there is often an implicit caveat to the effect of "Even if we did want people to get healthy they would need housing," or "People with stable housing tend to seek out help more frequently than those without." Such statements imply that HF is a deserving program by appealing to the moral imperative of interventionist narrative in providing the basis on which a recipient could become deserving and redemption be made possible. Intervention, however, as it intersects the world of mental health, addictions and homelessness, is a very complex narrative that blurs the disciplines of traditional medicine and psychiatry with social welfare into a maelstrom of heated debates about what kinds of interventions are permissible and what outcomes we can realistically expect.

In Houston the epicenter of these debates is the grassroots work done by non-profits charged with caring for the thousands of street poor, places such as Healthcare for the Homeless Houston (HHH) where I met its founder, Dr. David Buck. (Dr. Buck is also president of the newly established Patient Care Intervention Center, a not-for-profit organization that provides health care for vulnerable people in Houston.) The HHH program offered integrated services to meet the medical, psychological and social transitional needs of homeless people. These included a seamless transition for people leaving prisons so that they had places to stay and continuous medication streams if needed.

Dr. Buck introduced me to Dr. William Fann, an authority on psychiatry and psychopharmacology. Dr. Fann is very critical of how twentieth-century psychiatry largely abandoned the needs of the mentally ill. Briefly put, he and others argue that the post-1920 movement in Freudian psychiatry, with its emphasis on early childhood experiences and outpatient treatments, made it possible for states and governments to reduce their financial commitments to long-term residential psychiatric institutions and to under-staff those that remained. According to Dr. Fann, the results were the "snake pits" we were witness to in the 1960s and '70s. That institutional model, battered by neoliberal reductions in funding, could only fail miserably; so much so that governments saw an opportunity to improve their political standing among the conservative and liberal demos by shuttering hospitals and downloading responsibility for care onto the patients themselves. In doing so, governments appeared both to be saving money and supporting innovative and progressive mental health approaches.

One of the reasons there are so many people on the streets with mental health issues today is that there are no longer many humane long-term residential spaces to care for them. Indeed, the narrative we have been encouraged to believe is that such institutions are undesirable. Certainly those snake pits *were* undesirable. But in the absence of proper facilities, other institutions, ones not designed to handle this particular population, have been forced to do so. Fann and Buck argue convincingly that prisons and shelters have fared poorly in fulfilling that role. And as I argued earlier, Housing First models in part serve to accommodate the historical displacement of long-term care populations.

Another reason it is now hard to conceive of supportive long-term care facilities for people with mental health issues is that, over the last 40 years or so, this contraction of services has been successfully hidden in the prevalent discourse that blames patients themselves for being sick, for going off their meds and for failing to seek help. This perspective does not acknowledge how disheartening and even inhumane the search for help can be for people already marginalized by diseased brain chemistries and struggling in extreme poverty. Freudian self-regulatory outpatient models are very effective for people who are well resourced and have viable social ties to support themselves; not so much for people with long histories of street engagement, addiction or maltreated underlying psychiatric conditions.

Something people tend to forget when criticizing an ill homeless person is that they are *ill*, not foolish. According to Dr. Fann, mental illness in the context of the streets usually means the spectrum of bipolar conditions or schizophrenia-like diseases. These are not socially constructed or behaviorally determined illness; they are brain *diseases* (at least in the medical model). So when one questions the "deserving" nature of a person so inflicted, one must remember that their following a set course of recovery is unlikely. Failure almost always results when "normal" discourses and expectations for "transitioning" are imposed on such people. Such expectations are unfair.

We must not blame victims for going off their meds or for anti-social behaviors exhibited when their brain chemistry shifts, say Dr. Buck and Dr. Fann. We must anticipate that people coping with mental illness will display a wide range of capacities to remain housed, something also true of those dealing with neurological conditions and developmental or behavioural disorders. There will be both smooth and rough patches. There are no miracle cures. In some cases, institutional care may be necessary, and, as Buck and Fann suggest, the need for long-term residential psychiatric care far outstrips the availability.

I told Fann and Buck the story I mentioned earlier of the psychiatrist who almost killed me 20 years ago by telling me that my addiction problems were too vast for psychiatry to address. They were not surprised. They hear such things all the time from the people they help. They say the problem is partly because service providers are overworked and under-resourced, leading to a certain vocational and emotional detachment on the part of those charged with carrying out medical and psychiatric interventions, such as social workers, doctors and nurses. The result, they told me, has been a cleaving of the service provider from his or her humanity:

> "We are creating mechanics," David said. "They're not familiar with their own humanity.... We are creating androids."
> "An android would have had better sense," I reply. "So how do you guys here, who are so successful with your patients, tell the government what they need to know about how to make this work?"
> Gesturing to his office, Dr. Buck says, "Well you know, this is what medicine used to be years ago. The person mattered the most. If the person leaves feeling much worse, then we wonder, you know, if we have been helpful." I ask Dr. Fann if he agrees and he does. David interjects, "And they come back. I get, from Angela House, a place we work intimately with, women that are releasees from prison, related

largely to (the fact that) they were sexually abused as children and shockingly they're prostitutes now. And they have mental problems, no surprise. And they come here and Dr. Fann will just say, 'Is this the way you treat yourself?'"

Dr. Fann nods in agreement.

Dr. Buck continues: "And they suddenly say, 'Wait, you know, I am doing this to myself.' But he doesn't say it in this off putting way."

So I reiterate the story of Shannon, a squeegee kid seen in one of my films. She would squeegee for 20 bucks, go buy a rock, then repeat. And she was pregnant.

"But why was she getting high?" Dr. Buck asks rhetorically. "Because they were treated badly their whole lives. They were treated, you know, their parents basically told them they were a piece of shit, so they treated themselves that way."

Dr. Fann interjects, "The big difference is the way Dave, the psychiatry he was exposed to in school, is that the Freudian taught you had to have the anamnesis, that is, you have to tell all about your background and your childhood because 'all this' started with childhood trauma, which is not always the case.... So you know that ... anybody that's having this kind of mental stress (prostitution, street life) has either been mistreated or feels that they have been. So we just assume that we're going to believe them. Dave and I take the stance that we believe you, you've been mistreated. And they say, 'I don't trust people. I can't trust people' And they feel very guilty about that."

David interjects, "So much so that the service provider will type— write in the chart—document—'paranoid ideations' and suggest that maybe 'you need to take medications' but they don't say, 'Well, of course you do! You were sexually abused, you were physically abused.'

I was left thinking that, not surprisingly, intervention sounds like a terrible thing to most people. It has generally been practiced in such a way that it seems like a moral judgment about one's character. The client, consumer —however we describe the person seeking help—is left to feel at fault for their own needs when, in fact, they are not.

I say, "So there's nothing paranoid about it."

"Yeah. Yeah. It's almost a social adaptation. But it is not their fault," Dr. Buck adds.

Dr. Fann tells me, "So we say to them, 'You expect someone who has been mistreated all their lives to suddenly start trusting people?' And they just break down and cry."

Dr. Buck adds, "They look like [they are in awe]. 'Wait a second, how could I have missed this? I've been to doctors for 40 years and nobody's told me that.' And they'll think: 'It's not all my fault.' And when they learn that it's not all their fault, and there are things they can do to anticipate these changes in their life and the feelings that they have, they start having hope. And [for example] they'll quit smoking, they'll lose weight, they'll adapt their behaviours."

As Dr. Buck and Dr. Fann told me how common this blame-the-self narrative was among the people they worked with, I could not help but recall how I had blamed myself for the beatings my father had laid into me; how, after those assaults (he always left the house afterward), I hid behind the living-room curtains, staring into the night, waiting for him to come home, because I worried that he might not come back. "Imagine that," I shared with them: "I was worried he would not come back, even though it meant jeopardy for me." This blaming narrative is rooted deeply in the unconscious; such deeply rooted issues cannot be self-managed and so Buck and Fann ask people to think about their own self-narratives, to free themselves of the burden of blame, after which it is much easier to work on getting (and remaining) housed.

The film *Good Will Hunting* includes a wonderful scene that illustrates this point well. Will Hunting, a troubled but brilliant could-be scholar, has all but thrown away the greatest opportunity a budding mathematician could hope for—and also a really loving relationship—because he did not know how to manage these kinds of self-affirming narratives. Early in his life he had been so abused and beaten that his brain lost the ability to create a sense of self-worth. He spends months working with a psychologist who actually cares about him; at the climax, the psychologist embraces Will, and, despite Will's rejection, the psychologist clings to him, repeating, "It's not your fault, it's not your fault," until Will finally breaks down into tears. Only then, after that epiphanal moment, after riding that razor's edge without tranquility, he has but to accept that "it was not his fault." He can move on from there. My sister told me these things during my recovery. I have repeated the same words to people I have worked with on the streets. It seems to work.

Self-governing—more than merely self-managing, but understood as conduct of the self—is not the same for all people. For those of us who have been beaten and abused, raped or exposed to violence, for those of us with mental health issues, or who suffer addictions, self-government looks different than it does for those untouched by such torments.

Fann and Buck argue that a number of narratives need to be changed to meet the needs of people on the streets in our cities. First, we need to recognize a diversity of self-conduct narratives, rather than one specific self-help narrative. We need to recognize that there are people with psychiatric issues who respond well to pharmacological interventions (bi-polar disorder is one) and others who do not respond well (schizophrenias are examples). We cannot hold generalized expectations about people with mental health issues and how they orient towards housing goals. But most people do generalize and defer to statistics that suggest that the rise of street homelessness is because of mental health issues, without any actual understanding of the underlying diversity. The problem is not just making the generalization. The problem is that deferring to this narrative places the responsibility for solving the issue in the hands of experts, and by so doing the average person eschews any responsibility for people who suffer. Furthermore, the narrative reinforces the myths we have just discussed: primarily, that drugs and interventions will solve the underlying condition and that only people who are willing to accept pharmacological interventions are worthy of housing.

Finally, we should not trade the dominant narrative about homelessness for another singular dominant narrative (Housing First, say, or shelters). We need to find a way to include a number of narratives to address the truly complex nature of such social problems. IHC has a place in this wider range of narratives. But as Dr. Fann suggests, we also need to bring back long-term mental health facilities that actually work. That means hiring enough trained physicians and psychologists to handle the complex care needs of their patients. Currently such facilities tend to have on staff one psychiatrist or physician for up to 300 patients, a ratio that is simply untenable. In some cases, we will need to intervene more, and in others less. But we cannot even consider options and alternatives if the necessary staff and service structures do not exist.

If our culture provided first-rate, humane care for people who suffer underlying psychiatric, addiction and behavioral conditions, homelessness would be reduced. But taking an interventionist stance conflicts with the narrative of individual rights.

It has also been suggested that the types of spaces set aside need to be diversified to accommodate different people with different needs. While most patients on the schizophrenia spectrum do not fare well in institutions, there is growing evidence that eco-villages and rural intentional housing communities are effective at integrating even the worst-off cases.

Most people are familiar with the story of Temple Grandin, an autistic person whose life story proves that working on farms and with animals can help people with difficult underlying conditions. Fann and Buck connected me to Grant Kennedy, who was a co-director of a Houston IHC called Magnificat House. Magnificat House is part of Clubhouse International, an internationally successful organization for people with mental health issues and homelessness, which has 320 clubhouses in 34 countries.

Based on my observations, this was exactly the kind of environment that Buck and Fann suggested we needed; it provided the social and other supports people required and helped them to find and sustain housing. Magnificat operated as a day center, but was linked to a rural IHC residence called the Dona Marie Clubhouse, which was grounded in the lesson that Grandin taught us about farming and animals. On this residence, located on the out-skirts of Houston, the same social and occupational services are provided, but people are allowed to live onsite and work on the farm. When I visited in 2014, the people housed there were in various stages of working toward their own unique housing goals. Some wanted to stay there, some to return to regular apartments or homes, but in the meantime they had a safe and dignified place to live. Away from the noise and hectic pace of urban life, the bucolic setting and purposeful duties about the farm helped anchor people who had not fared well in more institutional settings. Each person with whom I spoke said this was the greatest community experience they could recall, because this particular housing community is oriented to the diverse mental health needs of the population that lives in it, rather than to prescribed administrative goals or outcomes.

Fann, Buck and most of the other people I work with would argue that the single most important shift needed in the narratives driving social policies today is a return to a patient- or person-centered discourse. That we now come across the term "human-centered design" more frequently in policy studies suggests that important needs we had forgotten are now re-emerging as central concerns.

A few days later I was in Galveston. I was fortunate enough to show some of my videos about Tent City to the resident women at Ada's House, a recov-ery home near the UTMB. The words of Dr. Buck and Dr. Fann had resonated with me. It was very interesting to show these women, all addicts of sorts, video of other women who did not benefit from the kind of therapeutic ser-vices offered by Ada House. The women in my films about Tent City were the kind of worst-off cases that spoke to Ada's residents; women who had not been able to see the choices that Buck and Fann spoke of; women who made the unfortunate choices they had been equipped to make, and to whom no one had said "It is not your fault." In particular, the story of Shannon was most heart-wrenching to the women at Ada's. In the film, Shannon is pregnant, loses her second child to Children's Aid, and reportedly ends up back on the streets. But Penny, a sex worker and addict, overcomes these behaviors because she got supportive housing in 2004 and was able to work through her problems with counselors.

In these stories, the Ada residents could literally and reflexively see and imagine themselves as parts of a continuum of possible life events rather than following inevitable trajectories in a fixed narrative leading to either recovery or homelessness. For some, seeing these other women addicts was a warning and reinforced the desire to get well. Others saw themselves at different times in their lives and began to share more openly with their therapists—the videos opened up new directions for discussion. And a few of the clients even had cause to admit that there were aspects of these women on film that remained attractive to them. That fact scared them. Perhaps most importantly, those who watched the film recognized they were not bad or unusual, and that their own stories could be informed by the stories of others. They were not passive victims of dominating self-narratives, but could have self-efficacy. For me, the obvious lesson was that images of various kinds can be doorways to new ways of constructing narratives of the self and of others. I felt that I was on the right track—we could use images to start conversations about social problems en route to changing narratives of inevitability.

With this in mind, I made my plans to return to Portland. With my colleagues Dan Price at the University of Houston and Jerome Crowder from UTMB, I had been working on converting VWIRE, an online visual elicitation tool they had created, for use as a narrative conduit for discussions about homelessness. It remained to be seen if the kinds of computer technology and Internet bandwidths in the camps were sufficient to provide the connectivity we would need to test the platform.

Visual elicitation techniques are not new in the social sciences. Ethnologists and anthropologists have been using photos and film to study others for over 130 years. I spoke earlier of the ethical requirements of visual ethnography, yet it may be useful to recall the incredibly powerful and convincing way in which seeing things helps humans tell stories. Henry Milgram proved that people have an undeniable tendency to look at something if others look at it; we are curious about what others see as curious. We say "I see what you mean" because it is often necessary for us to visualize ideas and propositions to make sense of them, to discard them, or to support them. Images can be quite deliberately selected or shot in certain ways to reinforce a premise or narrative.

Important recent visual representations of the homeless addict, such as Bourgois and Schonberg's *Righteous Dopefiend* (2010), use striking photography—junkies thrusting syringes into a friend's neck, infected abscesses at the injection site, and American flags draped over shanties—in order to evoke an emotional response to clear signs of what Bourdieu called a structural violence imposed on the worst-off of our citizens by a corrupt and unequal system of accumulation. Newspapers, magazine articles and photo-essays testify to the compelling force of images of the homeless and of dark places in otherwise normal city life. We use images to jar people out of old ways of thinking. Studies such as that carried out by Nielsen et al. (2012) clearly demonstrate that such pieces target conventional citizens and rarely if ever those in the images themselves.

While much of this use bespeaks the sincere attitudes of scholars, the press, activists and others to raise the issue of homelessness to a public level, it is rare that the semantic and rhetorical commitment (what we think and talk to ourselves about what we see—the stories we imagine in the public images) of the visual subjects, the homeless person, for example, or the addict, are understood. Do we tell the same stories, and if so, about everything? Observers who do not suffer from addictions and homelessness utilize and interpret images of addiction or the human condition of homelessness very differently than we who have suffered it.

The point is that addicts and the homeless are also visually savvy and for them the images have impact too. These impacts are rarely understood. We rarely ask those who suffer what they make of our images of suffering, or the stories we tell ourselves about *them*. The converse is also true. There were the simple but profound reactions of Dignity Villagers when they saw Nigel's photographs in my book. People saw themselves differently, and so after the dissertation I wondered: Could we not use the same technique to change other people's perceptions about homeless narratives? If over the web we could connect different kinds of people, housed and unhoused, using images to prime a serious discussion about IHC, would that help people fighting for housing get off the streets?

So off I had gone to Portland and everything had gone well, except that on the last day I had turned right to visit R2DToo, instead of turning left to the mall, and in the camp E. had died, and our hearts had broken, and the cops and EMS had been joking, and these guys I hadn't met before had smudged me, and I had just wanted to crawl out of my skin and into a bottle of something. And so there you have it. An event, an unpredictable moment, a tragic moment in one narrative causes the inevitability built into another to warp into myriad possibilities. I didn't drink. Instead I went to that restaurant and ate too much sashimi and vomited the field notes you read in the introduction to this book, as I pondered the various inevitable nightmares my having had a drink or snorting a blast might have had. In certain recovery fellowships they call this process "playing the old tapes," reminding ourselves just where a single choice out of the myriads possible might lead. Had I drunk, I would have been off and running, and that razor's edge is too sharp for me.

When I returned to Galveston I was different. The way I saw my work was different. I taught two courses while there: one a seminar on visual narratives, and the other a seminar on public ethnography. I enjoyed teaching but secretly I was disturbed by these other matters and reticent to write up my research. And in fact I did not look at the notes again until I started this book. I found out a few weeks later that I had won the 2104 Canadian Association of Graduate Studies Distinguished Dissertation Award in the Social Sciences and Humanities. That was a shock and I was grateful. The award forced me to revisit the meaning of this prior work. As gratifying and mysterious as the award was to me, I was feeling a strong sense of anomie in Texas, and had a sincere desire to come back to Canada. I want to argue that I was traumatized by the experience in that camp, but then I think of all the stories I have heard on the streets and in dark spaces: the women who have been raped and beaten, the men who have survived IEDs in Iraq, the adult children fleeing sexual abuse and the others cast out of their homes because their bodies didn't fit with how they felt about themselves, and I am left thinking that maybe my skin just wasn't thick enough. I had thought my problems quite trite and myself quite silly; selfish, perhaps. And I imagined I needed to get back to doing something good, something helpful and less pensive.

When I heard of a teaching position in Prince George, B.C., I leapt on it, applied, interviewed and was hired as a sessional faculty member in sociology at the College of New Caledonia. IMH graciously let me depart ahead of schedule, and in August, I packed my gear, loaded my car and began the journey out of Texas. Though I had left a number of projects unfinished by leaving early, I made some important connections and that work goes on, in fits and starts.

I had made contact with Jennifer Paulsen of the Texas Homeless Network in Austin, and she suggested I visit a place there called Community First Village (CFV). On my drive out of Texas, we met there and were given a tour by Alan Graham, a founder of the parent non-profit, Mobile Loaves and Fishes, that runs the village. According to the Austin *Culture Map*:

> Community First [Village] is a groundbreaking development de-
> signed for the homeless population of Austin. Located on Hog Eye
> Road near Walter E. Long Park, the community is 27 acres containing
> 140 tiny homes. Each home is 180 square feet with a porch, and
> residents have access to communal outdoor kitchens, private bath-
> rooms, showers, and laundry facilities.[166]

CFV is ambitious and remarkable enough to constitute its own book. So I will just speak to it in passing. It is nothing like Dignity Village, except that each uses tiny homes to house people. CFV is less a discursive site than a planned real-estate play for poor people. It is in fact the *über*-hybrid of the kinds of models I have been suggesting. It was built by a non-profit using donor funding mechanisms (http://mlf.org/community-first/) and was pitched as a sustainable tiny home village for homeless people. At Dignity Village these things are just ideas. At CFV they are making them real. In addition, Mobile Loaves and Fishes is a grassroots but Christian-flavoured mission to help the homeless with ties to extensive sponsorship and service networks that give it advantages over less affiliated sites. Most importantly to my thinking, it hasn't the burden of proving a constitutional argument, or defending itself against definitions of freedom, rights and autonomy. As Alan said when I met him in the state of the art office-trailer, "This is not an activist site, or a political claim. This is a real estate deal, Eric. It's affordable housing for the poor." At

$225 a month for a fully detached cottage, it seemed to me a totally suitable and reasonable form of accommodation, and exactly what IHC would want to be if all the necessary financial and managerial parts had been in place. In fact, at that time, CFV was so promising that other American cities took note and there was some chatter in the housing community that it might be the way to go looking forward.

9.6 Canada

The drive out of Texas was a very long ordeal. Just outside Austin my car broke down. Later, at the Kia dealership, they told me it had suffered a "catastrophic heat failure in the electric steering column." I was stuck in ranch country, in 40°C heat. A vicious thunderstorm approached. It sounds clichéd but tumble-weeds flew by, a plank from a fence rattled off my hood. I saw but three or four vehicles pass by. I had nowhere to go. I was parked next to an old, apparently

vacant ranch house. As lightning flashed all around, I called 911 to tell the dispatcher who I was, and where they could find my body if a tornado came through. It was that bad. Two hours into this, waiting for a tow truck that never arrived, after a lightning bolt hit so close that my ears rang, I ignored the 911 dispatcher's order to stay in my car, ran up the driveway of the old house and banged on the door.

I peered in a window. It was dark inside and looked empty. I decided to break into the garage to find shelter. I was thinking that this was exactly what homelessness was all about: desperation, fear, mortality, death. And just then 84-year-old Mary Juby opened the door and invited me in. "In 84 years, that's the first time I ever had a stranger come knockin' on my door," she said. When I told her who I was and that I was Canadian, she laughed heartily and commented that she had never met a Canadian before: "Guess y'all find it mighty warm round here." "Yes ma'am," I replied. She was pleasant enough and when she finally turned on the lights, I was shocked to see that her entire living room was filled with chickens: cardboard chickens, porcelain chickens, big ones, little ones, baby ones—chickens everywhere. She was all alone now; her friends and family visited but her

Juby ranch sign (top); Mary Juby's chickens. Photos: Eric Weissman.

husband was gone and they didn't run the cattle any longer, so she didn't have many visitors. Just her chickens. Eight generations of her husband's family had run that land. We sat there saying very little, watching the black skies and the lightning, wondering when the twister might touch down. But it did not. After three more hours, I told her I was getting tired of waiting for a tow truck, and she said, "You mean to say all's y'all need is a tow?" And she got on the phone and called her son-in-law, a tow-truck driver in the next town, who was there in 20 minutes. The storm passed and he drove me back to Austin, where I had to wait four days for a part to arrive for my car. Four more days stuck in Texas. When the part arrived and my car was fixed, I got in and just started driving.

I made it from Texas to Canada in four days. Along the way, I stopped in Sweetwater, Texas, Raton, New Mexico, Castle Rock, Colorado, Casper, Wyoming, then Lethbridge, Alberta, Kamloops, B.C. and finally Fort St. John and Prince George. On my drive, especially in the U.S., I was struck by how many empty and decaying factories, plants and warehouses I saw along the way. Refineries and mills shut down, whole districts of small cities boarded up. Labour eradicated over the years by capital's abandonment of the American Way. By my reckoning, in that nine-month period I had travelled over 10,000 kilometres and visited four provinces, ten states and 50 cities. And everywhere I went I saw homeless people. That did not change when I got to Prince George.

The school term at CNC started in September, just a few days after my award was officially announced. In the interim, the Texas Homeless Network had asked me to give a keynote address at their conference on ending homelessness in late September. I arranged to do so and also to bring Ibrahim Mubarak and Mitch Grubic to San Antonio for the talk. In my keynote I asked almost 500 people whose work revolved around emergency HF paradigms in the context of ten-year plans to end homelessness why they felt they could actually end homelessness. "You cannot end homelessness," I said. The room went silent. So I told them the short version of the story I presented here, including my own journey out of addiction, and, at the end of the talk, I challenged them to think about the possibility that IHC might become widespread and sanctioned as part of city strategies to end homelessness throughout the U.S. There was some doubt, and most felt IHC was a very limited housing model, but almost 100 people attended our breakout session on Tent City, Dignity Village and Right 2 Dream Too. At the very least, there was great interest in the role IHC could play even in interim planning.

A few weeks later, I flew to St. John's, Newfoundland to receive my dissertation award. They asked me to speak to the future of the Ph.D. My talk was equally challenging. I spoke to the fact that most of us with Ph.D.'s are out of work or forced to slave in adjunct or research positions, mostly because universities are not hiring and when they do, they hire people with more junior degrees or as part-timers. The Ph.D. was for me a personal goal, part of my redemption narrative. The press picked up on that and in a few hours, I was on CBC talking about having been homeless and commenting on the 2014 Homeless Report, which came out the same day. The Canadian Press ran a story about an addict and homeless man who recovered and became a professor. The redemption narrative had real legs and the story ran in outlets in the U.S., Canada and even in France. I did interviews with radio, TV, print and even the French edition of *Reader's Digest*. All of this was far more than I had anticipated, and to be honest it irked me that rather than focus on my work they focused on my personal story. The implication of my story— the compelling narrative that fuels reality television shows, too—is that even the most doomed narrative inevitabilities are not fixed but alterable. I was proof of that.

There was some justice in the award, too. A dean from York University who some eight years earlier told me that York's program in communication and culture would never accept me was in the audience, and when congratulating me afterward had turned white as a sheet when finally recollecting who I was. I was polite. The CAGS team treated me very well, so did Concordia, and I returned to CNC hopeful that I might have a bright future.

When I returned I was on the front page of the *Prince George Citizen*— "Ph.D. from the Edge" the story said—some other stuff about an addict and homeless man now teaching at CNC ... blah, blah. I got about the work of teaching four courses per term, leaving any other work I wanted to do for another time, and if the truth be known, I had a hard time in Prince George, even though I had fished in northern B.C. for over two decades and continue to do so. It is one of my favourite places on Earth, but I didn't fit well into the town. I demonstrated the VWiRE project to various housing groups, including Community Partners Addressing Homelessness (CPAH), and even helped set up a conference for them about Housing First, with noted scholar Jeanette Wagemakers Schiff from the University of Calgary. On my free nights I would sometimes drive around downtown on my way home from fellowship meetings. I saw the homeless men and women, mostly people of First Nations ancestry, sleeping in laneways, huddled around the fire pit, a community center, and sometimes sleeping along the Nechako River where I had fished for Sockeye. Prince George is still a rough town and had the dubious reputation as the most violent city in Canada between 2011 and 2014.

Much of the crime and homelessness is the direct result of Prince George's hub status. As the largest city in northern B.C., on the western leg of the highway to the west coast, as a key service hub for oil, mining and forestry companies, a lot of money flows through the town. This has led to a thriving illegal economy comprised of drugs and drug dealing, prostitution and racketeering and theft. An unknown number of the rental units and homes in Prince George have been subject to a phenomenon called "unit takeovers" (CPO 2013), in which drug dealers take over people's homes and living spaces. It's an area under-researched in North America, but a pervasive problem with which all front-line housing workers are familiar. I am currently research lead on a project in Toronto for the Dream Team that looks at this issue. In Prince George, the problem had been subsumed under the problem of flophouses; recently the RCMP raided a flophouse where more than 10,000 used needles were found. This shocked people in Prince George but for those of us who do research in this area, the fact that flophouses and takeovers should occur is not surprising at all. Nor was it a conceptual leap to understand why so many First Nations persons would end up the most visible reminder of homelessness in that city. In the last year, the tragic suicides of young people in the Attawapiskat First Nation highlighted the struggle of young people with depression, anomie and drug abuse across Canada's First Nations. In driving through First Nations lands near Lethbridge and observing how rundown many of the homes had become, coming to resemble the larger structures at Dignity Village, I surmised a relationship between decay of the soul and decay of the house.

There had been a real tension in the First Nations around Prince George too, one that paralleled the comments made by Robert, Jeff and Michael in Galveston. Non-Aboriginal persons blamed these homeless folks for being useless addicts, and expressed a complete sense of frustration about what to do about them. Native leaders I worked with understood the systemic and structural violence that 200 years of colonial tampering had wrought on their peoples, but looked at their own successful narratives as proof that the addicts and alcoholics had made their own bad choices. When I brought up stories people told me about abuses in residential schools, prisons or at home, I often heard that such stories, valid as they were, did not excuse the individual from responsibility as an adult. It angered me. It still does. One elder I worked with seemed to be the ideological doppelganger for Michael Jackson. Into this context of interchangeable blame-the-state, blame-the-self and blame-the-victim discourses, I inserted visual elicitation to conjure up new ways of imagining the causes and ways out of the problems facing Prince George. Clearly the stories they were using to deal with social problems were inaccurate or faulty.

Just as the project was beginning to get legs, my contract ended, and I was informed that my mom back in Toronto had cancer. In April 2015, I returned post haste to Toronto, and spent that summer living with my mom and stepdad. I applied for several teaching positions in Toronto and Montreal and was interviewed but refused. I had hoped to return to CNC in the fall but they interviewed me again and then hired someone else for the same position I had held. These were hard months that left me doubting the choices I had made, the intense mental, spiritual and physical toil that the Ph.D. and the travel had taken on me. And I was left wondering what it all had meant.

But I had time to start this book, and somewhere in writing it I remembered that U.S. vet who somehow tracked me down after reading about the dissertation award and from his bed in a Veterans Administration hospital reached out to me for advice about how he could make his recent acceptance into grad school work for him. I understand that he made it to school but I haven't heard anything since. I recalled Eduard from Montreal who read the same piece, whose son was lost to the streets in Vancouver, and who had in turn reached to me for help. I had suggested meeting him in Vancouver to help him find his son, but he managed to do so on his own, and they reunited in Montreal for a time. But the inevitability of the street narrative proved too strong. Presumably he is still riding the razor's edge on the lower East Side.

In August 2016, the city of Dallas announced its first IHC, the Cottages at Hickory Crossing, portending the emergence of the IHC as a larger phenomenon than previously anticipated. In order to see what was happening in Portland I went back in February 2016. The city of Portland had made yet another offer to Ibrahim and R2DToo. This time they had been offered a piece of land serviced with electricity and plumbing, adjacent to public transportation, and until recently it looked like the site would move there. But that is not the only story to come out of Portland. There are a number of camps that have emerged and are fighting for city sanction so that they can also help the several thousand people living on the streets. Hazelnut Grove and Forgotten Realm are two that are close to being situated. Interestingly, an unnamed camp for women, situated in the Lent District, was disbanded by the city after being up for only two days. The residents were immediately placed in a hotel because they were women. It is safe to say that certain categories of gender, age, infirmity and past civic duty will remain more deserving in the symbolic imaginaries of U.S. cities, and others less so. But perhaps that is not the crisis it once was because, looking forward, there will likely be many more IHC for people to live in.

At the Portland mayoral candidates' meeting in February, each of the (then) seven candidates said that rest areas like Right 2 Dream Too and IHC like Dignity Village had a place in their future housing strategies. Many cities are building such camps, accessing the Dignity Villagers and Ibrahim's group as planning resources. As I write this, Ibrahim is in San José where the city, several NPOs and homeless activists are currently crafting a temporary housing model that can help people live in sober and safe transitional spaces while they wait for housing. Tomorrow the city representatives will travel to Portland to see what variation of the R2DToo theme they will pitch in their $450-million bid to fund more than 20 of these spaces in San José alone.

For me, the best news is that Dignity Village, 16 years after it was formed, has finally institutionalized the role of an external manager into its internal managerial structure, and is operating better than it had for the last few years. I spoke with Katie Mays, an employee of JOIN, which I earlier mentioned as a non-profit that helps street people find and maintain housing. They too are part of the advisory board at Dignity Village. Katie has been the official manager at Dignity Village for almost 18 months. She helps people there get IDs, driver's licenses, and medical insurance, and she does many of the bureaucratic things needed to have a functional identity in the modern world. She also helps the village do the reporting and bookkeeping it had previously failed to do so miserably.

One of the issues she is working on is the upcoming contract renewal. Contract renewal is a sort of regulatory device that the city uses to keep the village in check. While popular opinion would not support a regime that ousted 60 vulnerable people, those same people must work towards complying with the contract or creating one that reflects—that is, "thirds"—the space of the village. So Katie is helping the village present a contract that reflects the reality of life there rather than appeasing the expectations placed on it. That

Katie has been there so long and that the villagers are pleased seems to indicate that they are closer to accepting the city's demand for a hybridized governance structure, one that includes external advisors in the village executive decision-making process. That is a big step. It is what other IHC are doing and it is what Dignity must do to evolve. As with everything in Dignity Village or any of these emerging IHC forms, every day is a learning experience and an opportunity to craft the narrative of intentional homeless communities.

The other end of the spectrum.
Redevelopment of social housing in Toronto's Regent Park, 2016. Photo: Eric Weissman.

As of March 2017, two of the village's leaders, Scott (the security chief) and Lisa (the CEO) are consistently engaged in external activism. After seven years in the village, they have come to realize that the village is, as I argued earlier, part of a larger debate. They are active members of Portland's Village Coalition, a group fighting for the rights of houseless people in the city. The city today has three sanctioned camps and is in negotiations with three others. Despite the fact that developers have staked out most of the city's available space to re-develop and gentrify, there are negative and empty spaces scattered around the city that, out of sheer necessity, are becoming legally zoned for emergency camps and tiny homes. This is real. Other cities are doing this too. Eugene has opened its second space, Emerald Village. And I have noted many others.

It is hard to say whether these legal sanctions reflect the fact that planners and politicians have "thirded" space and yielded to what it tells them, or if they have decided that IHC is a cost-effective way to look like they are doing something, but in any event IHC is on the rise. With proposed cuts to HUD's budget, the need for such spaces may increase.

I recently joined a working group in Toronto investigating the possibility of a tiny home complex in the central core. A division exists in the group as to whether the housing should be for homeless people or a model of affordable housing that could be marketed to new home owners. This debate will have implications on whether or not the project secures enough popular support to go ahead. The City of Toronto has expressed interest and supporters have offered up resources to build a test site. Currently the project is mired in exactly the same kind of debates and battles over location we read about in the case of Dignity Village. However, with housing all but out of reach to most Torontonians, with widespread support for row houses and a persistent problem with people moving in and out of homelessness, the narratives we have constructed about how to house people are shifting. It takes time to see the effects of critique. But it is safe to say that the critical movement around housing and homelessness is alive and powerful in North American cities, including Toronto.

A final note on R2DToo is called for. I spoke with Ibrahim just yesterday. Based on struggles within its board of directors, R2DToo is less stable than it was before. A change in mayor in Portland has resulted in uncertainty regarding policies related to the camp, and plans to move the camp to another site have gone nowhere. Ibrahim's feeling is that R2DToo will be shuffled to another poorly resourced site far away from downtown, because that is what city officials seem to be saying behind closed doors. In fact, developers still plan to bring the "mega-shelter" model (similar to Haven of Hope) to Portland.[167] Currently the developers are suggesting buying a golf course near the airport, next to a composting facility and Dignity Village. If this mega-shelter is built there, it might be that Dignity Village, R2DToo and all the other camps which currently stand in the way of other developers might be subsumed under the gigantic roof of Haven for Hope Portland. Ibrahim tells me that he personally feels this is likely to happen. He says, as if to cap off my book: "It's inevitable, Eric, it makes sense to the city and to the developers."

We will see.

In any event, in early April 2017 R2DToo was served eviction papers by the landowner. The land is now worth $1.2 million and developers are poised to gentrify Chinatown. R2DToo will be moved to a temporary site across the river, next to a bridge and out of the way—no one knows for how long or what will come next. But whether or not these types of spaces are permanent is no longer important to me. The very idea of permanence is a conventional imaginary. Permanence is not a measure of success in unconventional experiences or critical movements. Innovative and critical spaces morph, shift, and in the process both succeed and fail. So permanence is too conventional a measure and therefore no longer a viable one for me for adjudicating inevitability in sites that are both discursive and practical. IHCs like R2DToo, like Dignity Village, like all the others are part of the construction of narratives about how cities look at major social problems such as homelessness, and as such will always be understood upon reflection as the outcome of competitions between powerful critiques on the use of city spaces and the constitution of deserving and undeserving character.

For me, the question is no longer "Is there room for IHC in U.S. and Canadian cities?" because cities in both countries are considering or adopting the model. Yet the same moral question remains: Are these places good or bad? There are ways to answer this question. In the course of this book, I have used ethnography to offer up some stories so that you could decide for yourself if you agree with this use of space. Elsewhere, history and policy discussions reveal just whose interests are served by the various narratives present in the debates over these sites. A number of theories and methodologies have been hybridized to offer tools for socially critiquing the tactical power displacements that fuel struggles over neoliberal self-governing narratives. My own story provides a context for judgments I have made about situations that are hard to discuss objectively.

I sit here today in my office of my rented apartment, underemployed and living month-to-month like many other Canadians. I sit here not in judgment of IHC or the people we have met, but as someone who understands the precariousness built into the very world we live in.

Endnotes

1. Smudging is a ritual practice that uses the smoke from native grasses to purify spaces and make them sacred.
2. As discussed on *Bill Maher*, HBO, February 22, 2013.
3. Based on various statistics from HUD 2012; State of Oregon, EHAC 2011; NAEH 2011.
⁴ See Don Mitchell, *The Right to the City* (2003) Jim Ward, *The Street is their Home, the hobo's manifesto* (1979), David Wagner, *Checkerboard Square* (1993).
5. The documentary *Hard Times: Lost on Long Island* (2011) suggests that over 5,000,000 personal bankruptcies and 8,000,000 home foreclosures took place in the 2½ years between the 2008 bust and the making of the film.
6. Eugene, Oregon is using that language when constructing the terms of Opportunity Village.
7. You can view the documentary at www.subtextproductions.ca.
8. Lacan had argued that ideas have both symbolic and imaginary dimensions to the degree that popular illusions through speech acts become fixed in symbolic imaginaries in this autonomous realm where the ego comes to understand itself as a reflection (the mirror stage) of the imaginary order; such popularized ideas appeal to the narcissistic and autonomous needs of the individual to comprehend reality (Lacan 1955: Seminar Three: The Psychoses; also *Ecrits*, 1966). Castoriadis (1987) builds a model of larger scale "symbolic imaginaries" upon this foundation, arguing that under capitalism, simple or magico-religious foundations of common belief are replaced by increasingly scientific and managerial, even moral symbolic representations of the acceptable social and political order, often contained in laws and expectations for normal economic behavior.

9. http://www.ohs.org/education/oregonhistory.
10. http://vbc.cityrepair.org. City Repair and its festive Village Building Convergence won early battles with city government resulting in ordinances for alternative communal spaces in the city.
11. http://newswatch.nationalgeographic.com/2012/12/10/tiny-house-happy-life/.
12. These figures oscillate monthly if not yearly. CNN recently announced a national rate of 15.7% while another news source stated 14.1%. The figures I offer are from nationally recognized sources, HUD, NAEH, NCH and others.
13. The reader is cautioned that the figures presented in this section are impossible to verify and differ depending on the sources cited. Go to http://www.oregon.gov/ohcs/isd/ra/docs/2010_oregon_poverty_report.pdf for some good figures.
14. http://voiceofrussia.com/2013_03_25/The-US-Government-sent-an-assassin-for-me-interview-333/.
15. http://www.oregonlive.com/opinion/index.ssf/2012/09/index_3.html.
16. http://www.portlandoccupier.org/?s=dignity+village.
17. http://streetroots.org.
18. Connecticut and Rhode Island are the first two states to pass such laws, but Oregon and California are currently very close to signing theirs.
19. See Burchell (1991), Gordon, (1991).
20. For EID: www.oregon.gov/oprd/HCD/PROGRAMS/docs/OMSC_2011_EIDBID.pdf. Ecodistricts: sustainablebusinessoregon.com/articles/2010/04/portland_group_proposes_eco-districts_plan.html. BID:oregonlive.com/opinion/index.ssf/2010/06/portland_business_improvement.html.
21. In recent years, the topic of liminality as critique is gaining more attention in anthropology and beyond.
22. Since the home and the household are key institutions to the management of citizens in capitalist systems (Engels 1847), failure to establish these renders one a failure. All social institutions organize social

relationships in one way or another and manage the movement of people through time and space (Van Gennep 1908; Merton 1949; Boltanski 2011).

23. As reported on *Bill Maher*, February 22, 2013.

24. Discussed at length in the next chapter, but essentially a destabilization of ethnographic truth.

25. Modern space in Lefebvre's account of it is socially created, but it still inheres an idea that space is, in the first sense, natural, a vector or a "substance" after all, in which or onto which places are located, if not defined by the social relations which create them.

26. It is tempting to refer to Dignity Village as governed by a form of Indirect Rule, whereby the community is permitted to exist as long as it meets certain basic requirements of more powerful governance. The argument is that the state determines laws and regulates community life when it deems it necessary.

27. One might surmise that the decision was due in part to the influence of BIDS and residents of Portland's redeveloping city core. From the very moment villagers moved to the outskirts of Portland to take up residence, the city had established that such manifestations or places of poverty were to be considered marginal to the core values of home and land use.

28. They would argue that all cultures develop categories of the safe and unsafe, the known and ambiguous, and also they create spaces where ritual or routinized processes for transiting individuals through these psychic and actual conditions can take place with few repercussions for the rest of the group. Holy ground, temples, churches, shamans' quarters, and perhaps in industrialized areas doctors' offices, therapists' couches and community centers might be such locations or places.

29. Bevir says: "A hostility to the subject runs throughout Foucault's oeuvre. Indeed, he himself said, 'it is not power, but the subject, which is the general theme of my research'; and he described as his main aim the attempt 'to create a history of the different modes by which, in our culture, human beings are made subjects,' and so to efface the idea of the self-constituting subject" (1999:65). In Foucault's later work, we saw that he more clearly discusses how power creates certain types of subjects as a matter of population management within spatial territories and so, as Bevir reminds us, we must look at the individual as "an effect of power" (ibid: 63; Foucault 1977: 98).

30. There is also the very real somatic drive that "coming down" or "getting high" creates. The village we are looking at has had a drug problem for some years, but during this fieldwork, and as recently as June 2013, villagers estimate as many as 60% of the village is hooked on methamphetamine.

31. Derrida had argued that democracy, understood as rule by the people, requires sovereignty; without it the demos is usurped by other power, and effective democratic rule cannot be achieved.

32. Curtis had called it *In the Land of the Head Hunters* but the Kwakiutl rejected his title.

33. His most commonly cited work, published posthumously under his authorship but by his former students.

34. Cort-Haddon's "Torres Straits" visual ethnographies are among the earliest of their kind.

35. Perhaps the most famous American hobo who starred at the Chicago school.

36. These moments are defined as the *traditional* (1900–1950), the *modernist* or golden age (1950–70), *blurred genres* (1970–1986), *the crisis of representation* (1986–1990), the *post-modern*, a period of experimental and new ethnographies (1990–1995), *post-experimental inquiry* (1995–2000), the *methodologically contested present* (2000–2004); and the *fractured future* (2005–now) (3). Of these, it is with the last I am most concerned, but understanding its roots in the critical turn is important.

37. http://canononline.org/archives/current-issue/marx-tocqueville-and-the-problem-of-emancipation/.

Endnotes

38. "Actant" is a concept used in narratology and semiotics and in the social sciences. In the former it refers to a character whose nature serves a structural role in a story, like a thief or a protagonist; and so you can see the key to this is connectivity and structural implications. Actants for Latour are the formations, which result from two or more social actors when they do something together. They are not permanent or very predictable, but they do constitute a basic module in the structural conditions of the social world.

39. In this sense, the individual's freedom and autonomy are to be found in the liberty to act morally, that is, to satisfy the expectations of a moral maxim perceived as a universal law (Paton, 1948: introduction). Kant's Enlightenment project's goal of rationalizing democracy as a step beyond the bloodied and oppressive era of monarchies, therefore, gave political weight to the moral proposition that to respect one's self means to respect others; to treat others as ends in themselves, rather than as means to an end.

40. Under the seminal work and influence of Roy Bhaskar (1975, 1993), critical realism links to Marxism by aligning the idea of reality within two dimensions: an intransitive form that exists beyond one's knowledge of it, and a socially constructed world known through, work, science, education and observable experience. Marxist theories of domination, critical theory being an example, tend to isolate critique in the ideological discrepancies this dualism creates for dominant and alienated classes (Sayer, 2000).

41. It is simplistic to say that cultural realism is simply a model for explaining how everything in nature, which stands independently of our knowledge of it, and therefore has an independent objective reality, is related to explaining special consequences, such as the events of one's day. This is not the case. The emergent nature of cultural reality in human actors is embedded across three axes: the *empirical*, the *actual* and the *real* (Sayer 2000:11).

42. Hence, a mechanism's total effect on action or agency is unpredictable, and the idea that empirical observation can possibly observe the entirety of human complexity that might be represented by it, is misdirection, which once again ties closely to Bourdieu's cautions.

43. Archer suggests that there are various types of ideal internal conversation, which in my way of thinking, would suggest that there are certain type of ideal ways of understanding inevitability. These modes of reflexivity are found in four types of internal conversation that are very important for the work at hand:

1. Communicative reflexives: people whose narratives or ideas need to be rejoined or completed by others before they turn into action.
2. Autonomous reflexives: people act on their own ideas without confirmation.
3. Meta-reflexives: people who are reflexively critical of their own ideas, and socially critical about effective action.
4. Fractured-reflexives: people who cannot conduct purposeful internal conversations and go around in ever-increasing circles of disorientation.

(2003; see Dr. Archer's homepage: http://www2.warwick.ac.uk/fac/soc/sociology/staff/emeritus/archer/msarcher/research/latest/).

44. In *Of Grammatology* (1967), Jacques Derrida introduces his idea of *deconstructionism*. Deconstructionism does not seek transcendence out of the reflexive paradox. Instead, he submits, that we remain within the "paradoxical terrain in order to explore its critical potential" (Biesta and Stams 2001: 66; Derrida 1973: 3–6). "Since it relies on language, and language relies on signifieds finding meaning through superior signifiers, then knowledge is fundamentally metaphysical; facticity is meaningful as things relate to superior external modes of reference" (Der-

Eric Weissman

rida 1995: 54; 1996:87).

45. In his concept of *différence*, Derrida builds on Saussure's (1993) seminal work on language and argues that the elements of language are meaningless on their own and find relevance only in so much that they make reference to one another in *the structure* of language. "What is excluded thereby returns to sign the act of its own exclusion" (Biesta and Stams 2001: 66). Deconstruction affirms what is excluded and forgotten.

46. There is a distinction and an alliance to be made here between critical ethnography and political activism ethnography. Taking Carspecken (1996) as an example of the former and George Smith (1990) as an example of the latter, I want to argue that the eighth moment requires finding ways to align practices that serve to the ultimate end, that is, being critical and having effect.

47. I understand reflexive writing and filmmaking have built-in power dynamics; one does the best one can to expose how decisions and edits and conclusions are drawn.

48. http://www.cbc.ca/thesundayedition/d ocumentaries/2012/09/30/1971-kingston-p en-riots/April 17 1971.

49. At 6:00:00, http://www.youtube.com/ watch?v=RC5LRioMmck, also DS DISC 1, Subtext *ROM Cut* at 00:42:24.

50. At 00:11:54, www.youtube.com/watch? v=wldh8kLy4AI.

51. DS DISC 3: "Spaces, Places" at 00:28:02–00:28:29.

52. In traditional textual ethnography, reflexivity is situated in the investigator's experience in several ways. First, in choosing the "field," the object of the investigation, the investigator brings personal attributes, past experience and perhaps theoretical or paradigmatic biases, and so even before the study begins, the results are in part affected by a preconditioning of "choice" (Hirschkind 1994).

53. Ethical Traces: www.youtube.com/ watch?v=vClepUlEyeM.

54. In *Camera Lucinda* (1979) Barthes explores the physical connection between

photons and images and the organs of sight, which are interconnected, by vision, touch and mind.

55. DS DISC 2, Ethical Traces at 7:42.

56. Of course, from this perspective, American pragmatists come to judge or understand the actions of people on the basis of religious penetration of systems of meaning, ethics and action that are aligned with Protestant work ethics and ideals. I am less concerned with these religious ties to the approach than I am to other ties that might be said to be of similar value: the U.S., American democracy, liberty and freedom, which one might argue stem from religious practices of the colonialists, but I do not address here. See Hamner (2003:40–41).

57. I have already described it thus: ethnography, from the Greek, *ethnos*, and *graphos*, quite literally means *writing people*, or, later, *writing culture*. What separates traveler-writers from the status of ethnographers is that ethnography refers to a systematic analysis of people and customs, usually presented in a written text (*Merriam Webster Dictionary* 2011).

58. Strathern (1987) refines this position by pointing out that there is no reason to assume that the conditioning of a Western observer to Western subcultures is likely the same as that of a non-Western observer to her subcultures. That is because cultures construct self-knowledge differently.

59. http://www.huffingtonpost.ca/2013/11/2 2/antidepressant-use-world-canada_n_432 0429.html.

60. Antidepressant utilization in Canada, *Social Psychiatry and Psychiatric Epidemiology* (2005) 40:799–807.

61. "The Rideau Regional Centre, located in Smiths Falls, Ontario, opened in 1951 as the Ontario Hospital School. Along with similar residential institutions throughout Ontario, it was designed to house individuals who were deemed to have cognitive and physical disabilities. Individuals could be admitted by parents and guardians, training schools, or the Children's Aid Society. At its peak, Rideau's population exceeded 2,600 people in 1955, even though it was

Endnotes

only built to accommodate 1,500. By the mid-1970s, the Ontario government operated 16 such facilities across the province" http://www.institutionalsurvivors.com/background/rideau/.

62. Dry flyfishing requires studying entomology and then tying replicas of insects onto hooks in order to catch trout. A person writing about this without having experience of which insects hatch and when would find the task quite impossible.

63. At first I was astonished. However, between 2001 and 2004 a popular satirical stage play, *Urine Town*, by Holliman and Kotis, ridiculed capitalism and social programming by presenting the struggle of the poor as a pre-revolutionary moment. It was quite successful with over 900 performances. It won three Tony awards. This was not the project I was working on (db.com/production.php?id=1293).

64. Essentially the figures vary according to the value systems presented by the number collectors. States tend to downplay the problem, advocates to inflate the numbers.

65. Loizos 1991 refers to this filmic method as a sort of reportage.

66. In the spring of 2000, the homeless began to appear in greater numbers than in previous years.

67. Street Health in Toronto had conservatively estimated numbers of people on the street per day as between 5,000 and 9,000, with shelter visits as high as 32,000 per annum. However, these numbers did not account for countless others in jeopardy or on the streets.

68. It is largely impossible to present incontrovertible or even matching numbers, but grassroots organizations in various cities such as Street Health and the TDRC in Toronto regularly reported numbers as high as 5,000 to 9,000 per night.

69. Television, Internet, activist newsletters, magazines and photo exhibitions, as examples.

70. Pascal, Janet B., *Jacob Riis: Reporter and Reformer* (New York: Oxford University Press, 2005).

71. http://www.acf.hhs.gov/programs/ohs/.

72. Bourgois and Shonberg 2010, *Righteous Dopefiend.*

73. Following Weber (1974), the social organization of the street families I met inhered organization and leadership, sometimes based on age, experience on the streets or physical prowess, but these individuals were able to lead and this suggested power to me.

74. This is not to argue that people should live on the streets to feel empowered, or that many informants shared this view. It suggests that of the 47 million people in the U.S. and the 3.8 million people in Canada, who live dangerously close to the streets because of their poverty, some will land on the streets, and some will find that experience more empowering than life in conventional communities.

75. As of June 2013, she is the village CEO and this after three years of moving up the political ladder at the village and also conspiring to impeach the past CEO mid-term.

76. Even under Johnson's War on Poverty, policy measures directed at encouraging broader participation by the disadvantaged in the labour market and access to education were suggested as means to restore "victims" to the status of functioning citizens. But concrete and effective plans to do so failed to materialize (Valentine 1968; Rainwater 1968; Lewis 1968; Harvey and Reed 1996).

77. Delanty (2011:81). It is not my intention to defend deconstruction against genealogy except to say that Schrift does a good job of showing how the methods of Derrida, Nietzsche and Foucault deconstruct binary assumptions by rethinking the way truth is manufactured in language, discourse and text.

78. During the 1960s, before his turn away from structuralism, Foucault described his method of writing the past as "archaeology" (1967, 1969). In *The Order of Things* (1967), Foucault argued that history itself is not a safely packaged record of events, but a telling story of how reality is constructed

by dominant epistemes of a place and a time, and converted into the way certain "eventalizations" of a time are treated or experienced, such as madness ([1961] 2006). History, then, was not about point in time events, but about thought and ideas, since history as written manifested these and not the essence of anything tangible per se. "What is madness?" is not as important a question as "How is schizophrenia now understood?"

79. Foucault's neoliberalism differs from traditional uses; it is more than what economists look at as reactivation of old classical theories; more than sociology's way of explaining how market relations take prominence in society; and more than political science's tendency to view the extending of the administrative acumen of the state (Foucault 2008:130).

80. One can see immediate linkages with the work of Mead (1934), Berger and Luckmann (1966), in the sense that governmentality sets out certain possibilities for social realities and relations with them, though which individuals can determine their worth and their normalcy in terms of having good government. Less a psychological impulse than a social response, enacted through behaviours, conduct suggests something essential to relations rather than merely awareness.

81. Under sovereign power, however, economic and demographic growth occurs. That disciplinary power should emerge from within the frame of sovereignty is therefore understandable in the sense that the problem of discipline remains, even if it is now a specialized function of the state.

82. Foucault also cautions us not to overvalue the state as a totalizing system in current neoliberal governmentality. It is not that the state has taken over society as much as the state has become governmentalized by what he would call "governmentalization of the state" (Dean 2010:36). In this sense, one might argue that to see power one must look at how people are politically activated since "power is exercised by virtue of things being known

and people being seen" (Foucault 1980:154).

83. Michel Foucault, *Technologies of the Self*, edited by Luther H. Martin, Huck Gutman and Patrick H. Hutton, pp. 16-49 (University of Massachusetts Press, 1988).

84. But so too can individual enact punitive measures such as yelling, withholding favours and so on to discipline failed conduct.

85. One of the main objectives of this approach is to remedy the cleaving of theory and ideas from practice. Thévenot (2009) stated this goal as reuniting the moral and philosophical character of the social scientist with his critical capacity to do research. While critical sociology has a somewhat unclear meaning in the rest of the world, loosely revolving around scholarly attempts to observe and critique social movements and social problems, in France it means the sociology of Pierre Bourdieu and his "habitus-field-capital" paradigm (Blokker 2011:252).

86. Bourdieu represents this domination frequently (1972, 1999, 2002) and as we have discussed, it suggests the domination of agency by structure. Pragmatic sociology of critique does not separate out the two "forces" in the first place. There are morally capable human agents, and there are structural forces, manifest in forms of knowledge, sometimes embodied in what we call "institutions" and they are linked insomuch as human agents make diverse moral decisions about how to engage in this unstable and threatening world of ideas and situations (Boltanski 2011:55).

87. On the one hand, capitalism requires a class of poor workers to fill roles as cheap labor, but at the same time it creates stigmatizing laws, spatial codes and other means to reduce the social capital of the very poor. Poverty is to be avoided, yet is necessary to the process of accumulation.

88. One of the most economically powerless persons on the planet is the homeless person. Once again, the study of power among the poor has focused on the big problems, the repression of farmers in Central America (Sachs 2005), the shanties

Endnotes

of Asia (Davis 2006) and so on. This is so because these large categorical groups are easily situated within critiques of globalization and global capitalism where the sheer size and isolation of the poor population in sites like *flavellas* and massive shanty-cities abets an easier description of the parties involved in the struggle for resources and power in well-established cases of alienation and marginalization (Bayat 2009; Sachs 2005; Harvey, 2003; 1989; 2005). Such massive power struggles in these places confront international aid organizations and the world banking system, so they have received great attention. Power struggles on these massive scales are generally defined as collective actions, actions defined by their numerous affiliations and tendency towards massive struggles or social movements (Bayat 2010), whereas looking at issues of power in the case of a homeless man in Toronto or family camped out in their car in Portland requires situating notions of power in a specific and highly transient localized personality.

Powerlessness in itself, however, is closely related to notions of disaffiliation, Bahr (1973); and it is, therefore, very much an expression of the street people 1 was studying in 2001.

89. Wagner (1993), Bourgois (1996, 2010), Wasserman and Clair (2010), and Caponi (1999) represent urban ethnographies that connect poor urban subjectivities to political economies as a way of overcoming the stigmatizing and reductionist tendencies of the culture of poverty legacy. But this means abandoning dogmatic positions about what freedom and worth might ideally mean, in favor of a messier understanding grounded in the shifting categories of experience amongst the people we are studying.

90. These positions of course influenced by the dominant discourse of dignity and poverty expressed in poor laws and labor reform acts which we discuss in the following chapters.

91. Fairbanks Jr. (2004 dissertation) takes a different route but arrives at the same conclusion. He states that the "urban ethnographies of an earlier era—built on the foundational ethos of a War on Poverty—were either tacitly or explicitly in support of direct state action to ameliorate the devastating immiseration of structurally produced urban poverty and racial exclusion" (60). He then calls for urban ethnographers to find inventive ways to understand how these conditions currently play out. That is what this book intends to do.

92. It was as result of this mindset that 1 began to entertain Foucault's work on governmentality that we address in chapter four.

93. http://www.christianiaooo.dk.

94. http://www.christiania.org, http://www.christianiaooo.dk/english.php.

95. http://www.stmichaelshospital.com/pdf/ crich/homelessness-canadian-cities.pdf.

96. http://riotimesonline.com/brazil-news /rio-politics/rios-favela-population-largest-in-brazil/#.

97. http://blogs.newschool.edu/epsm/2012/ 05/24/orangi-town-karachi/. See also: A. Hasan (2003), *Urban Slums Reports: The Case of Karachi, Pakistan: Global Report on Human Settlements*; A. Hasan (2006), Orangi pilot project: The expansion of work beyond Orangi and the mapping of informal settlements, *Environment and Urbanization*, 18(2), 451–480.

98. My film, *Subtext: Real Stories* contains stories of these bottle diggers.

99. In my film, *Subtext: Real Stories*, 1 gathered images from the City of Toronto Archives of shanties built by immigrants from 1902 to 1938. They were set up in many places, next to the original city hall on College Street and on Bathurst next to the rail lands. My own ancestors recall the shacks and shanties belonging to friends and relatives during the depression. This is an underexplored part of Canadian urban history.

100. Even the Toronto Disaster Relief Committee (TDRC), which had

championed Tent City, had closed its doors as of 2012.

101. The TDRC's proposal to move Tent City to land owned by the city was rejected by city staff and the community and neighborhood services committee. Instead, the city selected a proposal from Homes First for the same site. It was to accommodate 32 homeless people in 29 prefab structures. "But [NOW Magazine reported] the tenants will be drawn primarily from Homes First's existing clientele, meaning that most of Tent City's 60 residents will be left squatting precariously on their current, heavily polluted site.... 'Of course we're happy that anyone is going to build affordable housing,' says TDRC member Beric German. 'But the people here [at Tent City] are the ones who have campaigned for this type of affordable housing. And the solution that is proposed won't house all those at Tent City who need housing'" (*NOW*, 21:8 (October 25–November 1, 2001). This site never materialized, yet the consideration of the project suggested to me that even the homeless had power when they coordinated their efforts with experienced organizers.

102. My film series, *Subtext: Real Stories 2002–2012* follows the residents of Tent City.

103. He was misguided. While the village had been legalized, it was rife with drugs, poor health and many of the issues facing Tent City. Until the film *Doorways to Dignity* (2010), no one really knew the extent to which the village had suffered.

104. I had envisioned this process as an "act of citizenship," following Isin (2008). However, a central tenet of their argument is that the act constitutes a break with habitus, and addressing the shantytown claim as a break with habitus would prove tautological in the sense that what activists had sought was a return to conventional lifestyles, using existing laws and practices to secure those rights democratically.

105. "Street Health is a non-profit community-based agency that improves the health

of homeless and under-housed people in Toronto. We offer both physical and mental health programs. Our work is focused in the neighborhood around Dundas and Sherbourne Streets, an area with the largest concentration of homeless shelters and drop-in centres in Canada" (www.streethealth.ca).

106. On September 26, 2002, the City of Toronto announced the Emergency Homelessness Pilot Project (http://www.toronto.ca/housing/pdf/tentcity5.pdf).

107. http://housepaint.typepad.com/housepaint/about-housepaint-phase-2-.html.

108. http://www.thegridto.com/city/localnews/counted-out-toronto-homeless-deaths/ offers a higher figure. The names from the TDRC are included in the *Blueprint to End Homelessness* (Wellesley Institute, 2006).

109. "Increasingly, cities across the nation are implementing punitive measures to sweep homeless people out of downtown areas." (http://www.nlchp.org/program.cfm?prog=4).

110. For Castoriadis, the social imaginary is pre-logical, a function of the individual's readiness to perceive and need to organize difference, yet is also conditioned by the forms of reason employed by a society at a given time and place (1987:145).

111. Lefebvre argued that the recognition of diversified spatial meanings is a departure from Cartesian models of space that cannot imagine spatial items without a body, in the sense that "We attribute a generic unity to the extension of the space, so that when the body which fills the space has been changed, the extension of the space itself is not considered to have been changed."

112. In Amos 8:4–6: "Hear this, O ye that swallow up the needy, even to make the poor of the land to fail, ... falsifying the balances by deceit. That we may buy the poor for silver, and the needy for a pair of shoes; and sell the refuse of the wheat." In Psalm 140:12, "I know that the LORD will maintain the cause of the afflicted, and justice for the poor." In Proverbs 19:17, "He

Endnotes

who is gracious to a poor man lends to the LORD, and He will repay him for his good deed." The position is supported by the *Encyclopedia of Homelessness* (2004) that offers extensive correlation between verses, laws and policies.

113. Mark Rathbone, Vagabond! *History Review*, March 2005 (Issue 51):8–13.

114. In addition to branding, "ear boring" was common; a hole one inch in diameter was drilled into the gristle of the ear (Snow and Anderson 1993:12).

115. Paul Slack, *Poverty and Policy in Tudor and Stuart England* (London: Longman, 1988).

116. See Marx and Engels (1970), Polanyi (1944), Wallerstein (2004), Polanyi (1949), Dean (1999; 2010), and Caton (1990).

117. The term "Skid Row" actually derives from the logging skids, ramps that carried logs from mill to river or sea and were elevated sufficiently for migrant workers to live underneath. They had been called "corduroy roads," then "skid rows," and later the term migrated to city spaces housing the itinerant.

118. Early studies of the homeless by Solenberger (1911) and Anderson (1923) revealed a largely male population sometimes of "intemperate manner," but very often suffering from mental illness of some sort; in some groups almost two-thirds suffered a major health problem such as blindness or deafness (see also Caton 1990:9).

119. Hoovervilles refer in a derogatory sense to President Herbert Hoover who was blamed for the depression, and who was perceived as less than sympathetic to those most affected by his mismanagement of the economy.

120. The Great Depression is understood as the result of irresponsible consumer spending, high household debt, falling commodity prices, bank failures, extreme unemployment, a stock market crash and various other events commensurate with a general economic collapse under liberal capitalism. Among other things, it helped

to call into question the liberal market values that, it was argued, had led to monopolistic and rapacious business practices.

121. There was little debate over who was deserving or not; though the displacement was massive and unprecedented, it was expected to be short-lived, and the millions of newly homeless were for the most part not blamed for their situation by the state, the police or media, and especially not in pubic imaginaries. While the dimension of the displacement was less dramatic in some other countries (England for example), it was still a universal experience among liberal democracies, and poverty, if not homelessness, became a defining caution under emerging neoliberal welfare policies.

122. State and municipal camps included.

123. Programs including minimum wages, encouragement of unions to fight for higher wages, and a reduction in farm production to raise farm incomes were seen as economic stimulators, while the introduction of social security and make-work programs was to provide relief on a broad scale to those hardest hit (Best 1991, 1993).

124. In the context of the discussion of neoliberalism presented earlier, housing policies were critiqued by conservative liberals for the impact they had on federal deficits and for spending government funds on economically defective segments of society.

125. While U.S. programs such as the Federal Housing Administration's rezoning laws in favour of single family dwellings can be seen as an ideological mechanism for transforming the labor base of the U.S. into manageable and contented populations, the result for poor individuals was that it became difficult to establish permanent residences because multi- and extended family modes were excluded (Leginski 2007:5). Such laws as the National Housing Acts of 1949 and 1954 created a legacy of gentrification in downtown cores where homeless people had congregated.

The 1949 and the 1954 acts continued to support new single family dwelling construction, but offered cities funding to purchase areas deemed to be "slums" under the principle of *eminent domain*, in order to encourage reinvestment in dilapidated city cores by private developers. Though termed "urban redevelopment" in the 1949 act, by 1954 it was deemed "urban renewal."

126. In the late nineteenth century, capitalist cities assigned the sprawling meadows and hillsides on the outskirts of town to the upper tiers of society while relegating the poor and destitute to the core (Jackson 1985: introduction).

127. This practice of intentional slum building started in New York City in 1935; developers were encouraged to build large housing projects for the working poor, but they did so under the condition that for each unit of slum housing, a unit of private dwelling would be demolished, creating both demand and sub-standard living conditions as they proceeded (New York Housing Authority, City of New York, retrieved November 16, 2011.

128. See Gareth Davies, *From Opportunity to Entitlement: The Transformation and Decline of Great Society Liberalism* (Lawrence, Kansas: University Press of Kansas, 1996); Michael B. Katz, *The Undeserving Poor: From the War on Poverty to the War on Welfare* (New York: Pantheon Books, 1989); Jill Quadagno, *The Color of Welfare: How Racism Undermined the War on Poverty* (New York: Oxford University Press, 1994).

129. Friedman argued for stronger basic legal (constitutional) protection of economic rights. See his *Inflation: Causes and Consequences* (1963) and George Stigler's *Memoirs of an Unregulated Economist* (1985).

130. See Burton Weisbrod, ed., *The Economics of Poverty: An American Paradox* (Englewood Cliffs, N.J.: Prentice-Hall, 1965). The policies of the War on Poverty, much like the housing acts previously discussed, can be seen as an extension of the New Deals and the Four Freedoms speech (they were freedom of speech, freedom of worship, freedom of want, and freedom from fear; the latter two were not guaranteed in the U.S. Constitution, and became the sources or access points for critics of Roosevelt's alleged socialism) (Rossi 1989; Best 1993).

131. While overall poverty rates declined to as low as 11% in the mid-1970s, by the late 1970s they had rebounded to 17%. Currently the rate is conservatively estimated to be close to 16% (HUD 2009; 2010; 2011).

132. In my film *Subtext*, homeless respondents recount similar expenses as recently as 2008. Rossi provides a fairly detailed account of the emergence of shelters as a loosely integrated system of municipal and private charitable accommodations for the homeless. For the most part, shelters run by private organizations like the Salvation Army were superior to those run by municipalities. Rossi suggests that this was in part because city shelters did not and could not restrict who entered the premises (except in terms of capacity limits) while private shelters could restrict who entered on the basis of inebriation or bizarre behaviour (36).

133. This is presumably because it has had a large population and a longer history of offering services associated to the poor. It is noteworthy that the majority of statistical information comes from Chicago and New York, both key sites for ethnographic sociology since the 1920s.

134. *On Justification* (2011:50–55).

135. Various studies, including Bahr and Caplow (1968), Solenberger (1911), Anderson (1923), Goodwin (1985, in Caplow 1990), Caton (1990) Street Health (2005–09), and NAEH (2011), cite the range of usage among the impoverished of alcohol and other substances at between 15% and 35% although such figures are not only unreliable, it is almost impossible to say with any certainty to what degree they differ from those of conventional populations. In Dignity Village, drug and alcohol use was close to 80%, though level of addiction per se was impossible to

Endnotes

discern.

136. See D. Levinson (ed.) *The Encyclopedia of Homelessness* (Thousand Oaks, Calif.: Sage, 2004); also Salem ebooks, *The Eighties in America*, section on "Homelessness."

137. "In 1983, a group of concerned leaders founded the National Citizens Committee for Food and Shelter to help meet the emergency needs of a growing population of homeless people across the country. By 1987, it was clear that despite the Committee's success, homelessness had taken root for a number of systematic reasons, and a 'hot and a cot' were not going to end the problem. At that time, the organization became known as the National Alliance to End Homelessness" (www.endhomelessness.org).

138. For example, The National Law Center on Homelessness and Poverty successfully litigated cases against the District of Columbia and the State of New York. See *Lampkin v. District of Columbia* 27 F.3d 605 (D.C. Cir. 1993).

139. Street counts are a common method of obtaining data from shelters, missions, food banks and walk-throughs in areas commonly frequented by homeless persons. The numbers are dubious.

140. http://www.sentencingproject.org/template/page.cfm?id=107.

141. In 1996 the Clinton administration introduced the Personal Responsibility and Work Opportunity Act (PRWORA). This act replaced the 1938 New Deal-era Aid to Families with Dependent Children Act (AFDC), which anchored national welfare strategies for close to 60 years. Elements of reforms included workfare provisions: recipients were to pursue or find work in order to receive supplements. While conservatives and liberals hailed such measures as a means to re-instill the American work ethic in welfare recipients, the policies can be seen as a way to associate self-worth with economic functionality.

142. "Consumers' perception of the Continuum of Care offers another divergent perspective. Consumers experience the continuum as a series of hurdles—specifically, ones that many of them are unable or unwilling to overcome. By leveraging housing on participation and treatment, continuum program requirements are incompatible with consumers' priorities and restrict the access of consumers who are unable or unwilling to comply with program terms" (Sam Tsemberis, founder of Housing First, http://www.ncbi.nlm.nih.gov/pmc/articles/PMC1448313/).

143. In *Subtext: Real Stories*, version two, (2008).

144. www.nlchp.org; www.nclej.org.

145. See NCH, "Tent Cities in America: A Pacific Report" (2010) and also www.ShareWheel.org.

146. http://vbc.cityrepair.org. "In 1996, neighbors in the Sellwood neighborhood of Portland at the intersection of 9th and Sherrett created a tea stand, children's playhouse and community library on the corner and renamed it 'Share-It Square.' In January 2000, the Portland City Council passed ordinance #172207, an 'Intersection Repair' ordinance, allowing neighborhoods to develop public gathering places in certain street intersections."

147. www.columbiaecovillage.or.

148. "In 1785, the Continental Congress passed the National Land Ordinance, which laid a Roman colonial grid over all lands west of the Ohio River. This included all future cities and towns. Public spaces and piazzas occur naturally at the intersection of pathways when communities are allowed to grow organically (http://cityrepair.org/about/why-city-repair).

149. Turner states that while his focus has been on preindustrial, traditional society, the "collective dimensions of communitas and structure are to be found at all stages and levels of culture and society" (113).

150. Michel de Certeau looked at real-life possible outcomes based on the *individuals* connected in the (always social) relation,

353

rather than on predictable relations governed by abstract terms. It is somewhere out of the negotiation of the rules and structures of the (urban) landscape that people (users) develop *tactics*, often undisclosed means of navigating and claiming the world around them.

151. For example, the Pathways web site suggests that the cost of a Housing First program is about $57 per night; a shelter $75, jail $164, hospitals and psychiatric wards $19 to $1185 (www.pathwaystohou sing.org/content/our_model). The cost of policing and delivery service to un-housed persons compounds the figures immeasurably.

152. Ten-year plans: "In 2000, the National Alliance to End Homelessness released *A Plan, Not a Dream: How to End Homelessness in Ten Years*—a bold, innovative strategy to end homelessness in the United States.... By developing—and subsidizing when needed—an adequate supply of affordable housing, communities can move people off of the streets and reduce homelessness effectively and permanently. The Homelessness Research Institute at the National Alliance to End Homelessness recently completed a study evaluating the completed plans. The report, *A Shifting Focus*, evaluates the elements and implementation of the plans. The Alliance maintains a database of the existing plans and encourages communities developing plans to submit theirs" (quoted from NAEH website; www.endhomelessness.org/pages/ ten-year-plan).

153. The number of worst-case needs in terms of housing assistance has jumped from 5.91 million to 7.10 million between 2007 and 2009, and includes renters in jeopardy of losing their housing. In all, 41 percent of poor renters in the U.S., or 17.1 million people, had what are called worst-case needs, caused by paying more than 50% of income on rent or suffering other hardships associated with sickness, low income and high costs. In this light, new housing or building affordable housing is a

concern lost in the translation of housing need across several categories of homelessness ranging from literally losing to in jeopardy of losing housing (HUD 2009, Report to Congress, www. huduser.org/Publications/pdf/worstcase_H sgNeeds09.pdf.

154. http://www.dallasnews.com/news/met ro/20150817-cottages-for-the-chronically- homeless-take-shape-in-south-dallas.ece.

155. Referring to my earlier summary of the tenets of neoliberalism, it is hard to imagine modern U.S. society in the absence of strong economic convictions; knowledge has been produced over time about inflation, trade deficits, tariffs, subsidies and budgets and also about the "need" for Americans to struggle alongside the economy during its latest reconstruction.

156. "II. INTRODUCTION TO THE DIGNITY MODEL. Why Dignity Village Works. A self-governed tent-village model has a number of advantages for everyone, particularly for homeless people, but also for taxpayers and businesses. In Portland, unless and until a homeless person becomes conventionally housed, there are basically only two options: (1) stay at a relatively conventional shelter (with curfews, early a.m. wakeups, close quarters, lack of privacy, lack of provisions for pets or couples to stay together, etc.), or (2) push a shopping cart around with your belongings all day and sleep in doorways or under bridges at night to be subject to harassment by police or be victimized by street thugs. To many homeless people, for whatever reasons, neither of these options is experienced as very attractive or helpful. An urban tented village offers a third alternative that is preferable to many homeless people and is beneficial for the broader community as well, offering the following advantages: Villagers gain a sense of community and human connection; Villagers enjoy a much safer environment, especially women, older people and people with disabilities or special needs; Villagers are able to form stable affinity groups and longer-term relationships; Villagers get to

have pets; Villagers gain the ability to cohabitate with spouses or intimate partners; Villagers find a sense of place, privacy, and personal space; Villagers recover from institutional dependency; Villagers enjoy a community-supported sanctuary from being criminalized due to very low economic status; Villagers work together to maintain a drug and alcohol free environment; Villagers use their skills, are enterprising and industrious; Villagers develop communication and leadership skills through involvement in the Village's self-governance; Business owners find less homeless people (not to mention their leavings) in their doorways; Taxpayers sleep better nights knowing that a very cost-effective and humane strategy for addressing homelessness was at least given a reasonable chance to prove itself, without being shut down prematurely by public officials; Even the police benefit by getting some positive press for a change, by cooperating with Village security to maintain a safe site.

"**Precedents: Seattle and Los Angeles:** The Dignity Village model is not without precedent. On the West Coast alone, at least two other tent cities have moved to more advanced stages of development [today both are gone]."

157. There is no way to reduce current practices of government to a principle or point of origin. Hence, as Dean suggests, practices need to be understood "as composed of heterogeneous elements having diverse historical trajectories, as polymorphous in their internal and external relations, and bearing upon a wide range of problems and issues" (40). "The term 'regime of practices' refers to these historically constituted assemblages, through which we do such things as cure, care, relieve poverty, punish, educate, train and counsel" (40).

158. The EHAC plan also notes an increase in the homeless population of over 75% between 2002 and 2007 with mental health indicators rising over 120% (EHAC 2008).

Oregon's Ten-Year Plan has 6 broad goals: (1) Prevent and divert people from becoming homeless; (2) Expand supply of affordable housing and supportive services; (3) Build capacity of persons experiencing homelessness through strategies that identify their risks and needs, and help them access appropriate housing and supportive services; (4) Identify and implement system of improvements for coordination at the program funding and delivery levels leading of measurable results; (5) Implement education and public campaign initiatives to remove societal stigma about homelessness to build community support and coordinated responses; (6) Improve data collection and methodology to better account for homeless persons.

159. First Monday Online Journal 15(1), January 2010 (http://firstmonday.org/ojs/index.php/fm/issue/view/301).

160. National At Home/Chez Soi Final Report,www.mentalhealthcommission.ca/English/document/24376/national-homechez-soi-final-report.

161. Peter Korn, "Police threaten complaint as calls mount at the commons," *Portland Tribune,* January 9, 2014 (http://portlandtribune.com/pt/9-news/206748-62953-police-threaten-complaint-as-calls-mount-at-the-commons).

162. In 2015, like New Orleans, Phoenix and Salt Lake City, Houston had claimed to have housed all its veterans in different stages of housing, sometimes understood as a COC or Continuum of Care system.

163. http://forabettertexas.org/images/EO_2014_ACSPovertyIncome_Charts.pdf.

164. http://www.galvestonislandtx.com/city/demo.htm.

165. http://www.city-data.com/poverty/poverty-Galveston-Texas.html.

166. http://austin.culturemap.com/news/city-life/04-04-16-community-first-new-east-austin-micro-village-opens-homeless-alan-

graham-mobile-loaves/#slide=o.
167. http://www.oregonlive.com/portland/i
ndex.ssf/2016/06/ portland_developers_pit
ch_100.html.

Bibliography

Abelson, Elaine. 2003. "Women who have no men to work for them: Gender and homelessness in the Great Depression." *Feminist Studies* 29(1):104–127.

Acciaioli, Greg. 1997. "Innocence lost: Evaluating an experimental era in ethnographic film." *The Australian Journal of Anthropology* 8(2):210–226.

Adorno, Theodor. 1985. "The sociology of knowledge and its consciousness." In Andrew Arato and Gebhardt Eike, eds. *The Essential Frankfurt School Reader*, pp. 452–466.

Adorno, Theodor W. 2007. *Negative Dialectics*. Translated by E.B. Ashton. New York: Continuum.

Albert, Hans. 1985. *Treatise on Critical Reason*. Princeton: Princeton University Press.

Alcoholics Anonymous (Anon.). 2001[1936]. *Alcoholics Anonymous: The Big Book*. New York: AA World Services.

Alinsky, Saul D. 1971. Rules for Radicals: A Pragmatic Primer for Realistic Radicals. New York: Vintage Books.

Allsop, Kenneth. 1967. *Hard Travelin': The Hobo and His History*. London: Pimlico.

Althusser, Louis & Étienne Balibar. 1998. *Reading Capital*. Translated by Ben Brewster London: Verso.

Amicht-Quinn, Regina, Maureen Junker Kerry and Elsa Tamez (eds.). 2003. *The Discourse on Human Dignity*. London: Concilium, SCM.

Amit, Vered. (ed.) 2000. *Constructing the Field: Ethnographic Fieldwork in the Contemporary World*. London and New York: Routledge.

Anderson, Nels. 1923. *The Hobo: The Sociology Of The Homeless Man*. Chicago: Phoenix Books.

Anderson, Nels. 1975. *The American Hobo: An Autobiography*. Leiden, Netherlands: E.J. Brill.

Apel, Karl–Otto. 1976. "The transcendental conception of language-communication and the idea of a first philosophy: Towards a critical reconstruction of the history of philosophy in the light of language philosophy." In H. Parret (ed.), *History of Linguistic Thought and Contemporary Linguistics*, pp. 32–61. Berlin: De Gruyter.

Apel, Karl-Otto. 1980. *Towards a Transformation of Philosophy*. London: Routledge and Kegan Paul.

Archer, Margaret. 1988. Culture and Agency: The Place of Culture in Social Theory. Cambridge: Cambridge University Press.

Archer, Margaret. 1995. *Realist Social Theory: The Morphogenetic Approach*. Cambridge: Cambridge University Press.

Archer, Margaret. 2000. *Being Human: The Problem of Agency*. Cambridge: Cambridge University Press.

Archer, Margaret. 2003. *Structure, Agency and the Internal Conversation*. Cambridge: Cambridge University Press.

Arendt, Hannah. 1977. *Between Past and Future: Eight Exercises in Political Thought*. Harmondsworth, UK: Penguin Books.

Arendt, Hannah. 1998. *The Human Condition*. Chicago: University of Chicago Press.

Arendt, Hannah 1990 [1965]. *On Revolution*. New York: Penguin Books.

Arhem, Kaj. 1993. "Millennium among the Makuna: An anthropological film adventure in the Northwest Amazon." *Anthropology Today* 9(3):3–8.

Aristotle. 1984. *The Complete Works*. Jonathan Barnes (ed.). Bollingen: Princeton University Press.

Asch, Timothy, John Marshall and Peter Spier. 1973. "Ethnographic film: Structure and function." *Annual Review of Anthropology* 2: 179–187.

Ashenden, Samantha and David Owen (eds.). 1999. *Foucault Contra Habermas*. London: Sage.

Atkinson, Paul, et al. 2007. *Handbook of Ethnography*. London: Sage.

Aull-Davis, Charlotte. 1999. *Reflexive Ethnography: A Guide to Researching Selves and Others*. London: Routledge.

Austin, John Langshaw. 1962. *How to Do Things with Words*. Oxford: Clarendon Press.

Badiou, Alain. 2001. *Ethics: An Essay on the Understanding of Evil*. London: Verso.

Bahr, Howard. M. 1968. *Homelessness and Disaffiliation*. New York: Columbia University Bureau of Applied Social Research.

Bahr, Howard, M. 1973. *Skid Row: An Introduction to Disaffiliation*. New York: Oxford University Press.

Bahr, Howard, M. and Theodore Caplow. 1973. *Old Men Drunk and Sober*. New York: New York University Press.

Bailey, Ron. 1973. *The Squatters*. Harmondsworth, UK: Penguin.

Bakhtin, Mikhail. 1981. *The Dialogic Imagination*. Trans. C. Emerson and M. Holquist. Austin: University of Texas Press.

Bakhtin, Mikhail. 1984. *Problems of Dostoevsky's* Poetics. Trans. C. Emersen and W. Booth. Minneapolis: University of Minnesota Press.

Bakhtin, Mikhail. 1986a [1979]. "Toward a methodology in the human sciences." In Mikhail Bakhtin, *Speech Genres and Other Late Essays*. Trans. V. McGhee. Ed. C. Emerson & M. Holquist (pp. 159–172). Austin: University of Texas Press.

Bakhtin, Mikhail. 1986b [1979]. "From notes made on 1970–71." In Mikhail Bakhtin, *Speech Genres and Other Late Essays*. Trans. V. McGhee. Ed. C. Emerson and M. Holquist (pp. 132–158). Austin: University of Texas Press.

Bakhtin, Mikhail. 1986c [1979]. "The problem of text in linguistics, philology, and the human sciences: An experiment in philosophical analysis." In Mikhail Bakhtin, *Speech Genres and Other Late Essays*. Trans. V. McGhee. Ed. C. Emerson and M. Holquist (pp. 103–131). Austin: University of Texas Press.

Bakhtin, Mikhail. 1990a [1979]. "Author and hero in aesthetic activity." In Mikhail Bakhtin, *Art and Answerability: Early Philosophical Essays*. Trans. V. Liapunov and K. Brostrom. Austin: University of Texas Press.

Bakhtin, Mikhail. 1990a [1975]. "Supplement: The problem of content, material, and form in verbal art." In Mikhail Bakhtin, *Art and Answerability: Early Philosophical Essays* (pp. 257–326).Trans. V. Liapunov and K. Brostrom. Austin: University of Texas Press.

Bakhtin, Mikhail. 1990. *Art and Answerability*. Ed. Michael Holquist and Vadim Liapunov. Trans. Vadim Liapunov and Kenneth Brostrom. University of Texas Press, Austin. [Written 1919–1924, published 1974-1979].

Bakhtin, Mikhail. 1993. *Toward a Philosophy of the Act*. Trans. Vadim Liapunov. Austin, Texas: University of Texas Press.

Balikci, Asen. 1989. "Anthropology, film and the Arctic peoples." *Anthropology Today* 5(2):4–10.

Bibliography

Banks, Marcus. 2001. *Visual Methods in Social Research*. London: Sage.

Banks, Marcus, and Morphy, Howard, Eds. 1997. *Rethinking Visual Anthropology*. New Haven: Yale University Press.

Barbalet, Jack. 1988. *Citizenship: Rights, Struggle and Class Inequality*. London: Open University Press.

Barbalet, Jack. 2009. "Pragmatism and symbolic interactionism." In Bryan S. Turner (Ed.). 2009. *Social Theory* (pp. 199-218). Boston: Wiley-Blackwell.

Barbash, Ilisa. and Lucien Taylor. 1997. *Cross-cultural Filmmaking: A Handbook for Making Documentary and Ethnographic Films and Videos*. Berkeley: University of California Press.

Barker, Jonathan 1999. *Street-Level Democracy: Political Settings at the Margins of Global Power*. Toronto: Between the Lines and Bloomfield, Conn.: Kumarian Press.

Barthes, Roland. 1982. *Camera Lucinda: Reflections on Photography*. Translated by R. Howard. London: Jonathan Cape.

Barthes, Roland. 1989. *Mythologies*. New York: The Noonday Press.

Basaure, Mauro. 2011. "An interview with Luc Boltanski: Criticism and the expansion of knowledge." *European Journal of Social Theory* 14: 361.

Bayat, Asef. 1994. "Squatters and the state: Back street politics in the Islamic Republic. *Middle East Report*, no. 191 (Nov.-Dec. 1994): 10-14.

Bayat, Asef. 2010. *Life as Politics*. Stanford, Calif.: Stanford University Press.

Beck, Ulrich 1992. *Risk Society: Towards a New Modernity*. London: Sage.

Beck, Ulrich and Johannes Willms. 2004. *Conversations with Ulrich Beck*. Cambridge: Polity.

Beck, Ulrich, Giddens, Anthony & Lash, Scott. 1994. *Reflexive Modernization: Politics, Tradition and Aesthetics in the Modern Social Order*. Cambridge: Polity.

Becker, Howard. 1963. *The Outsiders*. New York: Free Press.

Becker, Howard. 2007. "How we deal with the people we study: 'The Last Seminar' revisited." In David Downes, et al. (Eds.). *Crime, Social Control and Human Rights* (pp. 26-36). Cullompton: Willan Publishing.

Behar, Ruth and D.A. Gordon. 1995. *Women Writing Culture*. Berkeley: University of California Press.

Benhabib, Seyla. 1992. Situating the Self: Gender, Community and Postmodernism in Contemporary Ethics. New York: Routledge.

Benhabib, Seyla. 1986. *Critique, Norm, Utopia*. New York: Columbia University Press.

Bennet, Jonathan. F. 1995. *The Act Itself*. Oxford: Clarendon Press.

Berger, Peter L. (ed.) 1999. *The Desecularization of the World*. Grand Rapids, Mich.: William B. Eerdmans Publishing Co.

Berger, Peter L. and Luckmann, Thomas. 1966. *The Social Construction of Reality: A Treatise in the Sociology of Knowledge*. New York: Anchor.

Bergson, Henry. 1911. *Creative Evolution*. Trans. A. Mitchell. New York: Modern Library.

Bergson, Henry. 2001. *Time and Free Will: An Essay on the Immediate Data of Consciousness*. Trans. F.L. Pogson. New York: Dover.

Best, Gary Dean. 1991. *Pride, Prejudice, and Politics: Roosevelt Versus Recovery, 1933-1938*. New York: Praeger.

Best, Gary Dean. 1993. *The Nickel and Dime Decade: American Popular Culture during the 1930s*. New York: Praeger.

Bhargava, Deepak. 2012. "Social justice movements in a liminal age." *Poverty and Race* 21(3):1–14.

Bhaskar, Roy. 1975. *A Realist Theory of Science*. Leeds, UK: Leeds Books.

Bhaskar, Roy. 1979. *The Possibility of Naturalism*. London: Routledge & Kegan Paul.

Biesta, Gert J.J., and Stams, Geert Jan J. M. 2001. "Critical thinking and the question of critique: Some lessons from deconstruction." *Studies in Philosophy and Education* 20:57–74.

Biesta, Gert J.J. 1995. "Postmodernism and the re-politicization of education." *Interchange* 26: 161–183.

Birth, Kevin. 2008. "The creation of coevalness and the danger of homochronism." *Journal of the Royal Anthropological Institute* 14:3–20.

Bishop-Stahl, Shaughnessy. 2004. *Down to This: Squalor and Splendour in a Big City Shantytown*. Toronto: Vintage.

Biswas-Diener, Robert and Ed Diener 2006. "The subjective well-being of the homeless, and lessons for happiness." *Social Indicators Research* 76(2):185–205.

Blau, Joel. 1992. *The Visible Poor: Homelessness in the United States*. Oxford: Oxford University Press.

Blok, Anders and Torben Jensen. 2011. *Bruno Latour: Hybrid Thoughts in a Hybrid World*. New York: Routledge.

Blokker, Paul. 2011. "Introduction. Pragmatic sociology: Theoretical evolvement and empirical application." *European Journal of Social Theory* 14(3):251–261.

Blokker, Paul and Brighenti, Andrea. 2011. "Politics between justification and defiance." *European Journal of Social Theory*: 1–18.

Blum, Alan. 2003. *The Imaginative Structure of the City*. Montreal: McGill-Queens University Press.

Blumer, Herbert. 1969. *Symbolic Interactionism: Perspective and Method*. Englewood Cliffs, N.J.: Prentice-Hall.

Boas, Franz. 1928. *Anthropology and Modern Life*. New York: Norton.

Boas, Franz. 1928. *The Mind of a Primitive Man*. New York: Macmillan.

Bogue, Donald J. 1961. *The Homelessness Men on Skid Row*. Chicago: Tenants Relocation Bureau (City Of Chicago).

Bogue, Donald, J. 1963. *Skid Row in American Cities*. Chicago: University of Chicago Press.

Bohman, James. 1991. *New Philosophies of Social Science: Problems of Indeterminacy*. Cambridge, Mass.: MIT Press.

Bohman, James. 1998. "Theories, practices, and pluralism: A pragmatic interpretation of critical social science." *Philosophy of the Social Sciences* 29(4):459–80.

Bohman, James. 2011. "Methodological and political pluralism: Democracy, pragmatism and critical theory." In G. Delanty and S. Turner (Eds.). *Handbook of Contemporary Social and Political Theory* (pp. 149–159). London: Routledge.

Boland, Tom. 2013a. "Towards an anthropology of critique: The modern experience of liminality and crisis." *Anthropological Theory* 13:222.

Boland, Tom. 2013b. *Critique as a Modern Social Phenomenon: The Critical Society*. New York: Edwin Mellen Press.

Boltanski, Luc. 2011. *On Critique: A Sociology of Emancipation*. Cambridge: Polity.

Boltanski, Luc and Eve Chiapello. 2002. *The New Spirit of Capitalism*. London: Verso.

Boltanski, Luc and Lauren Thévenot. 1999. "The sociology of critical capacity." *European Journal of Social Theory* 2(3):359–77.

Bibliography

Boltanski, Luc and Lauren Thévenot. 2006. *On Justification: Economies of Worth.* Princeton, N.J.: Princeton University Press.

Bonner, Kay. 1997. *A Great Place to Raise Kids: Interpretation, Science, and the Urban-Rural Debate.* Montreal: McGill-Queen's University Press.

Bourdieu, Pierre. 1958. *The Algerians.* Boston: Beacon Press.

Bourdieu, Pierre. 1972. *Outline of a Theory of Practice.* Cambridge: Cambridge University Press.

Bourdieu, Pierre. 1984. *Homo Academicus.* Cambridge: Polity Press.

Bourdieu, Pierre. 1990. *The Logic of Practice.* Stanford, Calif.: Stanford University Press.

Bourdieu, Pierre and Loic Wacquant. 1992. *An Invitation to Reflexive Sociology.* Chicago: The University of Chicago Press.

Bourdieu, Pierre. 1998. *Acts of Resistance: A Tyranny of the Marketplace.* New York: New Press.

Bourdieu, Pierre. 1999. "The social definition of photography." In Jessica Evans and Stuart Hall (Eds.). *Visual Culture: The Reader* (pp. 162-180). London: Sage.

Bourdieu, Pierre. 2004. *Science of Science and Reflexivity.* Chicago: The University of Chicago Press.

Bourgois, Phillip. 2001. "Culture of poverty." In Levinson, David (Ed.) 2004 [2001]. *The Encyclopedia of Homelessness.* Thousand Oaks, Calif.: Sage.

Bourgois, Phillip. 2005. *In Search of Self-Respect: Selling Crack in El Barrio.* Cambridge: Cambridge University Press.

Bourgois, Phillip and Jeffery Shonberg 2009. *Righteous Dopefiend.* Berkeley: University of California Press.

Bowler, Gary M., Jr. 2010. "Netnography: A method specifically designed to study cultures and communities online." *The Qualitative Report* 15(5):1270-1275.

Brady, John. 1976. *The Craft of Interviewing.* New York: Vintage.

Briggs, Jean L. 1970. *Never in Anger: Portrait of an Eskimo Family.* Chicago: Aldine.

Brown, Wendy. 1995. *States of Inquiry: Power and Freedom in Late Modernity.* Princeton: Princeton University Press.

Brown, Wendy. 2008. *Regulating Aversion: Tolerance in the Age of Identity and Empire.* Princeton: Princeton University Press.

Brunt, Lodewijk. 2004. "Into the community." In Paul Atkinson et al. (Eds.). *The Handbook of Ethnography* (pp. 80-92). Los Angeles: Sage.

Burchell, Graham, et al. (Eds.). 1991. *The Foucault Effect: Studies in Governmentality.* Chicago: University of Chicago Press.

Burchell, Graham. 1996. "Liberal government and techniques of the self." In A. Barry et al. (Eds.). *Foucault and Political Reason: Liberalism, Neoliberalism and Rationalities* (pp. 19-36). Chicago: University of Chicago Press.

Burt, M., et al. (1999). *Homelessness: Programs and the People They Serve.* Findings of the National Survey of Homeless Assistance Providers and Clients. Washington, DC: Interagency Council on the Homeless.

Burt, M., & Aron, L. (2000). "Millions still face homelessness in a booming economy." Retrieved from http://www.urban.org/publications/900050.html.

Burt, M., et al. (2005). Strategies for preventing homelessness. Retrieved from: www.huduser.org/Publications/pdf/Strategies_for_preventing_Homelessness.pdf.

Butler, Judith. 1990. *Gender Trouble.* London: Routledge.

Butler, Judith. 2004. *Undoing Gender.* New York: Routledge.

Cadman, Louisa. 2010. "How (not) to be governed: Foucault, critique, the political environment and planning." *Society and Space* 28:539–556.

Caplow, Theodore. 1968. "Homelessness." In *International Encyclopedia of the Social Services*. New York: Crowell-Collier.

Capponi, Pat. 1997. *Dispatches from the Poverty Line*. Toronto: Penguin.

Capponi, Pat. 1999. *The War at Home: An Intimate Portrait of Canada's Poor*. Toronto: Penguin.

Carlos, Manuel L. 1973. "Fictive kinship and modernization in Mexico: A comparative analysis." *Anthropological Quarterly* 46(2):86.

Carspecken, Phil F. 1994. *Critical Ethnography in Educational Research: A Theoretical and Practical Guide*. London: Routledge.

Casey, Edward S. 1993. *Getting Back To Place: Toward a Renewed Understanding of The Place-World*. Bloomington: Indiana University Press.

Castells, Manuel. 1977. *The Urban Question: A Marxist Approach*. Trans. Alan Sheridan. London: Edward Arnold.

Castells, Manuel. 1978. *City, Class and Power*. London: Macmillan.

Castells, Manuel. 1983. *The City and the Grassroots: A Cross-cultural Theory of Urban Social Movements*. Berkeley: University of California Press.

Castoriadis, Cornelius. 1987. *The Imaginary Institution of Society*. Cambridge: MIT Press.

Castoriadis, Cornelius. 1991. *Philosophy, Politics, Autonomy: Essays in Political Philosophy*. Oxford: Oxford University Press.

Castoriadis, Cornelius. (1997) "Democracy as procedure and democracy as regime." *Constellations* 4(1):1–18.

Caton, Carol. 1990. *Homeless in America*. New York: Oxford University Press.

Chambers, Edward T. 2004. *Roots for Radicals*. New York: Continuum.

Chaplin, Elizabeth. 1994. *Sociology and Visual Representation*. New York: Routledge.

Chiozzi, Paolo. 1990. "What is ethnographic film? Remarks about a debate." *Society for Visual Anthropology Review* 6(1):26–28.

Chilton, Marianna. 2005. "Human rights are a joke: Perspectives from the poor on health and human rights." Paper presented at Lessons Learned from Rights-Based Approaches to Health Conference, Atlanta.

Church, Kathryn. 1995. *Forbidden Narratives*. Amsterdam: Gordon and Breach.

Church, Kathryn et al. (Eds.). 2008. *Learning through Community: Exploring Participatory Practices*. Toronto: Springer.

City of Toronto. 2004. "Next step guidelines."

City of Toronto, Staff Report. 2005. "Street needs assessment: Results and key findings." Toronto, June 20, 2006.

City of Toronto. 2005. "The Toronto drug strategy: A comprehensive approach to alcohol and other drugs." Toronto, December 2005.

Clifford, James and George E. Marcus. 1986. *Writing Culture: The Poetics and Politics of Ethnography*. Berkeley: University of California Press.

Clifford, James. 1988. *The Predicament of Culture: Twentieth-Century Ethnography, Literature, and Art*. Cambridge: Harvard University Press.

Cody, M. L. 1973. *Competition and Community Structure*. Princeton: Princeton University Press.

Bibliography

Coffey, Amanda. 1999. *The Ethnographic Self: Fieldwork and the Representation of Identity*. London: Sage.

Cohen, A., Rappaport N. 1995. *Questions of Consciousness*. Routledge: London.

Collier, John, Jr., and Collier, Malcolm. 1986. *Visual Anthropology: Photography as a Research Method*. Albuquerque: University of New Mexico Press.

Collins, Peter. 2002. "Connecting anthropology and Quakerism: Transcending the insider/outsider in post-socialist Saxony-Asnhladt." In E. Arweck and M. D. Stringer (Eds). *Theorizing Faith: The Insider/Outsider Problem in the Study of Ritual* (pp. 77–95). Birmingham: Birmingham University Press.

Collins, Peter, and Anselma Gallinat. 2010. "The ethnographic self as resource: An introduction." In Peter Collins and Anselma Gallinat (Eds.) *The Ethnographic Self as Resource* (pp. 1–25). New York: Berghan.

Collins, Peter, and Anselma Gallinat (Eds.). 2010. *The Ethnographic Self as Resource*. New York: Berghan.

Collins, Peter. 2010. "The ethnographic self as resource." In Peter Collins and Anselma Gallinat (Eds.). *The Ethnographic Self as Resource* (pp. 228–246). New York: Berghan.

Connell, Raewyn W. 1995. *Masculinities*. Berkeley: University of California Press.

Connor, Linda. 2001. "Margaret Mead, Gregory Bateson, and Highland Bali: Fieldwork photographs of Bayung Gede, 1936-1939." *Oceania* 72 (1):87ff.

Conquergood, Dwight. 1991. "Rethinking ethnography: Towards a critical cultural politics." *Communication Monographs* 58:179–194.

Crawford, Peter Ian, and Jan Ketil Simonsen. 1992. *Ethnographic Film Aesthetics and Narrative Traditions: Proceedings from NAFA 2*. Aarhus, Denmark: Intervention.

Crawford, Peter Ian, and David Turton (Eds.). 1992. *Film as Ethnography*. Manchester: Manchester University Press.

Crosby Joy. 2009. "Liminality and the sacred: Discipline building and speaking with the other." *Liminalities: A Journal of Performance Studies* 5 (1).

Cruikshank, Barbara. 1996. "Revolutions within: Self-government and self-esteem." In A. Barry et al. (Eds.). *Foucault and Political Reason: Liberalism, Neoliberalism and Rationalities* (pp. 231–51). Chicago: University of Chicago Press.

Cruikshank, Barbara. 1999. *The Will to Empower: Democratic Citizens and Other Subjects*. Ithaca: Cornell University Press.

Crystal, Stephen and Mervyn Goldstein. 1984. *Correlates of Shelter Utilization*. New York: City of New York.

Cuomo, Mario M. 1983. *Never Again: A Report to the National Governor's Association*. Portland, Maine: Task Force on Homelessness.

Dahrendorf, Ralf. 1968. *Essays in the Theory of Society*. London: Routledge and Kegan Paul.

Davies, Gareth. 1996. *From Opportunity to Entitlement: The Transformation and Decline of Great Society Liberalism*. Lawrence: University of Kansas Press.

Davis, Mike. 1984. "Forced to tramp: The perspective of the labor press, 1870-1900." In Eric H. Monkonnen (Ed.). *Walking to Work: Tramps in America, 1790-1935*. Lincoln: University of Nebraska Press, 1984.

Davis, Mike. 1986. *Prisoners of the American Dream*. New York: Verso.

Davis, Mike. 2006. *Planet of Slums*. London: Verso.

Dean, Mitchell. 1991. *The Constitution of Poverty*. New York: Routledge.

Dean, Mitchell. 1994. *Critical and Effective Histories: Foucault's Methods and Historical Sociology*. New York: Routledge.

Dean, Mitchell. 1999. *Governmentality, Power and Rule in Modern Society*. London: Sage.

De Certeau, Michel. 1988. *The Practice of Everyday Life*. Berkeley: University of California Press.

DeFilippis, James. 2004. *Unmaking Goliath: Community Control in the Face of Global Capital*. New York: Routledge.

Delanty, Gerard and P. Strydom (Eds.). 2003. *Philosophies of Social Science: The Classic and Contemporary Readings*. Buckingham: Open University Press.

Delanty, Gerard. 2011. "Varieties of critique in sociological theory and their methodological implications for social research." *Irish Journal of Sociology* 19(1):66–92.

Deleuze, Gilles and Félix Guattari. 1983. *Anti-Oedipus: Schizophrenia and Capitalism*. Minneapolis: University of Minnesota Press.

Deleuze, Gilles and Félix Guattari. 1987. *A Thousand Plateaus*. Minneapolis: University of Minnesota Press.

Denzin, Norman K. 1977. *Interpretive Ethnography: Ethnographic Practices for the 21st Century*. Thousand Oaks, Calif.: Sage.

Denzin, Norman K. 1995. "The experimental text and the limits of visual understanding." *Educational Theory* 45(1).

Denzin, Norman K. and Yvonna Lincoln. 2005; 2011. *The Sage Handbook of Qualitative Research Methods*. Los Angeles: Sage.

Denzin Norman K. and Michael Giardini. 2010. *Qualitative Inquiry and Human Rights*. Walnut Creek, Calif.: Left Coast Press.

DePastino, Todd. 2003. *Citizen Hobo*. Chicago: University of Chicago Press.

Derrida, Jacques. 1992. "Force of law: The 'mystical foundation of authority.'" In D. Cornell et al. (Eds.). *Deconstruction and the Possibility of Justice*. New York and London: Routledge.

Derrida, Jacques. 1996. "Remarks on deconstruction and pragmatism." In C. Mouffe (Ed.). *Deconstruction and Pragmatism* (pp. 77–88). New York and London: Routledge.

Derrida, Jacques. 1999. "Hospitality, justice, and responsibility: A dialogue with Jacques Derrida." In R. Kearney and M. Dooley (Eds.). *Questioning Ethics: Contemporary Debates in Philosophy* (pp. 65–83). New York and London: Routledge.

Derrida, J. and F. Ewald. 1995. "A certain 'madness' must watch our thinking: An interview with Jacques Derrida." *Educational Theory* 45:273–291.

Derrida, Jacques. [1974] 1997. *Of Grammatology. Corrected Version*. Trans. Gayatri Spivak. Baltimore: Johns Hopkins University Press.

Derrida, Jacques. 2001. *On Cosmopolitanism and Forgiveness*. New York: Routledge.

Derrida, Jacques. 2005. *Rogues: Two Essays on Reason*. Stanford: Stanford University Press.

De Saussure, Ferdinand. 1986. *Course in General Linguistics*. Trans. R. Harris. La Salle, Ill.: Open Court.

De Tocqueville, Alexis. 1961. *Democracy in America*. 2 vols. New York: Shocken.

Dewey, John. 1999. *The Essential Dewey*. 2 vols. Ed. L. Hickman and T. Alexander. Bloomington: Indiana University Press, 1999.

Diener, E., and R. Biswas-Diener. 2002. "Will money increase subjective well-being? A literature review and guide to needed research." *Social Indicators Research* 57: 119–169.

Bibliography

Doherty, Joe, et al. 2008. "Homelessness and exclusion: Regulating public space in European cities." *Surveillance and Society* 5(3):290-314.

Douglas, Mary. 1966. *Purity and Danger: An Analysis of Concepts of Pollution and Taboo*. London: Routledge & Kegan Paul.

Downing, J. 2001. *Radical Media, Rebellious Communication and Social Movements*. Thousand Oaks, Calif.: Sage.

Drache, Daniel. 2008. *Defiant Publics*. Cambridge: Polity Press.

Dumm, Thomas, L. 2002. *Michel Foucault and the Politics of Freedom*. London: Rowman and Littlefield.

Dumont, Louis. 1980. *Homo Heirarchus*. Chicago: Chicago University Press.

Durkheim, Emile. 1964. *The Division of Labour in Society*. New York: The Free Press.

Durkheim, Emile. 1982 [1895]. *Rules of Sociological Method*. London: The Free Press.

Dworkin, Ronald. 1996. *Freedom's Law*. Cambridge, Mass.: Harvard University Press.

Edwards, Elizabeth (Ed.). 1992. *Anthropology and Photography, 1860-1920*. New Haven: Yale University Press.

Edwards, Elizabeth. 2001. *Raw Histories: Photographs, Anthropology and Museums*. Oxford: Berg.

Edwards, Elizabeth. 2002. "Material beings: Objecthood and ethnographic photographs." *Visual Studies* 17(1): 67-75.

Eisenhart, Margaret and Kenneth Howe. 1992. "Validity in educational research." In M. LeCompte et al. (Eds.). *The Handbook of Qualitative Research in Education* (pp. 642-680). San Diego: Academic Press.

Elden, Stuart and W. Jeremy Crampton. 2007. *Space Knowledge and Power: Foucault and Geography*. Burlington, Vermont: Ashgate.

Elder, Sarah. 1995. "Collaborative filmmaking: An open space for making meaning, a moral ground for ethnographic film." *Visual Anthropology Review* 11(2):94-101.

Elder, Sarah. 2001. "Images of Asch." *Visual Anthropology Review* 17(2):89-109.

Englehart, Lucinda. 2003. "Media activism: The significance of viewing locations, facilitation and audience dynamics in the reception of HIV/AIDS films in South America." *Visual Anthropology Review* 19 (1 and 2):73-85.

Enjolras, B. and R.H. Waldhal (Eds.). 2008. *Non-Governmental Organizations and Public Policy*. Oslo: Novus Forlag.

Etzioni, A. 1993. *The Spirit of Community: Rights, Responsibilities, and the Communitarian Agenda*. New York: Crown Publishers.

Etzioni, Antonio (Ed.). 1995. *New Communitarian Thinking: Persons, Virtues, Institutions, Communities*. Charlottesville and London: University Press of Virginia.

Evans, Fred. 2009. *The Multivoiced Body*. New York: Columbia University Press.

Fabian, Johannes. 1971. "Language, history, and anthropology." *Journal for the Philosophy of the Social Sciences* 1(1):19-47.

Fabian, Johannes. 1983. *Time and the Other: How Anthropology Makes Its Object*. New York: Columbia University Press.

Fabian, Johannes. 1995. "Misunderstanding and the perils of context." *American Anthropologist*, new series 97(1):41-50.

Fabian, Johannes. 1996. *Remembering the Present: Painting and Popular History in Zaire*. Berkeley: University of California Press.

Fabian, Johannes. 2007. *Memory against Culture: Arguments and Reminders.* Durham, N.C.: Duke University Press.

Fabian, Johannes. 2008. *Ethnography as Commentary: Writing from the Virtual Archive.* Durham, N.C.: Duke University Press.

Fairbanks, Robert P., II. 2004. *Communal Re-Appropriation of Blighted Spaces: Governmentality and the Politics of Everyday Life in the Kensington Recovery House Movement.* (Dissertation.) University of Pennsylvania.

Fetterman, D. 1998. *Ethnography: Step by Step* (2nd ed.). Thousand Oaks, Calif.: Sage.

Feld, Steven and Keith Basso (Eds.). 1996. *Senses of Place.* Santa Fe, N.M.: SAR Press.

Ferguson, Robert M. 1911. *The Vagrant: What to Do with Him.* London: J. Nisbett and Co.

Fine, Gary A. 1983. *Shared Fantasy.* Chicago: University of Chicago Press.

Finley, Susan. 2003. "The faces of dignity: Rethinking the politics of homelessness and poverty in America." *Qualitative Studies in Education* 16(4):509-531.

Fisher, R. and E. Shragge. 2000. "Challenging community organizing: Facing the 21st century." *Journal of Community Practice* 8(3):1-19.

Flaherty, Robert J. 1922. "How I filmed 'Nanook of the North.'" *World's Work* (October):632-640.

Foley, Douglas E. 2002. "Critical ethnography: The reflexive turn." *International Journal of Qualitative Studies in Education* 15(4):469-490.

Foley, Douglas E. (Ed.) 2002. Writing Ethnographies: Some Queries and Reflections. Special issue of the *International Journal of Qualitative Studies in Education* 15(4): 383-495.

Foley, Doug. 2002. In Y. Zou and H. T. Trueba (Eds.). *Advances in Ethnographic Research: From Our Theoretical and Methodological Roots to Post-Modern Critical Ethnography.* Lanham, Maryland: Rowman & Littlefield.

Foley, Grif. 1999. *Learning in Social Action: Contribution to Understanding Informal Education.* London: Zed Press.

Foucault, Michel. 1969. *The Archeology of Knowledge.* Trans. A.M.S. Smith. New York: Pantheon.

Foucault, Michel. 1975. *Discipline and Punish: The Birth of the Prison.* Trans. A. Sheridan. New York: Random House.

Foucault, Michel. 1980. *Power/Knowledge: Selected Interviews and Other Writings 1972-1977.* Ed. C. Gordon. Brighton, UK: Harvester.

Foucault, Michel. 1982. "Technologies of the self." In Luther H. Martin et al. (Eds.). *Technologies of the Self: A Seminar with Michel Foucault.* Amherst: University of Massachusetts Press.

Foucault, Michel. 1982. "The subject and the power." In Hubert Dreyfus and Paul Rabinow, *Michel Foucault: Beyond Structuralism and Hermeneutics* (pp. 208-226). Brighton, UK: Harvester.

Foucault, Michel. 1984. "What is enlightenment?" In Paul Rabinow (Ed.). *The Foucault Reader* (pp. 32-50). New York: Pantheon.

Foucault, Michel. 1985a. *The Use of Pleasure.* New York: Pantheon.

Foucault, Michel. 1986a. "Of other spaces." *Diacretics* 16:22-27.

Foucault, Michel. 1986b. *The Care of the Self: History of Sexuality, Volume 3.* New York: Vintage.

Foucault, Michel. 1991. "Governmentality." Trans. Rosi Braidotti, revised by Colin Gordon. In Graham Burchell et al. (Eds.). *The Foucault Effect: Studies in Governmentality* (pp. 87-104). Chicago: University of Chicago Press.

Foucault, Michel. 1997. *Ethics: Subjectivity and Truth.* Ed. Paul Rabinow. New York: New Press.

Bibliography

Foucault, Michel. 2004. *The Birth of Biopolitics: Lectures at the Collège de France 1978–1979*. Paris: Palgrave.

Foucault, Michel. 2007[1997]. *The Politics of Truth*. Los Angeles: Semiotexte.

Foucault, Michel. 2007. "What is critique?" In M. Foucault, *The Politics of Truth* (pp. 41–82). Ed. S. Lotringer. New York: Semiotext(e).

Frampton, Caelie, et al. (Eds.). 2006. *Sociology for the Changing World: Social Movements/Social Research*. Halifax: Fernwood.

Freud, Sigmund. 1964. *Civilization and its Discontents*. London: Vintage and Hogarth Press and the Institute of Psychoanalysis.

Gallant, Gloria, et al. "From tent city to housing: An evaluation of the City of Toronto's Emergency Homelessness Pilot Project." Toronto: City of Toronto.

Gans, Herbert. 2010. "Public ethnography: Ethnography as public sociology." *Qualitative Sociology* 33:97-104.

Gans, Herbert. 1995. *The War against the Poor: The Underclass and Antipoverty Policy*. New York: Basic Books.

Gans, Herbert. 1991. *People, Plans and Policies: Essays on Poverty, Racism and Other National Urban Problems*. New York: Columbia University Press.

Gans, Herbert. 1969. "Culture and class in the study of poverty". In D.P. Moynihan (Ed.). *On Understanding Poverty: Perspectives from the Social Sciences* (pp. 201-228). New York: Basic Books.

Gardiner, Michael. *The Dialogics of Critique: M.M. Bakhtin and the Theory of Ideology*. London: Routledge.

Garfinkel, Harold. 1972. "Conditions of successful degradation ceremonies." In J. Manis and B. Meltzer (Eds.). *Symbolic Interactionism* (pp. 201-208). New York: Allyn and Bacon.

Garfinkel, Harold. 1967. *Studies in Ethnomethodology*. Englewood Cliffs, N.J.: Prentice-Hall.

Garfinkel, Harold. 1963. "A conception of, and experiments with, 'trust' as a condition of stable concerted actions." In O. J. Harvey (ed.). *Motivation and Social Interaction* (pp. 187-238). New York: The Ronald Press.

Geertz, Clifford. 1973. *The Interpretation of Cultures*. New York: Basic Books.

Geertz, Clifford. 1983. *Local Knowledge: Further Essays in Interpretive Anthropology*. New York: Basic Books.

Giddens, Anthony. 1973. *The Class Structure of the Advanced Societies*. London: Hutchinson.

Giddens, Anthony. 1976. *New Rules of Sociological Method: A Positive Critique of Interpretative Sociologies*. London: Hutchinson.

Giddens, Anthony. 1977. *Studies in Social and Political Theory*. London: Hutchinson.

Giddens, Anthony. 1979. *Central Problems in Social Theory: Action, Structure and Contradiction in Social Analysis*. London: Macmillan.

Giddens, Anthony. 1984. *The Constitution of Society: Outline of the Theory of Structuration*. Cambridge: Polity Press.

Giddens, Anthony. 2006. *Sociology*. 5th edition. Cambridge: Polity.

Glaser, Barney, and Anselm Strauss. 1967. *The Discovery of Grounded Theory: Strategies for Qualitative Research*. Chicago: Aldine Publishing Company.

Glasser, Irene. 1994. *Homelessness in Global Perspective*. New York: G. K. Hall.

Godechot, Olivier. 2009. "Luc Boltanski and Laurent Thévenot (trans. Catherine Porter), *On*

Justification: Economies of Worth: Book Review. *Cultural Sociology* 3 (1).

Goffman, E. 1974. *Frame Analysis: An Essay on the Organization of Experience*. New York: Harper & Row.

Goffman, Erving. 1959. *The Presentation of Self in Everyday Life*. New York: Anchor.

Goffman, Erving. 1961. "Role distance." In *Encounters: Two Studies in the Sociology of Interaction* (pp. 84–152). Indianapolis: Bobbs-Merrill.

Goffman, Erving. 1963. *Stigma*. New York: Anchor.

Goffman, Erving. 1967. *Interaction Ritual*. New York: Doubleday.

Goffman, Erving. 1969. *Strategic Interaction*. Philadelphia: University of Pennsylvania Press.

Goffman, Erving. 1979. [1976]. *Gender Advertisements*. London: Macmillan.

Goffman, Erving 1997. *The Goffman Reader*. New York: Wiley-Blackwell.

Gottdiener, Mark. 1995. *The Social Production of Urban Space*. Austin: University of Texas Press.

Gordon, Colin. 1991. "Governmentality and rationality: An introduction." In G. Burchell et al. (Eds.). *The Foucault Effect*. Chicago: University of Chicago Press.

Gounis, Kostas. 1996. "Urban marginality and ethnographic practice: Ethnography's interest." *City & Society*: 108–118.

Government of Canada. "Canada-Ontario affordable housing programme: Housing allowance/rent supplement program guidelines."

Gramsci, Antonio. 1971. *Selections from the Prison Notebooks*. New York: International Publishers.

Griffiths, Allison. 2002. *Wondrous Differences: Cinema, Anthropology and Turn-of-the-Century Visual Culture*. New York: Columbia University Press.

Grimshaw, Anne. 2001. *The Ethnographer's Eye: Ways of Seeing in Modern Anthropology*. Cambridge: Cambridge University Press.

Guthrie Woody. 1943. *Bound For Glory*. New York: Plume.

Gutting, Gary (Ed.). 2005. *The Cambridge Companion to Foucault*. 2nd ed. Cambridge: Cambridge University Press.

Habermas, Jürgen. 1970. *Toward a Rational Society*. Trans. J.J. Shapiro. Boston: Beacon. [German, 1968a, 1969]

Habermas Jürgen. 1971. "Knowledge and human interests: A general perspective." In *Knowledge and Human Interests* (pp. 301–17). Trans. Jeremy J. Shapiro. Boston: Beacon Press, 1971.

Habermas, Jürgen. 1987. *The Philosophical Discourse of Modernity*. Trans. Frederick Lawrence. Cambridge: Cambridge University Press.

Habermas, Jürgen. 1990. *Moral Consciousness and Communicative Action*. Trans. C. Lenhardt and S.W. Nicholson. Cambridge: MIT Press.

Habermas, Jürgen. 1998. "Actions, speech, acts, linguistically mediated interactions and the lifeworld." In M. Cook (Ed.). *On The Pragmatics of Communication*. Cambridge, Mass.: MIT Press.

Habermas, Jürgen. 2006. "Political communication in media society: Does democracy still enjoy an epistemic dimension? The impact of normative theory on empirical research." *Communication Theory* 16:411–26.

Hacking, Ian. 2004. *Historical Ontology*. Cambridge, Mass.: Harvard University Press.

Hall, Chase G. 2012. "Portland's Dignity Village expects to win contract extension." *The Oregonian*, July 10, 2012.

Halstead, Narmala, et al. (Eds). 2008. *Knowing How to Know: Fieldwork and the Ethnographic*

Bibliography

Present. New York: Berghahn Books.

Hammersley, M., & Atkinson, P. 1983. *Ethnography Principles in Practice.* London: Tavistock.

Hamner, M. Gail. 2002. *American Pragmatism: A Religious Genealogy.* New York: Oxford University Press.

Hamner, Gail. 2003. "What is an act?: Reflective action in pragmatism and praxis philosophy." *PoLAR* 26(2):38-60.

Hannerz, Ulf. 1990. "Cosmopolitans and locals in world culture." *Theory Culture Society* 7:237.

Haraway, Donna. 1988. "Situated knowledges: The science question in feminism and the privilege of partial perspectives." *Feminist Studies* 14(3):575-99.

Harman, Lesley. 1989. *When a Hostel Becomes a Home: Experiences of Women.* Toronto: Grammond Press.

Harrington, Michael. 1962. *The Other America: Poverty in the United States.* New York: Penguin.

Harvey, David. 1989. *The Condition of Postmodernity.* New York: Blackwell.

Harvey, David. 2008. "The right to the city." *New Left Review* 53 (September):23-41.

Hastrup, Kirsten. 1992. "Writing ethnography: State of the art." In Judith Okely and H. Callaway (Eds). *Anthropology and Autobiography* (pp. 116-133). London: Routledge.

Hastrup, Kirsten. 1992b. "Out of anthropology: The anthropologist as object of dramatic representation." *Cultural Anthropology* 7(3):327-345.

Haver, William. 1996. *This Body of My Death: AIDS and Historical Consciousness.* Stanford: Stanford University Press.

Hawley 1963. "Community power and urban renewal success." *American Journal of Sociology* 68:423.

Hay, D. 2006. "Economic arguments for action on the social determinants of health." Toronto: Canadian Policy Networks.

Hayek, Frederich A. 1960. *The Constitution of Liberty.* London: Routledge.

Hayek, Frederich A. 1944. *The Road to Serfdom.* London: Routledge.

Headley, Bernard D. 1990-91. "Race, class and powerlessness in world economy." *The Black Scholar* 2(1):14-21.

Hegel, Georg Wilhelm F. 1969. *Hegel's Science of Logic.* Trans. A.V. Miller. London: Allen and Unwin.

Hegel, Georg Wilhelm F. 1977. *Phenomenology of Spirit.* Trans. A.V. Miller. Oxford: Oxford University Press.

Heidegger, Martin. 1927. *Seit and Zei.* Tubingen Niemeyer: Verlag.

Heider, Karl G. 1976. *Ethnographic Film.* Austin: University of Texas Press.

Hilgers, Mathieu. 2009. "Habitus, freedom and reflexivity." *Theory and Psychology* 19(6):728-755.

Hindess, Barry. 1996. *Discourses of Power: From Hobbes to Foucault.* Oxford: Blackwell.

Hindmarsh, John, and Christian Heath. 2000. "Sharing the tools of the trade: The interaction constitution of workplace objects." *Journal of Contemporary Ethnography* 295: 517-556.

Hirschkind, Lynn. 1994. "Bedeviled ethnography." *American Ethnologist* 21(1):201-204.

Hobbes, Thomas. 1991[1651]. *Leviathan.* Ed. Richard Tuck. Cambridge: Cambridge University Press.

Hockings, Paul, ed. 1995. *Principles of Visual Anthropology.* New York: Mouton de Gruyter.

Holquist, Michael 2002. *Dialogism: Bakhtin and His World.* 2nd ed. New York: Routledge.

Honneth, Axel. 2000. "The possibility of a disclosing critique of society: The 'dialectic of enlightenment' in light of current debate in social criticism." *Constellations* 7(1):116–27.

Honneth, Axel. 2002. "An interview with Axel Honneth: The role of sociology in the theory of recognition." *European Journal of Social Theory* 5(2): 265–77.

Honneth, Axel. 2004. "Organized self-realization: Some paradoxes of individualization." *European Journal of Social Theory* 7(4):463–78.

Hook, Derek. 2001. "Discourse, knowledge, materiality, history: Foucault and discourse analysis." (online). London: LSE Research Online.

Hopper, Kim. 1990. "Advocacy for the homeless in the 1980's." In Caton, 1990. *Homeless in America* (pp. 160–74). New York: Oxford University Press.

Hopper, K. 1991. "A poor apart: The distancing of homeless men in New York's history." *Social Research* 59(1):107–132.

Hopper, Kim. 1998. "Housing the homeless." *Social Policy* 28(3):64.

Hopper, Kim. 2003. *Reckoning with Homelessness*. Ithaca, N.Y.: Cornell University Press.

Hopper, Kim and Jim Baumohl. 1994. "Held in abeyance: Rethinking homelessness and advocacy." *American Behavioral Scientist* 3(7): 522–52.

Hopper, Kim, and Baumohl, Jim. 1996. "Redefining the cursed word: A historical interpretation of American homelessness." In J. Baumohl (Ed.), *Homelessness in America* (pp. 3–14).Westport, CT: Oryx Press.

Hopper, Kim, and Baumohl, Jim. 2004. "Liminality." In D. Levinson (Ed.). *Encyclopedia of Homelessness* (pp. 354–356). Thousand Oaks, Calif.: Sage.

Horkheimer, Max. 1985. "The End of reason." In Andrew Arato and Eike Gebhardt (Eds.). *The Essential Frankfurt School Reader* (pp. 26–49).

Housing Liberation Front (HLF) Website. http://homelessliberation.wordpress.com/tag /oregonian/.

Hughes, Everett. C. 1971. *The Sociological Eye*. Chicago: Aldine.

Hulchanski, David. 2009. Homelessness in Canada: Past, Present, Future. Keynote Address, University of Calgary, February 2009.

Hulchanski, David, et al. 2009. "What's in a word?" Toronto: Cities Centre, University of Toronto.

Hull, George. 2009. "Book review: The new spirit of capitalism." *Huma-Mente*, issue 10 (July 2009).

Husserl, Edmund. 1910. "Philosophy as rigorous science." In Q. Lauer (Ed.). *Phenomenology and the Crisis of Philosophy*. New York: Harper.

Husserl, Edmund. 1960. *Cartesian Meditations*. Trans. D. Cairns. The Hague: Martinus Nijoff.

Husserl, Edmund. 1999. *The Essential Husserl*. Ed. D. Welton. Bloomington: Indiana University Press.

Hwang, Stephen, and A. Cheung. 2004. "Risk of death among homeless women: A cohort study and review of the literature." *CMAJ*, April 13, 2004:1708.

Innis, Harold. A. 2007. *Empire and Communications*. Toronto: Dundurn Press.

Interagency Council on Homelessness (n.d.). The 10-year planning process to end chronic homelessness in your community: A step-by-step guide. http://www.ich.gov/ slocal/plans/toolkit.pdf.

Interagency Council on the Homeless. 1992. *Outcasts on Main Street*. Washington, D.C.: Author.

Interagency Council on Homelessness. 2005, February 3. Interagency Council on Homelessness e-newsletter. http://www.ich.gov/newsletter/archive/02-03-05_e-newsletter.htm.

Interagency Council on Homelessness. 2006, July 11. Web posting of executive director's

Bibliography

comments to the National Summit for Jurisdictional Leaders. http://www.ich.gov/2006.html.

Institute for the Study of Homelessness and Poverty at the Weingart Center. 2005. Homeless counts in major US cities and counties. http://www.weingart.org/center/pdf/200512-city-county-homeless-counts.pdf.

Isin, Engen. F. 1992. *Cities without Citizens*. Montreal: Black Rose Press.

Isin, Engen 2002. *Being Political: Genealogies of Citizenship*. Minneapolis: University Of Minnesota Press.

Isin, E. F. and P.K. Wood. 1999. *Citizenship and Identity*. London: Sage.

Isin, E. F. and G. Nielsen, G. (Eds.). 2008. *Acts of Citizenship*. London: Zed.

Jay, Martin 1984. *Marxism and Totality: The Adventures of a Concept from Lukács to Habermas*. Cambridge: Polity.

Jackson, Kenneth, T. 1985. *Crabgrass Frontier: The Suburbanization of the United States*. New York: Oxford University Press.

James, William. 1977. *The Writings of William James*. Ed. John J. McDermott. Chicago: University of Chicago Press.

James, William. 1978. *Pragmatism and the Meaning of Truth*. A. J. Ayer, intro. Cambridge, Mass.: Harvard University Press.

James, William. 1982. *Varieties of Religious Experience: A Study in Human Nature*. New York: The Modern Library.

James, William. 1983. *The Principles of Psychology*. George Miller, intro. Cambridge, Mass.: Harvard University Press.

Jencks, Christopher. 1994. *The Homeless*. Cambridge, Mass.: Harvard University Press.

Johnson, Peter. 2012. "Heterotopia studies." Web paper.

Joint Center for Housing Studies, Harvard University. 2006. *America's Rental Housing*. Cambridge, Mass.: Author.

Jones, Richard G., Jr., and Christina R. Foust. 2008. "Staging and enforcing consumerism in the city: The performance of othering on the 16th Street Mall." *Liminalities: A Journal of Performance Studies* 4(1).

Jones, Hannah. 2007. "Exploring the creative possibilities of awkward space in the city." *Landscape and Urban Planning* 83: 70–76.

Joseph, Miranda. 2002. *Against the Romance of Community*. Minneapolis: University of Minnesota Press.

Kant, Immanuel. 1983. *Perpetual Peace and Other Essays*. Trans. T. Humphrey. Cambridge: Hackett.

Kant, Immanuel. 1992. *Critique of Pure Reason*. Trans. N. Kemp Smith. New York: St. Martin's Press.

Kant, Immanuel. 1992b. "An answer to the question: What is enlightenment?" In P. Waugh (Ed.). *Postmodernism: A Reader* (pp. 89–95). London: Edward Arnold.

Kant, Immanuel. [1785], 1993. *The Metaphysics of Morals*. Trans. Mary J. Gregor. Cambridge, Mass.: Cambridge University Press.

Karnas, F. 2007, March 1. Discussant comments: Historic and contextual influences on the U.S. response to contemporary homelessness. National Symposium on Homelessness Research. Washington, D.C.

Kateb, George. 2010. *Human Dignity*. Cambridge, Mass.: Belknap Press.

Katz, Michael B. 1989. *The Undeserving Poor: From the War on Poverty to the War on Welfare*. New York: Pantheon Books.

Katz, Michael. B. 2001. *The Price of Citizenship: Redefining the American Welfare State*. New York: Holt, Rinehart and Company.

Kelman, Herbert C. 1976. "Reflections on the history and status of peace research." Presidential address for the Peace Science Society, Ann Arbor, Mich.

Kelman, Herbert. C. 1977. "The conditions criteria and dialectics of human dignity: A transnational perspective." *International Studies Quarterly* 21: 529–552.

Kemp, Stephen. 2005. "Critical realism and the limits of philosophy." *European Journal of Social Theory* (2):171–91.

Kerr, Daniel. 2003. "We know what the problem is: Using oral history to develop a collaborative analysis of homelessness from the bottom up." *The Oral History Review* 30(1): 27–45.

Kincheloe, J.L. & McLaren, P. 2000. "Rethinking critical theory and qualitative research." In N.K. Denzin and Y.S. Lincoln (Ed.). *Handbook of Qualitative Research*, 2nd edition. Chicago: Sage.

Kluback, William. 1989. *The Legacy of Hermann Cohen*. Atlanta: Scholars Press.

Kleinman, Arthur. 2004. "Ethics and Experience: An Anthropological Approach to Health Equity." In S. Anand et al. (Eds.). *Public Health, Ethics, and Equity* (pp. 269–82). New York: Oxford University Press.

Kerouac, Jack. 1950. *On the Road*. New York: Penguin.

Kerouac, Jack. 1959. *The Dharma Bums*. London: Flamingo.

Kerouac, Jack. 1962. *Lonesome Traveller*. London: Pan Books.

Knight, Peter, T. 2002. *Small-Scale Research: Pragmatic Inquiry in Social Science and the Caring*. London: Sage.

Koegel, Paul and Beck, David. 2004. "Houston." In D. Levinson (Ed.). *The Encyclopedia of Homelessness*. London: Sage.

Kolnai, Aurel. 1976. "Dignity." *Philosophy* 51(197):251–271.

Koselleck, Reinhart. 1988. *Critique and Crisis: Enlightenment and the Pathogenesis of Modern Society*. Cambridge, Mass.: MIT Press.

Krauss, C. 2002. "Amid prosperity, Toronto shows signs of fraying." *The New York Times*, June 16.

Kristeva, Julia. 1986. *The Kristeva Reader*. Oxford: Basil Blackwell.

Kroker, Arthur. 1984. *Technology and the Canadian Mind: Innis/McLuhan/Grant*. Montreal: New World Perspectives.

Kuper, Adam. 1990. "Coming of age in anthropology?" *Society for Visual Anthropology Review* 6(1):22–25.

Kusmer, Kenneth. 2003. *Down and Out, On the Road: The Homeless in American History*. New York: Oxford University Press.

Lacan, Jacques. 2001. *Ecrits*. Trans. Alan Sheridan. London: Routledge.

Laclau, E., and Mouffe, C. 1985. *Hegemony and Socialist Strategy: Towards a Radical Democratic Politics*. London: Verso.

Lacroix, Marie, and Eric Shragge 2003. "Community capacity building and leadership at the grassroots." Ottawa: Human Resources Development Canada.

Larsen, Lars. 2011. "Turning critique inside out: Foucault, Boltanski and Chiapello on the tactical displacement of critique and power." *Distinktion: Sacandinavian Journal of Social Theory* 12(1):37–55.

Bibliography

Lather, Patti. 1991. *Getting Smart: Feminist Research and Pedagogy with/in the Postmodern.* New York: Routledge.

Lather, Patti. 1993. "Fertile obsession: Validity after poststructuralism." *The Sociological Quarterly* 34:673-94.

Lather, Patti. 2000. "Reading the image of Rigoberta Menchu: Undecidability and language lessons." *Qualitative Studies in Education* 13(2):153-162.

Lather, Patti. 2001. "Validity as an incitement to discourse: Qualitative research and the crisis of legitimation." In V. Richardson (Ed.). *Handbook of Research on Teaching*, 4th ed. (pp. 241-250). Washington, D.C: AERA.

Lather, Patti. 2004a. "This is your father's Paradigm: governmental intrusion and the case of qualitative research in education." *Qualitative Inquiry* 10(1):15-34.

Lather, Patti. 2004b. "Scientific research in education: A critical perspective." *British Educational Research Journal* 30(6):759-771.

Lather, Patti. 2004c. "Foucauldian 'indiscipline' as a sort of application: Qu(e)err(y)ing re-search/policy/practice." In B. Baker and K. Hayning (Eds.). *Dangerous Coagulations: The Uses of Foucault in the Study of Education.* New York: Peter Lang.

Lather, Patti. 2005. "From competing paradigms to disjunctive affirmation: Teaching research methodology in education." In C. Hancock and P. Paul (Eds.). *Essays on the Role and Nature of Research within the Ph.D. Program in Education.* Columbus: The Ohio State University.

Lather, Patti. 2006. "Paradigm proliferation as a good thing to think with: Teaching research in education as a wild profusion." *International Journal of Qualitative Studies in Education* 19(1):35-57.

Lather, Patti. 2007. "Post-modernism, post-structuralism and post(critical) ethnography: Of ruins, aporias and angels." In Paul Atkinson et al. (Eds.). *Handbook of Ethnography* (pp. 477-493). London: Sage.

Latour, Bruno. 1986. "The powers of association." In John Law (Ed.). *Power, Action and Belief* (pp. 264-80). London: Routledge & Kegan Paul.

Latour, Bruno. 1987. *Science in Action: How to Follow Scientists and Engineers through Society.* Cambridge, Mass.: Harvard University Press.

Latour, Bruno. 1991. *We Have Never Been Modern.* Cambridge: Harvard University Press.

Latour, Bruno. 2004. "Why has critique run out of steam? From matters of fact to matters of concern." *Critical Inquiry* 30(2):225-258.

Latour Bruno. 2004b. *The Politics of Nature: How to Bring Science into Democracy.* Trans. Catherine Porter. Cambridge: Harvard University Press.

Latour, Bruno. 2005. *Reassembling the Social.* New York: Oxford University Press.

Law, John and John Hassard. 1999. *Actor Network Theory and After.* Oxford: Blackwell.

Law, John. 2004. *After Method: Mess in Social Science Research.* London: Routledge.

Law, John. 2007. "Actor network theory and material semiotics." Version of April 25, 2007, available at http://www. heterogeneities.net/publications/Law2007ANTandMaterialSemio tics.pdf.

Lefebvre, Henri. 1981. *The Survival of Capitalism.* Berlin: Schocken Books.

Lefebvre, H. [1974] 1991. *The Production of Space.* Oxford : Editions Anthropos.

Lefebvre, Henri. 1996. *Writings on Cities.* Translated and edited by E. Koffman and E. Lebas. Oxford: Blackwell.

Lefebvre, Henri. 2000. *Everyday Life in the Modern World*. Trans. Sacha Rabinovitch. London: Athlone.

Lefebvre, Henri. 2003. *The Urban Revolution*. Trans. Roberto Bononno. Minnesota: University of Minnesota Press.

Leginski, Walter. 2007. "Historical and contextual influences on the U.S. response to contemporary homelessness." 2007 National Symposium on Homelessness Research. U.S. Department of Health and Human Services.

Lemke, Thomas. 2001. "The birth of bio-politics: Michel Foucault's lecture at the Collège de France on neo-liberal governmentality." *Economy and Society* 30(2):190-207.

Lemke, Thomas. 2001. "Foucault, governmentality, and critique." Paper presented at the Rethinking Marxism Conference, University of Amherst (Mass.), September 21-24, 2000. Some sections contain revised versions of previously published material (see Lemke 2001).

Lemke, Thomas. 2007. "An indigestible meal? Foucault, governmentality and state theory." *Distinktion* 15:43-64.

Lemann, N. 1996. [2004 edition]. "Kicking in groups." In W.A. Martin (Ed.). *The Urban Community*. Englewood Cliffs, N.J.: Prentice Hall.

Levi, Primo. 1984. *The Periodic Table*. New York: Penguin.

Levi, Primo. 1989. *The Drowned and the Saved*. New York: Vintage.

Levinas, Emmanuel. 1978. *Otherwise than Being or Beyond Essence*. Trans. A. Lingis. Dondrecht: Kluwer.

Levinas, Emmanuel. 1989. "Ethics and politics." In S. Hand (Ed.). *The Levinas Reader*. Oxford: Blackwell.

Levinson, David (Ed.). 2004. *The Encyclopedia of Homelessness*. Thousand Oaks, Calif.: Sage.

Lewis, Herbert. S. 1998. "The misrepresentation of anthropology and its consequences." *American Anthropologist* 100: 716-731.

Lewis, Oscar. 1959. *Five Families: Mexican Case Studies in the Culture of Poverty*. New York: Mentor.

Lewis, Oscar. 1961. *The Children of Sanchez*. New York: Vintage.

Lewis, Oscar. 1996 [1966]. "The culture of poverty." In G. Gmelch and W. Zenner (Eds.). *Urban Life*. Longrove, Ill.: Waveland Press.

Lewis, Oscar. 1966. "The culture of poverty." *Scientific American* 215:19-25.

Liebow, Elliot. 1967. *Tally's Corner: A Study of Street Corner Negro Men*. Boston: Little, Brown.

Lincoln, Yvonna S. and Egon G. Guba. 1985. *Naturalistic Inquiry*. London: Sage.

Lipset, Seymour Martin, et al. 1959. *Union Democracy: The Internal Politics of the International Typographical Union*. New York: Free Press.

Lipset, Seymour Martin. 1960. *Political Man: The Social Bases of Politics*. New York: Doubleday.

Lipset, Seymour M. and G. Marks. 2000. *It Didn't Happen Here: Why Socialism Failed in the United States*. New York: W.W. Norton.

Little, Adrian. 2002. *The Politics of Community: Theory and Practice*. Edinburgh: University of Edinburgh Press.

Lizardo, Omar. 2009, April 7. "The cognitive origins of Bourdieu's habitus. University of Arizona (olizardo@email.arizona.edu). Unpublished paper.

Locke, John. 1982. *Second Treatise on Government*. Ed. Richard Cox. Wheeling: Harlan Davidson.

Locke, John. 1989 [1689]. *An Essay Concerning Human Understanding*. 1689. Ed. Peter H. Niddick. Oxford: Clarendon Press.

Bibliography

Logan, John R. and Harvey L. Molotch. 2007. *Urban Fortunes*. Berkeley: University of California Press.

Loizos, Peter. 1993. *Innovation in Ethnographic film: From Innocence to Self- Consciousness, 1955–85*. Chicago: University of Chicago Press.

Lomax Alan. 1966. *The Folk Songs of North America*. London: Cassell.

London, Jack. 1905. *The War on Classes*. New York: Regent Press.

Lukács, Georg 1968. *History and Class Consciousness*. Cambridge, Mass.: MIT Press.

Lutz, Catherine, and Jane Collins. 1991. "The photograph as an intersection of gazes: The example of *National Geographic*." *Visual Anthropology Review* 7(1): 134–149.

MacDougall, David. 1998. *Transcultural Cinema*. Princeton: Princeton University Press.

Mackenzie, Iain. 1994. Limits, liminality and the present: Towards a Foucauldian ontology of social criticism. Ph.D. thesis. University of Glasgow.

Madison, D. Sonyi. 2012. *Critical Ethnography*. 2nd ed. London: Sage.

Malinowski, Bronislaw. 1922. *Argonauts of the Western Pacific*. London: Routledge.

Malinowski, Bronislaw. 1967. *A Diary in the Strict Sense of the Term*. Stanford: Stanford University Press.

Mann, J. 1998. "Dignity and health, the UDHR's revolutionary first article." *Health and Human Rights* 3(2):31–36.

Marchand, Trevor H.J. 2010. *"Making Knowledge": Explorations of the Indissoluble Relation between Mind, Body and Environment*. Malden: Wiley-Blackwell.

Marcus, George E. and Dick Cushman. 1982. "Ethnographies as texts." *Annual Review of Anthropology* 11:25–69.

Marcus, George E. and Michael M.J. Fischer. 1986. *Anthropology as Cultural Critique: An Experimental Moment in the Human Sciences*. Chicago: University of Chicago Press.

Marcus, George E. 1990. "The modernist sensibility in recent ethnographic writing and the cinematic metaphor of montage." *Society for Visual Anthropology Review* 6(1):2–12.

Marcuse, Herbert, 1941. *Reason and Revolution: Hegel and the Rise of Social Theory.*

Marcuse, Peter. 1988. "Neutralizing homelessness." *Socialist Review* 18(1):69–95.

Marcuse, Peter. 1990. "Homelessness and housing policy." In Caton. 1990. *Homeless in America* (pp. 134–160). New York: Oxford University Press.

Marin, M.V., and E.F. Vacha. 1995. "Self-help strategies and resources among people at risk of homelessness: Empirical findings and social services policy." *Social Work* 39(6):649–657.

Marshall, T.H. 1950. *Citizenship and Social Class and Other Essays*. London: Cambridge University Press.

Marx, Karl and Frederick Engels. 1848. *The Communist Manifesto*. London: Penguin.

Massey, Doreen and N. Denton. 1993. *American Apartheid: Segregation and the Making of the Underclass*. Cambridge: Harvard University Press.

Massey, Doreen. 1994. *Space, Place, Gender*. Minneapolis: University of Minnesota Press.

Massey, Doreen. 2007. *World City*. Cambridge: Polity Press.

Mayer, M. 2003. "The onward sweep of social capital: Abuses and consequences for understanding cities, communities and urban movements." *International Journal of Urban and Regional Research* 27:110–32.

McClagan, Meg (Ed.). 2006. "Introduction: Making human rights claims public." *American Anthropologist*, 108(1):191–220.

McGee, Patrick. 2002. *Telling the Other: the Question of Value in Modern and Post-Colonial Writing.* Ithaca: Cornell University Press.

McGranahan, Carole. 2006. "Introduction: Public anthropology." *India Review* 5(3-4): 255-267.

McLuhan, Eric, and F. Zingrone (Eds.) 1995. *Essential McLuhan.* New York: Basic Books.

Mead, George. H. 1934. *Mind, Self, and Society.* Chicago: University of Chicago Press.

Mead, Margaret. 1928. *Coming of Age in Samoa.* New York: Morrow.

Mead, Margaret, and Gregory Bateson. 1977. "On the use of the camera in anthropology." *Studies in the Anthropology of Visual Communication* 4(2):78-80.

Merleau-Ponty, M. 1962. *Phenomenology of Perception.* Transl. C. Smith. London: Routledge.

Mental Help Net, a service of CenterSite, LLC. 2002. "The self-help group sourcebook: Your guide to community and online self-help support groups."

Merton, Robert K. 1949. *Social Theory and Social Structure.* New York: The Free Press.

Merton, Robert K. 1973. "Sociology of science." In N.W. Storer (Ed.). *The Sociology of Science: Theoretical and Empirical Investigations.* Chicago and London: University of Chicago Press.

Michels, Robert [1915] 2001. Political Parties: A Sociological Study of the Oligarchic Tendencies of Modern Democracy. Kitchener: Batoche.

Miller, Peter, and Nikolas Rose. 1990. "Governing economic life." *Economy & Society* 19(1):1-31.

Miller, Peter, and Nikolas Rose. 1995. "Political thought and the limits of orthodoxy: A response to Curtis." *The British Journal of Sociology* 46(4):590-597.

Mills, C. Wright. 1970. *The Sociological Imagination.* London: Penguin.

Min, Enjun (Ed.). 1999. *Reading the Homeless: The Media's Image of Homeless Culture.* Westport, Conn.: Praeger.

Mingione, Enzo (Ed.). 1996. *Urban Poverty and the Underclass: A Reader.* Malden: Blackwell.

Mitchell, Don. 1995. "The end of public space, people's park, definitions of the public and democracy." *AAAG* 85(1):108-33.

Mitchell, Don. 2003. *The Right to the City: Social Justice and the Fight for Public Space.* New York: The Guilford Press.

Moor, J.H. 1989. "How to invade and protect privacy with computers." In C. C. Gould (Ed.). *The Information Web* (pp. 57-70). Boulder, Col.: Westview Press.

Moor, J. H. 1989. "The ethics of privacy protection." *Library Trends* 39(1-2):69-82.

Morgan, Lewis Henry. 1993. *The Indian Journals, 1859-62.* Ed. Leslie A. White. New York: Dover Publications.

Morphy, Howard. 1994. "The interpretation of ritual: Reflections from film on anthropological practice." *Man* 29(1):117-146.

Mouffe, Chantal. 2005. *On the Political.* London: Routledge.

Morson, Gary and Caryl Emerson. *Mikhail Bakhtin: Creation of a prosaics.* Stanford: Stanford University Press.

Moynihan, Daniel P. 1965. *The Negro Family: The Case for National Action.* Washington, D.C.: U.S. Department of Labor.

Myerhoff, B. 1982. "Life history among the elderly: Performance, visibility and remembering." In J. Ruby (Ed.). *A Crack in the Mirror: Reflective Perspectives in Anthropology.* Philadelphia: University of Pennsylvania Press.

Myerhoff, B. 1986. "Life not death in Venice: It is second life." In V. Turner and E. Bruner, E. (Eds.). *The Anthropology of Experience.* Chicago: University of Illinois Press.

Bibliography

National Alliance to End Homelessness. 2000. *A Plan, Not a Dream: How to End Homelessness in Ten Years.*

National Alliance to End Homelessness. 2006a. *Housing First: A New Approach to Ending Homelessness for Families.*

National Alliance to End Homelessness. 2006b. *Promising Strategies to End Family Homelessness.*

National Alliance to End Homelessness. 2006c. *A New Vision: What Is in Community Plans to End Homelessness?*

National Coalition for the Homeless. 2003. *Poverty Versus Pathology: What's "Chronic" About Homelessness.*

National Governors Association Center for Best Practices, Health Division. Issue Brief: State Strategies to Address Chronic Homelessness. Retrieved April 27, 2007.

Nielsen Greg. 2002. *The Norms of Answerability: Social Theory between Bakhtin and Habermas.* Albany, N.Y.: State University of New York Press.

Nietzsche, Friedrich W. 1887. *On the Genealogy of Morals.* Trans. W. Kaufmann. New York: Viking.

Nilson, Jakob and Sven-Olov Wallenstein (Eds.). 2013. *Foucault, Biopolitics and Governmentality.* Stockholm: Sodertorn University.

North, C.S. and E.M. Smith. 1993. "A comparison of homeless men and women: Different populations, different needs." *Community Mental Health Journal* 29(5):433–522.

Okely, J. and Callaway, H. (Eds.). 1992. *Anthropology and Autobiography.* London: Routledge.

Ostor, Aikos. 1989. "Is that what forest of bliss is all about? A response." *Society for Visual Anthropology Newsletter* 5(1):4–8.

Park, Robert E. 1936. "Human ecology." *American Journal of Sociology* 42(1):1–15.

Park, Robert, E. 1915. "The city: Suggestions for the investigation of human behavior in the city environment." *American Journal of Sociology* 20(5):577–612.

Parsons, Talcott. 1968. *The Structure of Social Action.* 2 vols. New York: Free Press.

Peirce, Charles, Sanders. 1931-1935. *Collected Papers of Charles Sanders Peirce.* Ed. Charles Hartshorne and Paul Weiss. 6 vols. Cambridge, Mass.: Harvard University Press.

Peirce, Charles Sanders. 1966. *Selected Writings.* Mineola: Dover Publications.

Phillips, Kendall R. 2002. "Spaces of invention: Dissension, freedom and thought in Foucault." *Philosophy and Rhetoric* 35(4).

Pink, Sarah. 2001. "Picturing culture: Explorations of film and anthropology." *Journal of the Royal Anthropological Institute* 7(3):592.

Pink, Sarah, et al. (Eds.). 2004. *Working Images: Visual Research and Representation in Ethnography.* New York: Routledge.

Pink, Sarah. 2007. *Doing Visual Ethnography: Images, Media and Representation in Research.* London: Sage.

Polanyi, Karl. [1944] 1957. *The Great Transformation.* Boston: Beacon Press.

Poole, Brian. 2001. "From phenomenology to dialogue: Max Scheler's phenomenological tradition and Mikhail Bakhtin's development from 'Toward a philosophy of the act' to his study of Dostoevsky." In Ken Hirschkop and David Shepherd (Eds.). *Bakhtin and Cultural Theory*, 2nd ed. (pp. 109-135). Manchester: Manchester University Press.

Popper, Karl. [1945] 1957. *The Open Society and Its Enemies.* London: Routledge and Kegan Paul.

Poverty, National Law Center on Homelessness and Poverty. 2009. Annual Report. Washington, D.C.

Proacci, Giovanni. 1991. "Social economy and the government of poverty." In *The Foucault Effect: Studies in Governmentality* (pp. 151–68). Ed. Graham Burchell et al. Chicago: University of Chicago Press.

Prosser, Jon, ed. 2003 [1998]. *Image-based Research: A Sourcebook for Qualitative Researchers.* London: Routledge.

Putnam, Robert. D. 2004. "Who bonds, who bridges, finds from the social capital benchmark survey." Paper given at American Political Science Association Annual Meeting, Chicago.

Rabinow, Paul. 1997. *Reflections on Fieldwork in Morocco.* Berkeley: University of California.

Rabinow, Paul. 2003. *Anthropos Today: Reflections on Modern Equipment.* Princeton: Princeton University Press.

Radcliffe-Brown, Alfred R. 1958. *Method in Social Anthropology: Selected Essays.* Chicago: University of Chicago Press.

Radthke, Wade. 2009. *Citizen Wealth.* San Francisco: Berret-Koehler.

Ranciere, Jean. 2004. "Who is the subject of the rights of man?" *The South Atlantic Quarterly* 103(2–3): 297–310.

Rapport, Nigel. 2010. "The ethics of participant observation: Personal reflections on fieldwork in England." In Peter Collins and Anselma Gallinat (Eds). *The Ethnographic Self as Resource: Writing Memory and Experience into Ethnography.* New York: Berghan.

Rapport, Nigel. 2003. *I Am Dynamite: An Alternative Anthropology of Power.* London: Routledge.

Rathbone, Mark. 2005. "Vagabond!" *History Review* no. 51:8–13.

Rawls, John A. 1971. *Theory of Justice.* Cambridge, Mass.: Belknap Press.

Reagan, Charles E., and David Stewart (Eds.). 1978. *The Philosophy of Paul Ricœur: An Anthology of his Work.* Boston: Beacon Press.

Reed, Lawrence W. 2008. *Great Myths of the Great Depression.* Midland, Mich.: Mackinac Center.

Reed-Danahay, Deborah (Ed.) 1997. *Autoethnography: Rewriting the Self and the Social.* New York: Oxford University Press.

Reed-Danahay, Deborah. 2004. "Autobiography, intimacy and ethnography." In Paul Atkinson et al. (Eds.). *The Handbook of Ethnography* (p. 407–426). Los Angeles: Sage.

Ricoeur, Paul. 1994. *Lectures III: Aux frontières de la philosophie.* Paris: Seuil.

Ricoeur, Paul. 1994b. "The plurality of sources of law." *Ratio Juris* 7(3):272–86.

Ricoeur Paul. 2007. *History and Truth.* Evanston, Ill.: Northwestern University Press.

Riles, Annelise. 2001. *The Network Inside Out.* Ann Arbor, Mich.: University of Michigan Press.

Riles, Annelise. 2003. "Ethnography in the realm of the pragmatic: Studying pragmatism in law and politics." *PoLAR* 26(2):1–7.

Riles, Annelise. 2006. "Introduction: In response." In A. Riles (Ed.). *Documents: Artifacts of Modern Knowledge* (pp. 1–40). Ann Arbor, Mich.: University of Michigan Press.

Rivlin, Leanne, and Imbimbo, Josephine. 1989. "Self-help efforts in a squatter community: Implications for addressing contemporary homelessness." *American Journal of Psychology* 17(6):705–28.

Robinson, Jill. 1994. "White woman researching/representing 'other' from apartheid to post-colonialism?" In Ann Blunt and Gillian Rose (Eds.). *Writing Women and Space* (pp. 197–226). New York: Guilford.

Rochberg-Halton, Eugene. 1982. "Situation structure and the context of meaning." *The Sociological Quarterly* 23:455–476.

Bibliography

Rorty, Richard 1980. *Philosophy and the Mirror of Nature*. Oxford: Blackwell.

Rose, Gillian. 2007. *Visual Methodologies: An Introduction to the Interpretation of Visual Materials*. London: Sage.

Rose, Nicolas. 1989. *Governing the Soul: The Shaping of the Private Self*. London: Routledge.

Rose, Nikolas, and Peter Miller. 1992. "Political power beyond the state: Problematics of government." *British Journal of Sociology* 43(2):173–205.

Rose, Nikolas. 1992b. "Governing the enterprising self." In Heelas and Morris (Eds.). *The Values of the Enterprise Culture: The Moral Debate* (pp. 141–164). New York: Routledge.

Rose, Nicolas. 1996. "Governing 'advanced' liberal democracies." In Andrew Barry et al. (Eds.). *Foucault and Political Reason: Liberalism, Neo-liberalism and Rationalities of Government* (pp. 37–64). London: UCL Press.

Rose, Nicolas. 1996b. *Inventing Our Selves*. Cambridge: Cambridge University Press.

Rose, Nicolas. 1999. *Powers of Freedom: Reframing Political Thought*. New York: Cambridge University Press.

Rose, Nicolas. 2000. "Community citizenship and the Third Way." *American Behavioural Scientist* 43(9).

Rossi, Peter H. and James D. Wright. 1987. "The urban homeless: Estimating composition and size." *Science* 235:1336–1341.

Rossi, Peter. 1989. *Down and Out in America*. Chicago: University of Chicago Press.

Rossi, P. 1990. "The old homeless and the new homelessness in historical perspective." *American Psychologist* 45:954–959.

Rotenberg, R. and G. McDonough. 1993. *The Cultural Meaning Of Urban Space*. Westport, Conn.: Bergin and Garvey.

Roth, Dee, et al. 1985. *Homelessness in Ohio: A Study of People in Need*. Columbus, Ohio: Department of Mental Health.

Rouch, Jean. 1975. "The situation and tendencies of the cinema in Africa, part II." *Studies in the Anthropology of Visual Communication* 2(2):112–121.

Ruby, Jay. 1975. "Is an ethnographic film a filmic ethnography?" *Studies in the Anthropology of Visual Communication* 2(2):104–111.

Ruby, Jay. 1980. "Exposing yourself: Reflexivity, anthropology and film." *Semiotica* 30(1–2):153–79.

Ruby, Jay. 1995. "The moral burden of authorship in ethnographic film." *Visual Anthropology Review* 11(2):77–82.

Ruby, Jay. 1996. "Visual anthropology." In David Levinson and Melvin Ember (Eds.). *Encyclopedia of Cultural Anthropology* (vol. 4, pp. 1345–1351). New York: Henry Holt.

Ruby, Jay. 2000. *Picturing Culture: Explorations of Film and Anthropology*. Chicago: University of Chicago Press.

Ruby, Jay. 2005. "The last 20 years of visual anthropology: A critical review." *Visual Studies* 20(2):159–170.

Rouch, J. 1974. "The camera and man." In *Studies in the Anthropology of Visual Communication*, 11:37–44. London: Routledge.

Sachs, Jeffrey. 2005. *The End of Poverty*. London: Penguin.

Salzman, Phillip. C. 1999. *The Anthropology of Real Life: Events in Human Experience*. Prospect Heights, Ill.: Waveland.

Salzman, Phillip. C. 2002. "On reflexivity." *American Anthropologist* 104(3):805–813.

Sanjek, Richard. 1990. *Fieldnotes: The Making of Anthropology*. Ithaca: Cornell University Press.

Sanjek, Richard. 1991. "The ethnographic present." *Man* n.s. 26 (4):609–628.

Sayer, Andrew. 2000. *Realism and Social Science*. London: Sage.

Scheler, Max. 1970 [1913]. *The Nature of Sympathy*. Trans. P. Heath. New York: Archon Books.

Schmitt, Carl. 1966. *The Concept of the Political*. Chicago: University of Chicago.

Schneider J.S. 1984. "Tramping workers, 1890–1920: A subcultural view." In E.H. Monkkone. *Walking to Work: Tramps in America, 1790–1935*. Lincoln: University of Nebraska Press.

Scholte, Bob [1969] 1972. "Toward a reflexive and critical anthropology." In Dell Hymes (Ed.). *Reinventing Anthropology* (pp. 43–57). New York: Pantheon.

Schütz, Alfred. 1964. *Collected Papers I: The Problem of Social Reality*. The Hague: Martinus Nijho.

Schütz, Alfred. 1967 [1932]. *The Phenomenology of the Social World*. Trans. G. Walsh and F. Lehnert. Evanston: Northwestern University.

Senate Committee on Appropriations. (2006, July 26). Senate Report 109-293. Washington, D.C.: Government Printing Office.

Sennett, Richard. 1970. *The Uses of Disorder: Personal Identity and City Life*. New York: W.W. Norton.

Sennett, Richard. 2003. *Respect in a World of Inequality*. New York: W.W. Norton.

Sennett, Richard. 2006. *The Culture of the New Capitalism*. New Haven: Yale University Press.

Shaw, Sarah K. 2011. Living in the Liminal: Case Studies in Ohio. Master's Thesis. Kent State University.

Sherover, Erica. 1979. "The virtue of poverty: Marx's transformation of Hegel's concept of the poor." *Canadian Journal of Political and Social Theory* 3(1).

Shorter, Edward and Charles Tilly. 1974. *Strikes in France, 1830–1968*. Cambridge: Cambridge University Press.

Shragge, Eric. 2003. *Activism and Social Change: Lessons for Community and Local Organizing*. Toronto: Broadview Press.

Shuman, Michael. 1998. Going Local: Creating Self Reliant Communities in a Global Age. New York: The Free Press.

Simmel, Georg. 1950. *The Sociology of Georg Simmel*. Compiled and translated by Kurt Wolff. Glencoe, Ill.: Free Press.

Simmel, Georg. 1971. *Georg Simmel: On Individuality and Social Forms*. Ed. D. Levine. Chicago: University of Chicago Press.

Simmel, Georg. 1997. *Simmel on Culture: Selected Writings*. Ed. D. Frisby and M. Featherstone. London: Sage.

Singer, Marc. 2000. *Dark Days*. Film. 94 (81) mins. Black and white. English. Directed and produced by Marc Singer.

Slack, Paul. 1988. *Poverty and Policy in Tudor and Stuart England*. London: Longman.

Snow, David A., et al. "The myth of pervasive mental illness among the homeless." *Social Problems* 33:407–423.

Snow, David A., et al. 1986. "Fieldwork roles and informational yield: A comparison of alternative settings and roles." *Urban Life* 15:377–408.

Snow, David and Leon Anderson. 1993. *Down on Their Luck*. Berkeley: University of California Press.

Snow, David A., et al. 1982. "Interviewing by comment: An adjunct to the direct question."

Bibliography

Qualitative Sociology 5:285-311.

Soja, Edward. 1989. *Postmodern Geographies: The Reassertion of Space in Critical Social Theory.* New York: Verso.

Soja, Edward. 1996. *Thirdspace: Journeys to Los Angeles and Other Real-and-Imagined Places.* Oxford: Blackwell.

Soja, Edward. 2010. *Seeking Spatial Justice.* Minnesota: University of Minnesota Press.

Solenberger, Alice. 1911. *One Thousand Homeless Men: A Study of Original Records.* New York Charities Publication Committee.

Spradley, James P. 1970. *You Owe Yourself a Drunk: An Ethnography of Urban Nomads.* Boston: Little, Brown.

Spradley, James, P. (1979). *The Ethnographic Interview.* New York: Holt, Rinehart & Winston.

Spry, Tammy. 2010. "Some ethical considerations in preparing students for performative autoethnography." In N. Denzin and M. Giardini (Eds.). *Qualitative Inquiry and Human Rights.* Walnut Creek, Calif.: Left Coast Press.

Stall, Susan and Randy Stoecker. 1998. "Community organizing or organizing community? Gender and the crafts of empowerment." *Gender and Society* 12(6):729-756.

State of Oregon. 2009. *A Home for Hope: A 10-year Plan to End Homelessness, Status Report, Year One.* Ending Homelessness Advisory Council.

Steinbeck, John. 1939. *The Grapes of Wrath.* New York: Penguin Books.

Stoller, Paul. 1992. *The Cinematic Griot: The Ethnography of Jean Rouch.* Chicago: University of Chicago Press.

Stoner, Alexander M. 2011. "Book review: *On Critique* by Luc Boltanski." *Catalyst: A Social Justice Forum* 2(1).

Strathern, Marilyn. 1987. "The limits of autoanthropology." In Anthony Jackson (Ed.). *Anthropology at Home* (pp. 16-38). New York: Tavistock.

Strathern, M. 1999. *Property, Substance and Effect: Anthropological Essays on Persons and Things.* London: The Athlone Press.

Strauss, Anselm. 1956. *The Social Psychology of George Herbert Mead.* Chicago: University of Chicago Press.

Street Health. 1998. "Homelessness, drug use and health risks in Toronto: The need for harm reduction housing." TDRC, Toronto.

Street Health. 2007. "Failing the homeless: Barriers in the Ontario Disability Support Program for homeless people with disabilities." Toronto.

Street Health Annual Reports 2006-2012. Toronto.

Street Roots. 2009, May 27. "Dignity Village today." Portland.

Substance Abuse and Mental Health Services Administration. 2003a. "Blueprint for change: Ending chronic homelessness for persons with serious mental illnesses and co-occurring substance use disorders."

Substance Abuse and Mental Health Services Administration. 2003b. "Assertive community treatment: Implementation resource kit." Retrieved from http://download.ncadi.samhsa. gov/ken/pdf/toolkits/ community/02.ACTusersguide.pdf.

Substance Abuse and Mental Health Services Administration. 2006. SAMHSA model programs. Retrieved from http://www.modelprograms.samhsa.gov.

Substance Abuse and Mental Health Services Administration. 2007. The national registry of based programs and practices (NREPP). Retrieved from http://nrepp.samhsa.gov/.

Suttles, Gerald D. 1968. *The Social Order of the Slum.* Chicago: University of Chicago Press.

Svenningsson, Elm M. 2008. "Understanding and studying Internet culture(s): Hybridity and interdisciplinarity." *Nordicom Review* 29(2):85–90.

Swithinbank, Tessa. 1997. "Homelessness, self-help, and social identity." *Gender and Development* 5(3):45–51.

Syme, William, H. 1904. *Honour All Men: A Plea for the Vagrant.* Watford: Michael.

Synnott, Anthony. 2009. *Re-Thinking Men: Heroes, Villains and Victims.* Burlington, Vermont: Ashgate.

Szakolczai, Arpad. 2000. *Reflexive Historical Sociology.* London: Routledge.

Tafari, Jack. 2005. "The ongoing transformation of Dignity Village." http://www.thestreetspirit.org /March2005/dignity.html.

Taylor, C. 1989. *Sources of the Self: The Making of Modern Identity.* Cambridge, Mass.: Harvard University Press.

Tylor, C. 1970. *The Pattern of Politics.* Toronto: McClelland and Stewart.

Terkel Studs. 1970. *Hard Times: An Oral History of the Great Depression.* New York: Penguin Press.

Thomas, Jim. 1993. *Doing Critical Ethnography.* Newbury Park: Sage.

Tilly, Charles. 1989. *Big Structures, Large Processes, Huge Comparisons.* New York: Russell Sage Foundation.

Townsend, Peter. 1979. *Poverty in the United States.* New York: Penguin.

Tsemberis, Sam. 2004. "Housing first approach." In D. Levinson (Ed.). *The Encyclopedia of Homelessness* (pp. 278–80). Thousand Oaks, Calif.: Sage.

Tully, Jim. 2009. *Shanty Irish.* Kent: Kent State University Press.

Turner, Stephen. 2008. "The future of social theory." In B.S. Turner (Ed.). *The New Blackwell Companion to Social Theory* (pp. 551–66). Oxford: Blackwell.

Turner, Bryan. S. 2001. "The erosion of citizenship." *British Journal of Sociology* 52(2):189–210.

Turner, Bryan S. 2006. *Vulnerability and Human Rights.* University Park, Penn.: Pennsylvania State University.

Turner, Bryan S. (Ed.). 2009. *Social Theory.* Boston: Wiley-Blackwell.

Turner, Bryan S. and C. Rojek. 2001. *Society and Culture: Principles of Scarcity and Solidarity.* London: Sage.

Turner, Stephen. 2009. "The future of social theory." In Bryan S. Turner (Ed.). 2009. *Social Theory* (pp. 551–567). Boston: Wiley-Blackwell.

Turner, Victor. 1967. *The Forest of Symbols: Aspects of Ndembu Ritual.* Ithaca: Cornell University Press.

Turner, Victor. 1969. *The Ritual Process: Structure and Anti-Structure.* Ithaca: Cornell University Press.

Turner, Victor. 1974. Dramas, Fields, and Metaphors: Symbolic Action in Human Society. Ithaca: Cornell University Press.

Turner, Victor. 1982 "Liminality and the performative genres." In F. Allan Hanson (Ed.). *Studies in Symbolism and Cultural Communication.* Lawrence: University of Kansas.

Turner, Victor. 1985. "The anthropology of performance." In Edith Turner, *On the Edge of the Bush* (pp. 177–204). Tucson: University of Arizona Press.

Turner, Victor W. and Edward M. Bruner (Eds.). 1986. *The Anthropology of Experience.* Urbana:

Bibliography

University of Illinois Press.

United Nations Centre for Human Settlements. 2000. *Strategies for Ending Homelessness.*

U.S. Department of Health and Human Services. 2003. Ending chronic homelessness: Strategies for action.

U.S. Department of Housing and Urban Development. 1994. Priority: Home! The federal plan to break the cycle of homelessness. Washington, D.C.

U.S. Department of Housing and Urban Development. 2001. Guide to continuum of care planning and implementation.

U.S. Department of Housing and Urban Development. 0203. Affordable housing needs: A report to Congress on the significant need for housing: Annual compilation of a worst case housing needs survey. Washington, D.C.

U.S. Department of Housing and Urban Development. HUD's fiscal year 2006 notice of funding availability policy requirements and general section to the superNOFA for HUD's discretionary U.S. Department of Housing and Urban Development, Department of Health and Human Services, and Department of Veterans Affairs. Notice of funding availability (NOFA) for the collaborative initiative to help end chronic homelessness. 68 Fed. Reg. 4017 (Jan. 27, 2003). Programs, 71 Fed. Reg. 3381 (Jan. 20, 2006).

U.S. Department of Housing and Urban Development. 2007. The annual homeless assessment report to Congress. Washington, D.C.

United States, Department of Housing and Urban Development [HUD]. 2013. The 2007, 2008, 2009, 2010, 2011, 2012, and 2013 annual homeless assessment reports to Congress.

Vahabzadeh, Peyman. 2009. "Ultimate referentiality: Radical phenomenology and the new interpretive sociology." *Philosophy and Social Criticism* 35(4):447–465.

Valentine, Charles. 1968. *Culture and Poverty: Critique and Counter Proposals.* Chicago: University of Chicago Press.

Vandenberg H. and W. Hall. 2011. "Critical ethnography: Extending attention to bias and reinforcement of dominant power relations." *Nurse Researcher* 18(3):25–30.

Vandenberghe, Frederic. 1999. "'The real is relational': An epistemological analysis of Pierre Bourdieu's generative structuralism." *Sociological Theory* 17:32–67.

Van Gennep, Arnold. [1908] 1960. *Rites of Passage.* London: Routledge.

Van Manen, Max (1990). *Researching Lived Experience: Human Science for Action Sensitive Pedagogy.* Albany: SUNY.

Venn, J., and J.A. Venn (Eds.). (1922–1958). "Haddon, Alfred Cort." *Alumni Cantabrigienses* (10 vols.) (online ed.). Cambridge: Cambridge University Press.

Visweswaran, Kamala. 1994. *Fictions of Feminist Ethnography.* Minneapolis: University of Minnesota Press.

Wacquant, Loic. 1996. "Red belt, black belt: Racial division, class inequality and the state in the French urban periphery and the American ghetto." In E. Mingione (Ed). *Urban Poverty and the Underclass* (pp. 234–270). Malden: Blackwell.

Wacquant, Loic. 2002. "Scrutinizing the street: Poverty, morality and the pitfalls of urban ethnography." *American Journal of Sociology* 107:1468–1532.

Wagner, David. 1993. *Checkerboard Square: Culture and Resistance in a Homeless Community.* San Francisco: Westview Press.

Wallerstein, Immanuel. 2004. *World-Systems Analysis: An Introduction.* Durham, N.C.: Duke

University Press.

Wallerstein, Immanuel. 2006. *European Universalism*. New York: The New Press.

Ward, Jim. 1979. *The Street Is Their Home: The Hobo's Manifesto*. London: Quartet.

Ware, Robert. 1973. "Acts and action." *The Journal of Philosophy* 70(13):403–18.

Wasserman, Jason A. and Jefferey M. Clair. 2010. *At Home on the Street: People, Poverty and a Hidden Culture of Homelessness*. London: Boulder.

Weber, Max 1963. *Max Weber: Selections from his Work, with an Introduction by S. M. Miller*. New York: Cromwell.

Weber, Max. [1946] 2009. *From Max Weber: Essays in Sociology*. Ed. G. Roth and C. Wright Mills. New York: Oxford University Press.

Wedderburn, Dorothy. 1974. *Poverty, Inequality and Class Structure*. Cambridge: Cambridge University Press.

Weisbrod, Burton (Ed.). 1965. *The Economics of Poverty: An American Paradox*. Englewood Cliffs, N.J.: Prentice-Hall.

Weissman, Eric. 2012. *Dignity in Exile: Stories of Struggle and Hope from a Modern American Shanty Town*. Mount Forest, Ont.: Exile Editions.

Weissman, Eric. 2010. "Are the streets male?" Unpublished manuscript. Montreal: Concordia University.

Wellesley Institute. 2006. "The blueprint to end homelessness in Toronto." Toronto: Wellesley Institute.

Wellesley Institute. 2007. *The Street Health Report 2007*.

Wils, J.P. 1989. "The end of human dignity." *Ethics Concilium* 203:29–54.

Willis, P. 2000. *The Ethnographic Imagination*. Cambridge, Mass.: Polity.

Woodgreen Community Services. 2005. "Woodgreen Community Services homelessness and housing help programs: Report of the Emergency Homelessness Pilot Project: Housing supports." Toronto.

Wolfe, T. (Ed.). 1973. *The New Journalism*. New York: Harper and Row.

Worth, Sol. 1981. *Studying Visual Communication*. Philadelphia: University of Pennsylvania Press.

WRAP—2010. "Strategizing the right to the city." WRAP Working Paper.

Wright, Talmadge. 1997. *Out Of Place: Homeless Mobilizations, Subcities, and Contested Landscapes*. Albany: State University of New York Press.

Wright, Talmadge and Mary Jo Huth. 1997. *International Critical Perspectives on Homelessness*. Westport, Conn.: Praeger.

Wright, Talmadge. 2000. "Resisting homelessness: Global, national, and local solutions." *Contemporary Sociology* 29(1):27–43.

Wright, Talmadge. 2000b. "New urban spaces and cultural representations: Social imaginaries, social space, and homelessness." In *Researching Urban Sociology*, vol. 5 (pp. 23–57). JAI Press. New Perspectives in Urban Sociology Series.

Wright Talmadge and Anne Roschelle. 2003. "Gentrification and social exclusion: Spatial policing and homeless activist responses in the San Francisco Bay area." In *Urban Futures: Critical Commentaries on Shaping Cities* (pp. 149–166). Ed. Malcolm Miles and Tim Hall. London: Routledge.

Wrightson, Keith and David Levine. 1995. *Poverty and Piety in an English Town*. Oxford: Oxford University Press.

Bibliography

Young, I.M. 1990. *Justice and the Politics of Difference*. Princeton: Princeton University Press.

Zimmermann, Ann and Adrian Favell. 2011. "Governmentality, political field or public sphere? Theoretical alternatives in the political sociology of the EU." *European Journal of Social Theory* 14(4):489–515.

Other Online Sources

- Government of Canada Human Resources and Skills Development Canada (hrsdc.gc.ca/)
- Subtext Productions (www.subtextproductions.ca)
- Dignity Village website (www.dignityvillage.org)
- Kwamba Productions website (www.kwamba.com)
- Street Health, Toronto (www.streethealth.ca)
- Government of Canada website (www.homelessness.gc.ca)
- *Oregonian* articles on Dignity Village:
  www.oregonlive.com/portland/index.ssf/2012/07/portlands_dignity_village_expe.html
  www.oregonlive.com/portland/index.ssf/2012/11/portland_grants_three-year_con.html
- www.sharewheel.org/
- www.columbiaecovillage.org
- www.wraphome.org/pages/
- http://wellesleyinstitute.com/files/homelesscount2009.pdf
- http://www.cbc.ca/news/canada/toronto/story/2006/06/23/to-homeless20060623.html
- http://www.thefreedictionary.com/shanty
- http://www.ic.org
- www.media.oregonlive.com/portland_impact/other/Dignity%20Village%20Evaluation%20Report%20Final%2003-22-10.pdf
- http://right2survive.wordpress.com/
- http://media.oregonlive.com/portland_impact/other/Dignity%20Village%20Evaluation%20Report%20Final%2003-22-10.pdf
- HUD: www.hud.gov/
- National Coalition for the Homeless: www.nationalhomeless.org

Index

Index